Henry Mason Baum

Church Reunion

discussed on the basis of the Lambeth propositions of 1888

Henry Mason Baum

Church Reunion
discussed on the basis of the Lambeth propositions of 1888

ISBN/EAN: 9783337735210

Printed in Europe, USA, Canada, Australia, Japan

Cover: Foto ©Lupo / pixelio.de

More available books at **www.hansebooks.com**

8 EAST FIFTEENTH STREET, NEW YORK,
AND LONDON, ENG.

STAINED GLASS==Colored designs for Memorial Windows specially prepared and estimates submitted free, in **English Cathedral, Geometrical, Gresaille,** or **Mosaic** glass, from the simplest to the most ...sign.

GIVEN BY

H. A. Dows

... estimates furnished for lighting ...d Chapels in **Gas, Lamps,** or **Elec**- **Gold, Silver,** and **Electro-plated** plate kept in stock,—also made ...sign. **Photos submitted.**

...ading **Desks, Chairs,** and **every** ... of **seating,** etc., for Churches, ... Schools. Estimate and designs

... Chapel **Curtains, Cushions.** Our ... **Rugging, Pads** and **Hassocks.**

...es, in **silk** or **stuff,** for Lutheran, ... Baptist ministers. **Academic Hoods.**

VESTMENTS== Eucharistic or Mass, in linen and silk; Cassocks, Surplices, Stoles, etc.

CLERICAL CLOTHING in every branch. We have made a specialty of this branch for over fifty years. Samples of cloths and Catalogue submitted post free.

.

ART WORK.

WE are specialists, established in 1857, and we do everything pertaining to the artistic side of the church interior. This includes Color Decoration for the walls, Stained Glass for the windows, and Furniture for the Chancel, or pulpit platform. Information, photographs, designs, and estimates will be submitted upon request.

We advocate honest work and materials for the church. What does this mean? It means Stained Glass, not paper imitation; it means good colors for the walls, not wall-paper; it means hard wood for furniture, not pine, grained; it means mosaic and marble, not cement imitations.

There is no reason why, even for a limited expense, the best materials cannot be secured. A good designer uses these in simpler ways to decrease the cost; he does not advocate the use of poor materials. We have always advised the best for the church, and our estimates and designs are arranged upon this basis.

Have you any questions to ask in regard to your church interior? It costs you nothing to consult us, and we can give you information that will be valuable. Correspondence solicited.

J. & R. LAMB,

59 Carmine St,

New York.

Send for illustrated hand-book of any department.

MAKERS OF

MEMORIAL ✣
✣ TABLETS,

IN

Brass, Bronze, and Marble.

CORRESPONDENCE INVITED.

641 BROADWAY, NEW YORK.

Stained Glass for Dwellings.

CHARLES BOOTH.

✣

Church Furnishings,

In Wood, Metal, and Stone.
Communion Plate, Basins, etc.

COLOR DECORATION

For Churches and Dwellings.

CHARLES F. HOGEMAN.

✣

OFFICE:
Churchman Building, 47 Lafayette Place, New York

WORKS:
12 Minton Pl., Orange, N.J., U.S.A.
115 Gower St., London W.C., Eng.

CHRISTIAN ART INSTITUTE
CONDUCTED BY R. GEISSLER,
318, 320, and 322 East 48th St., New York.

CHURCH FURNITURE
OF EVERY DESCRIPTION.

WALL DECORATION
IN OIL AND FRESCO.

STAINED GLASS, MEMORIAL WINDOWS,

FABRICS, FRINGES, EMBROIDERIES.

STONE, MARBLE, AND METAL WORK.

SEND FOR CIRCULAR.

NOTICE.

The rapid and unexpected growth of the patronage extended, compels us to arrange so as to obtain increased facilities for production.

Our extensive Show-rooms at the above address are being converted into additional work-rooms; and as suitable and commodious quarters for other Show-rooms could not be obtained in that immediate neighborhood, we shall remove

ON OR ABOUT DECEMBER 1,

to the new, fine, large, fire-proof buildings,

Nos. 52 and 54 Lafayette Place, New York.

NEW BOOKS.

LONGMANS, GREEN, & CO.'S
ANNOUNCEMENTS.

Messrs. LONGMANS, GREEN, & CO., having purchased the old-established business of Messrs. RIVINGTON, will in future supply most of the books hitherto published by that firm. Revised Catalogues of Works in General Literature, and Theological Works, are in active preparation, and will be sent when ready to any address forwarded to 15 East Sixteenth Street, New York, for that purpose.

CARDINAL NEWMAN'S AUTOBIOGRAPHY AND CORRESPONDENCE.

THE LETTERS AND CORRESPONDENCE OF JOHN HENRY NEWMAN DURING HIS LIFE IN THE ENGLISH CHURCH. With a brief Autobiographical Memoir. Arranged and Edited, at Cardinal Newman's request, by the Editor of the *Letters of the Rev. J. B. Mozley, D.D., Regius Professor of Divinity in the University of Oxford*. Two vols. Crown 8vo. (In the press.)

Cardinal Newman wrote to his sister in 1863, saying: "It has ever been a hobby of mine, though perhaps it is a truism, not a hobby, that the true life of a man is in his letters. . . . Not only for the interest of a biography, but for arriving at the inside of things, the publication of letters is the true method. Biographers varnish, they assign motives, they conjecture feelings, they interpret Lord Burleigh's nods; but contemporary letters are facts." This book is such a biography of the early years of the Cardinal's life as he himself wished for. It contains an autobiography, supplemented by abundant extracts from his correspondence. It was prepared during his life and with his sanction.

WORKS BY THE LATE CARDINAL NEWMAN.

APOLOGIA PRO VITA SUA	$1.25	**THE IDEA OF A UNIVERSITY DEFINED AND ILLUSTRATED**	$2.50
PAROCHIAL AND PLAIN SERMONS. 8 vols., sold separately, each	1.75	**HISTORICAL SKETCHES.** 3 vols., each	2.00
FIFTEEN SERMONS. Preached before the University of Oxford, between A.D. 1826 and 1843	1.75	**DISCUSSIONS AND ARGUMENTS** on Various Subjects	2.00
SERMONS BEARING UPON SUBJECTS OF THE DAY	1.75	**AN ESSAY ON THE DEVELOPMENT OF CHRISTIAN DOCTRINE.**	1.25
SELECTION, Adapted to the Seasons of the Ecclesiastical Year, from the *Parochial and Plain Sermons*	1.75	**CERTAIN DIFFICULTIES** Felt by Anglicans in Catholic Teaching Considered. Vol. I. Vol. II.	2.50 2.00
LECTURES ON THE DOCTRINE OF JUSTIFICATION	1.75	**THE VIA MEDIA OF THE ANGLICAN CHURCH.** Illustrated in Lectures, etc. 2 vols., each	2.00
SELECT TREATISES OF ST. ATHANASIUS, in Controversy with the Arians. 2 vols.	5.00	**ESSAYS,** Critical and Historical. 2 vols	2.50
VERSES ON VARIOUS OCCASIONS	1.25	**ESSAYS** on Biblical and Ecclesiastical Miracles	1.25
CALLISTA. A Tale of the Third Century	1.25	**AN ESSAY** in Aid of a Grammar of Assent	2.50
THE PRESENT POSITION OF CATHOLICS IN ENGLAND	2.50	**THE ARIANS OF THE FOURTH CENTURY**	1.25
		THE DREAM OF GERONTIUS. 16mo. Sewed, 20 cents; cloth.	.35

THE CHRIST, THE SON OF GOD. A Life of Our Lord and Saviour Jesus Christ. By the ABBÉ CONSTANT FOUARD, Honorary Cathedral Canon, Professor of the Faculty of Theology at Rouen, etc., etc. Translated from the fifth edition, with the author's sanction, by George F. X. Griffith. With an Introduction by Cardinal Manning. In two volumes, with Maps. Small 8vo. (Very shortly.)

THE DIVINITY OF OUR LORD AND SAVIOUR JESUS CHRIST. Being the Bampton Lectures for 1866. By HENRY PARRY LIDDON, D.D., D.C.L., Chancellor and Canon of St. Paul's. Fourteenth edition. With a new Preface having reference to Dr. Martineau's *Seat of Authority in Religion*. Crown 8vo. $2.00.

THE STEPS OF THE SUN. Daily Readings of Prose. Selected by AGNES MASON. 16mo, cloth, 329 pages, $1.25. (Just ready.)

LYRA CONSOLATIONIS. From the Poets of the Seventeenth, Eighteenth, and Nineteenth Centuries. Selected and arranged by CLAUDIA FRANCES HERNAMAN. Fcp. 8vo, cloth, gilt top, $2.00. (Just ready.)

The selection of verse in this volume is designed to comfort mourners from the first hours of their bereavement, and is based on those clauses of the Apostles' Creed in which the Church confesses her belief in her LORD's crucifixion, death, and burial, in His resurrection, ascension, and coming again. Poets of the last three centuries have been laid under contribution, but only when their writings fell in with the design of the book.

For sale by all booksellers. Sent on receipt of price by the Publishers,

LONGMANS, GREEN, & CO., 15 East Sixteenth Street, NEW YORK.

 # NEW BOOKS.

Thomas Whittaker's
NEW BOOKS.

HISTORY OF THE AMERICAN EPISCOPAL CHURCH: From the Planting of the Colonies to the End of the Civil War. By Rev. S. D. McConnell, D.D. 400 pages, octavo, cloth, $2.00; with gilt top, $2.25; half calf or half morocco, $3.00.

> We congratulate the author on giving us the most brilliant history of the Episcopal Church, and the most readable, that has ever appeared. — *Southern Churchman.*

GOD INCARNATE. The Bishop Paddock Lectures for 1890, by Rt. Rev. H. T. Kingdon, D.D., Bishop-Coadjutor of Fredericton, N. B. 8vo, cloth, $1.75.

> When we say we do not know of a work which within anything like the small compass covers the ground with all equal thoroughness of comprehension and clearness of statement, we are no doubt saying a good deal, but we think not too much. — *St. Andrew's Cross.*

A SECOND SERIES OF TUCK'S "HANDBOOK OF BIBLICAL DIFFICULTIES." Uniform with the first series. 8vo, cloth, $2.50.

> The *Handbook of Biblical Difficulties* supplies a help which all intelligent and devout Bible readers have long felt the need of, — namely, a manual which takes the various difficulties they meet with in reading the Word of God, and gives a reasonable solution of them in an intelligible manner without evasion of that which is difficult or which may seem contradictory.
> ... It supplies a distinct and widely felt want. — *Christian Chronicle.*

THE VOICES OF THE PSALMS. By Rt. Rev. W. Pakenham Walsh, D.D., Bishop of Ossory. 12mo, cloth, $1.50.

> A careful and devout commentary upon the Psalter, one fresh in thought and expression, not overburdened with the machinery of the newer criticism, but aiming to instruct as well as edify, and withal put forth in a popular form, — such a work is the subject of a large desire, and such a work is *The Voices of the Psalms.* ... Bishop Walsh long ago gained the reputation of an unusual ability in clearness and adaptability, and these are the most striking characteristics of the present work. — *The Christian Union.*

THE WORLD AND THE MAN. Being the Baldwin Lectures for 1890, delivered at Ann Arbor, Mich., by the Rt. Rev. Hugh Miller Thompson, D.D., LL.D. 12mo, cloth, $1.25.

> And what a rich and rare style he has of putting his thoughts! Every line of shining clearness, familiar in expression, full of nerve, bears the mark of ripest contemplation, is stamped with the fresh, singular individuality of the man. — *Living Church.*

THOMAS WHITTAKER, Publisher,
2 and 3 BIBLE HOUSE, NEW YORK.

 NEW BOOKS.

MACMILLAN & COMPANY'S
NEW THEOLOGICAL BOOKS

THE EPISTLE TO THE HEBREWS. With Notes by C. J. VAUGHAN, D.D., Dean of Llandaff, Master of the Temple. 12mo, $2.25. ✶✶✶ A companion volume to that on the Epistle to the Romans, of which the seventh edition has lately been published.

Dr. Vaughan is one of the ablest of living scholars in the department of exegesis. His contributions during the past forty years have fully shown this, and his volumes on the Epistles to the Romans, the Philippians, etc., are highly esteemed by competent judges everywhere. The present volume is the result of his latest efforts in Biblical studies. The exegesis is clear, consistent, and animated by the best spirit of Churchmanship; and as the volume is well printed in good-sized Greek type and with surprising accuracy, it deserves our warmest commendation. — *Living Church.*

LECTURES ON THE COMPARATIVE GRAMMAR OF THE SEMITIC LANGUAGES. From the papers of the late WILLIAM WRIGHT, LL.D., Professor of Arabic in the University of Cambridge. Edited by W. ROBERTSON SMITH. 8vo, $3.50.

THE CHRISTIAN YEAR. Thoughts in Verse for Sundays and Holydays throughout the Year. With a Memoir and Portrait. Red lines. Cloth, gilt edges, $1.50.

IMITATION OF CHRIST. Four Books. By THOMAS À KEMPIS. With an Introductory Essay on the authorship of the work, and an engraved portrait from contemporary sources. Red lines. Cloth, gilt edges, $1.50.

STUDIA BIBLICA ET ECCLESIASTICA. Essays chiefly in Biblical and Patristic Criticism. By Members of the University of Oxford. Vol. II. 8vo, $3.25.

CHARLES KINGSLEY'S SERMONS. New editions. 12mo. Uniformly bound in cloth, $1.25 each vol.
- Sermons for the Times.
- Water of Life, and Other Sermons.
- Village Sermons, and Town and Country Sermons.
- Sermons on National Subjects, and the King of the Earth.

Works of the RIGHT REV. BROOKE FOSS WESTCOTT, D.D., D.C.L., Bishop of Durham.

THE EPISTLES TO THE HEBREWS. The Greek, with Notes and Essays. 8vo, $4.00.

This noble commentary on the subject of the noblest of the Epistles will be welcomed by all lovers of profound and accurate scholarship. . . . Among the choicest products of English Biblical criticism in the latter half of the nineteenth century. — *Manchester Examiner.*

THE EPISTLE OF ST. JOHN. The Greek, with Notes and Essays. Second edition, revised. 8vo, $3.50.

INTRODUCTION TO THE STUDY OF THE FOUR GOSPELS. 12mo, $2.25

THE NEW TESTAMENT IN THE ORIGINAL GREEK. The Text revised by L. F. WESTCOTT, Bishop of Durham, and Prof. F. J. A. HORT, D.D. 18mo, cloth, $1.00; bound in leather, $1.25; bound in morocco limp, gilt edges, $1.75.

Students' Edition of the above, with Lexicon, in strong leather binding, $1.90.

∴ *Macmillan's NEW COMPLETE CATALOGUE will be sent free by mail to any address on application.*

MACMILLAN & CO., 112 Fourth Avenue, NEW YORK.

 # NEW BOOKS.

NEW THEOLOGICAL BOOKS.

LUX MUNDI. A Series of Studies in the Religion of the Incarnation. Edited by Rev. CHARLES GORE, M.A., Principal of Pusey House, and Fellow of Trinity College, Oxford. pp. 550. 8vo, cloth.

    CONTENTS:— 1. Faith, Rev. H. S. Holland, M. A.; 2. The Christian Doctrine of God, Rev. Aubrey Moore, M. A.; 3. The Problem of Pain: Its bearing on Faith in God, Rev. J. R. Illingworth, M.A.; 4. The Preparation in History for Christ, Rev. E. S. Talbot, D.D.; 5. The Incarnation in Relation to Development, Rev. J. R. Illingworth; 6. The Incarnation as the Basis of Dogma, Rev. R. C. Moberly, M. A.; 7. The Atonement, Rev. and Hon. Arthur Lyttelton, M. A.; 8. The Holy Spirit and Inspiration, Rev. C. Gore, M. A.; 9. The Church, Rev. W. Lock, M. A.; 10. Sacraments, Rev. F. Paget, D. D.; 11. Christianity and Politics, Rev. W. J. R. Campion, M. A.; 12. Christian Ethics, Rev. R. L. Ottley, M. A.

WHAT IS CHRIST'S CHURCH? CHURCH OR CHAPEL? An Eirenecoi. By the Rev. JOSEPH HAMMOND. 12mo, cloth. $2.00.

    The most complete manual. We can thoroughly recommend it to tell with "devout Non-conformists," and certainly there will be many Churchmen who may study and keep it at hand with profit. The whole is very ably and well done. — *The Guardian.*

    No one can read *Church or Chapel?* without a feeling of respect for the writer, and few without thinking better of the Church which he champions. It sets out the case with a lucidity and a moderation that are deserving of all praise. Will be found to have great value. — *Spectator.*

SUNLIGHT AND SHADOW IN THE CHRISTIAN LIFE. Sermons preached for the most part in America. By the Rev. W. J. KNOX-LITTLE. pp. 310. 12mo, cloth, $1.75.

    " They cannot help interesting and inspiring those who read them."

A New and Cheaper Edition of
THE EVIDENTIAL VALUE OF THE HOLY EUCHARIST. By the Rev. G. F. MACLEAR, D. D., author of *A Class-Book of Old and New Testament,* etc. Second Edition, revised and corrected. pp. 352. 12mo, cloth, $1.50.

    Extract from a letter to the author by the Rt. Rev. A. Cleveland Coxe, D.D., LL.D., Bishop of Western New York. (Reprinted by permission.)

    "I have been reading since Mid-Lent your masterly work on The Holy Eucharist as evidence, etc.: and long and lovingly as I have studied the Passion and Resurrection of our blessed Lord, I have just closed this work of yours, feeling how you have freshened and amplified what I knew before, and how much *you have made me know*, which I ought to have studied out and discovered for myself. I feel as if I ought to begin all over again, with new helps and suggestions, the study of my Greek Testament."

A HISTORICAL INTRODUCTION TO THE STUDY OF THE BOOKS OF THE NEW TESTAMENT. By GEORGE SALMON, D. D. Fourth and cheaper edition. pp. 678. 12mo, cloth, $3.50.

ILLUSTRATED NOTES ON ENGLISH CHURCH HISTORY. By the Rev. C. ARTHUR LANE. 2 vols., 16mo, cloth, 40 cents each.

    VOL. I. — From the Earliest Times to the Dawn of the Reformation.
    VOL. II. — The Reformation and Modern Church Work.

    The two volumes traverse the whole range of Church History in Britain. They contain over two hundred illustrations, including every Cathedral in England and Wales, and many notable Abbeys and Churches.

THE INCARNATION AS A MOTIVE POWER. Sermons by WILLIAM BRIGHT, D. D., Canon of Christ Church, Oxford. 12mo, cloth, $1.75.

    An admirable volume from one of the ablest living theologians in the Church of England. . . . It is superfluous to commend such a book as this; it needs no praise at our hands. — *Living Church.*

    The above may be obtained from any bookseller, or will be sent free by mail on receipt of price.

E. & J. B. YOUNG & CO.,
COOPER UNION, FOURTH AVENUE, NEW YORK.

 # NEW BOOKS.

RECENT PUBLICATIONS

OF THE

LONDON SOCIETY FOR PROMOTING CHRISTIAN KNOWLEDGE.

THE MONUMENTAL HISTORY OF THE BRITISH CHURCH. By J. ROMILLY ALLEN. With Illustrations. 16mo, cloth, $1.25.

In this volume is collected together a mass of information on the archæological side of the question as to how and when Christianity was first introduced into the British Isles, giving new light on the story of our Mother Church

THE TITLE-DEEDS OF THE CHURCH OF ENGLAND By T. P. GARNIER, M.A. 16mo, cloth, $1.25.

An historic vindication of the position and claims that the Church of England is the true lineal descendant of the first fellowship of the disciples on the Day of Pentecost.

ST. BERNARD, Abbot of Clairvaux, A.D. 1091-1153. By the Rev. S. J. EALES, 16mo, cloth, 80 cents.

This volume is the last issue of *The Fathers for English Readers*, and is a clear and interesting account of the "last of the Fathers," and of his great influence over the age in which he lived.

A SKETCH OF THE HISTORY OF EUROPE, chiefly International. By A. R. ROPES, M.A. 16mo, cloth, $1.00.

A sketch of the history of Europe as a system of States from the time when the Roman Empire gave that history unity down to the present day.

THE EVIDENTIAL VALUE OF THE HOLY EUCHARIST. By the Rev. G. F. MACLEAR, D.D. Author of *Class-Book of Old and New Testament*, etc. Second Edition, revised and corrected. 12mo, pages 352, cloth, $1.50.

Extract from a letter to the Author by the Rt. Rev. A. CLEVELAND COXE, D.D, LL.D., Bishop of Western New York. (Reprinted by permission.)

I have been reading, since Mid-Lent, your masterly work on 'The Holy Eucharist' as evidence, etc., and long and lovingly as I have studied the Passion and Resurrection of our blessed LORD, I have just closed this work of yours, feeling how you have freshened and amplified what I knew before, and how much *you have made me know* which I ought to have studied out and discovered for myself. I feel as if I ought to begin all over again, with new helps and suggestions, the study of my Greek Testament.

THE CHURCH CATECHISM; with Notes by E. M. Illustrated with twelve colored and many wood-cut engravings. 18mo, illuminated paper boards, 40 cents

NATURAL HISTORY OF THE ANIMAL KINGDOM. Adapted from the German of Professor Von Schubert by W. F. KIRBY, F.L.S. Illustrated with 91 full-page colored plates containing nearly 850 figures of animal life, and 120 page of descriptive matter, interspersed with numerous wood cuts. 3 vols, folio, $3.00 per vol

Vol. I. **MAMMALIA**; 31 colored plates, including 171 figures.

Vol. II. **BIRDS**; 30 colored plates including 115 figures.

Vol. III. **REPTILES, AMPHIBIA, FISHES, INSECTS,** etc.; 30 colored plate, including 480 figures

The work will also be supplied, the 3 vols. in 1, handsomely half bound, cloth sides, red edges, $4.50.

SCRIPTURE PICTURE-BOOK. The Story of the Old Testament. Printed in large type. Numerous full-page and other illustrations. Small 4to, limp cloth, 50 cents. cloth boards, illuminated side, red edges, 80 cents.

TWELVE TINY TALES. By Mrs. MOLESWORTH. A charming series of books, with colored illustrations by Harrison Weir and W. J Morgan. Small 4to, cloth, side in gold and colors, $1 00.

THE PETRINE CLAIMS. A Critical Inquiry by RICHARD FREDERICK LITTLEDALE, LL.D., D.C.L. 16mo, cloth, $2.00.

This is the most unanswerable book ever written on the Roman controversy. It gives Roman definitions and Roman authorities, and by them unanswerably proves that there has not been a legal Pope for 400 years. Let them answer this—if they can. — The Rev. J. H. HOPKINS, D D.

TWO EXCELLENT BOOKS FOR THE STUDY OF CHURCH HISTORY. Illustrated Notes on English Church History. By the Rev. C. ARTHUR LANE. 2 vols., 16mo, cloth, 40 cents each.

Vol. I **FROM THE EARLIEST TIMES TO THE DAWN OF THE REFORMATION.**

Vol. II. **THE REFORMATION AND MODERN CHURCH WORK.**

The two volumes traverse the whole range of Church History in Britain. They contain over 200 illustrations, including every Cathedral in England and Wales, and many notabl Abbeys and Churches.

A STORY OF THE CHURCH OF ENGLAND. Vol. II. Illustrated. 16mo, cloth, 60 cents.

The above may be obtained from any bookseller, or will be sent free by mail on receipt of price, by

E. & J. B. YOUNG & CO.,

COOPER UNION, FOURTH AVENUE, NEW YORK.

 REFERENCE BOOKS.

ENCYCLOPAEDIA FOR SELF-EDUCATORS.

JOHNSON'S UNIVERSAL CYCLOPÆDIA has long enjoyed an enviable reputation for comprehensiveness and correctness. To enable it to meet the demand for the latest obtainable data on the subjects treated, the publishers have prepared a new and revised edition, giving the most careful attention to every detail. Of the eight thousand articles contained in the volumes, one hundred and fifty were written by the editors-in-chief, President Barnard, of Columbia College, and Prof. A. H. Guyot, of the College of New Jersey. Eminent specialists have edited the various scientific and literary departments, men whose names signed to the articles are a guarantee of their accuracy. In biography the volumes are especially rich, three hundred American names appearing, and four hundred foreign. The industrial arts come next in the amount of space occupied, sixty-two subjects being treated under that head. The departments of public and civil law, in charge of Presidents Woolsey and Dwight, are particularly valuable. Astronomy, botany, geography, history, medicine, music, mythology, physics, politics, and zoölogy each receive full attention. There is an entire avoidance of the expression of critical opinions, thus keeping it within the limits which were set for it, as simply a book of facts. This vast amount of material is well arranged with reference to saving the time of the reader, a praiseworthy feature being the many sub-divisions of subjects, by which is avoided the necessity of reading the whole of a long article when but one point is sought. The maps and illustrations are many and excellent. Taken as a whole, the Cyclopædia is as nearly perfect as the best work of its scholarly editors and contributors could make it.—*The Chautauquan.*

From the Rt. Rev. F. D. Huntington, S.T.D., LL.D., Bishop of Central New York:

"So many of the editors, associate editors and special contributors of JOHNSON'S UNIVERSAL CYCLOPÆDIA, are known to me personally as scholars and writers in their several departments, that I have no hesitation in certifying to the great value and unquestionable accuracy of the work as a whole, though I have been able to give it only a cursory examination. The scope of the undertaking goes much beyond that of any of the class that I am acquainted with. I have exchanged my subscription for the volumes of Encyclopædia Britannica, as far as published, even, for Johnson's."

A. J. JOHNSON & CO., Publishers,

11 Great Jones Street, New York, N. Y.

REFERENCE BOOKS.

WORCESTER'S.
THE GREAT DICTIONARY OF THE ENGLISH LANGUAGE.

THE Standard Authority in use in American Schools and Colleges; American Orators, Writers, Poets, and Statesmen, people of education, and all the leading American newspapers and magazines, scores of the most brilliant men of the day can be named who make use of WORCESTER'S UNABRIDGED DICTIONARY.

IT CONTAINS THOUSANDS OF WORDS NOT TO BE FOUND IN ANY OTHER DICTIONARY.

The *New York Tribune* of March 26, 1890, says:—

"The Tribune has itself for fifteen years used Worcester's as its own authority in spelling and pronunciation. Every other large New York paper, as well as a great multitude of other publications, makes use of Worcester's Unabridged, and as the latter publication is the largest American dictionary in existence, we offer it to our readers unhesitatingly. One word ought to be said about the cheap reprints of old dictionaries, on which the copyrights have expired. No American citizen would want one of those antiquated volumes in the house. They contain a great number of errors in spelling. They do not have the new words or the new definitions. The only dictionary worth having is the unabridged (Worcester's) of 1890."

CHAMBERS'S ENCYCLOPÆDIA.
Vols. I., II., III., IV., and V. Ready.
ENTIRELY NEW EDITION, REVISED AND REWRITTEN.

A DICTIONARY of Universal Knowledge. Edited and Published under the Auspices of W. & R. CHAMBERS, Edinburgh, and J. B. LIPPINCOTT COMPANY, Philadelphia. To be completed in ten volumes. Issued at intervals of a few months. Price, per vol.: cloth, $3.00; cloth, uncut, $3.00; sheep, $4.00; half morocco, $4.50.

Of the many books of its kind that have been published in the English language, this is by far the most convenient and the most serviceable; and in its handsome new type, its large page, and its finer printing, to say nothing of its bringing every theme of which it treats down to date, the work in its revised form cannot be replaced in its usefulness in a working library. — *Boston Globe.*

No better book of the kind exists for household use than Chambers's Encyclopædia, which is now coming out anew in enlarged form. Its articles are clearly and pleasingly written, and are never too technical or abstruse. It ought to be in every family and office, for it will be found of daily use. — *Cincinnati Commercial Gazette.*

Whatever other cyclopædic literature may be produced in the years to come, we do not expect to be able to dispense with Chambers's. — *New York Observer.*

The price is such as to place this valuable work within the reach of almost every one who cares enough for the means of knowledge to spend a little upon their possession. — *New York Tribune.*

The list of staff writers and special contributors to this edition is unsurpassed, even by the great *Britannica*, and for people of average learning and moderate means this promises to be, when completed, the most satisfactory book of reference of its kind. — *New York Examiner.*

Specimen pages and testimonials of either of the above works mailed free on application.

FOR SALE BY ALL BOOKSELLERS.

J. B. LIPPINCOTT COMPANY, PUBLISHERS,
715 & 717 MARKET STREET, PHILADELPHIA.

THE CHURCH REVIEW,
For 1891.

The Church Review will be published quarterly during 1891, in the months of January, April, July, and October. Each quarterly issue forms a complete volume of 320 pages of text and 32 pages of advertising.

TERMS:—Library Edition (each quarterly issue bound in cloth), $5.00 a year in advance. Paper covers, $4.00 a year in advance. The price of a single copy, library edition, $1.50; paper covers, $1.25.

The CHURCH REVIEW was founded in April, 1848, and is the leading periodical of the Anglo-American Church. The American Bishops (fifty-nine, all that were present at the General Convention of 1883), in commending the REVIEW to Churchmen, say: "At the head of our current Church literature stands the CHURCH REVIEW . . . It is as comprehensive in its tone as the Church itself. All schools of thought that may lawfully claim recognition are welcome to its pages. The most vital questions of the day have been discussed by it with dignity, learning, and commanding ability." During the past ten years of the present editorial management its standard of scholarship in the field of religious journalism has been gradually raised, until to-day it undoubtedly stands at the head of religious periodical literature in this country. It does not confine its topics for discussion to religious questions, but considers the great social, intellectual, and philosophical problems of the age. Questions not strictly within the province of theology are treated by the most competent writers, whether or not they are members of the Anglican Communion. Thus it claims to represent not only the Anglo-American Church in the domain of religion and theology, but also the moral and intellectual side of American life and thought. It reviews more books of real worth in the various departments of literature than any other one periodical, either secular or religious, in the United States. This department of the REVIEW has received the highest commendation from the religious and secular press, and from the leading scholars of this country and England.

As each issue is a volume of large proportions, specimen copies cannot be sent out free, but upon application a copy will be sent for examination to be returned if the person making the request does not become a subscriber.

Address all communications to

THE CHURCH REVIEW CO.,
1 AND 3 UNION SQUARE, NEW YORK.

SEND 10c. IN STAMPS FOR THREE WEEKS' TRIAL.

PUBLIC OPINION

Is an attractive weekly publication of 36 pages, and the only one in America giving a broad, well-classified, and perfectly unbiassed

DIGEST OF THE CURRENT THOUGHT OF THE WORLD,

as expressed by the Leading Reviews, Magazines, and Newspapers.

$1000 a year expended for periodicals, and 18 hours' work a day reading them, would not give you what you can get in Public Opinion for $3.00 per year and 15 minutes a day.

It keeps the reader thoroughly in touch with the thought of the day on all subjects of interest.

Its corps of editors and translators read carefully all the principal daily papers of the nation, and the magazines, reviews, and prominent weeklies of this country and Europe. From this great mass of contemporaneous matter the most noteworthy articles and opinions upon topics chiefly occupying public attention in the fields of

POLITICS, SOCIOLOGY, SCIENCE, FINANCE, RELIGION, LITERATURE, AND ART,

are gathered into PUBLIC OPINION, and so arranged that the reader may catch the trend of public thought with but a slight expenditure of time, and at a cost of a fraction over *5 CENTS A WEEK.*

PUBLIC OPINION is in the tenth volume of its successful existence. It is taken by many thousands of the most intelligent people. Its circulation is world-wide, and its popularity universal. Its neutrality in all things has never been questioned.

L. S. METCALF, Editor "The Forum," says: Formerly, to keep informed of the drift of editorial views, I was obliged to read regularly a considerable number of newspapers; now I rely almost entirely upon PUBLIC OPINION, and obtain the information I need with the expenditure of but a small fraction of the time.

Rev. JAMES McCOSH, D.D., LL.D., says: The best journal existing for those who have not money to buy or time to read a great number of newspapers.

Hon. WILLIAM T. HARRIS, U.S. Com. Education, says: It ought to circulate a million a week.

HARPER'S WEEKLY: Whoever wishes to know the movement of public opinion will find it happily summarized in this publication.

BOSTON TRANSCRIPT says: The large circulation of PUBLIC OPINION is one of the surest signs of as high civilization in the United States.

Rev. CHARLES F. DEEMS, D.D., says: If I could take but one paper, it would be PUBLIC OPINION. If I took a hundred, I should still need it.

TO BE A READER OF PUBLIC OPINION IS TO BE WELL INFORMED.

SEND 10c. FOR 3 WEEKS' TRIAL SUBSCRIPTION.

If you are not already a subscriber to PUBLIC OPINION, send 10 cents in stamps for three weeks' trial. Yearly subscription, $3 per year. Subscription to January 1, 1891, free to those who subscribe for one year.

Mention CHURCH REVIEW.   **THE PUBLIC OPINION CO., Washington, D.C.**

 PERIODICALS.

The Lutheran Observer,

A RELIGIOUS FAMILY PAPER,

PUBLISHED WEEKLY AT

No. 524 WALNUT STREET, PHILADELPHIA.

EDITORS:
Rev. F. W. CONRAD, D.D., LL.D.
Prof. V. L. CONRAD, Ph.D., D.D.

WITH A LARGE NUMBER OF ABLE AND POPULAR WRITERS AS CONTRIBUTORS.

The LUTHERAN OBSERVER is the oldest, the largest, and most influential journal of the Lutheran Church in the United States. Its circulation greatly exceeds that of all the other English Lutheran Church papers in this country.

TERMS CASH IN ADVANCE.

One copy, per annum, including postage $2.00
One copy, six months 1.00
On trial, for three months 50

No new names are entered on the subscription book without the first payment in advance.

Remittances must be made in Post-Office Money Orders, Bank Checks, or Drafts. If these cannot be obtained, send the money in a Registered Letter. Postal Notes are not safe for transmission by mail. All postmasters are obliged to register letters when requested.

ORGANS AND PIANOS.

MASON & HAMLIN
ORGANS.

TESTIMONIALS FROM

Theo. Thomas. John K. Paine. S. B. Mills. Wm. L. Tomlins. Geo. W. Morgan. Sam'l P. Warren. Dudley Buck. Eugene Thayer. P. S. Gilmore. Franz Liszt. Saint-Saëns. Ch. Gounod. Campanini. Christine Nilsson. Marie Rose. Dr. Stainer. Johann Strauss. X. Scharwenka.

HIGHEST HONORS AT EVERY GREAT WORLD'S EXHIBITION,
PARIS, 1867, TO LONDON, 1885, INCLUSIVE.

FASHIONABLE MODELS.

LISZT ORGAN. — The finest and most powerfully toned Reed Organ made. The first one made expressly for the late Abbé Liszt. The Organ *par excellence* for the drawing-room, and used largely in churches and chapels. With one and two manuals.

THREE-MANUAL and 32-feet PEDAL ORGAN. — The most complete Reed Organ Manufactured. Contains 32 stops, composition pedals, etc. Used in Westminster Abbey.

QUEEN'S MODEL. — So called from the fact that it was made from furnished specifications expressly for, and sold to, Her Majesty, VICTORIA, Queen of England.

EOLIAN HARP ORGAN. — This style combines the effect of a stringed orchestra with the organ. It is possible to produce the undulating effect of stringed instruments with the one hand, while the other gives the organ tone.

An Illustrated Catalogue of over 100 Styles, suitable for - - - - - - Churches, Chapels, Sunday Schools, etc., sent free on application.

PIANOS.

The improved method of piano construction, invented by MASON & HAMLIN in 1882, has been fully proved, many excellent experts pronouncing it the greatest improvement in pianos of the century.

Send for full information.

MASON & HAMLIN ORGAN AND PIANO CO
BOSTON. NEW YORK. CHICAGO.

Organs and Pianos sold for Cash, Easy Payments, and Rented.

Royal Bavarian Establishment.

HANKEY MEMORIAL WINDOW,
BRANCH LIBRARY COLUMBIA COLLEGE, 121 W. 23D STREET, NEW YORK.

MAYER & CO.

MUNICH, LONDON,
AND
NEW YORK.

Memorial Windows,

Mural Paintings,

Statuary

in

*Marble, Wood,
and Terra Cotta.*

*Executed in our
Munich Studios
by Artists of the
Royal Academy.*

DESIGNS SUBMITTED.

DISCUSSED

ON THE

BASIS OF THE LAMBETH PROPOSITIONS

OF 1888

✠

*Reprinted from The Church Review for April
and October, 1890*

NEW YORK
THE CHURCH REVIEW CO.
1 AND 3 UNION SQUARE
1890

Copyright, 1890,
BY THE CHURCH REVIEW CO.

University Press:
JOHN WILSON AND SON, CAMBRIDGE.

TO

The Bishops Assembled in General Convention,

AT CHICAGO, IN OCTOBER, 1886,

AND AT

LAMBETH PALACE, LONDON, IN JULY, 1888,

THIS VOLUME

IS RESPECTFULLY DEDICATED BY THE EDITOR
OF THE CHURCH REVIEW.

PREFACE.

CHURCH REUNION is an object worthy of the best efforts of all who call themselves Christians. It is evident from the consideration of the subject in the following pages by men who will be recognized in all parts of America as among the foremost leaders of their respective Communions, that we can only hope for Church Reunion on the lines, and as the result, of historical investigation. It is necessary that there should be a common basis proposed, and a full understanding as to how much of such basis would be accepted by all, upon due proof of its being essential. The readers of this volume will not be in doubt on either of these points.

We have accomplished all we had in mind when we invited these distinguished leaders of religious thought to discuss the subject of Church Reunion in the CHURCH REVIEW. It was but natural that the articles should be put in the convenient form of a single volume. In this form they should have a wide circulation and careful reading among and by all thoughtful Christians.

But little is known of the great Holy Eastern or Greek Church, as it is sometimes called, and we thought it would add to the interest and value of this volume to add thereto an article on the Holy Eastern Church by the Hon. Francis J. Parker, which appeared in the January issue (1890) of the CHURCH REVIEW. We do not agree with Mr. Parker in his views on the *Filioque*, and he is at variance with the doctors of the Anglican Church. A man for whom the whole Anglican Communion has great respect, wrote us on learning of our intention to add this article to the volume, that he holds that "we are theologically right, and that our authorized *doctrine* and the authorized doctrine of the Orthodox East does not differ on this point. We have an incorrect text, and historically we are in the wrong. But I believe with Dr. Pusey and Dr. Liddon that for us to *remove* the *Filioque* under existing circumstances would shake the faith of many of our people in other articles of the Creed. They need to know more before it is done." But Mr. Parker gives a vast amount of information that is not to be found elsewhere within the limits of a single volume.

If the Anglican Church addresses herself chiefly to our Protestant brethren, it is also true, as Bishop Coxe has pointed out, that Church Reunion with the Church of Rome can only come when she is ready to restore the Historic Episcopate to its rightful place in the Church. For that reason we have also added an article in review of the late Dr. Littledale's great work on the "Petrine Claims," by Dr. John Henry Hopkins. In this article we have the advantage of the views of the two most celebrated controversialists on the subject of the Papacy that this century has produced.

We send this volume out, hoping and believing that it will incite many to a careful examination of the questions that now divide numbers of our fellow-Christians.

HENRY MASON BAUM,
Editor of The Church Review.

NEW YORK, November, 1890.

CONTENTS.

Church Reunion on the Basis proposed by the Lambeth Conference.

	PAGE
Lambeth Conference Report, Encyclical Letter	11
Definite Teaching of the Faith	12
Home Reunion	14
Relation to the Scandinavian Church	15
To Old Catholics and Others	15
To the Eastern Churches	16
Authoritative Standards	16

Reports of Committees.

Home Reunion	21
Scandinavians.—Old Catholics	26
Eastern Churches	31
Authoritative Standards	35

The Basis for Church Reunion proposed by the Lambeth Conference of 1888

	40
Prof. Charles A. Briggs, D.D.	41
Prof. Egbert C. Smyth, D.D.	72
Rev. Edward T. Horn, D.D.	77
Rev. Robert S. MacArthur, D.D.	82
Prof. William F. Mann, D.D.	92
Prof. E. F. Wolf, D.D.	97
Rev. William V. Kelley, D.D.	105

	PAGE
Prof. George R. Crooks, D.D.	112
Rev. Henry F. Van Dyke, D.D.	117
Rev. Thomas Armitage, D.D.	125
Rev. Henry M. Dexter, D.D.	129
Rev. James McCosh, D.D., LL.D.	132
Rev. John Hall, D.D., LL.D.	134
Rev. Lyman Abbott, D.D.	136
Rev. J. M. Buckley, D.D.	138
Rev. Howard Crosby, D.D., LL.D.	139
Rev. Talbot W. Chambers, D.D.	140
Rev. Thomas S. Hastings, D.D., LL.D.	141
Rev. William M. Taylor, D.D.	142
Rev. Edward B. Coe, D.D.	143

Historic Presbyterians.
    Rt. Rev. Arthur Cleveland Coxe, D.D., LL.D. 145

The Historic Episcopate.
    Rt. Rev. William Croswell Doane, D.D., LL.D. 158

What is Meant by the "Historic Episcopate" in the Resolutions of the House of Bishops in 1886 and the Lambeth Conference of 1888.
    Rt. Rev. William Stevens Perry, D.D., LL.D., D.C.L. 165

The Historic Episcopate.
    Rt. Rev. George F. Seymour, D.D., LL.D. 174

The Holy Scriptures as the Basis of Church Unity.
    Rev. William D. Wilson, D.D., LL.D. 191

The Faith Which Was Once for All Delivered.
    Prof. Joseph F. Garrison, D.D. 220

The Holy Eucharist the Lord's Eirenicon.
    Prof. J. J. Elmendorf, D.D. 231

The Validity of Non-Episcopal Ordination.
    Rev. Thomas F. Gailor, M.A., S.T.B. 244

The Voice of the Church of England on Episcopal Ordination.
    Rev. Arthur Lowndes 259

Contents.

	PAGE
BISHOP LIGHTFOOT ON THE HISTORIC EPISCOPATE.	
Rev. Thomas F. Gailor, M.A., S.T.B.	319
THE NICENE CREED AS THE SUFFICIENT STATEMENT OF THE CHRISTIAN FAITH.	
Prof. Frederick W. Davenport, S.T.D.	329
"THREE POINTS."	
Rev. John Henry Hopkins, S.T.D.	337
THE HOLY EASTERN CHURCH.	
Hon. Francis J. Parker	356
THE PETRINE CLAIMS.	
Rev. John Henry Hopkins, S.T.D.	387

 NEW BOOKS.

MACMILLAN & COMPANY'S
✷ *Publications* ✷

Works by the RIGHT REV. J. B. LIGHTFOOT, D.D., D.C.L., LL.D., Late Bishop of Durham.

ESSAYS ON THE WORK ENTITLED SUPERNATURAL RELIGION. 8vo, $2.50.

 It is almost impossible to give an adequate idea of the thoroughness with which the task of exposing the inaccuracy and the sophistry of *Supernatural Religion* has been accomplished. Those interested in the subject must consult the book itself, which they will find a work of triumphant scholarship from the hand of an expert, and in doing so they will also find that apart from the controversy involved, it has an independent value as a synopsis of patristic opinions. — *Churchman.*

 Every earnest student of the Christian evidences will feel grateful to Dr. Lightfoot, not only for his championship of the truth when assailed in the book to which he replies, but for the exceedingly valuable *résumé* he supplies of the whole argument as respects the authenticity of the New Testament books. It is a great service to the cause of sacred learning which the accomplished Bishop of Durham here renders, and is sure to be appreciated as such in America no less than in his own country. — *Chicago Standard.*

 It may confidently be affirmed that this book is the most notable contribution to the evidences which has been made in the present generation. — *Standard of the Cross.*

 We can almost thank the author of *Supernatural Religion*, mischievous as that book is, for provoking this most valuable contribution to the support of the authenticity of the Gospel. . . . A volume that no scholar can afford to do without in his library. — *Living Church.*

 Of the utmost importance to those interested in the great discussions of the age. — *Christian Advocate.*

 A permanent contribution to the most erudite and exact historical criticism. — *Advance.*

 Scholarly and unanswerable criticisms on the anonymous work called *Supernatural Religion.* — *Chicago Tribune.*

LEADERS IN THE NORTHERN CHURCH. 12mo. (Just ready.)

ST. PAUL'S EPISTLE TO THE GALATIANS. A Revised Text, with Introduction, Notes, and Dissertations. Tenth edition, revised. 8vo, $4.00.

ST. PAUL'S EPISTLE TO THE PHILIPPIANS. A Revised Text, with Introduction, Notes, and Dissertations. Ninth edition, revised. 8vo, $4.00.

ST. PAUL'S EPISTLE TO THE COLOSSIANS AND TO PHILEMON. A Revised Text, with Introductions, Notes, and Dissertations. Eighth edition, revised. 8vo, $4.00.

THE APOSTOLIC FATHERS. Part II. S. Ignatius. S. Polycarp. Revised Texts, with Introductions, Notes, and Dissertations. Second edition. Three vols. 8vo, $16.50.

 Dr. Salmon, in the *Academy*, of the previous edition said: "The book is characterized throughout by the admirable thoroughness with which Bishop Lightfoot does all his literary work, for I do not know any writer who inspires his readers with more just confidence that no work has been scamped, that on every question all the available evidence has been laid before them, and the arguments on both sides fairly presented."

THE APOSTOLIC FATHERS. Abridged edition. With short Introductions. Greek Text and English Translations. 8vo. (In the press.)

ST. CLEMENT OF ROME. The Two Epistles to the Corinthians. A Revised Text, with Introduction and Notes. Two vols. 8vo. (In the press.)

∴ *Macmillan & Company's NEW COMPLETE CATALOGUE will be sent free by mail to any address on application.*

MACMILLAN & CO., 112 Fourth Avenue, NEW YORK.

THE
Church Review

VOLUME LVII. ✠ APRIL, 1890

Church Reunion.

On the Basis Proposed by the Lambeth Conference.

Conference of Bishops of the Anglican Communion, holden at Lambeth Palace in July, 1888. Encyclical Letter from the Bishops, with Resolutions and Reports. London: Society for Promoting Christian Knowledge. New York: E. and J. B. Young and Company.

WE thought it would be not only a courteous act, but that it was due to representative men of the chief Protestant Communions in this country, to offer them an opportunity to say in the pages of the CHURCH REVIEW how far they are willing to accept the basis for Church Reunion proposed by the Lambeth Conference. Invitations to write were sent out to several leading clergymen of each Communion here represented, and we are glad to state that they were accepted, with but three or four exceptions.

Before entering upon the discussion of the basis proposed for Church Reunion, we give so much of the Report of the Lambeth Conference of 1888 as relates to the subject.

EDITOR.

ENCYCLICAL LETTER.

TO THE FAITHFUL IN CHRIST JESUS, GREETING: —

WE, Archbishops, Bishops Metropolitan, and other Bishops of the Holy Catholic Church, in full communion with the Church of England, one hundred and forty-five in number, all having superintendence over Dioceses or lawfully commissioned to exercise Episcopal functions therein, assembled from divers parts

of the earth, at Lambeth Palace, in the year of our LORD 1888,
under the presidency of the Most Reverend Edward, by Divine
Providence Archbishop of Canterbury, Primate of all England
and Metropolitan, after receiving in the chapel of the said palace
the Blessed Sacrament of the LORD'S Body and Blood, and
uniting in prayer for the guidance of the HOLY SPIRIT, have
taken into consideration various questions which have been submitted to us affecting the welfare of GOD'S people and the condition of the Church in divers parts of the world.

We have made these matters the subject of careful and serious
deliberation during the month past, both in general Conference
and in Committees specially appointed to consider the several
questions; and we now commend to the faithful the conclusions
at which we have arrived.

We have appended to this letter two sets of documents, the
one containing the formal Resolutions of the Conference, and the
other the Reports of the several Committees. We desire you to
bear in mind that the Conference is responsible for the first alone.
The Reports of Committees can only be taken to represent the
mind of the Conference in so far as they are reaffirmed or directly adopted in the Resolutions; but we have thought good to
print these Reports, believing that they will offer fruitful matter
for consideration.

. . . .

Definite Teaching of the Faith.

Recognizing thus the primary importance of maintaining the
moral precepts and discipline of the Gospel in all the relations
of life and society, we proceed to the consideration of the means,
within the reach and contemplation of the Churches, for inculcating the definite truths of the Faith, which are the basis of
such moral teaching.

We cannot escape the conviction that this department of work
requires great attention and much improvement. The religious
teaching of the young is sadly deficient in depth and reality,
especially in the matter of doctrine. This deficiency is not confined to any class of society, and the task of remedying the default is one which the laity must be prepared to share with the
clergy. On parents it lies as a Divine charge. Godfathers and
godmothers should be urged to fulfil the duty which they have

undertaken for the children whose sponsors they have been, and to see that they are not left uninstructed, or inadequately prepared for Confirmation. The use of public catechising and regular preparation of candidates for Confirmation is capable of much development. The work done in Sunday Schools requires, as we believe, more constant supervision and more sustained interest than, in a great many cases, it receives from the clergy. The instruction of Sunday School teachers, and of the pupil-teachers in Elementary Schools, ought to be regarded as an indispensable part of the pastoral work of a parish priest; and the moral and practical lessons from the Bible ought to be enforced by constant reference to the sanctions, and to the illustrations of doctrine and discipline belonging to them, to be found in the same Holy Scripture. It would be possible, to a greater extent than is now done, to make sermons in Church combine doctrinal and moral efficiency and, by illustrating the rationale of Divine service, lead on the congregations to the perception of the definite relations between worship, faith, and work, — the lessons of the Prayer-Book, the Catechism, and the Creeds.

It is not, however, with reference to the young alone, or to the recognized members of their own flock, that the clergy have need to look carefully to the security of definiteness in teaching the Faith.

The study of Holy Scripture is a great part of the mental discipline of the Christian, and the Bible itself is the main instrument in all teaching of religion. Unhappily, in the present day there is a wide-spread system of propagandism hostile to the reception of the Bible as a treasury of Divine knowledge; and throughout society in all its ranks, misgivings, doubts, hostile criticisms, and sceptical estimates of doctrinal truths as based on revelation, are very common.

The doubts which arise from the misapprehension of the due relations between science and revelation may be, and ought to be, treated with respect and a sympathetic patience; and where minds have been disquieted by scientific discovery or assertion, great care should be taken not to extinguish the elements of faith, but rather to direct the thinker to the realization of the fact that such discoveries elucidate the action of laws which, rightly conceived, tend to the higher appreciation of the glorious work of the CREATOR, upheld by the word of His power.

The dangers arising from the hostile or sceptical temper and attitude are increased by the difficulty of determining how far our teaching and the popular acceptance of it can be harmonized with a due consideration for the views on inspiration, and especially on the character of the discipline of the Old Testament dispensation, which, although they have never received definite sanction in the Church, have been long and widely prevalent.

We must recommend to the clergy cautious and industrious treatment of these points of controversy, and most earnestly press upon them the importance of taking, as the central thought of their teaching, our LORD JESUS CHRIST, as the sacrifice for our sins, as the healer of our sinfulness, the source of all our spiritual life, and the revelation to our consciences of the law and motive of all moral virtue. To Him and to His work all the teachings of the Old Testament converge; and from Him all the teachings of the New Testament flow, in spirit, in force, and in form. The work of the Church is the application and extension of the blessings of the Incarnation, and her teaching the development of its doctrinal issues as contained in the Creeds of the Church.

Home Reunion.

After anxious discussion we have resolved to content ourselves with laying down certain articles as a basis on which approach may be, by GOD'S blessing, made toward Home Reunion. These articles, four in number, will be found in the appended Resolutions.

The attitude of the Anglican Communion toward the religious bodies now separated from it by unhappy divisions would appear to be this: We hold ourselves in readiness to enter into brotherly conference with any of those who may desire intercommunion with us in a more or less perfect form. We lay down conditions on which such intercommunion is, in our opinion, and according to our conviction, possible. For however we may long to embrace those now alienated from us, so that the ideal of the one flock under the one Shepherd may be realized, we must not be unfaithful stewards of the great deposit intrusted to us. We cannot desert our position either as to faith or discipline. That concord would, in our judgment, be neither true nor desirable which should be produced by such surrender.

But we gladly and thankfully recognize the real religious work which is carried on by Christian bodies not of our Communion. We cannot close our eyes to the visible blessing which has been vouchsafed to their labors for CHRIST's sake. Let us not be misunderstood on this point. We are not insensible to the strong ties, the rooted convictions, which attach them to their present position. These we respect, as we wish that on our side our own principles and feelings may be respected. Competent observers, indeed, assert that not in England only, but in all parts of the Christian world, there is a real yearning for unity, — that men's hearts are moved more than heretofore toward Christian fellowship. The Conference has shown in its discussions as well as its resolutions that it is deeply penetrated with this feeling. May the Spirit of Love move on the troubled waters of religious differences!

Relation to the Scandinavian Church.

Among the nations with whom English-speaking peoples are brought directly in contact are the Scandinavian races, who form an important element of the population in many of our Dioceses. The attitude, therefore, which the Anglican Communion should take toward the Scandinavian Churches, could not be a matter of indifference to this Conference. We have recommended that fuller knowledge should be sought, and friendly intercourse interchanged, until such time as matters may be ripe for a closer alliance without any sacrifice of principles which we hold to be essential.

To Old Catholics and Others.

Nor, again, is it possible for members of the Anglican Communion to withhold their sympathies from those Continental movements toward Reformation which, under the greatest difficulties, have proceeded mainly on the same lines as our own, retaining Episcopacy as an Apostolic ordinance. Though we believe that the time has not come for any direct alliance with any of these, and though we deprecate any precipitancy of action which would transgress primitive and established principles of jurisdiction, we believe that advances may be made without sacrifice of these, and we entertain the hope that the time may come when a more formal alliance with some at least of these bodies will be possible.

To the Eastern Churches.

The Conference has expressed its earnest desire to confirm and to improve the friendly relations which now exist between the Churches of the East and the Anglican Communion. These Churches have well earned the sympathy of Christendom, for through long ages of persecution they have kept alive in many a dark place the light of the Gospel. If that light is here and there feeble or dim, there is all the more reason that we, as we have opportunity, should tend and cherish it; and we need not fear that our offices of brotherly charity, if offered in a right spirit, will not be accepted. We reflect with thankfulness that there exist no bars, such as are presented to communion with the Latins by the formulated sanction of the Infallibility of the Church residing in the person of the Supreme Pontiff, by the doctrine of the Immaculate Conception, and other dogmas imposed by the decrees of Papal councils. The Church of Rome has always treated her Eastern sister wrongfully. She intrudes her bishops into the ancient Dioceses, and keeps up a system of active proselytism. The Eastern Church is reasonably outraged by these proceedings, wholly contrary as they are to Catholic principles; and it behooves us of the Anglican Communion to take care that we do not offend in like manner.

Individuals craving fuller light and stronger spiritual life may, by remaining in the Church of their baptism, become centres of enlightenment to their own people.

But though all schemes of proselytizing are to be avoided, it is only right that our real claims and position as a historical Church should be set before a people who are very distrustful of novelty, especially in religion, and who appreciate the history of Catholic antiquity. Help should be given toward the education of the clergy, and in more destitute communities extended to schools for general instruction.

Authoritative Standards.

The authoritative standards of doctrine and worship claim your careful attention in connection with these subjects. It is of the utmost importance that our faith and practice should be represented, both to the ancient Churches and to the native and growing Churches in the mission-field, in a manner which shall neither give cause for offence, nor restrict due liberty, nor present any stumbling-blocks in the way of complete communion.

In conformity with the practice of the former Conferences, we declare that we are united under our Divine Head in the fellowship of the one Catholic and Apostolic Church, holding the one Faith revealed in Holy Writ, defined in the Creeds, maintained by the primitive Church, and affirmed by the undisputed Ecumenical Councils; as standards of doctrine and worship alike, we recognize the Prayer-Book with its Catechism, the Ordinal, and the Thirty-Nine Articles, — the special heritage of the Church of England, and, to a greater or less extent, received by all the Churches of our Communion.

We desire that these standards should be set before the foreign Churches in their purity and simplicity. A certain liberty of treatment must be extended to the cases of native and growing Churches, on which it would be unreasonable to impose, as conditions of communion, the whole of the Thirty-Nine Articles, colored as they are in language and form by the peculiar circumstances under which they were originally drawn up. On the other hand, it would be impossible for us to share with them in the matter of Holy Orders, as in complete intercommunion, without satisfactory evidence that they hold substantially the same form of doctrine as ourselves. It ought not to be difficult, much less impossible, to formulate articles in accordance with our own standards of doctrine and worship, the acceptance of which should be required of all ordained in such Churches.

We close this letter rendering our humble and hearty thanks to Almighty GOD for His great goodness toward us. We have been permitted to meet together in larger numbers than heretofore. Contributions of knowledge and experience have been poured into the common stock from all parts of the earth. We have realized, more fully than it was possible to realize before, the extent, the power, and the influence of the great Anglican Communion. We have felt its capacities, its opportunities, its privileges. In our common deliberations we have tested its essential oneness amid all varieties of condition and development. Wherever there was diversity of opinion among us there was also harmony of spirit and unity of aim; and we shall return to our several Dioceses refreshed, strengthened, and inspired by the memories which we shall carry away.

But the sense of thanksgiving is closely linked with the obligation of duty. This fuller realization of our privileges as members of the Anglican Communion carries with it a heightened sense of our responsibilities, which do not end with our own people or with the mission-field alone, but extend to all the Churches of GOD. The opportunities of an exceptional position call us to an exceptional work. It is our earnest prayer that all — clergy and laity alike — may take GOD'S manifest purpose to heart, and strive in their several stations to work it out in all its fulness.

With these parting words we commend the results at which we have arrived in this Conference to your careful consideration, praying that the HOLY SPIRIT may direct your thoughts and lead you to all truth, and that our counsels may redound through your action to the glory of GOD and the increase of CHRIST'S kingdom. Signed, on behalf of the Conference,

EDW: CANTUAR.

C. J. GLOUCESTER & BRISTOL, *Episcopal Secretary.*
RANDALL T. DAVIDSON, Dean of Windsor, *General Secretary.*
B. F. SMITH, Archdeacon of Maidstone, *Assistant Secretary.*

The following Resolutions were formally adopted by the Conference.

11. That, in the opinion of this Conference, the following Articles supply a basis on which approach may be by GOD's blessing made toward Home Reunion : —

(*a*) The Holy Scriptures of the Old and New Testaments, as 'containing all things necessary to salvation,' and as being the rule and ultimate standard of Faith.

(*b*) The Apostles' Creed, as the Baptismal Symbol ; and the Nicene Creed, as the sufficient statement of the Christian Faith.

(*c*) The two Sacraments ordained by CHRIST Himself, — Baptism and the Supper of the LORD, — ministered with unfailing use of CHRIST'S words of institution, and of the elements ordained by Him.

(*d*) The Historic Episcopate, locally adapted in the methods of its administration to the varying needs of the nations and peoples called of GOD into the unity of His Church.

12. That this Conference earnestly requests the constituted authorities of the various branches of our Communion, acting, so far as may be, in concert with one another, to make it known that they hold themselves in readiness to enter into brotherly conference (such as that which has already been proposed by the Church in the United States of America) with the representatives of other Christian Communions in the English-speaking races, in order to consider what steps can be taken, either toward corporate Reunion, or toward such relations as may prepare the way for fuller organic unity hereafter.

13. That this Conference recommends as of great importance, in tending to bring about reunion, the dissemination of information respecting the standards of doctrine and the formularies in use in the Anglican Church, and recommends that information be disseminated, on the other hand, respecting the authoritative standards of doctrine, worship, and government adopted by the other bodies of Christians into which the English-speaking races are divided.

14. That in the opinion of this Conference, earnest efforts should be made to establish more friendly relations between the Scandinavian and Anglican Churches; and that approaches on the part of the Swedish Church, with a view to the mutual explanation of differences, be most gladly welcomed, in order to the ultimate establishment, if possible, of intercommunion on sound principles of ecclesiastical polity.

15. (*a*) That this Conference recognizes with thankfulness the dignified and independent position of the Old Catholic Church of Holland, and looks to more frequent brotherly intercourse to remove many of the barriers which at present separate us.

(*b*) That we regard it as a duty to promote friendly relations with the Old Catholic Community in Germany, and with the 'Christian Catholic Church' in Switzerland, not only out of sympathy with them, but also in thankfulness to GOD who has strengthened them to suffer for the truth under great discouragements, difficulties, and temptations; and that we offer them the privileges recommended by the Committee under the conditions specified in its Report.

(*c*) That the sacrifices made by the Old Catholics in Austria deserve our sympathy, and that we hope, when their organization is sufficiently tried and complete, a more formal relation may be found possible.

(*d*) That, with regard to the reformers in Italy, France, Spain, and Portugal, struggling to free themselves from the burden of unlawful terms of communion, we trust that they may be enabled to adopt such sound forms of doctrine and discipline, and to secure such Catholic organization, as will permit us to give them a fuller recognition.

(*e*) That, without desiring to interfere with the rights of bishops of the Catholic Church to interpose in cases of extreme necessity, we deprecate any action that does not regard primitive and established principles of jurisdiction, and the interests of the whole Anglican Communion.[1]

16. That, having regard to the fact that the question of the relation of the Anglican Church to the *Unitas Fratrum*, or Moravians, was remitted by the last Lambeth Conference to a Committee, which has hitherto presented no Report on the subject, the Archbishop of Canterbury be requested to appoint a Committee of Bishops who shall be empowered to confer with learned theologians, and with the heads of the *Unitas Fratrum*, and shall report to His Grace before the end of the current year, and that His Grace be requested to take such action on their Report as he shall deem right.

17. That this Conference, rejoicing in the friendly communications which have passed between the Archbishops of Canterbury and other Anglican bishops, and the patriarchs of Constantinople and other Eastern patriarchs and bishops, desires to express its hope that the barriers to fuller communion may be, in course of time, removed by further intercourse and extended enlightenment. The Conference commends this subject to the devout prayers of the faithful, and recommends that the counsels and efforts of our fellow-Christians should be directed to the encouragement of internal reformation in the Eastern Churches, rather than to the drawing away from them of individual members of their Communion.

18. That the Archbishop of Canterbury be requested to take counsel with such persons as he may see fit to consult, with a view to ascertaining whether it is desirable to revise the English version of the Nicene Creed or of the *Quicunque Vult*.[2]

19. That, as regards newly constituted Churches, especially in non-Christian lands, it should be a condition of the recognition of them as in complete intercommunion with us, and especially of their receiving from us Episcopal succession, that we should first receive from them satisfactory evidence that they hold substantially the same doctrine as our own, and that their clergy subscribe Articles in accordance with the express statements of our own standards of doctrine and worship; but that they should not necessarily be bound to accept in their entirety the Thirty-Nine Articles of Religion.

---

[1] Resolutions (*a*), (*b*), (*c*), (*d*), (*e*), were carried *nemine contradicente*.
[2] Carried by 57 votes to 20.

REPORTS OF COMMITTEES.

No. 9.—HOME REUNION.

Report of the Committee[1] appointed to consider what steps (if any) can be rightly taken on behalf of the Anglican Communion toward the reunion of the various bodies into which the Christianity of the English-speaking races is divided.

The Committee was appointed to consider 'what steps (if any) can be rightly taken, on behalf of the Anglican Communion, toward the reunion of the various bodies into which the Christianity of the English-speaking races is divided.'

I. On entering upon their duty, they had at once brought to their notice evidence of a strong *consensus* of authoritative opinion, from various branches of the Anglican Communion, that the time for some action in this matter, under prayer for GOD'S guidance through many acknowledged difficulties and dangers, has already come; and that the Conference — speaking, as it must speak, with the greatest weight of moral authority — should not separate without some such utterance as may further and direct such action.

In the Convocation of Canterbury the subject has been under discussion, at intervals, for nearly thirty years. In the year 1861 a resolution, on the motion of the Rev. Chancellor Massingberd, was carried *nem. con.* in the Lower House, praying the bishops to commend the subject of 'the Reunion of the divided members of CHRIST'S Body' to the prayers of the faithful.

In 1870, at the instance of the Lower House, a Committee was appointed on Reunion, with power to confer with any similar Committee which might be appointed in the Northern Province. The Committee, in its Report, recommended the use of the special Prayer for Unity, appointed for the day of the Queen's Accession, and the consideration of the propriety of communication on the subject with the chief Non-Con-

---

[1] Names of the members of the Committee: —

Bishop of Sydney (*Chairman*).	Bishop of Minnesota.
" Adelaide.	" Nelson.
" Antigua (Coadjutor).	" New York.
" Brechin.	" Ripon.
" Edinburgh.	" Rochester.
" Hereford.	" Rupertsland.
" Jamaica.	" S. Andrew's.
" Lichfield.	" Wakefield.
" Manchester.	

formist bodies; and these recommendations, after a singularly interesting debate, were adopted by the house.

The Report contained the following passage: 'The Committee do not recommend that we should set out with proposing alterations of our existing formularies of faith and worship, while they by no means deny that concessions might be admitted hereafter, as the consequence of negotiations carried on in a spirit of love and unity.' It also suggested that on the day of the Queen's Accession 'all classes of Non-Conformists should be invited to institute similar prayers' for unity, and that the subject might be brought by sermons before our own people.

In 1887 the subject was again taken up, and a Resolution carried, on the motion of Canon Medd, that 'His Grace the President be requested to direct the appointment of a Joint Committee to consider, and from time to time to report upon, the relations between the Church and those who in this country are alienated from her Communion; and generally to make suggestions as to means which might tend, by GOD's blessing, to the furtherance of union of all among our countrymen who hold the essentials of the Christian Faith.' In the speech of the mover of the Resolution special reference was made to the probability of the discussion of the subject at the Lambeth Conference.

In the Convocation of York, the Committee have reason to know that similar action has been taken; but under pressure of time they have been unable to obtain detailed information of the actual proceedings.

From various Synods of the Colonial Church, similar, and even stronger, expressions of a desire to make some movement on the part of the Anglican Communion in this direction have been brought before the Committee. The General Synod of the Church in Australia and Tasmania, in 1886, 'desired to place on record its solemn sense of the evils of the unhappy divisions among professing Christians, and, through His Grace the Archbishop of Canterbury, respectfully prayed the Conference of bishops to be assembled at Lambeth in 1888 to consider in what manner steps should be taken to promote greater visible unity among those who hold the same Creed.' A Resolution was passed in almost the same words by the Diocesan Synod of Montreal; and similar Resolutions by the Provincial Synod of Rupertsland, and the General Synod of New Zealand. At the Session of the Provincial Synod of Canada in 1886, a Joint Committee was appointed, to confer with any similar Committees, which might be appointed by other religious bodies, on the terms upon which some honorable union might be arrived at.

But the most important and practical step has been taken by our brethren of the American Church in the General Convention of 1886, in accordance with the prayer of a petition signed by more than a thousand clergy, including thirty-two bishops. At that Convention a Committee of the House of Bishops presented a remarkable Report, which, after stating emphatically that the Church did 'not seek to absorb other Communions, but to co-operate with them on the basis of a common Faith and Order, to discountenance schism, and to heal the wounds of the Body of CHRIST;' and that she was prepared to make all reasonable concessions on 'all things of human ordering and of human choice,' dwelt upon the duty of the Church to preserve, 'as inherent parts of the sacred deposit of Christian Faith and Order committed by CHRIST and His Apostles to the Church, and as therefore essential to the restoration of unity,' the following : —

'1. The Holy Scriptures of the Old and New Testaments, as the Revealed Word of GOD.

'2. The Nicene Creed, as the sufficient statement of the Christian Faith.

'3. The two Sacraments, — Baptism and the Supper of the LORD, — ministered with unfailing use of CHRIST's words of institution, and the elements ordained by Him.

'4. The Historic Episcopate, locally adapted in the methods of its administration to the varying needs of the nations and peoples called of GOD into the unity of His Church.'

The Report concluded with the following words : —

'Furthermore, deeply grieved by the sad divisions which afflict the Christian Church in our own land, we hereby declare our desire and readiness, so soon as there shall be any authorized response to this Declaration, to enter into brotherly conference with all or any Christian bodies seeking the restoration of organic Unity of the Church, with a view to the earnest study of the conditions under which so priceless a blessing might happily be brought to pass.'

This Report was adopted by the House of Bishops, and communicated to the House of Clerical and Lay Deputies; and at the instance of the latter House it was resolved —

'That a Commission consisting of five bishops, five clerical and five lay deputies, be appointed, who shall at their discretion communicate, to the organized Christian bodies of our country, the Declaration set forth by the bishops on the twentieth day of October; and shall hold themselves ready to enter into brotherly conference with all or any Christian bodies seeking the restoration of the organic unity of the Church.'

After consideration of these significant documents, and of memorials from certain Associations which have already done good service in this cause, it was decided by the Committee that they were more than justified in recommending to the Conference that some steps should be taken by it in the direction specified in the Resolution constituting the Committee.

II. In considering how this could best be done, it appeared to the Committee that the subject divided itself naturally into two parts : first, the basis on which the united Church might, in the future, safely rest ; secondly, the conditions under which present negotiations for reunion, in view of existing circumstances, could be carried on.

The Committee with deep regret felt that under present conditions it was useless to consider the question of Reunion with our brethren of the Roman Church, being painfully aware that any proposal for reunion would be entertained by the authorities of that Church only on condition of a complete submission on our part to those claims of absolute authority, and the acceptance of those other errors, both in doctrine and in discipline, against which, in faithfulness to GOD'S Holy Word, and to the true principles of His Church, we have been for three centuries bound to protest.

But in regard to the first portion of the subject, the Committee were of opinion that with the chief of the Non-conforming Communions there would not only be less difficulty than is commonly supposed as to the basis of a common faith in the essentials of Christian doctrine, but that even in respect of Church Government, many of the causes which had originally led to secession had been removed, and that both from deeper study and from larger historical experience there was in the present day a greater disposition to value and to accept the ancient Church Order. It did not, indeed, appear to them that the question before them, which was of the duty, if any, of the Anglican Communion in this matter, was to be absolutely determined by these considerations; but they seemed, nevertheless, to give important encouragement to the Church in the endeavor to do what might appear to be her duty in furthering this all-important matter.

Accordingly, after careful consideration, they determined to take as the basis of their deliberations on this part of the subject the chief articles embodied in the Report of the Committee of the House of Bishops in the American Church; and after discussion of each, they submit them to the wisdom of the Conference, with some modifications, as supplying the basis on which approach might be, under GOD'S blessing, made toward Reunion : —

1. The Holy Scriptures of the Old and New Testaments, as 'containing all things necessary to salvation,' and as being the rule and ultimate standard of Faith.

2. The Apostles' Creed, as the Baptismal Symbol; and the Nicene Creed, as the sufficient statement of the Christian Faith.

3. The two Sacraments ordained by CHRIST Himself, — Baptism and

the Supper of the LORD, — ministered with unfailing use of CHRIST'S words of institution, and of the elements ordained by Him.

4. The Historic Episcopate, locally adapted in the methods of its administration to the varying needs of the nations and peoples called of GOD into the unity of His Church.

The Committee believe that upon some such basis as this, with large freedom of variation on secondary points of doctrine, worship, and discipline, and without interference with existing conditions of property and endowment, it might be possible, under GOD'S gracious providence, for a reunited Church, including at least the chief of the Christian Communions of our people, to rest.

III. But they are aware that the main difficulty of the subject lies in the consideration of what practical steps can be taken toward such reunion under the actual religious conditions of the community at home and abroad, complicated, moreover, in England and Scotland by legal difficulties. It appears to them, moreover, clear that on this subject the Conference can only express an opinion on general principles, and that definite action must be left to the constituted authorities in each branch of our Communion, acting, as far as possible, in concert.

They therefore respectfully submit to the Conference the following Resolution : —

'That the constituted authorities of the various branches of our Communion, acting, so far as may be, in concert with one another, be earnestly requested to make it known that they hold themselves in readiness to enter into brotherly conference (such as that which has already been proposed by the Church in the United States of America) with the representatives of other chief Christian Communions in the English-speaking races, in order to consider what steps can be taken, either toward corporate reunion, or toward such relations as may prepare the way for fuller organic unity hereafter.'

IV. They cannot conclude their Report without laying before the Conference the following suggestion, unanimously adopted by the Committee : —

'That the Conference recommend as of great importance, in tending to bring about Reunion, the dissemination of information respecting the standards of doctrine and the formularies in use in the Anglican Church ; and that information be disseminated, on the other hand, respecting the authoritative standards of doctrine, worship, and government adopted by the other bodies of Christians into which the English-speaking races are divided.'

They also desire — following in this respect the example of the Convocation of Canterbury — to pray the Conference to commend this matter of Reunion to the special prayers of all Christian people, both within and (so far as it may rightly do so) without our Communion, in preparation for the Conferences which have been suggested, and while such Conferences are going on; and they trust that the present Lambeth Conference may also see fit to issue, or to pray His Grace the President to issue, some pastoral letter to all Christian people, upon this all-important subject. For never certainly did the Church of CHRIST need more urgently the spirit of wisdom and of love, which He alone can bestow, who is 'the Author and Giver of all good things.'

Signed on behalf of the Committee,

ALFRED SYDNEY, *Chairman.*

No. 10.—SCANDINAVIANS.—OLD CATHOLICS.

Report of the Committee[1] *appointed to consider the relation of the Anglican Communion (A) to the Scandinavian and other Reformed Churches, (B) to the Old Catholics and other Reforming Bodies.*

A.

Your Committee consider that, in view of the increasing number of Swedes and other Scandinavians now living in America and in the English Colonies, as well as for the furtherance of Christian unity, earnest efforts should be made to establish more friendly relations between the Scandinavian and Anglican Churches.

In regard to the Swedish Church your Committee are of opinion that, as its standards of doctrine are to a great extent in accord with our own and its continuity as a National Church has never been broken, any approaches on its part should be most gladly welcomed with a view to mutual explanation of differences, and the ultimate establishment, if possible, of permanent intercommunion on sound principles of ecclesiastical polity.

Greater difficulties are presented as regards communion with the Norwegian and Danish Churches by the constitution of their ministry; but there are grounds of hope, in the growing appreciation of Church

---

[1] Names of the members of the Committee:—

Bishop of Winchester (*Chairman*). Bishop of Dunedin.
" Gibraltar.
Archbishop of Dublin. " Iowa.
Bishop of Albany. " Lichfield.
" Cashel " Lincoln.
" Central Africa. " North Carolina.
" Cork. " Salisbury.
" Derry. " Western New York.

order, that in the course of time these difficulties may be surmounted. It is much to be desired that a basis of union should be formed with a people who are distinguished by great devotional earnestness and uprightness of character.

B.

By the name Old Catholics we understand, in general terms, those members of foreign Churches who have been excommunicated on account of their refusal, for conscience' sake, to accept the novel doctrines promulgated by the authority of the Church of Rome, and who yet desire to maintain in its integrity the Catholic Faith, and to remain in full communion with the Catholic Church. As in the previous Conference, held in 1878,[1] we declare that 'all sympathy is due from the Anglican Church to the Churches and individuals protesting against these errors;' and 'to those who are drawn to us in the endeavor to free themselves from the yoke of error and superstition we are ready to offer all help and such privileges as may be acceptable to them and are consistent with the maintenance of our own principles, as enunciated in our formularies.'

Ten years have passed since this declaration was issued, and we are now called to consider more in detail our relations to the different groups comprehended under this general title.

I.

First of all, it is due to the ancient Church of Holland, which in practice accepts the title of Old Catholic, to recognize the fact that it has uttered energetic protests against the novel dogmas of the Immaculate Conception of the Blessed Virgin Mary, and of the universal bishopric and infallibility of the Bishop of Rome. It is to this Church that the community usually termed Old Catholic, in the German Empire, owes in the providence of GOD the Episcopal succession. We recognize with thankfulness the dignified and independent position which the Church of Holland maintained for many years in almost absolute isolation. It has now broken through this isolation, as regards its neighbors on the Continent. As regards ourselves, the Church of Holland is found on inquiry to be in agreement with our Church in many points, and we believe that with more frequent brotherly intercourse many of the barriers which at present separate us might be removed.

---

[1] Official Letter of 1878 in *Origin and History of the Lambeth Conferences*, pp. 135 and 136. S. P. C. K. 1888.

II.

The Old Catholic community in Germany differs from the Church of Holland, in this respect, among others, that it does not retain possession of the ancient Sees. The bishop of that community has wisely refrained from assuming a territorial title; we are not, however, without hope that the Old Catholic body may be, with the Divine guidance and in GOD'S good time, instrumental in restoring to that country the blessing of a united national Church. It may be noted that Bishop Reinkens, shortly after his consecration, was recognized as a Catholic bishop by the civil power in Prussia, Baden, and Hesse.[1] He and the parochial clergy under him have the right and duty, recognized by the State, of teaching the children of their own confession in the public schools. They are also in undisturbed possession of a number of ancient churches and benefices, and receive for the present a subsidy granted by Parliament.

As regards the form of doctrine actually professed by this body, we believe that its return to the standards of the undivided Church is a distinct advance toward the reunion of Christendom. We learn that it formulates the fuller expression of its belief in catechisms and manuals of instruction, rather than in articles or confessions, because it desires to avoid any methods which might create or perpetuate divisions.

We cannot consider that it is in schism as regards the Roman Church, because to do so would be to concede the lawfulness of the imposition of new terms of communion, and of the extravagant assertions by the Papacy of ordinary and immediate jurisdiction in every Diocese. For ourselves we regard it as a duty to promote friendly relations with the Old Catholics of Germany, not only out of sympathy with them, but also in thankfulness to GOD, who has strengthened them to suffer for the truth under great discouragements, difficulties, and temptations. We owe them our intercessions, our support, and our brotherly counsel; and we have reason to believe that aid from individual members of our Church may be most beneficially given toward the training of their future clergy.

We see no reason why we should not admit their clergy and faithful laity to Holy Communion on the same conditions as our own communicants, and we also acknowledge the readiness which they have shown to offer spiritual privileges to members of our own Church.

---

[1] The documents in question are printed at length in *Der Altkatholikismus*, published in 1887 by J. F. von Schulte, pp. 405, 415, 416. The Prussian Old Catholic law is to be found on pp. 44-46. Cp. pp. 549 foll. (Staatszuschuss für die Altkatholiken).

We regret that differences in our marriage laws, which we believe to be of great importance, compel us to state that we are obliged to debar from Holy Communion any person who may have contracted a marriage not sanctioned by the laws and canons of the Anglican Church. Nor could we, in justice to the Old Catholics, admit any one who would be debarred from communion among themselves.

III.

The 'Christian Catholic Church' in Switzerland, which has adopted a title long used by the Church in that country, has a recognized civil position of much the same character as that possessed by the Old Catholics of Germany. We consider that it is a body now sufficiently established to receive the assurance of the same sympathy and the offer of the same privileges from ourselves.

IV.

The Old Catholic Community in Austria has been recognized by the State as a distinct religious association, in accordance with the law of May 20, 1874.[1] Its constitution provides for the presidency of a bishop; but no election has as yet taken place, not from any indifference on the part of its members, but on account of the difficulty of securing the stipend required by law. In the mean time it has many of the rights secured by law to the German body. The Austrian Old Catholics have made great sacrifices, and deserve great sympathy from us, which we hope may be expressed in a practical manner. They have, we believe, an important future before them, if rightly guided. We cannot, however, regard the organization in Austria as sufficiently tried and complete to warrant a more formal relation on our part at the present time.

V.

The same remark applies with even greater force to the smaller groups of brave and earnest men of the Latin races, driven under somewhat similar circumstances to associate themselves in separate congregations in Italy, France, Spain, and Portugal. We sympathize with their efforts to free themselves from the burden of unlawful terms of communion. We have reason to believe that there are many who think with them, but have not seen the way to follow the outward steps which they have taken. We trust that in time they may be enabled to adopt such sound forms of doctrine and discipline and to secure such Catholic organization as will permit us to give them a fuller recognition. We desire, in our outlook into the future, to call to mind

---

[1] Von Schulte, *Der Altkatholikismus*, p. 435.

the well-known declaration of the Gallican clergy of 1682,[1] and also the advances made by Archbishop Wake in correspondence with the Doctors of the Sorbonne,[2] toward establishing a basis for intercommunion between the Churches of France and England. If some such principles could now be revived, we have reason to believe that they would be welcomed by many both in France and Italy, and they might again form the basis for hopeful negotiations.

In concluding this portion of our Report, we feel it our duty to express the opinion that the consecration, by bishops of our Communion, of a bishop, to exercise his functions in a foreign country, within the limits of an ancient territorial jurisdiction and over the natives of that country, is a step of the gravest importance and fraught with enduring consequences, the issues of which cannot be foreseen. While the right of bishops of the Catholic Church to interpose under conditions of extreme necessity has always been acknowledged, we deprecate any action that does not carefully regard primitive and established principles of jurisdiction and the interests of the whole Anglican Communion.

VI.

Lastly, the Committee have been asked at the last moment to consider the subject of the orders of the United Brethren, commonly called the Moravians. At the last Conference a number of the bishops ' were

---

[1] See Bossuet's *Défense de la Declaration du Clergé de France, &c.* 2 vols., 4to. Amsterdam, 1745, and Dupin's *Manuel du Droit public ecclésiastique français*, pp. 97-100, ed. 5, Paris, Henri Plon, 1860.

[2] Archbishop Wake wrote as follows to Mr. Beauvoir, on Nov. 18, 1718, in regard to this correspondence : ' If we could once divide the Gallican Church [from the Roman], a reformation in other matters would follow as a matter of course. The scheme that seems to me most likely to prevail, is, to agree in the independence (as to all matters of authority) of every national Church on any others ; and in their right to determine all matters that arise within themselves ; and for points of doctrine, to agree as far as possible in all articles of any moment (as in effect we already do, or easily may) ; and for other matters, to allow a difference till GOD shall bring us to a union in those also. One only thing should be provided for, to purge out of the public offices of the Church such things as hinder a perfect communion in the service of the Church, that so, wherever any come from us to them or from them to us, we may all join together in Prayers and the Holy Sacraments with each other. In our Liturgy there is nothing but what they allow, save the single rubric relating to the Eucharist ; in theirs nothing but what they agree may be laid aside, and yet the public offices be never the worse or more imperfect for the want of it. Such a scheme as this I take to be a more proper ground of peace at the beginning than to go to more particulars.'

The correspondence of Archbishop Wake with Mr. Beauvoir, Dr. Dupin, Dr. P. Piers Girardin, and others, is printed in the fourth Appendix to Dr. Maclaine's translation of Mosheim's *Church History*, vol. vi., pp. 126, foll., London, 1828. The above letter will be found in full on p. 172, and is quoted in Rev. G. G. Perry's *History of the English Church, third period*, p. 48, London, 1887.

recommended to associate with themselves such learned persons as they might deem eminently qualified to assist them by their knowledge of the historical difficulties involved.'[1] These bishops have not been able to act upon this recommendation, and no Report is before the Conference. Your Committee, in the short time allowed them, have not found it possible to inquire into the details of this subject with such care as would enable them to propose to the Conference any sufficient basis for the expression of an authoritative opinion.

It must not, however, be overlooked, that from time to time, up to the present day, very friendly relations have existed between Moravians and members of our Communion. In their greatest trials they have received from eminent English bishops and Churchmen the sympathy and support due to a zealous body of Christians, imbued with a primitive spirit, and claiming to possess a valid Episcopate.

The labors of Moravian missionaries are known to all the world. We should therefore welcome any clearer illustration of their history and actual status on the part of their own divines.

The subjects committed to the consideration of this Committee have embraced, as will be seen, a very wide range of interests, and we have reluctantly been compelled, on this account, to confine our Report almost entirely to the bodies specified in the terms of our commission.

Signed on behalf of the Committee,

E. HAROLD WINTON, *Chairman*.

No. 11.— EASTERN CHURCHES.

Report of the Committee[2] *appointed to consider the relation of the Anglican Communion to the Eastern Churches.*

Your Committee regard the friendly feelings manifested toward our Church by the Orthodox Eastern Communion as a matter for deep thankfulness. These feelings inspire the hope that at no distant time closer relations may be established between the two Churches. Your Committee, however, are of opinion that any hasty or ill-considered step in this direction would only retard the accomplishment of this hope. Our expectations of nearer fellowship are founded upon the friendly

---

[1] *Origin and History of the Lambeth Conferences*, p. 137.
[2] Names of the members of the Committee:—
Bishop of Winchester (*Chairman*).   Bishop of Limerick.
Bishop Blyth.   " Meath.
Bishop of Gibraltar.   " Springfield.
" Iowa.   " Travancore

tone of the correspondence which the Archbishop of Canterbury and his predecessors have held from time to time with patriarchs of the Orthodox Church, and upon the cordiality of the welcome given by the heads of that Church to Anglican bishops and clergy, such as the Bishop of Gibraltar, who have travelled in the East. Additional grounds of hope are furnished by the visit of Archbishop [1] Lycurgus to England in 1870, by the conversation which passed between him and the present Bishop of Winchester at Ely, by the words which Archbishop Lycurgus used at the conclusion of the second Conference held at Bonn;[2] and by the request which the Orthodox Patriarch of Jerusalem recently addressed to the Archbishop of Canterbury, that the Anglican Bishopric in Jerusalem should be reconstituted, and that the headquarters of the bishop should be placed in that city rather than at Beyrout or elsewhere.

We reflect with thankfulness that there exist no bars, such as are presented to communion with the Latins by the formulated assertion of the infallibility of the Church residing in the person of the Supreme Pontiff, by the doctrine of the Immaculate Conception, and other novel dogmas imposed by the decrees of later councils.

We must congratulate the Christian world that, through the research of a Greek metropolitan, literature has been lately enriched by the recovery of an ancient document which throws unexpected light upon the early development of ecclesiastical organization.

It would not be right, however, to disguise from ourselves the hindrances which exist on either side. The first and most formidable of these is the disputed clause inserted in the Creed of Constantinople, erroneously called the Nicene Creed, without any Conciliar authority, by the Latin Church. This clause, which has the prescription of centuries, and is capable of being explained in an orthodox sense, it may be very difficult to remove. Another barrier to full understanding between the Orthodox Eastern Church and ourselves would be the extreme importance attached by that Church to trine immersion in the rite of Baptism, which practice, however, there is nothing to prevent

---

[1] Lycurgus, late Archbishop of Syra and Tenos.

[2] At the end of the Conference at Ely (1870), Archbishop Lycurgus said, —

'When I return to Greece I will say that the Church of England is not like other Protestant bodies. I will say that it is a sound Catholic Church very like our own; and I trust that by friendly discussion union between the two Churches may be brought about.'

At the end of the Bonn Conference (1875), he said to Dr. von Döllinger, —

'In the name of all those of my own Communion I thank you, Mr. President, for your marvellous efforts in the work of reuniting the several Churches, of bringing together again the so numerous divisions of the Rock of our REDEEMER. Our joy is full; and there will be great joy in our homes also. We earnestly pray GOD for His further blessing.'

our Church from formally sanctioning. We, on the other hand, experience a somewhat similar difficulty as regards the Eastern rite of Confirmation, which we can hardly consider equivalent to ours, inasmuch as it omits the imposition of the bishop's hands, and is usually conferred upon unconscious infants; yet we do not regard this as requiring members of the Orthodox Church to receive our Confirmation. It would be difficult for us to enter into more intimate relations with that Church so long as it retains the use of icons, the invocation of the saints, and the cultus of the Blessed Virgin; although it is but fair to state that the Greeks, in sanctioning the use of pictorial representations for the purpose of promoting devotion, expressly disclaim the sin of idolatry, which they conceive would attach to the bowing down before sculptured or molten images. Moreover, the decrees of the Second Council of Nicæa, sanctioning the use of icons, were framed in a spirit of reaction against the rationalizing measures, as they were regarded, of the iconoclastic emperors. The Greeks might be reminded that the decrees of that Council, having been deliberately rejected seven years afterward by the Council of Frankfort, and not having been accepted by the Latin Church till after the lapse of two centuries, and then only under Papal influence, cannot be regarded as binding upon the Church.

Your Committee would impress upon their fellow-Christians the propriety of abstaining from all efforts to induce individual members of the Orthodox Eastern Church to leave their own Communion. If some be dissatisfied with its teaching or usages, and find a lack of spiritual life in its worship, they should be advised not to leave the Church of their baptism, but by remaining in it to endeavor to become centres of life and light to their own people, — more especially as the Orthodox Eastern Church has never committed itself to any theory that would make it impossible to reconsider and revise its standards and practice.

Your Committee think it desirable that the heads of that Communion should be supplied with some authoritative document setting forth the historical facts relating to our orders and our position in the Catholic Church, as much misconception appears still to prevail on this subject. Your Committee feel that the position which England now occupies in Cyprus and in Egypt places in our hands exceptional opportunities of elevating the moral and spiritual life of our Eastern brethren. Especially may this be done by introducing or promoting higher education; any help given in this way we have reason to believe would be warmly welcomed. We rejoice to know that schools have lately been established at Constantinople and elsewhere for the purpose of supplying education to those who are in training for the ministry. In the more general diffusion of knowledge among the instructors of the people lies the best hope of that mutual understanding and esteem for which the heads of the Orthodox Church have shown so much desire.

Your Committee cannot be expected to deal separately with the other Churches of the East, among which the Armenian appears to be the largest and most important. Approaches have been made to us from time to time by bishops and other representatives of this Communion, appealing for aid in support of educational projects for the instruction of their own people. The Armenian Church lies under the imputation of heresy; but it has always protested against this imputation, affirming the charge to have arisen from a misconception of its formularies. The departure from orthodoxy may perhaps have been more apparent than real; and the erroneous element in its creed appears now to be gradually losing its hold upon the moral and religious consciousness of the Armenian people.

In regard to other Eastern communities, such as the Coptic, Abyssinian, Syrian, and Chaldean, your Committee consider that our position in the East involves some obligations. And if these communities have fallen into error, and show a lack of moral and spiritual life, we must recollect that but for them the light of Christianity in these countries would have been utterly extinguished, and that they have suffered for many centuries from cruel oppression and persecution. If we should have opportunity, our aim should be to improve their mental, moral, and religious condition, and to induce them to return to the unity of the faith without prejudice to their liberty. This we take to be the purpose of the Assyrian Mission set on foot by the late Archbishop of Canterbury, and continued by his successor.

In conclusion, we would call attention to the fact that in the East advance is slow, and even in the West we find differences perpetuate themselves, owing to national peculiarities, hereditary prejudices, and other causes, in spite of real wish for unity. We think that Christians need to be cautioned against impatience in expecting quick results. Such impatience argues imperfect trust in the ultimate fulfilment of our LORD'S prayer for His people, that they 'all may be ONE.'

Signed on behalf of the Committee,

E. HAROLD WINTON, *Chairman*.

No. 12.—AUTHORITATIVE STANDARDS.

Report of the Committee[1] appointed to consider the Subject of Authoritative Standards of Doctrine and Worship.

In considering the subject of the Authoritative Standards of Doctrine and Worship, which are the primary means of securing internal union among ourselves, and of setting forth our Faith before the rest of Christendom, we acknowledge first of all with deep thankfulness to Almighty GOD the vital and growing unity of the great Communion to which we belong.

We acknowledge also with the same heartfelt thankfulness the increasing intercourse which is taking place between our own Churches and other Churches of Christendom, and the extension of our own Communion into many non-Christian countries, to which GOD has especially called us to minister by the diffusion of the English-speaking race throughout the world.

The consideration of the new conditions thus created seems to call for a careful statement of our own position in regard to authoritative standards of doctrine and worship.

This statement is divided into three parts: first, as to standards of doctrine and worship which unite us with the great body of the Church Universal; second, as to those which regulate our internal union or should be imposed upon Missionary Churches; third, as to a manual of doctrine for general use, but which should not be authoritative.

I.

We recognize before all things, and amid all discouragements and divisions, the great bond of an essential unity which exists among all Christians who own the one LORD JESUS CHRIST as their Head and King, who accept the paramount authority of Holy Scripture, who confess the doctrine of the Nicene Faith, and who acknowledge one Baptism into the Name of the Blessed Trinity.

[1] Names of the members of the Committee.—
Bishop of Ely (*Chairman*).   Bishop of Meath.
" Aberdeen.   " Nassau.
" Albany.   " Qu'Appelle.
" Arkansas.   " Rupertsland.
" Derry.   " Salisbury.
" Dover.   " S. David's.
" Edinburgh.   " Sydney.
" Grahamstown.   " Western New York.
Bishop in Japan.

But we cannot regard this measure of unity as adequately fulfilling our LORD's prayer that His followers should be one, and we feel, therefore, that it is our duty to explain our own principles as regards standards of doctrine and worship, in the humble hope of preparing the way, so far as in us lies, for the reunion of Christendom.

We have a duty to the Church Universal; we have a duty also toward those who are now distinctly within our own Communion or who may hereafter be so closely allied to it as to form practically one body with ourselves.

As in former Conferences,[1] we declare that we continue 'united under one Divine Head in the fellowship of the one Catholic and Apostolic Church, holding the one Faith revealed in Holy Writ, defined in the Creeds, maintained by the primitive Church,' and 'affirmed by the undisputed' Ecumenical 'Councils.'

In defining our own position more explicitly, we recognize, with the general consent of the Fathers, that the canonical books of the Old and New Testaments 'contain all things necessary to salvation,' and are the rule and ultimate standard of all Christian doctrine.

In addition to the Creed commonly called the Nicene Creed, to which we have already referred, we, as a part of the Western Church, have a common inheritance in the 'Apostles' Creed,' confessed by us all in the Sacrament of Baptism. In like manner we accept the hymn *Quicunque Vult*, whether or not recited in the public worship of our Churches, as resting upon certain warrant of Scripture, and as most useful, both at home and in our missions, in ascertaining and defining the fundamental mysteries of the Holy Trinity, and of the Incarnation of our Blessed LORD, and thus guarding believers from lapsing into heresy.

In relation to the doctrine of the Procession of the HOLY SPIRIT, while we believe that there is no fundamental diversity of faith between the Churches of the East and West,[2] we recognize the historical fact that the clause *Filioque* makes no part of the Nicene Symbol as set forth by the authority of the undivided Church.

We are of opinion that, as opportunity arises, it would be well to revise the English version of the Nicene Creed and of the *Quicunque Vult*.

---

[1] See *Origin and History of the Lambeth Conferences*, pp. 62 and 119. S. P. C. K. 1888.

[2] The Committee beg to refer, in illustration of this statement, to the important propositions, accepted by members both of the Eastern and Western Churches, which were agreed to at the Reunion Conference held at Bonn, Aug. 16, 1875, under the Presidency of Dr. J. J. I. von Döllinger. See the *Report of the Proceedings, &c.*, with a Preface by Dr. Liddon.— Pickering, London, 1876, pp. 103, 104.

We suggest to the Conference that the President be requested to appoint a Committee for this purpose.

With regard to the authority of the Ecumenical Councils our Communion has always recognized the decisions of the first four Councils on matters of faith, nor is there any point of dogma in which it disagrees with the teaching of the fifth and sixth.

The Second Council of Nicæa, commonly called the Seventh Council is, however, not undisputed, and while we recognize the historical circumstances of the eighth century, which naturally led to the strong protest against iconoclasm made there, it is our duty to assert that our Church has never accepted the teaching of that Council in reference to the veneration of sacred pictures.

II.

From the standards of doctrine of the Universal Church which the whole Anglican Communion has always accepted [1] we now pass to those standards of doctrine and worship which are specially the heritage of the Church of England, and which are, to a greater or less extent, received by all her sister and daughter Churches. These are the Prayer-Book with its Catechism, the Ordinal, and the XXXIX. Articles of Religion.

All these are subscribed by our clergy at ordination or admission to office, but the XXXIX. Articles are not imposed upon any person as a condition of communion. With respect to the Prayer-Book and Articles, we do not consider it an indispensable condition of intercommunion that they should be everywhere accepted in their original form, or that the interpretation put upon them by local courts or provincial tribunals should be received by every branch or province of the Anglican Communion. In illustration of this principle, we would refer to the differences from the English Order of the Administration of the Holy Communion which have long existed in the Scottish and Ameri-

---

[1] Let Preachers take care that they never teach anything in a sermon which they wish to be religiously held and believed by the people, except what is in accord with the doctrine of the Old or New Testament and what the Catholic Fathers and ancient Bishops have collected from the same doctrine. — *Canon of 1571, concerning Preachers.*

Such person &c. . . . shall not in anywise have authority or power to order, determine, or adjudge any matter or cause to be heresie, but onely such as heretofore have been determined, ordered, or adjudged to be heresie, by the authority of the Canonical Scriptures or by the first four general Councils or any of them, or by any other general Council wherein the same was declared heresie by the express and plain words of the said Canonical Scriptures, or such as hereafter shall be ordered, judged, or determined to be heresie, by the High Court of Parliament of this realm, with the assent of the Clergy in their Convocation; anything in this Act contained to the contrary notwithstanding. — 1 *Eliz.* 1, § *XXXVI.*

can Churches, and to the facts that the XXXIX. Articles of Religion were only accepted in America in the year 1801 with some variations, and in Scotland in 1804, and that the Church of Ireland, as well as the Church in America, has introduced some modifications into the Book of Common Prayer.

We, however, strongly deprecate any further material variation in the text of the existing Sacramental offices of the Church, or of the Ordinal, than is at present recognized among us, unless with the advice of some Conference or Council representing the whole Communion.

With regard to the daily offices and such further forms of service as the exigencies of different Churches or countries may demand, we feel that they may be safely left for the present to the action of the bishops of each Province. We do not demand a rigid uniformity, but we desire to see the prevalence of a spirit of mutual and sympathetic concession, which will prevent the growth of substantial divergences between different portions of our Communion. With regard to those Dioceses which are not yet united into Provinces, we recommend that the Bishop of the Diocese should not act in the way of revision of, or additions to, such offices without the advice of the Archbishop of Canterbury; or in the case of foreign missionary jurisdictions of the American Church, without the advice of its presiding bishop.

With regard to the XXXIX. Articles of Religion, we thank GOD for the wisdom which guided our fathers, in difficult times, in framing statements of doctrine, for the most part accurate in their language and reserved and moderate in their definitions. Even when speaking most strongly and under the pressure of great provocation, our Communion has generally refrained from anathemas upon opponents, and we desire in this to follow those who have preceded us in the Faith. The omission of a few clauses in a few of the Articles would render the whole body free from any imputation of injustice or harshness toward those who differ from us. At the same time we feel that the Articles are not all of equal value, that they are not, and do not profess to be, a complete statement of Christian doctrine, and that, from the temporary and local circumstances under which they were composed, they do not always meet the requirements of Churches founded under wholly different conditions.

Some modification of these Articles may therefore naturally be expected on the part of newly constituted Churches, and particularly in non-Christian lands. But we consider that it should be a condition of the recognition of such Churches as in complete intercommunion with our own, and especially of their receiving from us our Episcopal succession, that we should first receive from them satisfactory evidence that they hold substantially the same type of doctrine with ourselves. More particularly we are of opinion that the clergy of such Churches should accept articles in accordance with the positive statements of our own standards of doctrine and worship, particularly on the substance and rule of Faith, on the state and redemption of man, on the office of the Church, and on the Sacraments and other special ordinances of our holy religion.

III.

In the foregoing resolutions we have confined ourselves to a consideration of existing authoritative formularies, and to such as may serve the like use under particular conditions. We are unable, after careful consideration of the subject, to recommend that any new declaration of doctrine should, at the present time, be put forth by authority. We are, however, of opinion that the time has come when an effort should be made to compose a manual for teachers which should contain a summary of the doctrine of the Church, as generally received among us. Such a manual would draw its statements of doctrine from authoritative documents already existing, but would exhibit them in a completer and more systematic form. It would also naturally include some explanation of the services and ceremonies of the Church. The whole might be preceded by a historical sketch of the position and claims of our Communion.

Such a manual would, we believe, be of great service both in maintaining the type of doctrine to which we have referred, and in enabling members of other Churches to form a just opinion of our doctrines and worship. We suggest that His Grace, the President, be requested to nominate three or more bishops to undertake such a work, and if it seem good to him and to the other archbishops, metropolitans, and presiding bishops of the Church, that they give the work, when completed, the sanction of their imprimatur. We do not suggest that the Conference should be asked to undertake this work, or that it should be regarded as an authoritative standard of the Church.

Signed on behalf of the Committee,

ALWYNE, ELY, *Chairman*.

THE BASIS FOR CHRISTIAN REUNION PROPOSED BY THE LAMBETH CONFERENCE OF 1888.

1. *The Holy Scriptures of the Old and New Testaments, as " containing all things necessary to salvation," and as being the rule and ultimate standard of Faith.*

2. *The Apostles' Creed, as the Baptismal Symbol; and the Nicene Creed, as the sufficient statement of the Christian Faith.*

3. *The two Sacraments ordained by* CHRIST *Himself, — Baptism and the Supper of the* LORD, *— ministered with unfailing use of* CHRIST'S *words of institution, and of the elements ordained by Him.*

4. *The Historic Episcopate, locally adapted in the methods of its administration to the varying needs of the nations and peoples called of* GOD *into the unity of His Church.*

The Historic Episcopate as a basis of Reunion.

PROFESSOR CHARLES A. BRIGGS, D.D. [PRESBYTERIAN],
UNION THEOLOGICAL SEMINARY, NEW YORK.

THE aspirations for the reunion of Christendom that have been felt by large numbers of Christians in most, if not all, the denominations, have reached the fullest and strongest expression in recent times in the four articles proposed by the House of Bishops of the Protestant Episcopal Church in the United States, Oct. 20, 1886, as a basis of approach for such reunion. These were subsequently adopted, with slight modifications, in 1888, by the Lambeth Conference, representing the Church of England and her daughters throughout the world.

In January, 1887, in the *Presbyterian Review*, I said that these articles " are in my judgment entirely satisfactory, provided nothing more is meant by their authors than their language expressly conveys."

In September last I reiterated this statement; namely:—

> The four terms that are set forth therein as 'essential to the restoration of unity among the divided branches of Christendom' are in my judgment entirely satisfactory, provided nothing more is meant by their authors than their language expressly conveys. There is room for some difference of interpretation; but these terms ought to be received in the same generous manner in which they are offered, in the hope that the differences will be removed by conference and discussion [*Whither?* p. 263].

I have seen no reason to change the judgment then expressed. The discussions of the subject that have been carried on from many different points of view, and the happy results of the conferences that have thus far been held, have confirmed it. The evolutions that are now taking place in the different denominations in the revision of Prayer-Book and of Creed, in the reorganization of Christian life and work, and in the adoption of new methods for evangelization and Christian nurture, all point in the same direction, and show that the Christian denominations are moving under the sway of an irresistible impulse into closer combinations that will ere long result in federation, and at last in consolidation. I shall spend no time upon the first three terms, for there will be little difficulty in agreeing upon them. I shall use the space assigned me for the discussion of the real point of difficulty.[1]

The great difficulty to be overcome is the Historic Episcopate. We ought not to be surprised at this, for the struggles of British Christianity since the Reformation have been centred in questions of the government and discipline of the Church. The debates about ecclesiastical government have been complicated with the contests over political government. The historical student traces the development of ecclesiastical government in Great Britain and America in the midst of the evolutions of civil government. Political parties and ecclesiastical parties have to a very great extent coincided in the history of Great Britain.

The Historic Episcopate has been historically complicated with the development of the intricate relations of Church and State. The same difficult relation is now one of the chief influences at work in favor of restoring the Historic Episcopate to those Churches that have neglected it or discarded it.

I. *Church and State.*

Even the greatest champions of the *jure divino* theory of Church government have not escaped the subtle Erastianism which, even when it declines to put the supreme authority over the Church in the hands of the civil magistrate, nevertheless insensibly assimilates the operations of Church courts to the civil courts, and the methods of administration of bishops and presbyters to those of magistrates and parliaments. The American Republic, when it severed for the most part the Church

---

[1] I feel very keenly the difficulties involved in the discussion of such a delicate question within the pages of a Review that represents another body of Christians than the denomination to which I belong. I fear lest I may say something that may be misunderstood, or may give offence to those who may differ from me. This article was written in compliance with the request of the Editor. It is my sincere desire and earnest purpose to remove misapprehensions and misunderstandings, and to promote so far as may be the reunion of Christendom I am endeavoring to mediate, and my effort should be judged from this point of view. I shall speak in the first person; for it is important that no one should say that I assume to represent any one but myself.

from the State, did not altogether avoid the influence of civil government upon ecclesiastical government. It is a pleasing fiction that the divorce of Church and State is complete in the United States. But it becomes evident so soon as strife breaks out in any congregation, or an irreconcilable battle is waged between parties in the denominations, that the civil courts are the courts of last resort even for ecclesiastical affairs. And now that the Church is becoming more ethical and less dogmatic, more practical and less theoretical, it is plain that the Church and the State must come to an understanding upon the great questions of Public Education, National Religion, Marriage and Divorce; the care of the sick, the disabled, the poor, and the criminal classes; and in the entire field of social and industrial life. This fiction of a divorce of Church and State has been a will-o'-the-wisp that has brought us into many difficult and dangerous places. It is necessary that Church and State should come into closer union, in order to accomplish the great aims of humanity as well as of Christianity. The Church cannot abstain from those ethical questions that are the controlling principles of all sound government. There must be harmony between Church and State, or else there will be conflict. The worst position that can be taken by the Church is indifference, isolation, and abstinence from the religious and moral obligations of public education, good citizenship, sound government, social life, and public morality. Christian ethics comprehend all these things. If the Church in America has neglected them, it is because it has not apprehended and practised the heights and breadths of Christian ethics. The evil effects of the divorce of Church and State are making it evident to thinking men in all denominations that in some way a concord must be established between the denominations, in order that the State may not obstruct the advance of Christianity in the nation, and put itself in opposition to the Church in the great religious and moral needs of humanity.

The so-called American theory of the separation of Church and State has had two results. 1. On the one side, the State has been relieved from the burdens of the support of the Church and the duties of religion. The influence of the Church upon the State is no longer direct, immediate, and pervasive as a recognized force influencing all actions; but it is indirect, subtile, and mediate, through the influence of the Church upon its adherents among the various officers of the government. The State has been relieved of the support of the Church, and also to a great extent of higher education and of public charities. This enormous burden has thus been shifted from the shoulders of the whole people to the shoulders of the pious, benevolent, and self-sacrificing citizens. The great mass of the indifferent, selfish, and irreligious, whether poor, comfortable, or rich, escape these burdens, which then fall upon a portion of the community in double measure. It is evident that many of the largest estates in America are in the hands of men who do little, if anything, for public charity, higher education, and religion. It is easy to see what enormous savings they make in this respect when compared with the land-owners and bond-holders of other countries. The great moral, religious, and educational forces which are most potent to protect their persons and property are supported by others; and to this extent many of our millionnaires are as truly dependent upon public charity as the beggars at their gates.

The United States Congress and the legislatures of the several States pay little, if any, attention to the desires of the Christian public, as expressed in the various Church courts. They are much more influenced by an organized body of merchants, whether these are composed of a few men at the head of great trusts, or of many voters in various trade associations. The splitting up of the Church into so many conflicting denominations, and the organization of ecclesiastical bodies without regard to the territorial divisions of the towns and States, have marred their influence. This has been overcome in recent years in several of the denominations by making the ecclesiastical territories correspond with the political. But much more needs to be accomplished in this regard. It is the better organization of the Roman Catholic Church that gives it more influence with politicians. Let us not deceive ourselves by imagining that it is all due to the wiles of the Jesuits, or to the power of priests to influence voters.

The Church has lost immensely in its influence upon the State. The Protestant Churches have less influence than the Roman Catholic, notwithstanding the Protestants are vastly greater in numerical strength, in wealth, in institutions of learning, and in literature.

2. The Church has lost largely in its power to influence the

State, but the State has gained largely in its influence over the Church. This has been in two directions: —

(*a*) The State has the supreme authority over the Church in all material affairs, — over its property, so far as the Church is a visible organization; and over its communicants and its office-bearers, as having rights of contract, and as having character and reputation. It is really only so far as the Church is immaterial that it is exempt from the authority of the State. The Church has no more freedom than a Masonic lodge, or an association of liquor-dealers.

(*b*) The State has also a subtile influence upon the Church. The civil government and the civil courts have exerted an irresistible influence upon the ecclesiastical government and the ecclesiastical courts, and thereby modified to a great extent all religious organizations in the United States.

The Episcopal Churches have the executive department of Church government efficiently organized and ever ready to speak and act through the bishops. The non-Episcopal Churches have no other executives than temporary moderators, presidents, and clerks who are unable to go beyond their instructions, and are not competent to act in the emergencies that may arise in the Church or the State, or in the complicated questions of education and social life. Banks and railroads, trusts and commercial companies, cannot get on without presidents. Academies have their principals, colleges and universities their presidents and chancellors. The city has its mayor, the State its governor, the United States their president. There can be no efficiency in commercial, social, educational, and civil life without the executive head. The Church never can be efficient without such executives in the several grades of the territorial organization. The inefficiency of Protestants is largely due to the neglect of the executive function of the Historic Episcopate.

Owing to the irresistible influence of the civil government upon the ecclesiastical government, the denominations have been gradually assimilated. Let any one compare the Congregationalists of New England with the Congregationalists of Old England, and he will see that the former have advanced very far in the direction of Presbyterianism, in the authority given to councils to license and to ordain ministers, to fellowship or disfellowship Churches, and to legislate as to the common affairs of the denomination. It is true there is the old

hostility to any claim of authority, but the authority is all the stronger that it is given in the form of counsel and fraternal advice.

The American Presbyterian Church has departed widely from the Westminster model in the constitution of the Presbytery, in the theory of the ruling eldership and in methods of government and discipline. The theory that the ruling elders represent the people is an American Presbyterian doctrine that has been adopted from the representative theory of the American Republic. The Protestant Episcopal Church is very different from the Church of England in its government. Its two houses, its conventions, Diocesan and General, and their methods of government are more like those of the American Presbyterian Church than those of the Church of England.

We are thus brought to this interesting situation, that the free Churches of the United States under the potent influences of the civil government, all the more powerful that it has been indirect and insensible, have assimilated themselves so far to the civil government and thereby also to each other, that in their ecclesiastical government they are at present not far apart, and that any one of the three types is nearer to the golden mean of parties in the seventeenth century. Why, then, should they any longer remain apart? It is my opinion that the process of assimilation is so rapid, and the constraint of external necessity is so great that it is inevitable that they will unite early in the twentieth century, in spite of all traditions and of every opposition of dogmaticians and ecclesiastics. When they unite, it is inevitable that the unity of the organism will find expression in the executive functions of the Historic Episcopate.

II. *The Historic Episcopate as a Term of Union.*

The Historic Episcopate is made the great question of difficulty by the fourth article of the proposition of the House of Bishops and the Lambeth Conference.

But it is really a no more difficult question than the *Historic Presbyter*. I apprehend that before the reunion is accomplished each one of these offices must pass through the fire. I am not sure that it makes any very great difference where we begin. Possibly it may be as well that the Episcopal Churches should settle the question of the Historic Episcopate, and that the

Presbyterian Churches should determine the question of the Historic Presbyter.

But it is just here that one of the most interesting features of the situation meets us. The Episcopal Churches are no more agreed as to the Historic Episcopate than are the Presbyterian Churches as to the Historic Presbyterate. The Greek Church will not agree with the Roman; neither of these will agree with the Anglican. Let any one consider the differences in the Church of England as represented by the three names, Hatch, Lightfoot, and Gore.

In view of this discord as to the Historic Episcopate, well known to the House of Bishops and the Lambeth Conference, it seems quite evident that these bishops, differing among themselves in their theory of the Episcopate, could not lay down a basis for the reunion of Christendom that would involve any particular theory of the Episcopate. They could only mean that which was essential to the Historic Episcopate, that to which divines like Hatch, Lightfoot, and Gore could agree.

Many Presbyterians and Congregationalists have the feeling that it is the Anglo-Catholic theory of the Episcopate that the House of Bishops and the Lambeth Conference are proposing. This is favored by the industry and boldness with which the Anglo-Catholic party are pressing their theory. But it seems incredible that the House of Bishops would propose a theory to which it would be difficult to rally a majority of the members of the Church of England. It was probably well known to them that Presbyterians, Methodists, Congregationalists, and Lutherans could not accept the Anglo-Catholic theory. But there are multitudes of ministers in all the non-Episcopal Churches who are willing to accept the theory of the Episcopate of the late Dr. Hatch, and there are many who could adopt the theory of the late Bishop Lightfoot.

The progress of the discussion as to the *Historic Episcopate* teaches two lessons: (1) The Anglo-Catholics who really desire the reunion of Christendom should beware lest they make their theory of the Episcopate *essential*. They are entitled to argue for it to the extent of their ability; but they should understand that if they make their theory essential there is no possibility of reunion. They must first conquer other parties in the Episcopal Churches before they can have any prospects of overcoming the hosts in the non-Episcopal Churches, who, so far as my observation goes, are unanimous against them. (2) On the other hand, those who hold that the Historic Episcopate is *jure humano* and not *jure divino*, that it has historic right, but no Biblical basis, should not make their views essential. The Anglo-Catholic theory has been in the Church of England from the beginning, and it would be an historical wrong to exclude it. I think that theory can be shown to be erroneous. Recent historical research is very damaging to all *jure divino* theories of Church government, but it is a tolerable error, and it should be recognized by all as a legitimate and a lawful theory of the Episcopate. These theories ought to co-exist, and be mutually tolerant and forbearing. The question is to be determined by historic research, and not by dogmatic statements or ecclesiastical decisions.

The view that I have taken of the meaning of the Historic Episcopate as proposed by the House of Bishops and the Lambeth Conference as the fourth term of union is confirmed by one who seems to speak with authority. Dr. Vincent, the Assistant Bishop of Southern Ohio, tells us plainly: —

> Nothing is said here of Episcopacy as of Divine institution or necessity, nothing of 'Apostolic succession,' nothing of a Scriptural origin or a doctrinal nature in the institution. It is expressly proposed here only in its 'historical character' and as 'locally adapted to the varying needs of God's people.' All else, unless it be its Scripturalness, is matter of opinion, to which this Church has never formally committed herself. Her position here is the same broad and generous one taken in the preface to her Ordinal. That phrase, 'the Historic Episcopate,' was deliberately chosen as declaring not a doctrine, but a fact, and as being general enough to include all variants. — [An Address on *Christian Unity*, p. 29. Published by the Cincinnati branch of the Church Unity Society.]

This platform, thus interpreted, is broad enough and strong enough for the feet of Presbyterians, and it contains nothing to which they can rightly object.

The non-Episcopal Churches are willing to consider the Historic Episcopate as *jure humano*, as not essential to the existence of the Church, but as important for its well-being. On that ground we can stand. Not a few Presbyterians agree with me that the Presbyterian form of government, as now used in the Presbyterian Church, is defective. It is impossible for a whole Presbytery to exercise Episcopal functions in any practical way. A committee of Presbytery is more efficient; but it has been the experience of committees that really the best committee is a committee of *one*, and practically in all committees the chairman or secretary does the major part of the work. The Presbytery needs an executive head who shall be relieved from the cares of a local Church and be consecrated to the superintendency of the whole Church in the limits of the Presbytery. Many Presbyterians feel the inefficiency of the Presbytery very keenly, and are prepared to advance to the permanent moderator or superintendent. Why not call him bishop? The tendency in the Presbyterian Church is toward such a bishop, who will give the Presbytery an executive head and make it more efficient. The Episcopate has in its favor the historical usage of the Christian Church from the second century until the sixteenth. The Episcopate has in its favor also its continuance in several national Reformed Churches, showing that it is not inconsistent with the Reformation. History is a powerful argument for the Episcopate. This, added to the practical argument, makes the future of the Episcopate sure unless the old blunders should be renewed and perpetuated.

III. *Grounds of Opposition to Episcopacy.*

There are four reasons for opposition in the non-Episcopal Churches to the Historic Episcopate:—

1. The claim that the Diocesan Episcopacy has the Divine right of institution by CHRIST and His Apostles.

2. The claim that the Diocesan bishops are the successors of the Apostles.

3. The claim that ordination by Diocesan bishops has in it special grace without which there can be no valid ministry.

4. The claim that Diocesan bishops have Divine authority to rule the Church.

These claims for the Diocesan Episcopate have been associated in the minds of the non-Episcopal ministry with all the tyranny and abuses that the Church has suffered at the hands of Diocesan bishops. These claims are not recognized by the ministry of other Protestant Churches, and it is not at all likely that they ever will be recognized. Unless the Historic Episcopacy can be eliminated from them, the reunion of Christendom is improbable.

1. There is agreement among recent historical critics of all parties that there is no record of the institution of the Diocesan bishop in the New Testament. The only bishops of the New Testament are presbyter-bishops, and these are ever associated in a college or Presbytery. Nowhere do we find a Church under the guidance of *one* of these presbyter-bishops. Nowhere do we find more than one Church in one city. Hatch, Lightfoot, Gore, Sanday, Harnack, and Schaff are agreed as to this point. Hence the battle-cries of all the parties in the seventeenth century have happily disappeared in this new concord of historical criticism. There is no ecclesiastical organization now in existence that corresponds with the organization of the Church in the New Testament. Where do we find the independent Church with a single pastor and a bench of deacons of modern Congregationalism? Where do we find the ruling elders with a presiding parochial bishop of modern Presbyterianism? Where do we find the Diocesan bishop with his subordinate priests and deacons of the Episcopal Churches? None of these are in the New Testament. All *jure divino* theories of Church government that base their orders on the authority of the New Testament are, if not yet buried, inanimate corpses, slain by historical criticism. *Jure divino* Congregationalism and Presbyterianism have but few advocates at the present time. It is probable that it is the failure of the *jure divino* theory of the Diocesan Episcopate that has a great deal to do with the advance of the Church of England and her daughters toward Church unity.

2. The claim that bishops are the successors of the Apostles is no longer defended on the ground of the New Testament, but on the ground of the history of the second Christian century. Early in the second century bishops appear at the head of colleges of presbyters in the leading Churches of Asia; but it is admitted that these do not appear so early in the Churches of Europe and Africa, where the Churches were governed by colleges of presbyter-bishops. It is admitted that these bishops of the cities of Asia are not yet full Diocesan bishops; they are parochial bishops, bishops of cities and towns where but one Church exists so far as can be determined. These parochial bishops are more like the pastors of Presbyterian and Congregational Churches than Diocesan bishops, save that they are at the head of colleges of presbyter-bishops, to which modern

Congregationalism has nothing to correspond except ruling deacons, and Presbyterianism has no sufficient substitute in ruling elders. Such deacons and such elders have no counterpart in the second Christian century; and the breaking up of the Church of CHRIST into a number of different organizations in the same city, even if these be in the same general ecclesiastical organization, was not dreamed of in the second century.

It is a plausible theory that the parochial bishops of Asia were ordained and installed either by the hands of the Apostles or by those prophets, teachers, and evangelists who had Divine inspiration, and who appear in the New Testament as the assistants and deputies of the Apostles in the organization of the Church.[1] It is also a legitimate theory that these parochial bishops were the historical successors of these assistants and deputies of the Apostles who were at first travelling apostles and evangelists, but who gradually became settled and permanent parochial bishops of the larger and more central Churches.[2] But giving all the importance to these theories to which they may be entitled, by pushing the evidence to the utmost extreme, we do not get any more than probable historical evidence for the parochial bishops as historical successors of the Apostles.

---

[1] Though the New Testament itself contains as yet no direct and indisputable notices of a localized Episcopate in the Gentile Churches, as distinguished from the movable Episcopate exercised by Timothy in Ephesus and by Titus in Crete, yet there is satisfactory evidence of its development in the later years of the Apostolic age; that this development was not simultaneous and equal in all parts of Christendom; that it is more especially connected with the name of S. John; and that in the early years of the second century the Episcopate was widely spread and had taken firm root, more especially in Asia Minor and in Syria. — LIGHTFOOT, *Epistles of S. Ignatius*, vol i., p. 376.

[2] "We have no determining evidence (in the New Testament) as to the exact form which the ministry of the future was to take. . . . Were the local bishops to receive additional powers, such as would make them independent of any higher order? Or were the Apostles and Apostolic men, like Timothy and Titus, to perpetuate their distinct order? And if so, was it to be perpetuated as a localized or as a general order? These questions are still open" [GORE, *Ministry of the Christian Church*, pp. 269, 270]. "In the West no more than in the East did the supreme power ever devolve upon the presbyters. There was a time when they were (as the epistles of Clement and Polycarp bear witness) the chief *local* authorities, — the sole ordinary occupants of the chief seat. But over them, not yet localized, were men either of prophetic inspiration or of Apostolic authority and known character — 'prophets' or 'teachers' or 'rulers' or 'men of distinction' — who in the sub-Apostolic age ordained to the sacred ministry, and in certain cases would have exercised the chief teaching and governing authority. Gradually these men, after the pattern set by James in Jerusalem or by John in the Churches of Asia, became themselves local presidents or instituted others in their place" [*l. c.*, p. 335].

We are not on the ground of the Divine right of the New Testament. We have nothing more than very ancient historic right for the Historic Episcopate, but no Divine right. On the other hand, the theory that the parochial bishop was a natural evolution of the college of presbyter-bishops; that it was inevitable that the college should have an executive head; and that with the growth of the Church, this presiding presbyter-bishop, who at first was temporary and changeable, or in the order of seniority would become a permanent parochial bishop, having the administration of the affairs of the Church of the city committed to his hands, without any ordering of the Apostles and without any Divine institution,— this theory accounts for all the facts of history as they appear in the ancient documents.[1]

The modern Church cannot safely commit itself to any of these theories, for it is within the range of possibility that ere long other early Christian documents may be discovered, of more importance than the Teaching of the Twelve Apostles, that will put the whole question in a new light. We cannot agree to any more than that the parochial bishop at the head of a Presbytery of presbyter-bishops was a historic fact of the first half of the second Christian century, and that it became universal at the close of the century. Whether it rests upon Apostolic authority, or the authority of the presbyter-bishops into whose hands the government of the Church was intrusted by the Apostles, it is not necessary for us to determine. The New Testament gives us no *jure divino* on the subject. If it were an essential question, it is reasonable to suppose there would have been a *jure divino* determination of it. We may agree upon the historic fact; we cannot agree upon the Divine institution.

The Apostles had a unique office,— to bear witness to what they had seen of the historic CHRIST, His life, His teachings, His

---

[1] We do not underrate the historical argument even when it comes so close to the Apostles themselves and the prophets who were associated with them. But we claim that it is necessary to carefully distinguish it from the Divine right of the New Testament. In the consideration of this difference I have been greatly impressed by the inconsistency in which many modern Presbyterians have become involved. The old Presbyterians were entirely consistent when they demanded a Divine right from the New Testament itself for the ministry and the canon of Scripture. But modern Presbyterians who have abandoned the argument from the testimony of the HOLY SPIRIT for the canonicity of Scripture, and rest the authority of the canon of Scripture upon the historical evidence connecting it with Apostolic penmen, can no longer with consistency demand a *jure divino* for Episcopacy, and refuse the candid and firm historical argument of Bishop Lightfoot.

death on the cross, His resurrection, His ascension, and the Christophanies of the enthroned SAVIOUR. No successors could fulfil this office. The other parts of their office, teaching, governing, and administration of the sacraments, they transmitted to others. In the New Testament the presbyter-bishops are seen doing all these things. They could transmit these things to their successors without any need of a higher order, superintending them and governing them. It seems to many historical critics that this very thing they did. If others find comfort in a theory that the Apostles or Apostolic men had a hand in instituting the parochial bishops, we have no objection to the theory, if held as a theory and not urged as essential to the existence of the Church. But the second century gives us only the parochial bishop. The Diocesan bishop and the village bishop were later developments. Certainly these had no institution from the hands of the Apostles or Apostolic men. We may accept the Diocesan bishop as a historic evolution in the growth of the Church under the guidance of the DIVINE SPIRIT, but we cannot accept the Diocesan bishop as linked by Apostolic succession as a distinct order to the ordaining hands of the Apostles. The ordination of presbyter-bishops may be linked to Apostolic hands by the testimony of the New Testament. The ordination of the parochial bishop may be linked to the Apostles' hands by a plausible interpretation of historical facts. But the Diocesan bishop is an evolution out of the parochial bishop, and the only Apostolic succession he has is through the parochial bishop, or possibly only through the presbyter-bishops.

3. The claim that ordination by Diocesan bishops has special grace, without which there is no valid ministry, is the most objectionable of all the claims that are put forth on behalf of the Historic Episcopate at the present time. We hold that there is no evidence for this in the New Testament, or in the second Christian century. The New Testament tells us of ordination by a Presbytery of presbyter-bishops, but gives us no example of ordination by a parochial bishop, still less of ordination by a Diocesan bishop. The Presbyterian Churches claim that their ordination by presbyter-bishops is in accordance with the example of the New Testament, and that the Apostolic succession has been regularly transmitted through the centuries in the laying on of hands of these presbyter-bishops. At the Reformation some of the National Churches of northern Europe laid

aside the Diocesan bishops, and by the highest authority in those Churches gave the entire authority of the ministry to the presbyter-bishops' meeting in Presbytery.

Presbyterian ministers have been ordained by the laying on of hands of presbyter-bishops, in regular succession from presbyter-bishops ordained by Diocesan bishops at the head of bodies of presbyter-bishops.

Gore admits "that the Church principle of succession would never be violated by the existence in any Church of Episcopal powers, whether free or conditional, in all the presbyters, supposing that those powers were not assumed by the individual for himself, but were understood to be conveyed to him by the ordination of the Church."[1] Now this is precisely the case with the Reformed National Churches of Europe. The Churches of Switzerland, Germany, and Scotland were reformed in doctrine and discipline by the same authority as the Church of England; namely, the authority lodged in the National Church itself. It is quite evident that the National Church was less free to reform itself and more hindered in its development in England than in any other Protestant country. The Diocesan bishops were deposed for tyranny, immorality, and heresy in many of the Reformed Churches in an orderly way. In those countries where Diocesan bishops led or followed the National Churches in their reform, they were retained. But where they were deposed, and discontinued in the interests of the good order and discipline of the Church, the whole authority of the Church was given over into the hands of the presbyter-bishops. Did these National Churches die with their deposed Diocesan bishops? Was there no inherent authority in the Church to govern itself when its historic bishops had left it in the lurch? Even granting that in the interests of good order ordination by a Diocesan bishop at the head of a Presbytery is necessary to a valid ministry, yet the disorders of the Reformation, and the separation of the bishops from the Churches of the Reformation, left the National Churches in such an abnormal condition that the only ordained ministry left to them were obliged to exercise all the functions of the ministry. Their acts, even if irregular and disorderly, were therefore valid, because they were not the usurped authority of individuals; they were the authority of organized National Churches, in accordance with national law and order.

[1] *Ministry of the Christian Church*, 1889, p. 143.

Principal Gore says, "It cannot be maintained that the acts of ordination by which presbyters of the sixteenth or subsequent centuries originated the ministries of some of these societies, were covered by their commissions or belonged to the office of Presbyter, which they had received."[1] But this is precisely what has been maintained in the Lutheran and Reformed Churches from the beginning. The Westminster Directory teaches, —

(1) No man ought to take upon him the office of a minister of the Word without a lawful calling [John iii. 27; Rom. x. 14, 15; Jer. xiv. 14; Heb. ix. 4]; (2) Ordination is always to be continued in the Church [Tit. i. 5; 1 Tim. v. 21, 22]; (3) Ordination is the solemn setting apart of a person to some publique Church office [Num. viii. 10, 11, 14, 19, 22; Acts vi. 3, 5, 6]; (4) Every minister of the Word is to be ordained by imposition of hands, and prayer with fasting, by those preaching presbyters to whom it doth belong [1 Tim. v. 22; Acts xiii. 3; xiv. 23]; (5) The power of ordering the whole work of ordination is in the whole Presbytery [1 Tim. iv. 14].

It is not presbyters gathered in societies who ordain, but presbyters organized in a Presbytery for the government and discipline of the Church. These presbyters claim Apostolic succession through the laying on of hands of presbyters in successive generations, leading back to the Apostles in the New Testament times. These Presbyteries claim succession to the Presbyteries that have governed the Church in all ages under various names. Their authority was not destroyed when the presiding bishops were lawfully deposed and the office of Diocesan bishops was for good reasons discontinued. The whole authority of ordination fell to the whole Presbytery or whole body of presbyters organized as National Churches.

Principal Gore also says, "Beyond all question they 'took to themselves' these powers of ordination, and consequently had them not."[2] But Presbyterians claim, on the contrary, that they did have these powers of ordination by right of succession and that they did not take them to themselves, and that they consequently had them. They not only had them by transmission in ordination by presbyters and Diocesan bishops, but they had them by becoming, through the deposition of the Diocesan bishops, and the commission into their hands by the General Assembly of the National Church, and by the consent of the National Parliament, the seat of the whole authority in the

[1] *Ministry of the Christian Church*, 1889, p. 344.   [2] Ibid., p. 345.

National Church. There was no more taking to themselves powers of ordination by Scotch, Swiss, Danish, Dutch, and German presbyters in these National Churches of Northern Europe than there was in the case of the Protestant bishops of the Church of England who were deposed by the Roman Church, and whose authority to ordain has never since been recognized by the Roman Church. Did the deposed Diocesan bishops retain in their hands the sole authority to ordain in the National Church, and were the whole body of presbyters and the people and Parliament doing unlawful acts in vindicating the purity of the Church, its orthodoxy, and the Divine rights of JESUS CHRIST? GOD forbid! The accident or good providence that enabled the Church of England to advance into the Reformation with her bishops at her head, does not entitle that Church to lord it over other National Churches, or to claim the only valid ministry in Protestantism. The Lutheran and Reformed Churches of the continent of Europe and the Presbyterian and Congregational Churches of Great Britain and America, challenge comparison with the Church of England and her daughters at this point, and at any other point. The ministry of those Churches who honor the names of Luther and Melancthon, Zwingli and Calvin, Knox and Alasco, and a host more of the greatest men of modern times, will never dishonor the memory of these heroes of the Faith by denying the validity of their ministry. The reunion of Christendom at such a cost would be a dishonorable transaction. Presbyterians and Congregationalists will continue to honor the memories of Cartwright and Travers in their contest with Whitgift and Hooker; of Marshall, Palmer, and Baxter in their contest with Laud, Hall, and Taylor; of Robinson and his band of Separatists who founded the Plymouth Colony; of the patriarch White of Dorchester and his associates, who founded the Massachusetts Bay Colony; of Melville, Welch, Livingston, and Rutherford, and a host of brave Presbyterians and Congregationalists, who battled against civil and ecclesiastical tyranny of bishops and king. Such names as Cartwright, Melville, Baxter, and Bunyan shine among the heroes of the Faith. Such lordly and tyrannous prelates as Whitgift and Laud no modern Church would tolerate for a moment. The English people of our day would hurl such bishops from their thrones with thunderbolts of wrath. Such prelacy is not the Historic Episcopate.

It should be definitely understood that the ministry of the non-Episcopal Churches will not in any considerable numbers dishonor the Apostolic succession of their ministry through such presbyter-bishops. If our brethren of the Episcopal ministry think there is any special grace in ordination by the hands of a Diocesan bishop, and offer that grace to us without exacting from us any renunciation of the ministry we have received as Presbyterians, by the laying on of the hands of the Presbytery, I am free to say that in order to the unity of the Church, and in order to the historical continuity that there is in the Diocesan Episcopate, honored through the centuries of Christian history, I would accept the offer of Episcopal ordination, and I doubt not that many ministers would follow me in such a step. But we cannot accept the doctrine that the grace of Apostolic succession drops only from the bishop's hands, or that the presbyters who take part in the ceremony of ordination are merely attendants, communicating nothing of the authority of the ministry from their share in the ceremony of ordination.

4. The claim that bishops have Divine authority to rule the Church was pressed in former times. But unless we mistake, it has been for the most part abandoned in Great Britain and America. The fight against Episcopal usurpation and tyranny has been fought to the end; and the Church of England and her daughters are now among the freest and most tolerant Churches in Christendom. There is much more of tyranny in modern Presbyterianism, and even in modern Congregationalism, than there is in the Historic Episcopate, as it is now known in Great Britain and America.

None of these four claims that have been associated with Historic Episcopacy would be recognized by the ministry of the non-Episcopal Churches. Many of us are willing that all who desire to make these claims may do so for their own comfort and edification, in so far as they do not force them upon us, or endeavor to make them the law of the Church of CHRIST. We do not follow the ancient Puritans in rejecting them as anti-Christian errors. We do not agree with the old Presbyterians in casting out *jure divino* Episcopacy in order to set up *jure divino* Presbytery. Cartwright and Travers were as much in error on the one side as Laud and Hall on the other.

We have to consider under the Historic Episcopate that which is essential to it as a bond of union, and not those unessential theories and claims that have been put forth by certain parties in its behalf. These are but the outer garments of the Historic Episcopate, that may be exchanged for other robes. These are the features that may be pleasant for some parties to look upon, and we shall not deny them their pleasure in them. But when the proposition of the House of Bishops is adopted, "the Historic Episcopate, locally adapted in the methods of its administration to the varying needs of the nations and peoples called of GOD into the unity of the Church," then, if we mistake not, all these unessential things will be referred to the special charge of the Anglo-Catholic party to nurse them and care for their future, while all other parties will agree with the Anglo-Catholics in rallying round the Historic Episcopate in its essential features as seen in all lands and in all times, taking form in the several Dioceses as the conditions and circumstances require.

IV. *Advantages of the Historic Episcopate.*

Where, then, is the advantage of the Historic Episcopate? Where is the *substance* in which all Episcopal Churches and parties are agreed, and to which it is probable non-Episcopal Churches will adhere, in order to the reunion of Christendom?

1. *The Historic Episcopate was a Historical Evolution in Church Government.* Although there were no other bishops in New Testament times than presbyters, yet it was a legitimate and inevitable result of a bench or body of presbyters that one should have the management of affairs, be the executive head, and preside over the government of the local Church. The presiding bishop therefore sprang up in the latter part of the first century, or early in the second century. At first this bishop was a parochial bishop. There was but one Church organization in the city, with missions in the suburban villages. The unity of the Church maintained itself with its increase in size, so that in the latter part of the second century, or early in the third century, the parochial Presbytery had grown into a Diocesan Presbytery, and the parochial bishop into a Diocesan bishop, and later chorepiscopi, or pastors of village Churches, came into the field. The system continued to develop in history until the archbishop and patriarch and pope, one after the other, gave expression to the higher unities of the

growing Church of CHRIST. The Historic Episcopate is a historical evolution. It has a vast variety of form in history. At what stage in the development shall we take it as a basis of union? The Roman Church presents us the system in its highest form in the Pope. The Greek and Oriental Churches give us an earlier stage in the patriarch. The Church of England presents us the still earlier stage in the archbishop. The American Episcopal Church does not rise higher than the Diocesan bishop. The Presbyterian Church goes farther back to the parochial bishop. What Church is there that goes back to the earlier form of government as it appears in the New Testament, with a bench of parochial presbyter-bishops under Apostolic oversight? Not one. They all have made the mistake of pleading a *jure divino*, while they all represent a later stage of *jure humano* development. At what stage, then, shall we take our stand for Church unity? What is the essence of the Historic Episcopate in which all can agree?

It seems to me that the solution is not in going backward, but *forward*. History speaks very strongly for the Historic Episcopate. My historic sense not only gives me great respect and veneration for the office, but also leads me to the opinion that the Church, guided by the DIVINE SPIRIT, did not err in its Episcopal government through all these centuries. The abandonment of the Episcopate was not a natural result of the Reformation. It was not a part of the Lutheran movement. The national Lutheran Churches of Denmark and Sweden have retained bishops until the present day.

Sweden claims Apostolical succession for her bishops. The Episcopal office was restored to Denmark, but the first bishops were ordained by Bugenhagen.[1] Bishops continued at the head of the Reformed Churches of Prussia and Brandenburg for a long time. England began with bishops. Scotland had superintending bishops. It was the jealousy that princes in Germany felt of the Episcopal prerogative that prevented the Lutheran Church from having Diocesan bishops. However, superintendents were appointed to exercise many of the functions of the Episcopate in the larger portion of Germany and Austria.

It was the tyranny of the bishops, and their close alliance with the Crown, that forced the reforming party in the State as well

---

[1] *Briefwechsel zwischen H. L. Martensen und I. A. Dorner*, Bd. i. s. 238.

as in the Church to take ground against them. The King was the supreme bishop of the Church of England, and became a national pope.

There was nothing in the principles of the Reformation that at all interfered with the Episcopal office. There was nothing in Puritanism that forced the abolition of the Episcopate. Some of the ablest archbishops and bishops of England and Ireland were Puritans. It was more the evolution of civil politics and the political complications of the bishops that made the difficulty in Great Britain. Whitgift and Laud did more to injure the Episcopate in Protestantism than any other agencies whatever. The opposition to the Episcopate in Presbyterian circles is a traditional opposition that goes back to the Laudian usurpation and the civil and religious wars that followed. The Episcopate of *Abbot* and *Ussher* Presbyterians are under historical bonds to accept.

The difficulty is not to be solved by stopping at any of the stages in the historical evolution of the Episcopate, whether with the parochial bishop, the Diocesan bishop, the archbishop, the patriarch, or the pope. The whole process is a natural evolution of the Historic Episcopate. As I have recently said: —

Christendom might unite with an ascending series of superintending bishops that would culminate in a universal bishop, provided the pyramid would be willing to rest firmly on its base, the solid order of the presbyter-bishops of the New Testament and of all history, and all Churches. But the pyramid will never stand on its apex, nor hang suspended in the air supported by any of its upper stages [*Whither?* p. 238].

2. *The Historic Episcopate is the Crown of Presbyterian Government.* It was so historically; it is so practically. Therefore Presbyterians should be willing to accept it as such. They are not willing to accept the theory of the *three orders*, but many are willing to accept the bishop as the executive head of the one order of ministers, — the first among his brethren, the most honored, the most efficient, of them all. It is the theory of Apostolic *orders* that makes the difficulty in the Historic Episcopacy. We can agree upon orders as differences in rank as *jure humano*, for the well-being of the Church, so far as these higher orders are higher by election of their breth-

ren, and not higher by descent of Apostolical succession. I could agree to bishop, archbishop, patriarch, and pope if these were all chosen by the Church in stage upon stage of advancement toward the executive head of the Church. But I could not agree that the bishops had any exclusive Divine right or historic right to transmit the Episcopal order, any more than that the Pope should transmit papal authority. The bishops should be simply the executive officers of the Church chosen by the Presbyteries. I am willing, in other words, to agree to the whole system of Episcopal orders even up to a papal head, but am not willing to agree to theories of higher orders, which are associate with prerogative, pride, ambition, tyranny, and despotism. Presbyterians might be willing to recognize all sorts of theories of the Episcopate and tolerate all kinds of human weakness and follies in bishops; they could not unite on any of the theories of the Historic Episcopate, but they might unite on the Historic Episcopate itself. And if the Anglo-Catholics desire to conserve their theory by any rites and ceremonies in the way of consecration and ordination by bishops, they should concede to others the Presbyterial election, Episcopal responsibility to synods or conventions in which presbyters shall have their rights; and they should put such checks upon Episcopal authority as will prevent any of those evils from which the Church suffered so much in the past.

It is interesting to observe just here two historical facts: (1) What the Presbyterians offered in 1661, as their ultimatum; and (2) What is the actual condition of the Historic Episcopate in America, when compared with this ultimatum.

The Presbyterial ultimatum of 1661 was given in the Proposals of the Presbyterian ministers, drawn up after nearly three weeks' debate, in Sion College, in which Edmund Calamy, Reynolds, Newcommen, and Baxter, had the chief hand.

That although upon just reasons we do dissent from that ecclesiastical hierarchy or prelacy disclaimed in the Covenant, as it was stated and exercised in these kingdoms, yet we do not, nor ever did renounce the true ancient and primitive presidency as it was ballanced and managed by a due commixture of presbyters therewith, as a fit means to avoid corruptions, partiality, tyranny, and other evils which may be incident to the administration of one single person, which kind of attempered Presidency, if it shall be your Majesty's grave wisdom and gracious moderation, be in such manner constituted as that the forementioned and other like evils may be certainly prevented, we shall humbly submit thereunto.

And in order to an happy accomodation in this weighty business, we desire humbly to offer unto your majesty some of the particulars which we conceive were unwise in the Episcopal government, as it was practised before the year 1640.

1. The great extent of the Bishop's Diocess, which was much too large for his own personal inspection, wherein he undertook a pastoral charge over the souls of all those within his bishoprick, which must needs be granted to be too heavy a burthen for any one man's shoulders, the Pastoral office being a work of personal ministration and trust, and that of the highest concernment to the souls of the people, for which they are to give an account to CHRIST.

2. That by reason of this disability to discharge their duty and trust personally, the bishops did depute the administration of much of their trust, even in matters of spiritual cognizance, to commissaries, chancellors, and officials, whereof some were secular persons, and could not administer that power which originally appertaineth to the pastors of the Church.

3. That those bishops who affirm the Episcopal office to be a distinct order, by Divine right from that of the Presbyter, did assume the sole power of ordination and jurisdiction to themselves.

4. That some of the bishops exercised an arbitrary power as by sending forth the Books of Articles in their Visitations, and therein unwarrantably enquiring into several things, and swearing the churchwardens to present accordingly. So also by many innovations and ceremonies imposed upon ministers and people not required by law, and by suspending ministers at their pleasure.

In reforming of which evils, we humbly crave leave to offer unto your majesty, —

1. The late most reverend primate of Ireland his Reduction of Episcopacy unto the Form of Synodical Government, received in the ancient Church : as a ground work towards an accommodation and fraternal agreement in this point of Ecclesiastical government : which we rather do, not only in regard of his eminent piety and singular Ability as in all other parts of Learning so in that especially of the Antiquities of the Church, but also because therein expedients are offered for healing these grievances.

And in order to the same end, we further humbly desire that the suffragans or chorepiscopi, mentioned in the Primate's Reduction, may be chosen by the respective Synods, and by that Election be sufficiently authorized to discharge their Trust. That the Associations may not be so large as to make the Discipline impossible, or to take off the ministers from the rest of their necessary imployments.

That no oaths or promises of obedience to the Bishops, nor any unnecessary subscriptions or engagements be made necessary to ordination, institution, induction, ministration, communion, or immunities of ministers, they being responsible for any transgression of the Law.

And that no Bishops nor any ecclesiastical governors may at any time exercise their government by their own private will or pleasure, but only by such rules, canons, and constitutions as shall be hereafter by Act of Parliament ratified and established; and that sufficient provision be made to secure both ministers and people against the evils of Arbitrary Government in the Church.

These Presbyterian Proposals were rejected by the bishops in 1661. But unless we mistake, every one of these Presbyterian Proposals has been complied with by the Protestant Episcopal Church in the United States. Baxter said in 1691, "Oh, how little would it have cost your Churchmen in 1660 and 1661 to have prevented the calamitous and dangerous divisions of this Land, and our common dangers thereby and the hurt that many hundred thousand souls have received by it? And how little would it cost them *yet to prevent the continuance of it*" [*Penitent Confession, Preface*]. Then I thank GOD that the Church of England and the American Protestant Episcopal Church are now willing to pay this small cost. I stand by Baxter; and I shall do all I can to reduce the cost. It is no time for Presbyterians to increase their demands. We should vie with our Episcopal brethren in generosity and self-sacrifice. I believe that Presbyterians will rise to the situation so soon as they understand it. I believe that ere long Presbyterians will accept the Proposals of the House of Bishops, and thus show that they have the same spirit of accommodation and desire for the unity of CHRIST'S Church that their fathers showed in the Proposals of 1661. We are thankful that after more than two centuries a House of Bishops has accepted all that our fathers proposed.

3. *Episcopal ordination and Presbyterial ordination are not inconsistent, but complementary.* A Presbyterian minister is ordained by the laying on of the hands of the Presbytery with a moderator at their head. The ordination is the act of the

whole body organized for the government of the congregations and presbyters within its bounds. The Episcopal minister is ordained by the laying on of the hands of the bishop, with two or more attending presbyters. We shall place the directory and the ordinal side by side for comparison.

ORDINAL.	DIRECTORY.
The bishop, with the priests present, shall lay their hands severally upon the head of every one that receiveth the order of priesthood, the receivers humbly kneeling upon their knees, and the bishop saying, " Receive the HOLY GHOST for the office and work of a priest in the Church of GOD, now committed unto thee by the imposition of our hands."	The candidate shall kneel down in the most convenient part of the Church. Then the presiding minister shall, by prayer, and with the laying on of the hands of the Presbytery, according to the Apostolic example, solemnly ordain him to the holy office of the gospel ministry. Prayer being ended, he shall rise from his knees; and the minister who presides first and afterward all the members of the Presbytery in their order, take him by the right hand, saying. in words to this purpose, "We give you the right hand of fellowship to take part of this ministry with us."

In this ceremony the presiding minister is to be compared with the bishop, and the Presbytery with the two or more presbyters associated with the bishop. There is the same ceremony essentially, but there are two striking differences: (*a*) In the one case the bishop presides and directs the ceremony of ordination. The bishop is the permanent head of the Diocese, and the authority of the Diocese centres in him. He has been chosen bishop because he is the most honored, the most revered, and the most efficient of the presbyters. His presidency is permanent, and thereby of higher rank, giving to the whole service dignity and unity. The presiding minister of the Presbytery may be, and often is, one of the least honored and least revered members of the Presbytery. He adds no dignity to the occasion, and if it should happen, as it not infrequently does, that he presides for the first time, his presiding in the ordination lacks grace and propriety, and in so far disturbs the solemnity of the occasion. Unless we mistake, it is a common experience in connection with the ceremony of Presbyterian ordination that candidates, presbyters, and people, all alike regret that some other more honored and more graceful presbyter had not been called upon to preside. A shifting moderator lacks the propriety, grace, and dignity attached to the presidency of the bishops in the government and in the ceremonies of the Church. Episcopal ordination therefore is greatly to be preferred to ordination by a temporary presiding presbyter.

(b) On the other hand, we have to compare the two or more presbyters who are associated with the bishop in Episcopal ordination, with the body of presbyters, organized as a Presbytery, who take part in Presbyterial ordination. This body of presbyters, embracing the pastors of the congregations and other grave and venerable members who may be present, all with their hands upon the head of the candidate, and subsequently giving him the right hand of fellowship, make the ceremony a very impressive one, that is never forgotten by the candidates. This impressiveness, this weight of authority, this extent of influence, seems to be lacking in the Episcopal ceremony. Presbyterian ordination is the official act of the entire body of ministers in the Presbytery, and therefore of the Presbyterian Church as such, in the exercise of its Presbyterial functions. Episcopal ordination lacks this authority of the organized Presbytery, and concentrates the attention upon the authority of the bishop. It is the common theory, if we mistake not, in the Episcopal Church that the presbyters are merely attendants on the bishop and that they do not represent the body of presbyters in their act. It seems to be the common opinion that the term "*our* hands" in the Ordinal does not refer to the hands of bishop and presbyters, but only to the bishop's hands, speaking as the head of the Church. We may be permitted to doubt, however, whether that was the original meaning of the phrase.

When the two ceremonies are compared, each has its advantages and its disadvantages. If the bishop took the place of the presiding minister in the Directory, and the Presbytery took the place of the two or more attending presbyters of the Ordinal, the two ceremonies would be equally improved by becoming identical. When the happy union is consummated, Episcopacy and

Presbytery may each contribute an equal share to a Church that will be higher, better, and more efficient than either.

The difficulty here is not as to the future; that will take care of itself. The difficulty is in making the transition. Let us see what that difficulty practically is. The difficulty is with the theory of the three orders of the ministry as resting on Divine right. Those in the Episcopal Churches who do not accept this theory would have little difficulty in recognizing the validity of Presbyterian ordination as to essence. Presbyterian ordination has all the virtue in it that the laying on of the hands of the presbyters can impart It only lacks that virtue that comes from the bishop's hands. There can be little doubt that ordination has been carefully guarded in Presbyterian Churches. No minister enters the Presbyterian Churches of Great Britain without the laying on of hands of the Presbytery, or body of presbyters, with a moderator presiding over them. The Presbyteries of the Presbyterian Churches of Great Britain when the Episcopal Church was disestablished had been ordained with few exceptions by Episcopal as well as Presbyterial ordination Those few had been ordained by the Presbyteries of Swiss, French, Dutch, and German Churches in the same orderly manner. The founders of the Presbyterian Church were regularly ordained, at least a sufficient number of them, even according to the highest theory of the Episcopal function. If these presbyters were entitled to share with bishops in the ordination of other presbyters, in accordance with the lawful practice of the ancient Churches and the Church of England and her daughters, so far as they could transmit authority as presbyters, they transmitted it to the presbyters that they ordained. If they transmitted anything when ordaining with bishops, they transmitted the same when ordaining without bishops. What is lacking, therefore, and the only thing that is lacking in the ordination of Presbyterian ministers, is that virtue and that alone that comes from the Diocesan bishop's hands. Presbyterial ordination therefore may be incomplete, but it is an ordination in part, so far as presbyters can ordain. If ordination belongs to the bishop alone, then Presbyterian ministers have not been ordained. If presbyters are simply the attendants of the bishop, and their participation adds nothing to the ordination, then Presbyterian ministers are not ordained. But if the participation of presbyters has some importance, if their participation in ordination communicates any grace or authority, then they may communicate that grace and authority whenever they are properly organized as a Presbytery to act. It may be asked which, indeed, is the more valid ordination, — that by presbyters without a bishop, or that by a bishop without the co-operation of presbyters. The authority of the Scriptures can be cited for the former, but the latter has been regarded as irregular, even in Episcopal Churches; and yet such irregular ordinations have taken place in the Church of England. Against them the Puritans rightly complained. And yet these ordinations by bishops alone, that were irregular, were not regarded as invalid. Why, then, should ordination by presbyteries alone be regarded as invalid? The Church of Scotland is an independent National Church, as truly a National Church as the Church of England, and so recognized at the settlement of the Revolution. Those who question the validity of the ordination of the ministry of that Church and her daughters from the point of view of the National Church of England and her daughters, have no more warrant so to do than the Church of Scotland would have to deny the validity of the ordination of the ministry of the Church of England and her daughters. The two Churches were organized by ecclesiastical and civil law, and are on an equality before the law in Great Britain. The Church of England is Episcopal, and the Presbyterian Church of England is Dissenting. The Church of Scotland is Presbyterian, and the Episcopal Church of Scotland is Dissenting. In the United States the daughters of these two National Churches are on an equality before the law; the one is as much the Church of the United States as the other. The two National Churches have different theories and methods of ordination. The one is as regular and lawful as the other, and there is as genuine Apostolical succession in the one as in the other. The Church of Scotland has her succession through the presbyter-bishops. The Church of England traces her succession through the Diocesan bishops. On the theory of two orders by Divine right the Presbyterial ordination is valid only so far as the ordination by presbyters is concerned, and invalid for the failure of the bishop's hands. But on the theory that the bishop is only *jure humano*, and therefore not necessary to the existence of the Church, where a National Church is organized without Diocesan bishops, ordination by presbyters is valid and orderly. All who do not accept the *jure divino* theory of the Episcopate should agree to this.

The difficulties in the way of the recognition of Presbyterian ordination are ancient difficulties that we should feel bound to respect and to remove if possible. The difficulty is practically this: If a Presbyterian should apply for admission to the Episcopal Church, it would be necessary for him to be confirmed and ordained. If an Episcopal minister should seek admission to the Presbyterian Church, it would be necessary for him to be voted upon after examination by the Session of a Presbyterian Church, and then received into a Presbytery after his subscription to the Westminster Confession. The difficulty in the one case would be *ceremonial*, in the other case it would be *doctrinal subscription*. These barriers are purely ecclesiastical ones. They are fences set up in the interest of the good order of the Church. Let us consider the additional difficulties our fathers had in their way. In 1661 two thousand parish ministers were thrust out of their charges in England because they could not take the following oaths: (1) Non-resistance and passive obedience to bishop and king; (2) Conformity to the Liturgy; (3) Renouncing the solemn league and covenant to which they had previously sworn. During the Presbyterian supremacy hundreds of parish priests had been removed because they refused to swear to the covenant. No one could be ordained during that period, and subsequently, according to the Directory, who did not take "the covenant of the three kingdoms." It was not simply a matter of ordination on either side. These ancient fences have been broken down; others still remain. It would be possible for the Presbyterian Session to waive its right of examination; it would be possible for the Presbyterian Church to reduce its subscription from the Westminster Confession to the Nicene Creed or the Apostles' Creed. I suppose it would be possible in the Protestant Episcopal Church to waive the ceremony of confirmation in the admission of members of Presbyterian Churches, and to waive the ceremony of ordination by those who had been ordained by the laying on of the hands of the Presbytery.

I was informed by high authority immediately after the adjournment of the Lambeth Conference that a very considerable proportion of that Conference would be willing to recognize Presbyterial ordination under certain conditions, but that the time had not come to take definite action. Bishop Vincent confirms this testimony when he says: —

But one expedient so far, has been proposed which promises to meet the difficulty in any practical way, and that is the proposition of Bishop Charles Wordsworth of the Scottish Church, made through a committee of the last Lambeth Conference. It was substantially this: that we should now recognize the full ministerial standing of clergymen presbyterially ordained, providing that hereafter all their ordinations should be by bishops. The report of the Committee says: 'While the Church in her XXIII. Article lays down the necessity of the ministry as a sacred order, commissioned by "those who have public authority given them in the congregation;" and while for *herself* she has defined this expression by insisting in her own Communion on *Episcopal* ordination, she has nowhere declared that all other constituted ministry is null and void.' This proposition was not accepted by the Conference, and probably for two good reasons, if for no other: because it was not prepared to act so suddenly in so serious a matter, and also because, being only a Conference, it had no authority so to act. But it should also be said that ten out of the twelve members of the Committee voted for it, and that the Archbishop of Canterbury expressed his 'very full and hearty sympathy with it' [VINCENT, *Address on Church Unity*, pp. 34–36].

I have been deeply interested in this matter of ordination in connection with the question of the reunion of Christendom, and it has come upon me as a surprise that the divided Church has been thinking of ordination from the same point of view as the Church used to do when there was but one Church in a nation. Presbyterians recognize the ordination of Roman Catholics and Episcopalians as well as other denominations.

They put up the barrier at doctrinal subscription. The Episcopal Church recognizes Roman Catholic ordination as well as her own, but refuses Presbyterial ordination. The Roman Catholics reject Episcopal ordination as well as Presbyterial. But after all, something more than ordination is required for the exercise of the ministry in all of our denominations. The Lord Bishop of London would not be received to the Presbytery of New York without subscription. His ordination would be recognized, but he would not be allowed to exercise his ministry in the bounds of the Presbyterian Church. He might preach, but so might a layman. He could not become a pastor of a congregation, and he could not rule as a presbyter in the Presbyterian Church. I apprehend that an Episcopal rector or bishop would have no difficulty in allowing a Presbyterian minister to preach a sermon or to deliver a lecture in an Episcopal church or cathedral. The question to him would be simply a matter of good order very much the same as if a lay-evangelist were to be admitted to a Presbyterian pulpit.[1]

The difficulty of ministerial recognition comes precisely where it would come in a Presbyterian Church; namely, in the exercise of government and discipline, and in the administration of the sacraments, for these are the functions of the presbyter's office. The preaching of the gospel is not in dispute. That may be done by laymen in all the denominations, but the office of presbyter can be entered upon only by ordination after examination.

The ordination in one denomination will not suffice for another denomination. Examination, and in many cases subscription also, will be required of all those who have been ordained in other denominations. The Church in this way gives authority to the candidate to exercise the office of presbyter. It gives its authority. But it can only impart the authority it has. The Presbytery of New York can give authority by examination, subscription, and ordination to a presbyter to labor as presbyter in the bounds of the Presbyterian Church, but it cannot give him authority to act as presbyter within the bounds of any other denomination. If I desired to be a presbyter in the Methodist Episcopal Church, it would be necessary for me to be received by a Conference and have its authority to serve in one of the Churches under its care. If I desired to serve as a presbyter in the Baptist Church, it would be necessary for me to be immersed and then recognized as a presbyter after examination before a council of Baptist presbyters called for the purpose. If I desired to serve as presbyter in the Protestant Episcopal Church, it would be necessary to be ordained by a Diocesan bishop. As it appears to me, there are obstacles in every case; the most difficult ones are with the Baptists. But

---

[1] I cannot find that the Canons of the Protestant Episcopal Church are any more exclusive than the Directory of Worship and Book of Discipline of the Presbyterian Church. It may be that the Episcopal clergy are stricter in their adherence to the laws of the Church, and the Presbyterian ministry are more independent in their attitude to their own rules. But it may be questioned whether good order is not better than license, even when the laws are wrong and ought to be repealed.

suppose that an Episcopal bishop were called to serve as a pastor within the bounds of the Presbytery of New York, he could not serve without examination before the Presbytery and subscription to the Westminster Confession. I doubt whether an Episcopal rector would find it any easier to become a Presbyterian presbyter than it would be for a Presbyterian pastor to become an Episcopal priest. The denominations are all proceeding on a theory of ordination in the Church which was sufficiently valid when there was but one National Church which could impart authority to a minister to exercise the functions of a presbyter anywhere in the land. But this is no longer the case. An Episcopal ordination does not give a minister as wide an opportunity of usefulness as Presbyterial ordination. Presbyterial ordination does not give as wide an opportunity of ministerial service as ordination to the ministry of the Methodist Episcopal Church. Each of the denominations ordains its own ministry, and the ministers thus ordained are divided into different camps. The question arises why ordained ministers should not go from the one denomination to the other? The difficulty in the way is a lack of organic union between the denominations. If there were such an organic union by way of federation in the constitution of a council representing the supreme courts of all the denominations, then the organic union thus consummated would be able to arrange for the mutual recognition of the ministry and work of the several branches of the reunited Church. I do not see any other way of overcoming the separation than by organic unity, by confederation first and consolidation afterward. The recognition of the validity of Presbyterial ordination will not remove the difficulty unless it is connected with federation or consolidation. It would remove a strife of words and misapprehensions of many kinds, but it would not make the presbyter of one denomination into a presbyter in another denomination. I see only two ways of accomplishing this. The one is for a considerable number of presbyters to become presbyters in two or more denominations at the same time, and thus become connecting links pulling them together. The other is for all organized bodies of presbyters to become members of a larger body, comprehending in one vast organism all the ministry of our country. That is the ideal that Christian men and women of all denominations should keep steadfastly in view, that we all may be one, having one Bible, one creed, one baptism, one

Table of the LORD, one ministry of bishops and presbyters, one HOLY SPIRIT, one reigning SAVIOUR, one GOD and FATHER of all, over all, through all, and in all.

CHARLES A. BRIGGS.

PROFESSOR EGBERT C. SMYTH, D.D. [CONGREGATIONAL], PROFESSOR IN THEOLOGICAL SEMINARY, ANDOVER, MASS.

EDITOR OF THE CHURCH REVIEW, SIR: —

ON account of special and pressing engagements, I was obliged to decline your invitation to contribute to the proposed Symposium on Church Reunion; but your subsequent urgent request that I would give at least some brief expression of my views leaves me no alternative, lest I should seem indifferent to your courtesy and unappreciative of the object you would promote.

My training and convictions lead me always to think of the Church as a Divine Kingdom, as a fellowship of men with GOD and with one another on the basis of the Incarnation, and of redemption, and to give supremacy to what is vital and spiritual according to the prayer of our LORD, — "That they may all be one; even as Thou, Father, art in Me, and I in Thee, that they also may be in us, ... I in them, and Thou in Me, that they may be perfected into one." Starting thus with what is spiritual, and anticipating its triumph in the consummation, I believe also, perhaps all the more firmly on this account, in an ever increasing *manifestation* of unity; for the spiritual life of the Church is a principle of fellowship and organization, and requires agencies and methods of organization, and is the one power, from and through the HOLY SPIRIT, capable of producing a real and manifested union of all disciples and Churches of CHRIST. I could not, at least without protest, belong to a society calling itself a Church, that excluded from its fundamental conception the ideal of one visible Catholic Church of CHRIST; and I believe that the progress of history, notwithstanding the schisms that exist or may arise, has been and will be toward this goal, — a manifested fellowship of all believers.

There are many signs of this movement to-day, particularly the changes which are becoming apparent in conviction and feeling. Among these I may mention an uneasy and growing sense that many present divisions are not only unnecessary, but wrong; that our denominationalism has much in it of sectarianism; that many causes and reasons of its existence have lost their original force; that it involves an immense waste of energy and means; that the calls for Christian work, in a world now open as never before to the gospel, require for their answer an immense increase in the spirit and agencies of Christian co-operation.

Among the most immediate and practical methods of promoting a Christian fellowship that will affect outward activities and find expression in organic forms, the one proposed by the American bishops in 1886, and indorsed by the Lambeth Conference, seems to me to be peculiarly suggestive and promising. It presents a noble example of a sincere and serious endeavor to promote Church unity by searching out and cultivating existing agreements; by a renunciation, as a condition of union, of many things which are deemed excellent in themselves and are not to be abandoned; by a recognition of steps and stages of union and the expression of readiness to enter into conference with other bodies for a better understanding of each other's positions. I regard this action as a most honorable and imperative challenge to the nobility of all other Christian Communions to do likewise, to enter upon a like process of self-examination, and to define to themselves in what ways they can promote the same end. If after this has been carefully done, there could be conferences as proposed, I should anticipate very beneficial results.

The first work is within each denomination, although it may be stimulated and clarified by contemporaneous and wider discussion. Each body, it seems to me, is now summoned by myriad voices to adjust itself to the great principle of Christian catholicity. This does not involve an abandonment of its own special treasures of thought or life or equipment for service. Unity is not uniformity in the Church any more than in Nature. But it does signify a strenuous, it may be a sacrificial, endeavor to put away as a term of Church communion, everything which cannot vindicate for itself the predicate of essentiality, everything which cannot fairly claim the sanction of S. Vincent's Rule, when this is interpreted so as to include the Apostolic Church and Age, and according to the nature and demeanor of a Christianity fitted to be universal. Whatever, in any body, is extra-Christian, as well as what is un-Christian, whatever goes beyond the simplicity of faith in CHRIST, and the demands of a fellowship on the basis of a common redemption, — however desirable in itself, however it may contribute to the enrichment of Christian life and the efficiency of Church organization, — should not stand as a barrier to the visible communion of Churches one with another, or, so far as this may be called for, their organic union or reunion. If each body would hold its acquisitions for the common good, and cultivate its agreements with every other, and guard its own treasures, that it may have the more to give, helping others to larger views of truth or nobler forms of worship, or more orderly and effective methods of administration, if each Communion would put by, in dealing with others where common confession or labor is desirable, all that interferes with such co-operation, the cause of reunion would receive an immense impulse.

I might, perhaps, stop here; yet as you suggest in your letter that each contributor is expected to speak only for himself, I judge that you desire some expression of opinion respecting the acceptability of the basis of agreement which you enclose.

For myself, I accept it as proposed, and should ask for no change in its terms. Considering it, however, as a means to an end, there are two points in respect to which discussion is likely to arise, and greater explicitness may be desirable.

One point is the reference to the Nicene Creed. As the proposed reunion is limited to English-speaking bodies of Christians, it may be that it is unnecessary to raise the question whether the original and Ecumenical or the Western form of the Creed is proposed. Yet it would seem to be desirable, in such a movement, to proceed from the outset on the broadest basis. I would, indeed, be thankful for any measure of success, and would not use the best as the enemy of the good. Yet the ideal method may be the most practical in the long run, and be attended on the whole with the least friction. The one decisive reason, I suppose, for singling out the Nicene Creed as a doctrinal statement is its ecumenical significance. It is in every way much to be desired that Oriental Christianity should receive impulse from, and come into closer relations with, Western. A union within the latter, by outward fellowship, by alliance, by organic reunion, by whatever may prove feasible or most excellent, is a great good to be specially sought for; but would not a better result still be to secure with this an open way to a larger fellowship? The Western doctrine of the SPIRIT would not thereby be disparaged. No Western creed would be changed. If one addition to the Ecumenical Creed is insisted upon, what shall be said to those who may ask for others? The power of the proposal lies in its breadth and catholicity. Any departure from this will prove, I fear, a disadvantage at the start. What is ultimately aimed at is not an Anglican reunion, but an ecumenical one; and a basis large enough for such a fellowship is likely to be most effective at every stage of the process.

From this point of view I should query whether the Nicene Creed — which I heartily accept in its Western form — even as originally put forth, might not be kept subordinate to the Apostles' in the discussion of terms of union. The former, indeed, has its own inestimable advantages, and I should regret its displacement in confession and worship. When historically interpreted, it simply adds to earlier creeds an unmistakable affirmation of the true Divinity of the SON and of the HOLY SPIRIT, — fundamental beliefs of the Christian Church. Yet I would not exclude from a scheme of Church union any body of Christians that acknowledges JESUS CHRIST as SAVIOUR and LORD, and seeks to do His will, and desires fellowship in Him and His SPIRIT, even if it were not ready to accept the definition of Nicæa. When some hesitated to apply to the HOLY SPIRIT the Nicene term, "co-essential," S. Basil waived it, and Athanasius justified him. Christian unity may require at times that the Church should go back of theological tests, however true they may be, to the fundamental facts of Christianity, to a confession which embodies them, and to the spirit of discipleship. Those who acknowledge JESUS' Lordship and strive to do the will of GOD may be trusted to the sure method of the Divine promise and to an authority that transcends that of the *Ecclesia docens*.

The other point is the "Historic Episcopate." The phrase is an elastic one, — intentionally so, I presume. It covers a fact, not a theory of its origin or significance. The discussion which is invited will inevitably reveal differences of interpretation, and perhaps will raise some delicate questions. For myself I am free to say that many years of study of the history of the Church leave little doubt in my mind that a distinction of office, or function, between bishops and presbyters, has its root in the Apostolic Age, and appears in the history of the Church of Jerusalem almost from the beginning, and elsewhere so close upon the same formative period as to imply a beginning within it. The institution of the Episcopate, moreover, is not only thus venerable, but it is the distinctive mark of a type of polity which can claim beyond all others steadfastness, continuity, power of survival and of adaptation. Other forms, whatever their special excellences, are comparatively untried and provincial. I cannot but think there is a good in such an institution for the Church Universal. Yet as an office it is not more continuous than that of the pastorate, nor as universal. I do not find it everywhere original with the Christian Church, nor even general in the primitive Churches, nor anywhere in Apostolic teaching made a *conditio sine qua non* of the being, nor even of the well-being, of the Christian Church. When, therefore, acceptance of it is made a condition of reunion, the scope of such unity is somewhat strictly defined, and the query is suggested whether a question of principle is not necessarily raised, — whether, for instance, the Episcopate, as distinct from the Presbyterate, or the pastorate, or the Christian ministry even, is not co-ordinated as a term of union with creed and sacraments. In such an issue there can be no question where the mass of the members of non-Episcopal bodies would be found. Probably few of them are prepared to welcome an Episcopal constitution as at present desirable or expedient; but if discussion should change their attitude here, it is not likely to alter it on the other question. On this line I should regard the prospect of reunion, organic or otherwise, as not much helped by the Lambeth proposal. But I do not thus understand this article. It treats of the Episcopate solely as a historic fact, and thus opens an inviting field for discussion. Probably here too the wisest method is for each body in the first instance to consider the question from its own point of view, and with reference to its own responsibilities, including that of doing what it can to promote the great end of Christian unity. In such a movement the proposal of the bishops and of the Lambeth Conference will have, I doubt not, a legitimate and helpful influence, raising an important question for each non-Episcopal body, stimulating any tendency that may already exist carefully to consider the essential value of the Episcopal office, and in still other ways contributing to a thoughtful consideration of this aspect of the problems of Church fellowship and unity.

Renewing the expression of a respectful and cordial recognition of the value of the proposals you enclose in your letter, and regretting that I am obliged to write under special disadvantages as to leisure and time,

I remain,

Yours very respectfully and truly,

EGBERT C. SMYTH.

REV. EDWARD T. HORN, D.D. [LUTHERAN], CHARLESTON, S. C., PRESIDENT OF THE UNITED SYNOD OF THE SOUTH.

I AM asked by the Editor of this REVIEW to "send my views on the subject of Christian Reunion in general, and how far the basis proposed (by the House of Bishops in 1886 and indorsed with slight modifications by the Lambeth Conference in 1888) meets with my approval." He adds, "Of course it will be understood that each writer will speak only for himself."

The *Basis for Reunion* proposed by the Lambeth Conference is an advance upon that of the House of Bishops. In this whole matter it is necessary that words should be used in one determinate sense; and vague terms should not be adopted with a view to the comprehension of a variety of opinions. I am far from believing that the House of Bishops intended to suggest a vague formula. From the beginning I have confided in their simplicity of purpose, and have thought that the Christian bodies they address should reply with the same simplicity and due frankness. But the first particular in the bishops' formula, "The Holy Scriptures . . . as the Revealed Word of GOD," seemed to me indefinite. To this the Lambeth Conference adds, "As containing all things necessary to salvation, and as being the rule and ultimate standard of Faith." The first clause is a quotation from the Article VI. of the Church of England, and doubtless indicates that the whole is to be accepted in the sense in which it is stated in the Articles. Add to this the *second proposition* of the BASIS, — the proposition of the Nicene Creed. This, of course, means not the Creed of Nicæa nor the more finished Creed of Constantinople, but the Nicene Creed as it appears in all the formularies of the Western Church, including those set forth by the bishops of these Churches, and therefore with the addition of the *Filioque*. This involves a disregard of the *Anathema* which the Council of Ephesus pronounced against all who should add to their Nicene Creed; it involves also an abandonment of the notion of the peculiar and binding authority of the councils of the first four centuries, of the councils of the "undivided" Church. It discards the opinion that the Universal Episcopate is endowed with infallibility or semi-infallibility as the depository of Apostolic tradition, and therefore is in harmony with the XIX. and XXI. Articles of the Church of England, by which it is confessed that "things ordained by General Councils as necessary to salvation have neither strength nor authority, unless it may be declared that they be taken out of Holy Scripture." This is the safe basis, acknowledged by us; and as thus amplified by the Lambeth Conference, and explained by the *second proposition*, I heartily indorse it.

In their second proposition, "The Nicene Creed as the sufficient statement of the Christian Faith," the bishops, as we see, went beyond the first four general councils; nor do I see how they or we could give up the *Filioque* without sacrificing the Truth of GOD. But the Lambeth Conference goes further: it adds, " The Apostles' Creed, as the Baptismal Symbol." The Apostles' Creed, as we have it, is the result of a gradual development lasting up to the middle of the sixth century, and I do not think ever has been acknowledged by an Ecumenical Council. I think the Lambeth Conference has done well in this; but is it enough? The Conference with Non-Conformists, reported on page 277 of the last number of this REVIEW, adds the words, " Including of necessity the doctrines of the Holy Trinity, the Incarnation, and the Atonement." But are the words, " The Holy Christian Church," in the Creed, to be defined in accordance with the Creeds of the time of the Reformation, or not? In the Rule of Faith proposed, as I have explicated it by the second member of the Basis, its position with reference to the authority of bishops and councils and the relative authority of Christian tradition, is a distinct acknowledgment of the formal principle of the Reformation; and no student of ecclesiastical history will deny that it could not have been enunciated before that time. Why, if we go so far, ignore the *material principle* of the Reformation, which is as real and valuable a development of Christian consciousness up to that time; why ignore the great doctrines of the nature and extent of the Redemption through CHRIST and of the nature and operation of the Means of Grace? I do not think it is possible to ignore any of the doctrines which have occupied the Faith of the Church, especially those which have been embodied in Creeds. Nor should we give up one conviction which has been begotten by the Word of GOD. The Scriptures, the acknowledged rule, dare be subordinated to no notion of convenience. Would it not be better to adopt the whole course suggested by the additions of the Lambeth Conference, and take as the point for the comparison of faiths the point of departure itself? In the original Confession the princes and cities set down, *first*, wherein they agreed with Rome in holding the historical Faith; and *secondly*, the errors and abuses of Rome which they were compelled to reject. In 1565 the Council of Trent gave Rome's final answer. Is it not possible to ascertain definitely whether we still hold that original Faith, — whether we agree with Rome in so far as the Reformers did, or whether we now reject a part of the earlier Faith? It will not be held, I think, that Rome has approached us in the mean time. Can we not discover whether we still reject as errors and abuses what were then rejected? But even at Augsburg there was disagreement among the opponents of Rome. Zwingli sent his own *Reckoning of Faith*, and the four cities united in a confession of their own. The English purposely modified the Confession of the Germans, after protracted negotiations had been broken off, in which the Germans insisted on their doctrine, and the English were always slower to admit it. Then we have confessions without number, — Helvetic, Belgic, Scottish, Dutch, Heidelberg, and Westminster, all of that age, or dealing with questions of that age. If all the Communions that then separated, as tenaciously hold their differences, we may dismiss the hope of reunion. Would it not be well to go back to the point of departure and discover how many of those differences endure, and which of them are required by the Rule of Faith, and which are the outcome of perversity? In my opinion, the Nicene Creed is not a sufficient statement of the Christian Faith; and it seems that very few are ready to admit that it is.

I have still greater objection to the *third proposition*, though the Lambeth Conference has not got so far in its course of wholesome amendment. It is to be observed that there is a good deal of sound doctrine in this proposition too. The requirement of the use of the *elements* excludes the Romish communion in one kind; the agreement to "minister" the Holy Sacrament would seem to forbid consecration without communion; and the insistence on the Words of Institution simply, as the only *sine qua non* of valid consecration, disposes of those prayers and invocations by which the Greek as well as the Roman Church believes a transmutation of the elements to be wrought. Here also the bishops recognize the development of doctrine which was registered in the confessions of the sixteenth century. But why stop here? On the one hand, why by such a proposition do they allow the addition to the Words of Institution of those prayers and ceremonies by which the Holy Communion is presented as a sacrifice for sin, an offering for the living and the dead? And on the other hand, are they able to ignore the historical Faith of the Church in the Real Presence of our LORD in the Holy Sacrament? Is not this of faith too, and can we, dare we, intimate that it is of secondary importance?

Now, of the *fourth proposition* I must frankly say that I think it is a matter of little importance. If agreement in the Faith can be secured, I would be very glad to consider whether a government by bishops, which is recommended by ecclesiastical history, might not be a good polity to adopt. But the proposition itself, suggesting the retention of the Episcopate as a matter co-ordinate with the Rule of Faith, the Confession of Faith, and the Sacraments instituted by CHRIST, causes us to hesitate. What do the bishops mean by the *Historic Episcopate?* Is this to be interpreted by the first proposition? Then we frankly reply, that we find the parity of the ministry taught in the Scriptures. Do they mean to insist that *the ministry of teaching the Gospel and administering the Sacraments was instituted by* GOD? Then we agree with them. Do they, in accordance with what is implied in the second proposition, give up all assertion of the semi-infallibility or the peculiar authority of the Universal Episcopate; or do they mean by the *Historic Episcopate* what this REVIEW taught in the last number, pp. 177–181 : "All the spiritual power to be found at any time or anywhere in the Church of CHRIST has come from that order or through that order?" Or is the Historic Episcopate to be defined by discovering what the Episcopate was like at any particular time in the history of the Church, or what it happens to be in any particular country, say in the Protestant Episcopal Church in the United States? I would not for a moment insinuate that the bishops proposed a submission to their own authority and jurisdiction as the one prerequisite of the unity of the Church. But we have a right to point to the fact that the Historic Episcopate has been the subject of a continuous development. The Episcopate in the time of Ignatius or Irenæus was not identical with the Episcopate of Ambrose; the Episcopate of Ambrose was different from that of the bishops in the time of the Reformation; and the Episcopate in the Roman Church has changed since then. The Episcopate in the Protestant Episcopal Church in the United States is historic in the sense that it is the last term in a long development from the original institution of a Christian ministry. But so is the Episcopate in England, and so is the Roman Episcopate, and so is the Swedish Episcopate, and so is the Episcopate of the Moravian Brethren; and yet all these Episcopates differ each one from every other of them. This is not a matter of name merely, nor simply of agents of consecration, but of function, powers, limitations, qualifications. We ask not merely who consecrated, but who *chose;* and suggest that under various constitutions men alike called bishops have been consecrated, some to one office, some to another. This fourth proposition therefore needs explanation. If it proposes Episcopacy as a convenient method of government, it is worthy of consideration; if it asserts it as a necessity because of Divine institution, then the bishops must make good their claim out of Holy Scripture against the conviction of the vast majority of their fellow Protestants and the equal but inconsistent claim of Rome.

I think I have made plain how far the proposed *Basis* is from satisfying me; but I would not have taken the trouble to do so if it were not for my hearty sympathy with this attempt on the part of the bishops, and with the object they have in view. The divisions of the Church are a hindrance and a scandal. To separate from our fellow Christians without warrant of Holy Scripture is a crime. And in this country especially, in proportion as a new nationality is being evolved out of all the elements of our Commonwealth, the hope of unity is growing. Some one had to take the first step; and the House of Bishops in taking it have shown a worthy conception of their office. And they are right in proposing that there must first of all be an agreement concerning the doctrine of the Gospel and the administration of the Sacraments. If such agreement can be secured, we may let the rest take care of itself. I do not understand that this basis is intended to be an *ultimatum*. On the other hand, we see that it is already undergoing modification. It should be studied, and the Commission on Unity should tell the meaning of each of their propositions. And I hope that the discussion and conference may continue until all shall be led to see what is the Faith once delivered to the saints, and to be ashamed of that which they hold without warrant of Scripture, and contrary to the law of love.

EDWARD T. HORN.

THE REV. ROBERT S. MACARTHUR, D.D. [BAPTIST], NEW YORK.

THE Basis of Christian Reunion proposed by the Lambeth Conference in 1888 is worthy of the careful consideration of all bodies of Christians. The principles formulated by that Conference no doubt received the prolonged consideration of men eminent for learning and character. That there is now a desire for closer union among different denominations of Christians, no one familiar with the facts can for a moment doubt. And that such a reunion is desirable, provided it can be secured in harmony with conscientious convictions as to the teaching of GOD'S Word, no one will for a moment hesitate to admit. We ought not, however, to depreciate the essential unity which now exists.

Essential unity may exist even where organic unity is wanting. As matters now are, organic unity is neither feasible nor desirable; but a fuller co-operation among Christians of every name for the salvation of souls and for the glory of God is both possible and desirable. Whatever will contribute toward securing this result is to be esteemed of value in all discussions on this general subject. Different denominations have made official responses to various overtures looking to this result. This writer does not presume to represent his denomination by any formal appointment, but he heartily believes that he will not seriously misrepresent it in what he may say on this subject.

1. The first statement made by this Conference, as to the authority of the Holy Scriptures of the Old and New Testaments, is one which most Baptists would like to recast so as to make it more authoritative than as given by this Conference. The Scriptures are not to be simply the "ultimate standard of Faith," but the only rule of Faith and Practice. We must have an infallible authority in all matters of religious faith. We repudiate the figment of an infallible man, but we rejoice in accepting the authority of this infallible Book. The Word of GOD is to be regarded as the clearest revelation of the will of GOD which men have received. To that Word we are to bow with unquestioning submission; what it clearly utters we unquestioningly believe; when it commands us to go forward, we joyfully obey. When the Bible speaks, we may not be silent; when it is silent, we may not speak. More and more must the Word of GOD be exalted as the only rule of Faith and Practice in the Church of CHRIST. Whatever comes between the believing heart and the authoritative Word of GOD is to be doubtfully received or entirely rejected. Creeds made by men are not authoritative standards. To the authority of GOD's Word three millions of members of Baptist Churches in these United States, and six millions of adherents to Baptist Churches, most joyfully submit. The famous dictum of Chillingworth is to be emphasized, — the Bible, and the Bible only, the religion of Protestants. Unfortunately many Protestants do not so regard the Word of GOD. They give tradition and churchianity an authority which tends to displace the Word of GOD as the only rule of Faith and Practice.

2. The so-called Apostles' Creed is an early summary of the Christian Faith, with most of whose statements Baptists are heartily agreed. We fully appreciate the high praise which Augustine gives it when he says regarding it, *Regula fidei brevis et grandis; brevis numero verborum, grandis pondere sententiarum.* We highly esteem it as a compendium of doctrine, for its intrinsic worth and for the veneration in which it has been so long and so deservedly held by many bodies of Christians. We can almost agree with Dr. Schaff when he says that though it is "not in form the production of the Apostles, it is a faithful compend of their doctrines, and comprehends the leading

articles of the Faith in the triune GOD and His revelation, from the creation to the life everlasting, in sublime simplicity, in unsurpassable brevity, in the most beautiful order, and with liturgical solemnity; and to this day it is the common bond of Greek, Roman, and Evangelical Christendom." We object, however, to its title. It is not, in any natural sense of the word, the Apostles' Creed. This title is an example of what has been called "a pious fraud." All investigators now heartily agree that the so-called Athanasian Creed was not the work of the famous Athanasius, although it bears his name. Dr. Swainson does not hesitate to ascribe the origin of this title to a deliberate purpose to practise an imposition. He classifies this purpose with that which led to the " False Decretals," and the " Donation of Constantine." The Apostles never saw the Creed to which their name is attached; they never heard of it, and perhaps would not be willing to indorse it in all its parts as we now have it. It may be said that the title is now used with the understanding that it is simply a truthful compend of Apostolic doctrine; that it sets forth Apostolic principles of faith in GOD and in His revelation. But the title was intended to convey quite a different meaning; it was intended to convey the idea, which the Roman Catholic Church now clearly teaches, that its clauses were actually contributed by the Apostles. This Church, on the authority of what is known now to be a spurious sermon of Augustine, undertakes to name the clauses given by the different Apostles. To the historical compiler and traditionalist Rufinus of the fourth century, we are indebted for the earliest accounts of the origin of this creed. He affirmed that the Apostles, before separating to the different nations, agreed upon "a form of sound words," and that when met together they composed this compend under the special influence of the HOLY GHOST. But no careful historic student attaches importance to-day to this testimony of Rufinus. There may have been, there doubtless were, various formulas of belief in existence from the earliest times; but no one can prove that the Apostles' Creed is so ancient by from four hundred to five hundred years. The most that can be claimed for the title is that it fairly represents the facts of Christian Faith as taught by the Apostles. We also know well that the clauses relating to the descent into hell, and to the communion of saints, are of later origin than are the other portions of this creed. It may be affirmed that the so-called Apostles' Creed was substantially in existence from the end of the fourth century; but in its completed form some authorities teach that it cannot be traced to a period earlier than about the middle of the eighth century. If this statement be correct, then it is about four centuries later in its present form than the earlier forms of the Nicene Creed. The clause, "He descended into hell," is one whose origin is involved in great doubt, and whose teaching is not accepted by many devout believers and profound scholars. We know that an alternative form is suggested, and if that form were universally adopted, fewer criticisms would be pronounced upon this ancient and confessedly beautiful compend of doctrine.

To the Nicene Creed more serious objection may be offered. The circumstances of its origin tend greatly to lessen the authority of its statements. We know that the controversies which began in the second century were prolonged into the third and fourth centuries under various phrases of belief and statement. This creed sprang out of the heart of this long and troublous conflict; it was literally a compromise, and it is to be received only as such. In the Council held in 325 at Nicæa, summoned by Constantine, there were three distinct parties,—the Athanasian, the Eusebian, and the Arian. The Arian, or heretical party was comparatively few in numbers, and its direct influence was not great at any time in the Council; but its indirect influence through the Eusebian, or middle party was marked at every stage of the discussion. For a time this middle party was able to hold the orthodox, or Athanasian party with a firm grasp. We all admit that there was much that was grand and imposing in the Nicene Council. No Church council so imposing had met previous to that time, and perhaps few of like character have met since. But we know also that at times this Council conducted itself in a manner altogether unbecoming a solemn assembly of Christian men met for a high and holy purpose. Drafts of creeds were torn in pieces by the excited assembly, and the "lord of misrule" reigned occasionally with uninterrupted sway. The Council was at times more like a ward caucus of average politicians than like a council of grave and reverent men.

It is also to be said that the Nicene Creed does not now appear in its original form; and the history of many of its later clauses is involved in great obscurity. Whether they are to be attributed to the Nicæno-Constantinopolitan Council is not generally known even by the most careful investigators. Some affirm that the enlarged creed appears in a work written before the meeting of this latter Council. The exact facts probably never will be known. It must be admitted also that these creeds are not to any great degree conservators of doctrine; they are often divisive rather than unitive. The Nicene Creed did not stop the sway of Arianism even at the time; it magnified, and in a certain sense dignified, Arianism, and led, for a time at least, to its more rapid spread. Creeds are not conservative of doctrine in England or America to-day. The Churches whose creeds are longest and strongest differ more among themselves as to their Faith and Practice than do Churches in which there is no creed, in the technical sense of that term. This is not the expression of an opinion; it is not the formulation of an argument; it is simply the statement of an historic fact. The Nicene Creed, moreover, is in some of its parts too abstruse, too metaphysical and philosophical, for general adoption. It is difficult for any man to give a clear interpretation of some of its expressions. There may be doubt as to whether the forms in which it appears in English properly represent the thought of the original; but the interpretation, after a true translation has been made, is much more difficult than the translation itself. It would puzzle any teacher of religion to make a statement of some clauses in this creed which would be intelligible to the minds of immature thinkers and inexperienced believers, or even to those of maturity and experience. That creeds have their use, we do not for a moment deny; that they should be thrust between the Christian and his Bible, we do not for a moment believe. Whatever tends to dethrone and to displace, or to disparage, the Word of GOD is so far to be rejected. We are unable to see the advantage of emphasizing the value of elaborate creeds. We cannot discover their practical use in Christian life and work, and we know that in many instances they have divided the Church, when a simpler statement of GOD'S Word would have united GOD'S people. It is often much more difficult to interpret the creeds than to interpret the Scriptures on which their statements are supposed to be based. We therefore favor the retention of GOD'S Word, and that alone, as the only rule of the

Faith and Practice of the Church; but we do not object to a brief, simple statement of its fundamental truths, expressed, for the most part, in its own words.

3. To this statement we have no special objection to offer. The term "sacrament" we do not use and do not indorse. It is not a Scriptural term. There is no reason why we should not use a Scriptural term when one is given us which is more appropriate than is this term. We believe that the Word of GOD clearly teaches that the only subjects of baptism are believers, and that the act of baptism is properly described in the language of the Apostle Paul when he says, "Buried with Him in baptism;" and in this belief we have the support, in large part, of the best scholarship of the world. The term "sacrament," both as to its origin and its associations, we reject. That the ordinances of the LORD'S house should be " ministered with unfailing use of CHRIST'S words of institution," we heartily believe. We strive so to minister these ordinances, and are ready to accept this statement as the manner in which the ordinances are to be observed.

4. The expression "Historic Episcopate" is one which is perhaps capable of several distinct meanings. In some of the senses in which it might be used, and in the one in which it was probably used by the Lambeth Conference, we cannot agree. If there is in the expression an implication of the so-called Apostolic succession, we shall be obliged to refuse our indorsement. If we were permitted to interpret the expression, we might give it our adherence. That the Apostles had or could have successors, strictly speaking, we wholly deny. With Dr. G. A. Jacob, late Head-Master of Christ's Hospital, and the author of the *Ecclesiastical Polity of the New Testament*, when he says, "The Apostles had no successors in their office; they stand alone as the Divinely inspired teachers, legislators, and rulers in CHRIST'S Church and Kingdom," we heartily agree. In the very nature of the case they could not have successors. The Word of GOD does not indorse the sense in which the word "bishop" is now used by some bodies of Christians. The meaning of the New Testament is so clear as scarcely to admit of intelligent differences of opinion. It is not possible that the great majority of believers could accept the " Historic Episcopate," as the term is ordinarily understood, as a basis of unity in the Church of JESUS CHRIST.

On the whole subject of Christian unity, four propositions may be laid down, which if accepted would greatly help to solve the perplexing problems involved.

1. The Word of GOD must be recognized as the only rule of Faith and Practice. We have already enlarged upon this thought in the earlier part of this article.

2. No denomination has a right to a separate existence, except it represents and teaches some important doctrine or doctrines of the Word of GOD which other denominations either oppose, reject, or inadequately present. Surely that is a reasonable proposition. No denomination has a right to exist as such, if it has no distinctive truth to teach to the world; no right to exist merely to gratify the personal vanity of its supporters, or to furnish a vocation for its preachers; no right merely to maintain a tradition, however honorable and venerable. The question must be asked regarding any Church, What truth has this organization to give us which other bodies of Christians do not teach? That is a fair question; to it each denomination, with the Word of GOD as its authority, ought to give an intelligent reply. The true Apostolic Church is that Church which best illustrates the spirit and the teachings of the Apostles, — that Church whose ordinances and worship most fully harmonize with the teaching and example of the Apostles. Why waste the LORD'S money in maintaining a separate organization for home and foreign mission work, except the particular body have a truth to teach which other Churches are not presenting to the world? It is fair to ask regarding some Churches this question, What truth of GOD'S Word would perish from the earth if these Churches should cease to exist as separate bodies? In regard to some organizations it must be said that the echo of the questioner's voice will be the only answer to his question. Why, then, should such organizations be maintained? Why should not the advocates of organic Christian union give their attention at once to this matter? Why might not some of them immediately illustrate their preaching by merging themselves and their Churches into other Christian bodies, which teach, in all essential respects, the doctrines which their own Church teaches? If we honestly apply this rule we shall certainly eliminate several denominations. The question is, are these principles sound, and if so, ought they not to be applied in the interest of a true economy

in the conduct of the LORD'S work, and also in the interest of a wholesome Christian union?

3. Akin to this proposition is another: Organic union ought first to be effected among all the wings and branches of each denomination itself. When that has been accomplished, that denomination can consistently and effectively urge organic union among the various bodies differing much more widely in name, in Faith, and in forms of worship. There are Free-will Baptists and Hyper-Calvinistic, Anti-Missionary and "Omissionary" Baptists, Seventh Day Baptists and several other wings and branches bearing some form of the denomination's name. Regular Baptists feel that they ought, if possible, to secure union among some of these divisions and subdivisions. In the case of some, such union is probably impossible. We ought to begin near home, and later we could consistently urge bodies differing more widely to come into a closer union.

Similar remarks will apply to the Presbyterian Church. The distinctions between Old School and New School have at least nominally passed away. Traces, however, of former divisions still remain; but there are yet many branches of the one Presbyterian Church. There are United Presbyterians, Cumberland Presbyterians, Covenanter and several other divisions of the one body. Some of these divisions are again subdivided; and some of the subdivisions are again subdivided. If one were to speak of the Reformed (Dutch) Church in this connection, the argument would be greatly strengthened. It would seem as if all these bodies which are Presbyterian in government, and which differ so little in faith and practice, might be brought into one great Pan-Presbyterian Church. There are also various bodies of Christians bearing the name "Methodist." We have Episcopal Methodists, Wesleyan Methodists, Calvinistic Methodists, and Protestant Methodists; and some of these divisions are also subdivided again and again. Let us have a great Pan-Methodists' organization, and then Methodism shall be able more effectively to make its appeal to other bodies not bearing its distinctive name. Congregationalists also have different wings. The line of cleavage may not be so marked by a separate terminology as it is by differences in Faith and Practice which cannot well be formulated into differences in nomenclature. These differences, however, are real; they are manifesting themselves in theological schools, in home mission work, and especially in the Board for foreign mission work. When we come to speak of the Protestant Episcopal Church, we have many illustrations of the necessity which there is of such a denominational unity as is here advocated. There are in this body wide differences, wider probably than in other denominations, in the essential spirit of different Churches, although there is outward unity. There is the High Church, and there is the Low Church and the Broad Church. There are Reformed Episcopalians and, in the opinion of those at least, presumably un-Reformed Episcopalians. There ought to be a Pan-Episcopal Church, which might perhaps include our Methodist friends so far as the term "Episcopal" is concerned, before the most effective form of appeal can be made for organic unity to those outside the Episcopal fold. We trust the effort toward a more permanent unity will be begun along all these denominational lines.

4. We venture to suggest another proposition. No form of organic union is to be advocated which gives to any Church the right to appropriate for itself such ecclesiastical titles, or to employ such historical assumptions, as practically to unchurch all other bodies of Christians. No titles should be used by any Church except such as are clearly given in the Word of GOD, and they are to be adopted in the sense in which they are used, according to the conclusions of the best scholarship in the Word of GOD. The assumptions which are here condemned are great barriers to Christian union. They sometimes simply excite laughter; they occasionally justify wholesome indignation. No officials in any Church are justified in appropriating to themselves titles implying appointment by authority over all Christians in a town, city, or State. Such assumptions are as unfraternal as they are un-Scriptural. No man has a right to claim for himself a title which has never been bestowed by those whose bestowment alone could justify him in its use. No union among denominations, which is simply absorption of one into another, except in the case of denominations which have no distinctive truth to teach, as we have already suggested, is to be commended. The question of legal and personal rights immediately obtrudes itself at these points. The lion said to the lamb, "Let us be one, and lie down together." The union was speedily effected, but when

the attitude of recumbency was secured, the relative positions of lion and lamb it is easy to understand. Such a relationship is not Christian union; it is simply absorption of one body into another without any real advantage to the cause of CHRIST as a whole. There must be fraternal consideration, there must be regard for the rights of all, in any attempt to unite the different denominations into one great whole. The assumptions which we here condemn are a great barrier to Christian union.

We have not advocated organic union; but we rejoice in all forms of co-operation, and in some forms of federation. But it is quite certain that if there is to be any form of organic union, it must begin at the baptistery. Every denomination in Protestant Christendom, and in the entire Roman and Greek Churches, can agree upon baptism, as taught by our LORD and His Apostles. The Greek Church, numbering eighty to ninety millions of adherents, has ever been a stout witness on behalf of baptism. The Roman Church joyfully accepts it, and all the Protestant Churches join hands with these two great bodies. On no substitute for baptism can all the denominations agree. We are not now arguing a point; we are simply stating an incontrovertible fact. Do men really want organic Christian union? Are they in earnest when they proclaim this desire? Are they willing to follow CHRIST into the waters of baptism? Are they willing to join hands with their brethren in all centuries and in all climes? Here is the opportunity; here is the truly Apostolic and Catholic ordinance. If they will but follow Apostolic injunction and example, then all can say, "We are buried with Him by baptism unto death." And then there may be, if it is desired, organic union without doing violence to the convictions of any, and in acknowledged harmony with the Word of GOD and its recognized interpretations. We are not arguing for an organic union of all the denominations as matters now are; we are simply stating the manner in which it is clearly possible. We could quote the most learned authorities of many faiths and countries and centuries in favor of this position. On but few points is the scholarship of the world so nearly a unit as it is in regard to the meaning of the word "baptism," and as to the practice of the Apostles and the early Church. It would be easy to fill pages with the names of learned authorities on all these points; and the simple-minded disciple of the LORD JESUS, with no guide but the New Testament, comes to the same conclusion. May the HOLY SPIRIT lead all believers into all truth!

R. S. MACARTHUR.

PROFESSOR WILLIAM J. MANN, D.D. [LUTHERAN], PHILADELPHIA.

EDITOR OF THE CHURCH REVIEW, SIR:—

THE Faculty of the Theological Seminary of the Lutheran Church at Mount Airy requested me to answer the invitation extended in your favor of March 22, 1890, to the Rev. C. W. Schaeffer, D.D. LL.D., Chairman of the Faculty. My answer makes no claim to express the sentiments of the Faculty, or of any portion of the Lutheran Church, but it is to be taken as the opinion of an individual member of that Communion.

I feel myself considerably embarrassed by the want of a definite conception of the object in view; namely, the reunion of the Church. Certainly, all Christians feel that the disunited condition of Christendom, as we witness it, does not correspond with that conception of the "communion of saints" which was in the mind of its Divine Author, but is in glaring contradiction to the fundamental ideas of Christianity as a system of religious and ethical principles, and to a large extent prevents Christianity from executing its mission, and from conveying to mankind its intended blessings. No enlightened Christian can therefore be indifferent toward a movement coming from so respected and influential an assembly as the Lambeth Conference of the Anglican Church, that has in view the extinction of evils inherent in the present condition, and that may serve better to enable our sacred religion to spread its blessings upon the world.

Examining that "Basis for Reunion" laid before me, I confess that its very broadness, its apparent liberality, is to me embarrassing. I agree to this, that the canonical writings of the Old and New Testament shall be the exclusive rule by which all teachers and all teachings shall be tested.

Of course, to apply this principle, it needs a certain unanimity in the interpretation of the Old and New Testament canonical writings to make it a practical rule. Certainly I acknowledge the Apostles' and the Nicene Creeds as statements of the fundamental principles of the Christian religion. If the task would consist simply in stating the points wherein Christianity differs from heathenism or from Gnostic and Arian errors, I would say these two creeds are "sufficient," and would not object to adding the Athanasian Creed, in spite of its scholastic treatment of the Trinitarian dogma.

The Church catholic was in those times necessitated to guard the true doctrine against certain errors, then endangering the existence and the character of Christianity. Other errors of various forms arose since then from time to time, and made inroads into the Body of CHRIST, sickening it and endangering its very life. Against these errors those Ecumenical Symbols offer no declaration and no guard, and to supplement this defect by adding (No. 3) the two sacraments, not only leaves the very important sacramental question, which more than any other divided Protestantism, unsolved, but ignores other questions which mere ignoring neither solves nor removes. To use in the administrations of the LORD'S Supper "CHRIST'S words of institution," will, harmless as it seems to be, never satisfy millions of Lutherans, since they know that under this form heresies affecting Christology and hereby the very centre of the Christian system of saving truth, have crept in and are retained, and since they consider the celebration of the Sacrament also an act and an occasion of professing their religious conviction. A unanimous testimony given by a very large part of Evangelical Christendom against errors affecting faith and life in our age might have weight with many, and prove that the Church not only rests on the achievements of bygone ages and repeats their formulas, but stands up with striking unanimity to-day, warning against errors opposing Divinely revealed truth, destructive to the Church, and poisoning individuals, families, and society. A mere attempt to prove that on some points various Christian denominations of the present generation are identified with the venerable relics of the past, while on those errors, which now powerfully oppose the truth as it is in CHRIST, and undermine the foundations of Christian life, an ominous silence is kept, only reveals the weakness of the Church and its inability to counteract the dangers of the times. If such a declaration is impossible or inadmissible, it is questionable whether any other form for a basis of reunion will promise a desirable result.

It is clear that any reunion on the basis of the one proposed by the Lambeth Conference would be a union intended to cover the differences existing. It would be an agreement to disagree. In every effort of such a character the seed of discord and disunion is inherent. There is in it a sort of charity at the expense of honesty; and in this case it amounts to a *suppressio veri*, which nowhere is more to be avoided than in matters of conscience and religion.

In No. 4 of the Lambeth Conference propositions, mention is made of the "Historic Episcopate," and it is presented as an integral part of the "Basis for Reunion." It stands to reason that those who would unite on this basis would have to come in under this *conditio sine qua non*, and to retain or accept the Episcopate as the only admissible form of Christian Church government.

I, as a Lutheran, feel no repugnance to the Episcopate as a principle of Church government. I am far from saying that the Episcopate is the only form of Church government admissible in the Christian Church. Denying this exclusive right of the Episcopate, I refer to the canonical books of the Old and New Testament "as the rule and ultimate standard of Faith." Time-honored as the Episcopate is, it is no article of Faith. It is in GOD'S Word nowhere demanded as a principle, by the consent to which is conditioned fellowship in the Christian community. I respect it as a historical growth. I can understand why it was retained in the Church of England in her connection with the State on the basis of Erastianism, and the aristocratic tendencies of the ruling classes of England, and why it was not retained in Scotland, where the prevailing elements were more tinged with democratic proclivities. I admit willingly that there is much to be said in favor of the Episcopate. But on the other hand, I cannot forget that out of the Episcopate grew Papacy and many concomitant evils, and that it did not save the Church of England from the inroads of Arminianism, the rising within her of Quakerism and Methodism, and the disturbing influences of Puseyism and Ritualism. In the United States of America it did not prevent a split in the Protestant Episcopal Church, and the origin of a Reformed Episcopal Church. These historical facts establish a right to doubt the wisdom of making acceptance of the Historic Episcopate an absolute condition of entering into a reunion agreement.

I do not wish to be understood as undervaluing the importance of the organization and government of the Church. But I insist on this point, that all that appertains to the governmental question is of secondary concern. We are not saved by any form of Church government, but by faith in CHRIST, by appropriating His merits and assimilating His personal qualities. The great end of CHRIST's incarnation is not the Church, but the Kingdom of GOD, the liberation of man from the dominion of the world and the acknowledgment of GOD's ruling, and submission through penitent faith to His will, to establish true morality as the common task of the human race and the basis of true happiness. Thus viewed, GOD'S Kingdom is the highest good, and the Church, with all that appertains to it, is the indispensable instrumentality for its actualization. To identify GOD's Kingdom and the Church is a portentous Roman error. Starting with these preliminaries, I say that the question of the organization and government of the Church is of secondary character, as I cannot maintain that the efficacy of the functions of the officers of the Church is dependent on the privileged character of a caste, endowed with peculiar supernatural powers. This none of the venerable men assembled at Lambeth would claim for the bishops. Consequently, the question of the Episcopate will ultimately be settled on the principle of expediency, as it originally grew out of it, whereby is excluded its absolute and unlimited necessity. It is with a view to this point that I do not wish to be understood as admitting the claims of the Episcopate as a *conditio sine qua non* for the existence of the true Church; while on the other hand, I do not wish to be misunderstood as ignoring the historic basis and the venerable character of the Episcopate and of the organization of the Church on this basis. I for one would give the preference to the *Historic Episcopate* before all other forms of Church government, and would, with proper limitations of its privileges and rights, to which the Committee of the Lambeth Conference alludes in its final observation, and with due regard for local conditions and traditions, advocate its adoption where it can be introduced without danger to equally or more important interests.

In conclusion, I say that much will have to be changed in the relation now existing between the different Church parties, before a practical result of reunion movements will be attained.

That each claims to be the Church, while every one produces in the average the same moral and social result, and not one of them all stands before the community without faults and blemishes, — this is simply calculated to mutually irritate and generally to make Christianity ridiculous in the eyes of the world. The zeal often manifested to make proselytes and to work for the increase of " the Church," is not always unalloyed love of GOD and souls, but only often another form of refined egotism. It is a pride, contributive to the ignorance which representatives of various denominations frequently reveal concerning the condition, the work, and the merits of others, and of the contempt based on gross ignorance with which the others are treated. Now, this is not Christian, neither is it expedient, provided we have the great thought of reunion at heart and are willing with a clear conscience to work in this direction.

There is one point more, to which I may be permitted to allude, provided I do not encroach too much upon your liberality. There are so very few symptoms observable which might indicate that we Protestants, in spite of all existing differences, have in common a certain historical origin, and form a practical antithesis to the errors of Romanism, without which antithesis our right of existence would be lost. I have often felt that it might be of advantage if all Protestants would unite on a day commemorative of the great world-historic fact of the Reformation, to be solemnly and religiously celebrated every year. I do not agree with many positions of Romanism, while I am no enemy of the Roman Catholics. But viewing their wisdom in showing the world that they are one great organization, their zeal to make progress and to gain influence and power, I think we Evangelicals are but too remiss in strengthening our own religious consciousness on the basis of that only rule of faith and life, the Word of GOD, and in feeling that in our antithesis to those errors which crept in while the watchmen slept, and which affect the corner-stone of our salvation, Justification by Faith, we are a unit and are willing to let the world know it.

Dii atque animam salvavi.

W. J. MANN.

PROFESSOR E. J. WOLF, D.D. [LUTHERAN], THEOLOGICAL
SEMINARY, GETTYSBURG, PA.

EDITOR OF THE CHURCH REVIEW, SIR:

IN your kind request that I should give you my views upon the subject of Christian Reunion in general, and state how far I would accept this " Basis on which approach might be, under GOD'S blessing, made toward reunion," you very properly serve notice that each writer speaks only for himself. I accept this understanding. Yet in discussing the acceptability of the bishops' overtures I cannot forget that this basis is proposed by the highest representatives of the Episcopal Church, nor suppress for the time my Lutheran consciousness. No other two Communions have in doctrine and worship so much in common as the Episcopal and the Lutheran. For proof of this, one need but lay the XXXIX. Articles alongside of the Augsburg Confession and take a look at the historic liturgies of the two Churches. So close were the sympathy and the intercourse between the Church of England and the Evangelical Church of Germany during the first period of the Reformation "that it cannot be doubted" if both Churches had been embraced in the same territory, there would have been but one Communion, and that without any compromises. It has been recognized also by Episcopal historians that if the bishops of Germany had joined in the reformatory movement, and if the English bishops had united in opposing it, the German Church would have been Episcopal, and the English Church would have been non-Episcopal.

This affinity made itself felt in the early history of this country. A number of Episcopal congregations in the neighborhood of Philadelphia enjoyed during the first decades of the eighteenth century the stated ministrations of Lutheran clergymen, — ministrations which they eagerly sought, " lest their children would become unchristened heathen or Quakers, and their Churches would be changed into stables alongside of Quaker meetinghouses." When, on the other hand, a later generation of German Lutherans demanded English preaching, distinguished pastors were known to direct them to the Episcopal Church as being properly the English Lutheran Church.

Closely as these great historic Churches approach each other on many points, nevertheless the very terms of this fraternal overture reveal the wide chasm which separates them. It lays down as fundamental at least one feature which the Lutheran Church has always regarded as an *adiaphoron*, while it passes by among other things the doctrine of justification by Faith alone, which to all Lutherans is the doctrine of a standing or falling Church. Lutherans do not object to the Historic Episcopate as an administrative institution. They, in fact, maintain it in various countries. The Apostolic legitimacy of the Swedish Episcopate is no more disputed than is that of the Church of England, and if this institution were deemed essential to the government of CHRIST'S Church, or believed to have any inspired authority, the Lutheran clergy and congregations of this country could readily avail themselves of its benefits. But holding that the ministry is simply the office of dispensing the Word and the Sacraments, that its incumbents have an essential equality, and that no form of Church polity is of Divine right, — some of its writers even teaching that every claim to a Divinely instituted polity is essentially Romish, believing the Scriptures to make the grace of salvation contingent upon naught but Word and Sacrament, and beholding in history the fruits of a pure and vigorous Christianity outside the domain of the Historic Episcopate, — the Lutheran Church would have to repudiate the principles under which she came into distinctive being, and turn her back upon four centuries signalized by the presence of the SPIRIT within her bosom, before she could accept the Historic Episcopate as indispensable to the integrity or the unity of the One Holy Christian and Apostolic Church.

That it is a very ancient institution; that it has often rendered inestimable service to the Christian cause; that it has been made illustrious by the ability and sanctity of many of its representatives, — no historical scholar will question. But if it must be accepted as "essential to the restoration of unity among the divided branches of Christendom," then I would humbly but firmly say it were far better to have these divisions continue, sad and reproachful as they seem, than to accord a Divine right to that which, so far as GOD enables us to see, is lacking the proper credentials for such a claim. The truth revealed from heaven is of greater moment to mankind than any human institution, however beneficial, and the moral inability of non-Episcopalians to abandon what they have always held to be the truth on this subject, is fortified by the admission of the foremost Anglican scholars that the Historic Episcopate derives no support from the Scriptures.

According to the teachings of such expositors as Lightfoot, Hatch, and even Plummer, on the origin of the Episcopate, the fourth proposition of the bishops' Basis, with all deference to the distinguished prelates who formulated it, stands in manifest conflict with the first, namely, "The Holy Scriptures of the Old and New Testaments containing all things necessary to salvation and being the rule and ultimate standard of Faith." This is the generic principle of Protestantism, its *raison d'être*, and of course must forever remain the first condition for unity among the Protestant Communions. But until the advocates of Episcopacy find it in the Scriptures, the acceptance of these as the ultimate authority, of necessity includes the rejection of Episcopacy as an essential. The converse of this is equally true.

Were the Scriptures alone a sufficient basis for union, as some fondly dream, the consummation so devoutly wished need be not a day longer delayed, for they are accepted unconditionally by every division of the Evangelical Church. But it being by general consent indispensable to have the essentials of the Christian Faith defined and formulated in exact and faithful expressions, I cannot see how Churches concerned for the purity and completeness of Evangelical truth can be content with the Nicene Creed as "the sufficient statement of the Christian Faith." While not according any authority to the creeds of Christendom, they arose as historical necessities for the confutation of error, they are the invaluable acquisitions which resulted from long and bitter conflict with the enemies of truth, and their distinct and comprehensive articulation and systematic arrangement of Scriptural verities are among the priceless treasures which the Church of to-day, under the law of continuity, has inherited from the Church of the past.

Recognizing as we do the Head of the Church upon the mediatorial throne governing all things for the advancement of His Kingdom, believing that He endowed His Church with the Spirit of the truth to guide it into all the truth, holding in eternal remembrance the company of faithful witnesses who in their devotion to unmistakable statements of the Gospel passed through water and through fire, I cannot conceive of an exigency that would justify the Church in casting overboard trophies for which her noblest servants in various critical periods hazarded their lives. Is it worthy of the Church, for any cause whatever, to treat as of no moment the grandest achievements ever made in the cause of truth? Does it become her character and her claims to extinguish the light which for ages illumined her path, to turn her back upon Scriptural doctrines and systems for which the whole of Christendom has felt its indebtedness to the fourth and fifth centuries, and to ignore those vital principles for which the Protestant world still commemorates the glorious Reformation?

Granted that the Evangelical Christian Church could as a whole adopt a measure so irreconcilable with her mission as the pillar and ground of the truth, suppose that Augustine and his immediate followers, with Luther, Calvin, Melancthon, and the other Reformers, could be relegated to oblivion as having contributed nothing to the illumination or compass of Evangelical doctrine, what intrinsic gain is to result from such a sacrifice? What enlargement of influence, what increment of spiritual power, would accrue to the communion of believers, marshalled in grand proportions of outward unity under such conditions?

Imagine for a moment the realization of this plan, and contemplate the advance of Christianity in the united body. One set of pulpits will teach the total wreck of humanity by sin, another set will glorify this similitude of deity, and denying its impotence, will hold that at its lowest it needs but a smile of encouragement to rise to the loftiest character. One class will hold all men to be under condemnation for original and actual sin, from which the mercy of GOD alone can redeem them; another will treat all with the complacent pity which regards mankind as unfortunate rather than guilty. Some will glory in the Cross of CHRIST as man's only hope, others will hold up the Nazarene's personal character, or perchance His sublime teachings, as the condition for the renewal of the world. Some will preach that faith alone brings salvation to the sinner, others that a holy life is the one thing that is acceptable to GOD. In some Churches men will hear that justification is simply the restoration of the condemned to GOD'S favor, in others that justification is of the nature of sanctification, and that its literal meaning, " making just," holds in theology. By some the sacraments will be interpreted as picturesque memorials, by others as having a supernatural content. Here eternal woe will be denounced on the impenitent; yonder it will be maintained that

God's infinite love cannot fail ultimately to draw to itself every creature.

What reverence or prepossession would such a spectacle inspire among them that are without? If our present divisions, due largely to diversity of doctrines, form melancholy stumbling-blocks to the world, what will the world think of our attempting to disguise these divisions under the garb of outward unity?

It becomes us to walk in wisdom toward those without, yet primarily the Church must guard the health and development of her own children. What, now, would be the inevitable effect on these of such discord in the Church's instructions on subjects that touch the very heart of Christian experience? It is probably a less serious calamity for souls to be entangled in some definite error, than to have such a jumbling of truth and error from recognized spiritual guides as must stagger the understanding and distract the conscience. Certainly, next to corruption of doctrine, the greatest harm must result from confusion of doctrine. Yet with no bulwark save the Nicene Creed against the brood of errors that spring up invariably in the path of the Gospel, the Church can have no guarantee against that confusion and corruption of doctrine which in the Middle Ages followed the obscuration of sound and clear views on sin and grace. While not holding the Episcopate responsible for it, we never can forget that the Church never sank so low as when it was an organic unity governed by the Historic Episcopate, but with Gospel truth neglected, obscured, or corrupted.

Desirable as the reunion of Christendom confessedly is, the acceptance of two propositions in this basis, it seems to me, is out of the question, with all those who value the precious doctrines of grace, which study and prayer and conflict and martyrdom have added to "the substantial deposit of Christian Faith." Among all the divisions of the Evangelical Church, there is not one which does not have many noble souls, who would part with their life's blood before they would consent to part in any measure or in any sense with these truths. It appears therefore to my mind impossible for "the chief of the Christian Communions" to reunite organically on any basis that does not include the common inheritance of Christian doctrine which is substantially embodied in the creeds of the Reformation. The Church is set for the defence of the truth, not for its displacement.

This does not sound like a voice in favor of Church union. These sentiments may be voted out of place in a Symposium on the Reunion of Christendom, and I very much regret if I shall strike a note of discord in a grand symphony concert. From the irrepressible agitation of this subject in the press, from a number of movements which express a powerful public sentiment, from many infallible signs of growing cordiality and charity between different denominations, one might conclude that an irresistible current in behalf of union has set in, and that those solicited to write upon it are expected simply to register its depth and volume. That any one should have the audacity to breast the current would reflect seriously upon his discretion. Yet is it wise, is it rational, in a movement so desirable and so momentous, to close our eyes to the colossal barriers which block its path? The scandal of the Church's divisions, like the monstrous iniquity of the liquor traffic, is so revolting that the intensity of our abhorrence may blind us to the insuperable difficulties by which it is beset. Before adopting visionary schemes or forming alliances which in the end may only retard the reunion of our divided ranks, it becomes us to take in if possible the situation, to measure the stupendous dimensions of the undertaking, and to gauge the depth and the significance of the feeling which is by many regarded as almost universal and therefore indicative of a providential impulse, a proof that the SPIRIT is impressing the cause upon the minds of Christians.

Far be it from me to offer a different interpretation or to belittle the sincerity or the strength of a wide-spread sentiment, yet I cannot fail to observe counter-tendencies which are sufficiently powerful to paralyze and counteract the wisest and noblest efforts to heal the wounds in CHRIST'S body. The respective denominations have as a rule shown no symptom of relaxing their hold on their doctrinal characteristics. The Baptists have no idea of uniting with Christians who regard anything besides the immersion of adult believers as baptism. The Lutherans have no thought of abandoning the doctrine of CHRIST'S presence in the Eucharist. The Congregationalists have but lately shown that they still hold to the Divine right of their polity. And the very Church which so honorably and fraternally makes overtures for reunion puts in the foreground as a condition its one distinctive feature. These facts remove the enchanting prospect of a united Evangelical Church into the remote future, although such adherence to convictions redounds really to the credit of those bodies. But alongside of this honorable adhesion to principle, there is a sectarian upholding of trifles which is tantamount to a glorying in diversities and divisions for their own sakes. As long as Evangelical Christians cannot agree on the language of the LORD'S Prayer, or use the same form of the Apostles' Creed, or study in the Sunday Schools the same Scripture lessons on the great Festivals which have been fountains of spiritual refreshing to the Church in all ages, there is hardly any occasion to hurry up the details which are to consummate the reunion of Christendom.

It is not pleasant to introduce these things here. It is not wise to ignore them. They show that, underneath the current which to the joy of many makes for union, there is a countercurrent which arrests the tide of Christian fellowship and insults the noblest aspiration of our age. A grave responsibility for the perpetuation of schism must rest upon those who in the face of the great multitude of Christians disturb the harmony of public worship by inserting a sectarian shibboleth into the common prayer and the common creed of believers, and upon those also who, when charged to select uniform lessons for the Sunday Schools of the world, put out from year to year a scheme which prevents the children from uniting in the universal triumph of Christendom on Easter morning. It is undeniable that as long as denominations are thus occupied with straining out gnats and puerilities that represent not a grain of principle, the weightier matter of a united Church must content itself with an occasional protest. If we are to keep on stickling for set phrases, for prejudices begotten of ecclesiastical or civil strife, for opinions and traditions that have no significance except that they have been for some time in vogue; if nothing is to be laid upon the altar; if the cause of Church union is not worth a single sacrifice, and its realization is expected without a Calvary,— then we may as well face the issue, and give up the contest as chimerical and hopeless.

From these emphatic negatives it is apparent that I have no plan of union to advocate, no definite proposal to suggest. I have at present no faith in any measure that has come to my notice; and I do not believe that the man has been born who is capable of devising a feasible measure. The insuperable character of the obstacles in the way remind me of the limitations of human expedients; the desirability of the object and the hope of its ultimate realization recall the truth that "with GOD all things are possible." And may not our extremity once again prove GOD'S opportunity?

At all events, in our zeal for this blessed cause are we not in danger of infringing upon Divine prerogatives? Is not this a case in which the hand of Divine wisdom and power must interpose? We are constantly quoting the SAVIOUR'S prayer in behalf of the unity of His followers; but we seem to forget that it was a prayer, and construe it into a command. We speak of it as if it had been addressed to His followers instead of to His FATHER, and we think it the bounden duty of the different denominations to answer it. The continued and wide-spread agitation of this issue has indeed produced a general conviction that this is a work of human achievement, that it devolves upon the teachers and leaders in the various Communions to institute measures by which the disruptions of CHRIST'S body may be healed, and the scattered fragments of His hosts become united. Are we not in peril of putting ourselves in the place of GOD, of taking upon ourselves what belongs to the FATHER, of intermeddling presumptuously with what GOD has reserved to His own season and His own power?

The preaching of the Gospel among all nations the REDEEMER intrusted to His disciples under the condition of His abiding presence with them; but when the work of uniting the redeemed in one fold lay as a mighty burden upon His heart, He addressed His memorable prayer to His FATHER in heaven. The creation of a united Church is not the product of men's hands; it is the work of that Omnipotence which in the beginning reduced the chaos of matter into the majestic unity of the universe.

Our only hope for the unity of the Church lies there, where our LORD Himself looked for it, — in the FATHER'S great heart. And we joyfully look for the day when all Christians shall be one, not because we have faith in what is devised or proposed from any quarter, but because the only begotten SON prayed for this result to His FATHER, and we know that the FATHER always heareth Him.

It becomes us, indeed, to be in accord with our MASTER'S prayer, — to have in this, as in all things, the same mind which dwelt in Him. The first duty and the first sign of promise for ultimate union in the Church is the cultivation of sympathy, charity, and concord with one another. It devolves on us indeed to pray as He prayed, to keep on repeating His prayer. And our conduct must be consistent with our praying, "endeavoring to keep the unity of the spirit in the bond of peace;" but we must distinguish between what is GOD'S province and what is ours, between that which He alone can accomplish and that which is clearly made our duty.

It will greatly help the cause so near to our hearts if we reverently bear this in mind. Nothing is gained by men attempting to run ahead of GOD'S leading, or by pushing at the slow wheels of the Divine chariot. Probably no marked advance in the relations of the different denominations need be expected until a signal is noted from above, and in conjunction with it a mighty moving of the HOLY GHOST upon the minds and hearts of men. It may come in the form of fire, in awful calamities.

JEHOVAH found a way of reuniting His ancient people through the terrible ordeal of a long captivity. He put an end to the monstrous strife which in the first century raged between Jewish and Gentile Christians by reducing to ashes the Holy Temple whose continuing worship blinded the Jews to the essentials of salvation. The fires of overwhelming catastrophes have in the past proved the all-potent agency for fusing together the diverse elements of GOD'S kingdom. And all the intimations of revelation and all the lessons of history induce the belief that in GOD'S own time His furnaces will consume our sectarian idols, extinguish the dissensions and contentions of His people, and melt them into a unity which has its ideal and prototype in the union of the SON with the FATHER.

E. J. WOLF.

Theological Seminary, Gettysburg.

THE REV. WILLIAM V. KELLEY, D.D. [METHODIST], BROOKLYN, N. Y.

EDITOR OF THE CHURCH REVIEW, SIR:

THIS article is invited by a request which presents as materials for consideration the overtures toward reunion put forth by the House of Bishops of the Episcopal Church in 1886, the Lambeth Conference indorsement of the same in 1888, and the conclusions of the London Conference of leading Anglicans and Non-Conformists held last December, as given in the CHURCH REVIEW for January, 1890. It is proper that our response to this courteous invitation should be with equal courtesy of spirit, as well as with such perfect candor as is necessary to personal honesty and to the value of any discussion. Nothing but good, and perhaps greater good than any of us foresee, can come of frank and fraternal debate. To save ourselves at the outset from the misfortune of being at any point misunderstood, we premise our conviction that fervent love, utter respect, and general co-operation between all Christian bodies, resulting in all possible effective unity, are parts of "a consummation devoutly to be wished;" and there is no prayer in which we join more earnestly than that of CHRIST for oneness among His disciples, in which petition we imagine that we hear the voice of Protestant Christendom uniting. We apprehend that the only difference of opinion will be over the kind and form of unity considered possible.

The first three quarters of the basis proposed for union by the House of Bishops and the Lambeth Conference is intelligibly clear, and, we think, not in the nature of things impossible to agree upon. Over the Holy Scriptures as the first foundation-stone there can be no dispute. Agreement upon the two creeds, which are virtually one, as a sufficient statement of Christian Faith, seems perhaps a not altogether unlikely or remote possibility; for undeniably the trend of the time is toward an abbreviation of creeds, contracting the required confessions of belief into narrower compass. Our personal sympathies and judgment move in that direction, and, if we mistake not, the persuasion grows throughout Protestant Christendom that wisdom lies that way. A firm adherence to the few items absolutely necessary to constitute Christian Faith, with range and verge for free opinion beyond, has obvious and great advantages. One advantage is that this course returns us toward the simplicity of the primitive Church, freeing us possibly from some things which may be of the nature of incrustation rather than growth, and tending to save us from the error of teaching for doctrines the commandments of men. Another gain in such abbreviation of creed-requirements is that it renders feasible a more extensive unity as fewer points of harmony are held requisite for union. Do not interest and justice both urge to this? Would not this larger inclusiveness put the Church in possession of its own by claiming and appropriating all those who vitally belong to it; while it would admit to Church privileges every one who is essentially Christian and therefore fairly entitled to recognition and membership? There can be no danger in this. A strengthening of the stakes of the Christian tent would make safe a lengthening of its cords to an enlarged comprehensiveness. Put loud and unanimous accent on the fundamentals. Let the solid emphasis of all Protestant Churches be massed on the few central essentials of faith, closely compacted in statement, instead of being distributed and dispersed over voluminous amplifications and peripheric variations, and there will be no peril in embracing all who loyally assent to those indisputable essentials. Another effect of a restriction of Christian creeds to the comprehensive fundamentals is an allowance of greater liberty in non-essentials, and in items of secondary importance, a larger range to individual thought and taste in what may be derived through experience or reasoned and constructed on the Divinely outlined foundations. We take it to be the general opinion of our day that such an allowance of freedom is in harmony with true progress. A formal union which does not permit liberty to individuality is mechanical, superficial, insincere, oppressive, and temporary. While we witness many efforts toward realizing brotherhood and organizing unity of various kinds, the most imperious voice that shakes the air of to-day is the one which demands recognition and protection for the rights of the individual, both in matters of thought and in matters of conduct. Protestantism and democratic institutions are responsible for that. It is essential to the soundness and stability of any sort of union that only so much concession toward concert of opinion and action be asked of each member as may be absolutely indispensable to the secure existence of that union.

The Lambeth Report's third condition of union, relating to the sacraments, may be passed with approval and without debate.

It is at the fourth and last point of the proposed basis that we are brought to a halt by what seems a lack of explicitness. The documents themselves give us no light as to what is intended by the "Historic Episcopate" in the overtures of the Episcopal bishops or their Lambeth indorsement. Is it our obtuseness or is it something else that causes perplexity or hesitation in us of "other Communions" over many Episcopalian and Anglican deliverances on the subject of Church union? When the American bishops say in a communication to the House of Deputies, "We believe that all who have been *duly* baptized with water in the name of the FATHER and of the SON and of the HOLY GHOST, are members of the Holy Catholic Church," we receive no clear message, because we are in doubt what is the precise thought behind that one word "duly." In like manner, when the same message says, "In all things of human ordering or human choice relating to modes of worship and discipline or to traditional customs, this Church is ready in the spirit of love and humility to forego all preferences of her own," for the sake of unity with others, while our hearts burn within us responsively to the sweet, gentle, winsome tone of the utterance, we are yet not informed by the message what things the House of Bishops regards as " of human ordering or human choice; " and just there lies a possibility of the reopening of an ancient debate from differences of opinion between the bishops and the unprelatical denominations.

We count it also a defect in many of the appeals for union that they fail to include a definition of the nature and degree of the desired unity. Collateral evidence, however, indicates that generally, if not always, it is organic union that is contemplated in such overtures. The CHURCH REVIEW in its last previous issue speaks of the resolutions adopted by the Conference of leading Anglicans and Non-Conformists in London last December as "the only practical result yet reached in the matter of organic unity."

The first and greatest obstacle in the way of such union is the diversity of opinion as to its possibility or desirability. Without any disposition to imply that it is impossible for the Anglican Church in Britain and the United States to be GOD'S chosen instrument to lead on a world-wide reform, we may yet remark that it seems somewhat strange that if the organic union of Christendom is a necessity, such intelligent and enterprising bodies as the great Presbyterian Church, the Congregational Church, and the Methodist Episcopal Church should not perceive its desirability, and with their characteristic zeal, practical habits of mind, and desire for the highest systematic efficiency, move for it. Is there any sign that these influential Churches regard organic union as a clear desideratum?

No fact is better known than that the non-Anglican Communions have not been in the habit of considering denominationalism in general an unmitigated evil; while of course each denomination thinks its own separate existence justifiable and necessary. It is not certain that any one of these religious bodies, if it had the power to destroy denominationalism by absorbing all other Churches and Christians into its own fold, would do so; the reason for this being a persuasion that denominationalism in itself has a mission the fulfilment of which has been and will be beneficent and variously advantageous. It is quite impossible for us to believe that the majority of Protestant Christians will ever be prepared to agree with the Rev. William Granger, a zealous and honorable advocate of Church union, that the Father of Lies is the author of denominationalism, any more than they will concede the assertion of the Romish Church that Protestantism is a work of the Devil.

The American Episcopal bishops say, "This Church does not seek to absorb other Communions," but if "any Christian bodies" seek "the restoration of the organic unity of the Church," the Church is ready "to enter into brotherly conference with" such bodies. If any prophet sees in the ecclesiastical sky a sign as big as a man's hand that any of those "bodies" are seeking or likely to seek organic union with the Church which now issues overtures, we shall be glad to have the token pointed out. In 1872 Dr. Campbell, the Primate of England, characterized it as visionary to "look forward to a time when all the various denominations throughout Britain are to come and desire admission into the Church of England."

The sagacity of this opinion is plain to minds of only ordinary discernment from less lofty points of observation than the Archbishopric of Canterbury.

The CHURCH REVIEW in its issue of January, 1890, remarking on the fact that no Methodists joined in the Conference of leading Anglican and Non-Conformists in London, in December last, says: "The Methodists are exactly those upon whom our claim is the strongest and who had least ground for quitting our fellowship." In a sermon in Christ Church, Bedford Ave., Brooklyn, a New York City rector said in presence of the Bishop of Long Island, "If we had treated the Methodists wisely and fairly, they would not have gone out from us." If the Methodists are especially in mind in the appeals for Church union, we can only say that the time of their probable return in a body to the Anglican Communion seems to us very remote; indeed, all reasonable expectation of such a return is as dead as the cause of the Stuarts, with whose restoration under Charles II., in 1661, the less liberal and more exclusive views toward non-Episcopalian bodies were fastened on the Anglican Church. The House of Hanover is as likely to abdicate in favor of the descendants of the Stuarts as the Methodist Church is to abjure its right of existence in deference to Anglican views. And surely the noble and intelligent men who are urging the overtures which are under consideration in this symposium are too wise to suppose that, in any approach toward union, any one of the non-Episcopalian bodies will be influenced in the slightest degree by a desire to recover connection, alleged to be lost, with a "Historic Episcopate." The day never can come which will find these large and powerful denominations dissatisfied with the validity and authority of their ministry, or the genuineness of their standing as proper and living parts of the Body of CHRIST. In these matters they will abide solidly on the foundations they have chosen. They believe, with some of the greatest leaders the Episcopal Church has ever had, that "Apostolic succession," so-called, is a myth entirely unprovable, and spiritually valueless even if it were proven. Nor have pretentions to superiority based on this notion always been put forth by the Anglican Church. If we mistake not, there were a hundred years during which, in the language of an eminent clergyman of that Communion, "no one in the Church of England thought of calling in question the validity of the orders and sacraments of the Reformed Churches," which were presbyterial in ordination and government, and from which ministers and members were received to immediate and equal standing in the Church of England.

We hold that there may be a vital and effective unity of Protestant Christendom without organic consolidation, and that in our time every sunrise finds that spiritual oneness more complete. It is absurd in these days to imply that denominationalism necessarily means "bitterness and unhallowed strife." The only strife it legitimately stimulates is an emulous rivalry in usefulness. The lamentable old dim days of mutual misconception, which were like that battle on dark Dundagil by the Cornish Sea, where —

> "Friend and foe were mingled in the mist,
> And friend slew friend, not knowing whom he slew" —

are long gone by, and more and more on all the circuit of great Zion's walls, the watchmen see eye to eye and concentrate hostilities upon the foe.

Whether an organic union of all, or of the principal, Protestant Communions is desirable or even possible, is matter for gradual elucidation by free and frank discussions like the present, in the spirit of love and meekness, with a disposition to make all possible concessions "for euphony's sake," as the college phrase puts it. While to us neither the possibility nor the desirability is clear, we offer to all sincere and earnest reasoners a hospitable mind open to light and conviction.

One thing, it seems to us, must occur to every reflective mind. In all attempts at reform, a logical order and natural sequence of consistent action should be preserved; and whether it be organic union or only a perfect fraternity and co-operation that is aimed at, all overtures are likely to be futile if unaccompanied by a full recognition, in utterance and bearing and action, of ecclesiastical equality, — a practical recognition by an even interchange of pulpits, ministers, and members. Negotiations for union ought to be conducted on a level, and not on an incline. The consulting group has difficulty in keeping its footing on the slope long enough to hold a conference, and the members of it tend to slide away from one another. Until every barrier to actual fraternity is thrown flat by the hands which now hold such barriers up, organic unity is certainly a Utopian dream. In a message to the House of Deputies, the Protestant Episcopal House of Bishops in 1886 avowed the "solemn purpose" to seek some practical plan for "terminating the unhappy divisions" which separate their "fellow-Christians in this land;" but in the same message the bishops declined to approve a resolution, adopted by the House of Deputies, sending mere cordial greetings to their "Congregational brethren" assembled at the same time in the same city. We must be pardoned if, like Mr. Lincoln, we are "reminded of a story." In Warren County, New Jersey, is a village named Harmony. At Martin's Creek one day a traveller asked a man whom he met on the road, "How far is it to Harmony, if I go straight ahead?" "Well," replied the man, "if you go straight ahead in the direction you are going, it is about twenty-five thousand miles; but if you will turn right around, it is three miles." We do not trifle. Our words are earnest, prayerful, and loving. Shameful would it be to write or speak otherwise on the sacred and momentous subject of Christian Unity. If there are any questions which men should consider upon their knees, this is one of them. If there be one desire which we ought to foster with hopeful and yearning hearts, making it dictate our prayers and our actions, it is that the great Head of the Church Universal will lead on His leagued hosts, ordered in whatever unity shall contribute most to widest and swiftest victory. We are bound to hold our doubts in check with the constant remembrance of the lesson history teaches, that it is possible for us to be living, without knowing it, on the eve of great events; and the perfect unification, in some form or other, of all Christian forces may be nearer now than we think.

WILLIAM V. KELLEY, D.D.

PROFESSOR GEORGE R. CROOKS, D.D. [METHODIST], DREW THEOLOGICAL SEMINARY, MADISON, NEW JERSEY.

EDITOR OF THE CHURCH REVIEW, SIR:

YOUR courteous request that I reply, as a Methodist, to the proposals of union put forth by the House of Bishops in 1886, and reissued by the "Conference of Bishops of the Anglican Communion," in 1888, demands of me, I assume, an explicit reply. The subject is so important that all the Churches interested must if possible come into a clear understanding with one another. The Basis of Reunion (we prefer the term "union") proposed is contained in the following points:—

1. The Holy Scriptures of the Old and New Testaments, as "containing all things necessary to salvation," and as being the rule and ultimate standard of Faith.

2. The Apostles' Creed, as the Baptismal Symbol; and the Nicene Creed, as the sufficient statement of the Christian Faith.

3. The two Sacraments ordained by CHRIST Himself,—Baptism and the Supper of the LORD,—ministered with unfailing

use of CHRIST'S words of institution, and of the elements ordained by Him.

4. The Historic Episcopate, locally adapted in the methods of its administration to the varying needs of the nations and peoples called of GOD into the unity of His Church.

To the first three statements there can be no objection; some might contend for the double procession of the HOLY SPIRIT, and urge its addition to the Nicene Symbol, but, I imagine, not many would make that a bar to union. The real difficulty will be in the fourth proposition,—the acceptance of "the Historic Episcopate," as you are supposed to understand the meaning of that term.

We take you to mean by this expression the Episcopate which, derived by a distinct line of succession from the Apostles, is the channel through which the grace of the HOLY SPIRIT is conveyed to the body of believers. Also, that the conveyance of grace through this channel is indispensable to a valid administration of the sacraments. Properly, it is incumbent on your bishops who make the offer of union to define terms, and if it were possible to obtain from them within reasonable time an exact account of the meaning which they place upon this form of language, I would rest here and write no more. But this cannot be done. I must therefore gather its sense from other parts of the Proceedings of the Pan-Anglican Synod of 1888. The address of all the bishops, signed by the Archbishop of Canterbury, contains these words:—

The attitude of the Anglican Communion toward the religious bodies now separated from it by unhappy divisions would appear to be this: We hold ourselves in readiness to enter into brotherly conference with any of those who may desire intercommunion with us in a more or less perfect form. We lay down conditions on which such intercommunion is, in our opinion, and according to our conviction, possible. For however we may long to embrace those now alienated from us, so that the ideal of the one flock under the one Shepherd may be realized, we must not be unfaithful stewards of the *great deposit* intrusted to us. We cannot desert our position either as to Faith or Discipline. That concord would in our judgment be neither true nor desirable which should be produced by such surrender.

So, also the report of the Committee on Home Reunion made at the same Conference speaks thus:—

The Committee were of opinion . . . that both from deeper study and from larger historical experience there was in the present day a greater disposition to value and to accept the *Ancient Church Order*.[1] Moreover, Resolution Nineteenth, and last of the series adopted at Lambeth, says: 'That, as regards newly constituted Churches, especially in non-Christian lands, it should be a condition of the recognition of them as in complete intercommunion with us, and especially of their receiving from us *Episcopal Succession*, that we should first receive from them satisfactory evidence that they hold substantially the same doctrine as our own, etc.'[2]

Here accord in doctrine and the acceptance of Episcopal Succession are put together as both indispensable to intercommunion.

I am confirmed in my opinion that this is your meaning of the words " Historic Episcopate " by the language of your bishops, just cited, put in comparison with the first three terms of union. Do you hold that the Holy Scriptures contain all things necessary to salvation? So do we. And that they are the rule and ultimate standard of Faith? So do we. Do you hold the Apostles' Creed as the Baptismal Symbol? So do we. And the Nicene Creed as the sufficient rule of Faith? So do we. Do you confess two sacraments only ordained by CHRIST? So do we. And ask that they be ministered in both kinds with the unfailing use of the words of CHRIST'S institution? So do we. There must be, then, the one point only — the Historic Episcopate — in regard to which we differ. Not an Episcopate merely, for I speak in the name of Methodists, who have an honored Episcopate, but one derived through a certain order of succession and holding a " deposit " of grace " intrusted " to its keeping.

You will excuse the care I have taken to define this phrase, in default of precise definition on your side. If I have rightly construed the meaning of the bishops at Lambeth, then I must say, in all kindness, that Methodists cannot accept union with you on this basis, and for the following reasons: —

1. We do not believe that the Anglican bishops hold " a great deposit [of grace] intrusted "[3] to them in a sense not applicable to other clergymen. Nor do we believe that the

---

[1] Page 36. The Italics in this article are my own.
[2] Page 28. [3] *Lambeth Conference*, p. 15.

succession which they claim from the Apostles is essential to the validity of the sacraments. We hold that all the offices and ministrations of the Church ordained by CHRIST are means of grace to the believer, but that the grace is ministered to him by the direct action of the SPIRIT. If in partaking of the LORD'S Supper he, according to the formula, "feeds upon CHRIST in his heart by faith, with thanksgiving," he has a valid sacrament, no matter if the minister who has pronounced the words of institution, and distributes the elements, was ordained by laymen. Whatever "the great deposit" intrusted to your bishops may be, we attach no importance to it. Our sacraments are in our estimation already valid sacraments. Children and adults baptized by us have, as we believe, a truly Christian baptism; our communicants who receive the memorials of CHRIST'S passion are nourished by the partaking of CHRIST "after a spiritual and heavenly manner." Therefore we say consistently of the separation now existing, we are no more "alienated" from you than you are "alienated" from us. Nor can we believe that "the ideal of one flock under one Shepherd" is to be realized by our accepting your Episcopacy. The Shepherd is one and unchangeable; the flock is already one in Him, and needs only to act in harmony with that Divine ideal to make the outward expression of its oneness what it ought to be.

2. I apprehend, from the terms employed in the Proceedings of the "Conference of Bishops," that we do not agree with you on the point of the essentials of unity. From the Report of the "Committee on Home Reunion," I gather the following expressions. They speak of a resolution passed in 1861, "praying the bishops to commend the subject of reunion to the divided members of CHRIST'S body" [p. 82]; of a joint committee appointed "to report upon the relations between the Church of this country and those who in this country are alienated from her Communion" [p. 82]; of a readiness to enter into brotherly conference with all or any Christian bodies *seeking the restoration of the organic unity of the Church* [pp. 84, 85]; of a confidence felt by them that the non-Episcopal bodies of the present day show a greater disposition "to value and accept the ancient Church order" [p. 86]; again, of a readiness to "consider what steps can be taken *either toward corporate reunion*, or toward such relations as may prepare the way *for organic*

unity hereafter." Am I right in inferring from these passages that you conceive the unity of the Church to consist in the acceptance of a certain external order, to wit, the Historic Episcopate? If you hold that the unity of the Church depends upon an external bond, we Methodists hold it to depend upon an internal bond. We believe the unity of CHRIST'S Body to be a Divine fact, in a sense which seems to separate us in opinion from you. Our doctrine is that CHRIST'S body is one, by virtue of His Divine life pervading all its members, wherever they may be, or under whatever forms of Church order they may worship. Its unity is something which we as human agents cannot establish. It is an "organic unity," because the Church is a body having a head, "even CHRIST," and members united to Him by an appropriating faith. From this head, "the whole body fitly joined together, and compacted by that which every joint supplieth, . . . maketh increase unto the building up of itself in love" [Eph. iv. 15, 16]. The head of the Church and the fountain of its life is CHRIST, and not a company of bishops acting as intermediaries between Him and believers. As we construe the Epistle to the Ephesians, the body makes increase directly from Him [ch. iv. 16].

If these convictions rest on a Scriptural basis, our business is not to try to create the unity of CHRIST'S Church through the acceptance of one external order rather than another, but to act in harmony with a fact already Divinely established. Being already made sons of GOD and brothers one with another, our duty is to recognize the brotherly bond, to come into the fellowship which is the legitimate product of a sense of unity. We ask nothing of you but brotherly love; and this is all we need offer on our side. But if anything we have can profit you, take it and welcome, in GOD'S name.

Pardon me, if at this point I speak candidly; but what I am about to say ought, I think, to be said. When I look through the *Proceedings of the Conference of the Bishops of the Anglican Communion*, I find a very halting manifestation of brotherliness. The avoidance of the recognition of the Christian bodies they address as Churches strikes me very painfully. The bishops tell us, "We thankfully recognize the real religious work which is carried on by Christian bodies not of our Communion;" so the Report of the Committee on Home Reunion designates us as "Christian bodies" [pp. 84, 85, 88]; the Committee also recommend that conferences be held, "such as that which has already been proposed by the Church in the United States of America, with the representatives of other chief Christian Communions in the English-speaking races." Are we to infer that you do not recognize these brethren whom you approach with proffers of love as true Churches in JESUS CHRIST? Must we presume you not to be aware that a proffer of union coming to us in this guise must necessarily be offensive? Let me assure you, then, that we believe our Churchly standing to be good and sufficient in the presence of Him who is head over all things. We say, then, in the language of your bishops, "We cannot desert *our* position either as to Faith or Discipline. That concord would, in our judgment, be neither true nor desirable which should be produced by such a surrender."[1]

Thanking you for the invitation to speak on this subject in the pages of the CHURCH REVIEW, believe me,

Yours most sincerely,

GEORGE R. CROOKS.

The Unity of the Visible Church.

THE REV. HENRY J. VAN DYKE, D.D. [PRESBYTERIAN], BROOKLYN, NEW YORK.

THE day for eulogizing the division of the Church of CHRIST into "denominations," has gone by. Thoughtful and earnest Christians are coming more and more to recognize and mourn over it as evil, in its origin and its results. We get the most vivid impression of the evil when we lay aside all abstract theories and look at the concrete facts as they exist before our eyes. We cannot embrace the Christian world in our view; but we can consider a part as the type of the whole. Here is a town, not a hundred miles from any of us, consisting of a thousand inhabitants, or about two hundred families, — just enough to make one parish or pastoral charge, able to sustain the ordinances of the Gospel for itself, and to contribute to the evangelizing of the world; but instead of one self-supporting

[1] *Proceedings*, etc., p. 16.

Church, this town has five sickly organizations, two or three of which are sustained by some Missionary Board. One of these Churches has a steeple surmounted with the cross, the common symbol of Christianity; the others, if they have steeples at all, have crowned them with a weather-cock. All these Churches claim to be Christian; but they all bear denominational names, and each is a rival of the others. Now, the evil of this state of things does not consist only nor chiefly in its waste of Christian resources; but the chief evil is its demoralizing effect upon religious experience and Christian character. It narrows men's souls by concentrating on a sect the sympathies and affections which ought to expand upon the whole Body of CHRIST; and this effect is the most shrivelling when men succeed in deluding themselves into the belief that their sect *is* the Body of CHRIST. It creates false tests and standards of personal piety. It mars the symmetrical growth of the soul in the knowledge of CHRIST by magnifying certain doctrines to the neglect or denial of others. The notion that it is the mission of different denominations to bear witness to *particular phases* of Divine truth, might be well enough if the people to whom this witness is borne were brought under the influence of all the witnesses. But to subject one Christian to the teaching of Divine Sovereignty, and another to the insistence upon human freedom, cultivates two different types of character, neither of which is according to the truth. The idea of a "witness-bearing Church," — that is, a body of Christians with a special Divine commission to bear testimony against other *bodies of Christians,* — while it is pleaded in defence of denominationalism, is in fact one of the worst fruits of the system.

The effect of the system upon the Sacraments is no less to be deplored. It obscures the true meaning of these holy ordinances by contracting the Table of the LORD to the close communion of a party in this Church, and by making baptism the badge of a sect; so that one says, "I was baptized an *Episcopalian*," and another, "I was baptized a *Presbyterian*," and another, "I was baptized a *Baptist*." The effect of denominationalism upon the ministry is no less deplorable. It too often degrades the servant and ambassador of CHRIST into the hired man of a voluntary association, and suspends his reputation and influence upon his success in making proselytes from other "societies." That minister must be a strong man, who, in adjusting his work to such conditions, does not lose somewhat of the spirit of his high commission, and shrivel his own mind to the dimensions of a *Gossip*.[1]

These evils are greatly aggravated by their complication with social distinctions and family pride. Denominational lines, in such communities as we have described, are very apt to follow the lines of class distinctions, and to deepen them with "the Gospel plough." Religious societies become social clubs, and get rid of the question about seating the poor man in vile raiment by making it practically certain that he will not come into the same assembly with the man in goodly apparel and a gold ring. "The Salvation Army," or any other outside effort, is good enough for him. And so we look with complacency upon the spasmodic movements of zeal without knowledge, and even patronize them from a distance, as a salve to our conscience, not perceiving that the plea for their necessity, and indeed fact of their existence, is a standing reproach to the Church.

What wonder, if in this state of things one half of our settled ministers in all denominations are unsettled in their minds, and waiting for "a call"! What wonder if the doors of vacant Churches are besieged by an army of candidates, composed not only of young men who are openly looking for their first charge, but largely of old soldiers, some of whom by unworthy devices conceal the fact of their candidacy? Surely if we need a civil-service reform in the State, there is no less need of a pastoral-service reform in the Church. And this reform, to be effective, must begin at the denominationalism which fills the land with feeble Churches and half-supported ministers, and wastes in sectarian rivalries what ought to go to the evangelizing of the world.

The first and most important step toward the correction of any evil is to see and acknowledge its existence; and the second is like unto it, — an earnest desire for a better state of things. The unity of Christendom — a unity that the world can see, and be convinced by it that the Father has sent His only begotten Son — is to-day a longing in the heart and a prayer on the lips of multitudes of Christians. We hail every expression of such desire as a prophecy of its fulfilment, according to

---

[1] *Gossip* is an ecclesiastical term, — a corruption of *Godsib*. It was first applied to sponsors in baptism, and its development into its present popular use is not without historic significance. See Brewer's *Dictionary of Phrase and Fable*.

others the same sincerity we claim for ourselves. We do not sympathize with those who view with squint suspicion the proposals for reunion by the American Episcopal Church indorsed by the Lambeth Conference; and while we cannot accept the terms proposed in their present form as sufficient and practicable, we do heartily embrace and respond to their spirit. The reunion of Christendom is a sublime idea, an inspiring hope. It is not necessary to the indulgence of this hope to forecast the precise form of its fulfilment; and therefore we need not exclude from its embrace any of those throughout the world who profess the true religion. The best things in the world are not *made*; they *grow*. The unification of Christendom, as a whole, or in part, cannot be accomplished by bargains and contracts between rival sects; neither can it be effected by the absorption of one denomination under the distinctive forms of another. The *Romanist* may cry, " Lay aside your private judgment, and submit to the infallible Pope." The *Episcopalian* may say, " Come and be ordained by our bishops; " the *Baptist* may say, " Come and be immersed; " the *Presbyterian* may say, " We acknowledge the validity of your orders and sacraments; only accept our Calvinism, and we will be one; " and the *Methodist* may respond, "Give up your Calvinism and accept our doctrine of free grace; " but what do all these invitations amount to? They cannot be accepted. Men cannot and ought not to renounce their personal convictions of truth. If you should dissolve all Christian denominations today, it would create not union, but anarchy. If you should renounce all creeds, the result would be, not a broader faith, but a confusion of tongues. Is there, then, no practicable way in which we may work toward the fulfilment of our hopes? Yes, certainly. We can hold to our distinctive forms, whether of discipline or of worship; but we can hold the form in subordination to the substance. We can hold our distinctive creeds until the time comes when they can be safely laid aside, meanwhile recognizing CHRIST, the incarnate Word, as above all written words, human and Divine, the confession of faith in Him as above all creed-subscriptions, and the Catholic Church, which is His Body, as above all Christian denominations. If these principles are accepted, not in word only, but in power, their dominance will show itself. There are three directions in which they may work themselves out gradually but mightily, like the dawning of the day, — Recognition, Co-operation, and Federation.

1. *Recognition.* The Church of Rome is the only Christian denomination which officially claims to be *the* Church in any exclusive sense; and this claim, coupled with her denial of any distinction between the Church as visible and invisible, necessarily precludes the Church standing, the Christian character, and the salvation of all who do not acknowledge her authority and participate in her sacraments. In this she is terribly logical and consistent. But what is to hinder any and all Protestant denominations from acknowledging one another individually and collectively as belonging to the Church of CHRIST, and treating one another accordingly? Theoretically, and aside from the sectarian spirit of which we are all more or less guilty, there are only two obstacles in the way, — the mode of *baptism*, and the mode of *ordination* to the ministry. But that these are not insuperable obstacles to mutual recognition is evident; because upon the supposition that the validity of the sacraments depends upon the specific mode of their administration, and the authority of the ministry to administer them, and their consequent efficacy, depend upon a particular mode of ordination to the ministry, it is not credible that CHRIST and His Apostles should fail to leave on record specific instructions which would prevent the possibility of mistake upon the subject. It may not be possible even for GOD to state an *abstract doctrine* in human language so that all human minds will apprehend it alike; but there is no such difficulty in the way of describing an act to be performed by human hands. If CHRIST was immersed Himself and meant all His disciples to follow His example in this respect, and if immersion is essential to the validity of baptism, why did He not say so? Why is it not so written in explicit terms? If any one answers, " He *did* say so, and it *is* so written," we respond, " We cannot see it." And the fact that millions of the holiest and wisest men in all the Christian ages, whose candor and love of truth are beyond question, have not been able to see it, is proof conclusive that it is not there. The same observations apply to ordination to the ministry. If Paul and the other Apostles believed that no ordination is valid unless it be performed by the hands of a Diocesan bishop, distinct from and superior in office to ordinary ministers, and that the succession of such ordinations is essential to the existence of the

visible Church and to the efficacy of her Sacraments, why did they not say so, and record the doctrine in explicit terms for the instruction of all ages? The fact that men equally learned and honest differ on the subject, is proof conclusive that there is no such record. When our Episcopal brethren in their overture for reunion insist upon "the *Historic*, meaning the *Diocesan*, Episcopate" as equally essential with the Holy Scriptures and the Holy Sacraments, we remind them that there is a *Prehistoric* Episcopate which is not Diocesan, and that by their own acknowledgment what they call the Historic Episcopate is not explicitly enjoined in the Scriptures, which "contain all things necessary to salvation, and are the rule and ultimate standard of Faith." Oh, is it not pitiful in the sight of GOD and angels that the mere mode of administering two outward ordinances, concerning which CHRIST has given no explicit instructions, should be magnified into partition walls between His disciples, for whom He prays that they all may be one? And the pity becomes more profound when we consider the fact that these two obstacles have not always and everywhere been regarded as insurmountable. It is only in this country that the Baptist denomination makes its mode of baptism a warrant for "close communion." It is only since the days of Charles I. and his prime minister, Archbishop Laud, that the Episcopal denomination has refused to recognize the validity of other ordinations beside its own.

We shall be reminded that now and here these partition walls are not so high as to prevent the different denominations from looking *over them* and mutually recognizing one another as Christians. We admit this, and rejoice in the growing spirit of inter-denominational comity, which is so characteristic of our times. But it is the unity of the visible *Church* that we are contending for. We long for *Church* recognition as the only legitimate and permanent embodiment of Christian fellowship. Mutual recognition aside from the organic life and work of the Churches, performed as a holiday parade, and upon platforms erected for that special purpose, is little more than a confession of the evils of denominationalism. It does not apply any practical remedy; sweet and pleasant in itself, it is only a sentiment, and unless it is embodied in deeds, it will evaporate in the words that express it. If it goes no farther, its practical effect is to disparage the Church, and to alienate thinking men from her life and her work. What we need is such a mutual recognition as will lead to co-operation.

2. And this *Co-operation* must be within and not outside of the visible Church. We do not undertake to forecast its methods; but we have a very distinct prevision of its results. *First* of all, it will prevent the needless multiplication of Churches, and the waste of Christian means and energies in particular localities. *Secondly*, it will elevate the ministry, and cultivate a nobler type of Christian character, by laying aside petty rivalries and strifes about words and forms of worship, whose only effect is the perversion of the hearers, and by insisting upon the great central facts and doctrines of Christianity. *Thirdly*, it will add immense resources and give a new impulse to the missionary work of the Church, which is the chief object of her existence; and it will give new efficacy to that work, by presenting a united front and lifting up high above all sectarian colors the common banner of Christianity before the heathen world.

3. As both an expression and a practical means of promoting this recognition and co-operation, we are heartily in favor of *Federation* between any and all denominations of Christians.

One thing seems clear, — that the unification of the Church cannot be accomplished by one denomination working upon another from without. Proselytism, whether by argument or persuasion, is a waste of time and strength. The converts made by such means are far-fetched and of little worth; neither, again, can the denominations be unified by any power separate from and above them all. The wrecks of that experiment are scattered along the whole path of history. The time for world empires, whether of the Church or the State, is past. The unity of the Church can be effected only by a vital power dwelling in every part and common to all. That power can be none other than the HOLY SPIRIT. But the SPIRIT OF GOD, in Nature and in grace, works by means. Cosmos, "the beautiful order," was not imposed upon, but evolved out of Chaos. The SPIRIT

> With mighty wings outspread,
> Dove-like, sat brooding on the vast abyss
> And made *it* pregnant.

The earth and the waters brought forth abundantly.

The unification of Christian denominations must be attained by bringing out into clearer recognition and adjusting to new relations that which is already in them. The first stage in the process is the practical acknowledgment that the things in which they agree, whether in doctrine, discipline, or worship, are not only more important in their bearing, but more and greater in themselves, than the things in which they differ. The conviction of this truth comes home to every candid mind in the careful study of the creeds of Christendom. But the thought of theologians and scholars needs to be embodied in a visible form in order to be apprehended by the popular mind. What more simple or safe embodiment of the idea can be invented than the Federation of Christian denominations? The possibilities of such Federation are unlimited. It does not involve the surrender of sectarian peculiarities, but simply the subordination of them for a time to that which is confessedly higher and more important. Under any plan which may be adopted, it will have this great advantage, that practice will go hand in hand with theory, and the experiment reach no farther than experience shall warrant. Beginning on a small scale, and embracing at first only the subdivisions of sects holding the same system of doctrine and order, and separated by distinctions as small as the difference between a psalm and a hymn, or between the sound of a pitch-pipe and the swell of an organ, who shall say that it will not enlarge its circumference and intensify its assimilating power until it embraces the Christian world in its circumference? It is easy to sit in the seat of the polemic, surmising difficulties and predicting failure; but it is far nobler to hope for and hasten unto the blessed time when out of many folds there shall be one flock and one Shepherd. The greatest living poet sang in his youth of a poetical millennium, —

> When the war-drums throb no longer, and the battle-flags are furled
> In the parliament of men, the federation of the world.

And though the vision has not yet come to pass, who will say there has been no progress toward its fulfilment? Behind and above all the kingdoms of the world is the Kingdom of our LORD and His CHRIST. Of the increase of His government and peace there shall be no end. Who shall say how near may be the time when the isles which wait for His law shall hail the light of His coming, and the troubled sea moaning on every

shore shall hear and be hushed at the stillness of His voice?
And above all, who will refuse to do what he can to prepare the
way of the LORD, to exalt every valley, to make low every
mountain, to gather out the stones and make smooth the rough
places in the highway of our GOD? I am a Presbyterian, not
only by birth, but by conviction, and yield to no man in loyalty
to the denomination in whose service my life has been spent,
and in whose bosom I hope to die; but I do not expect to be
a Presbyterian nor anything of the kind in heaven. And as
my sun grows larger and more mellow toward its setting, I
would gladly exchange everything that is not essentially Christian for a few of the days of heaven on earth, in the unity and
peace of the Church of GOD, which He hath purchased with His
own blood.

HENRY J. VAN DYKE.

Brooklyn.

THE REV. THOMAS ARMITAGE, D.D. [BAPTIST], NEW YORK CITY.

EDITOR OF THE CHURCH REVIEW, SIR:

YOU ask how far the Basis of Christian Reunion, made by the bishops of the Protestant Episcopal Church in America, and the Lambeth Conference in England, is likely to commend itself to the approbation of the various Christian Communions?

There is great room for fear that its influence for practical benefit will be very limited; and chiefly because it makes no attempt to remove the radical differences which exist between the Communions, and to which they severally cling with all the tenacity which the human conscience can command. No subject is worthy of more patient thought than that submitted by these two bodies of learned and venerable men. They breathe the spirit of the age in striving for a higher unity than has been yet attained, and express a strong conviction that the present fragmentary state of things is unsatisfactory, and so far, their loving aim at oneness must bring the several Communions into that closer relationship which follows a better knowledge of one another. No broad and catholic meeting-plan can be found for them, where the truest mutual respect is not cultivated, where a holy self-respect is not retained, and where the mutual recognition of Christlikeness is denied. To these good influences the suggestions of these godly thinkers will contribute. Yet it requires little precedent sobriety of mind to see, that the present disjointed condition of these bodies disqualifies them for promoting organic oneness. The elements of strife and division must cease to exist in the bosom of each Communion, so that each is at peace with itself, before it can blend with the others in a common unity. Those discords which threaten so often to tear each individual denomination asunder, arise out of a moral condition which cannot be made to harmonize with the spirit, much less with any given form, of oneness. Instead of moving sweetly, as in the music of the spheres, the exterior bond of unity, in such cases, often becomes grievous. That bond does not attract to one centre, so that there is no real fellowship, where it should be found in its strongest and tenderest forms. All this is evinced in the various factions which now mark all the great Protestant bodies, as well as those of the Roman Catholic Communions.

True fellowship is deep and thoroughly inter-dependent, with great inwardness, but little surface. It implies all that makes oneness of mind and fundamental soul-sympathy. Many sound and true men are longing with enthusiasm for something to which they can give no name. Hence, when they meet with genuine Christian kindness, for want of a more appropriate cognomen, they call it Christian Unity, while still it is not clear what is wanted, much less does it appear how exactly it can be attained. The true-hearted are feeling their way to answer the question: "How can the *disjecta membra* of GOD'S family come back into one grand unity?" In the formal, the ceremonial, the verbal basis of union, there is no depth, no warmth, nor can it be made an effectual antidote to division. In such union there may be beauty, even sentiment and some truth, but there is no fervent fellowship. Such methods only lead us into that loose way of talking about Christian unity, where there is in reality no abiding agreement. We often mistake manly kindness, and that gentlemanly refinement which permit us to worship peacefully in the same place, for the oneness which is essentially true unity. This may hide from us the sin and the shame of disturbing disunion, but it does not work in us that for which our LORD prayed, although we may all be numbered in the same ecclesiastical fold: "That they all may be one, as Thou, Father, art in Me, and I in Thee, that they also may be in us."

The Lambeth Conference, in its kindly spirit, proposed the Bible as the "rule and ultimate standard of Faith," with the Apostles' Creed and the Nicene Creed "as the sufficient statement of the Christian Faith." But in their present divided state, all the great Protestant bodies verbally hold to the Bible as the only standard of truth, and how can it more perfectly reunite them to reaffirm this position? As to the acceptance of the two creeds named, being "the sufficient statement of the Christian Faith," those creeds came into existence, especially the Nicene, as the result of long and bitter divisions; and as they never have wrought union heretofore, by what power can they accomplish it at this late day? Besides this, neither of these creeds state the entire body of Christian doctrine, about which the Christian world is divided; and some of the tenets on which one denomination of Christians is divided from another are not noticed in either of them. The "Basis of the Bishops recommends that Baptism and the LORD'S Supper shall be administered in the use of CHRIST'S words of institution, and of the elements ordained by Him." In the latter centuries, these two ordinances have been the subjects of more controversy than any other two points in Christianity, while they were vital in the ancient times, between the Latin and Greek Churches. Yet the bishops submit nothing touching the manner in which the Apostolic Churches administered the ordinances. So also of the "Historic Episcopate, locally adapted in the methods of its administration to the varying needs of the nations and peoples." But surely they would not have all the various views and methods now held in all the Communions blended into one, from the archbishop down to the simple pastor of a single congregation, and call that union, simply for the sake of calling it so. This, of itself, would create such contentions as have never yet existed in a Christian body, so that division would become more rife than ever. In a real union of the several Christian bodies, somebody must give up something; but the bishops fail to tell us what they will give up themselves, or what their Churches will yield, nor is it clear what points they wish others to abandon in non-Episcopal Communions.

All the different denominations of Christians hold their right to separate existence on the ground that they represent some Scripture truth which is not clearly represented in some other Church; for this reason they came into being and have remained as distinct bodies, most of them at great cost of suffering, and some of them at a greater cost of life, in martyrdom. Who of them are to abandon this position, and what supposed truths are they to cast aside, in order to secure the proffered boon of organic ecclesiastical union? Neither meekness, love, nor fidelity, but only discord and distraction would follow such reunion as this, and at once the division of tongues would turn Zion into Babel. The various Communions are divided now in respect to the *meaning* of the Bible, and they never can be united in one body until some of them are convinced that they do not interpret the Bible properly. Who, then, shall work that change, and on what platform shall it be wrought? Oneness on vital truths cannot bring this about so long as a large number of relative truths remain in dispute.

The prayer of our blessed REDEEMER throws a light upon the nature and methods of oneness, among Christian believers, which the Lambeth Conference does not. From this we may catch a powerful illumination, because the oneness of CHRIST our SAVIOUR with the FATHER is to be the type of our unity with one another. Here, uniformity is made the mere negation of unity. The FATHER and the SON are one in likeness and disposition, one in character and love, one in aim and endeavor. When reciprocal fellowship between believers springs from an inward life, from unity of conviction, purpose, and hope, then, and not till then, can there be a perfect agreement in Christian doctrine and duty. "This unity," says Alford, "has its true and only *ground* in faith in CHRIST, through the Word of GOD, as delivered by the Apostles, and is, therefore, not the mere outward uniformity, nor can such uniformity produce it." As men, believers have already a oneness of essence in themselves, as the FATHER and the SON had essential unity. But believers have not a oneness in interest, thought, feeling, and action, concerning truth and salvation, as have the FATHER and the SON. "That they also may be in us," and so are one among themselves. Our LORD was not speaking of the absolute unity of the Godhead, or He could not have prayed that believers should be taken into that unity; but He does pray that we may be taken into the oneness of the FATHER and the SON in all that relates to the truth and to a life of holiness, under the reign of truth. That unity may be outstanding and visible in the spiritual life of CHRIST'S disciples, in their purity, zeal, and consecration. When these are seen, then "the world will believe that Thou has sent Me." But this can never be done by a formal, creedal, mechanical unity of ecclesiastical agreement. The entire Christian world is laid under debt to the bishops for their devout utterances in the direction of reunion among the Communions, but their plan cannot work an answer to the prayer of JESUS. If these noble men will show us how His intercessory prayer can be answered by the common co-operation of all Christians, then, but not till then, may we hope to see the reunion of all Christians in Church relations.

THOMAS ARMITAGE.

THE REV. HENRY M. DEXTER, D.D., EDITOR OF THE *Congregationalist*, BOSTON.

EDITOR OF THE CHURCH REVIEW, SIR:

IT seems to me that Christian Reunion must be that of the heart, in the spirit, not in the letter; and that such reunion is perfectly possible under any outward circumstances, and will be attained whenever the HOLY SPIRIT shall so work mightily upon the hearts of all believers as to lead them to forget those lesser things as to which they differ, in the joy and strength of remembering those larger things in which they are at one. Πολλαὶ μὲν θνητοῖς γλῶσσαι, μία δ' ἀθανάτοισιν. Ought not those portions of the varying polities of CHRIST'S followers which seem inharmonious and immiscible to be regarded as the devise of the Fall to theology; as the many languages of earth are legacies from Babel — like those to be outgrown whenever that which is perfect is come and that which is in part shall be done away?

Meanwhile what is better — what indeed *can* honestly and honorably be otherwise done — than that each believer follow, as to Church detail, such Divine leadings as he is conscious of within himself, in his own essential tastes and convictions? At the same time let him feel that so long as he does so in perfect love and charity toward all his Christian brethren whose like endeavor may not lead them precisely to reproduce his own experience, he is nevertheless in real union with them and they with him; as he that hath faith to eat all things may be in perfect love and charity with his weak brother that eateth herbs, provided he judge him not, and acknowledge that the LORD hath received him.

I have never been able to believe that the Great Head of the Church intends all Christian people to be of one earthly fold, only of one heavenly. He has endowed and conditioned them too diversely for such comfortable unity. The sedate, order-loving, noise-hating believer, and the restless, itinerative shouting Christian only discomfort and disturb each other by seeking to be formally at one. Each is happier, each will be better edified, and be more drawn out to a larger work, when associated mainly with those who are like himself, and when positioned externally to his mind. The scout with his long rifle, the artillery-man serving his great gun, the cavalry-man with his flashing sabre, the marine with his musket, and the common sailor with his hand-spike on the war-ship, each may serve his country with as true a heart and as valiant a hand as the other. And all together, so only they be equally obedient under one controlling leadership, and alike determined that it shall be victorious, are more useful than if, with identical weapons and drill, massed together. If the whole body were an eye, where were the hearing? If the whole were hearing, where were the smelling? But now hath GOD set the members, each one of them, in the body even as it pleases Him. And if they were all one member, where were the body? But now they are many members, but one body.

With these views I can but regard the "Basis for Christian Reunion proposed by the Lambeth Conference" as conceived in, and designed for, a lower than the true and only possible plane of such infinitely to be desired reunion.

Yet to express, as has been most courteously desired, some opinion as to how far the religious Communion to which I belong could accept that proposed basis, I desire to say that so far as I have knowledge of the fundamental principles of Congregationalism, and some familiarity with the general feeling and judgment of the body, it seems to me safe to state: —

1. That Congregationalists can heartily accept the first and third articles of that basis, which make the Holy Scriptures to

"contain all things necessary to salvation," and to be "the rule and ultimate standard of Faith; " and which accept the two Sacraments of Baptism and the LORD'S Supper, "ministered with unfailing use of CHRIST'S words of institution, and of the elements ordained by Him."

2. That, "for substance of doctrine" — using that phrase to suggest that the lack felt in these formulæ, if any, would be in the direction of understatement rather than overstatement of the contained truth — Congregationalists could accept the second article, which names "the Apostles' Creed as a Baptismal Symbol," and "the Nicene Creed as a sufficient statement of the Christian Faith."

3. As to the remaining fourth article, "the Historic Episcopate, locally adapted in the methods of its administration to the varying needs of the nations and peoples called of GOD into the unity of His Church," nothing could better express the conviction of Congregationalists, if only they be permitted to interpret the phrase the "Historic Episcopate" as intending its early sense, as distinguished from the later superinduced significance. Like the New Testament Revisers, they regard the word ἐπίσκοπος in the four instances of its use in the Acts and Epistles as purely synonymous with the word translated "presbyter," or "pastor." And they understand the lately discovered *ΔΙΔΑΧΗ ΤΩΝ ΔΩΔΕΚΑ ΑΠΟΣΤΟΛΩΝ* [lines 277–281], "Now appoint for yourselves bishops and deacons worthy of the LORD, men meek and not avaricious, and upright and proved; for they too render you the service of the prophets and teachers," as carrying that "historic sense" well along into the second century. Moreover, when we find Chrysostom and Jerome, both of whom died in the fifth century, the one, in explanation of Paul's words [Hom. Phil. i. 1], answering the question, "Were there several bishops of one city?" by saying, "Certainly not, but he calleth the presbyters so;" and the other [*Ad Lang. Epist. c. i.*] remarking, *Apostolus perspicue docet eosdem esse presbyteros quos Episcopos*, we are constrained to feel that we should do right to decline, by the acceptance of the Episcopate which should exercise authority beyond that scripturally given to pastors of Churches, to become entangled again in a yoke of bondage which neither our fathers nor we were able to bear. We would not indeed much object to bishops chosen on the theory of an Archbishop of Canter-

bury of 350 years ago [Cranmer, *Questions and Answers concerning the Sacraments*, etc. 9], thus, " Sometimes the people did choose such as they thought meet thereunto; and when any were appointed or sent by the Apostles or others, the people of their own voluntary will, with thanks, did accept them, — not for the supremity, impery, or dominion that the Apostles had over them to command as their princes or masters; but as good people, ready to obey the advice of good counsellors, and to accept anything that was necessary for their edification and benefit."

In these views I hope it is not irreverent for me, not animated by an overpowering faith in the success of a movement with which yet every good man must be in sympathy, to conclude by adopting S. Paul's hortation: " Brethren, let each man wherein he was called, therein abide with GOD. Art thou bound under obligation of love and duty unto a bishop, seek not to be loosed; art thou loosed from a bishop, seek not a bishop. But and if led in conscience, or by taste, thou do so, thou hast not sinned."

HENRY M. DEXTER.

THE REV. JAMES MCCOSH, D.D., L.L.D. [PRESBYTERIAN], EX-PRESIDENT OF PRINCETON COLLEGE.

Federation of Evangelical Churches.

I TAKE it very kind that the Editor of the CHURCH REVIEW has asked me to write on Church Reunion. I am sorry to be obliged to begin by saying that I do not see any prospect of an immediate full reunion. I am not to inquire who are to blame for this state of things, or whether we may not all be so far in fault.

As requested, I have weighed carefully the overtures proposed in evident kindness by the Lambeth Conference. With most of them there would be a general accordance. But there will be a decided aversion to the Fourth Article as to the Historic Episcopate as it is understood by the Churches. Churches not Episcopal interpret it as meaning that their ministers must be reordained before they can be admitted into the united Church. I am not authorized to speak for my own Church, the Presbyterian, or any other denomination. But from a large acquaintance with the Churches of Europe and America," I know, as a matter of fact, that the great body of the non-Episcopal Churches are not prepared to submit to these conditions, and that it is utterly useless to try to persuade them to do so. In these circumstances I have been led to inquire whether, though not able to obtain all that we wish, we may yet secure some of the most valuable advantages of a union, these being good in themselves, and fitted to lead to something farther and higher.

If we cannot have an incorporation of the Churches, let us have a federation. It is known to all who have looked around them that there are dense districts in all our great cities, and they are increasing in number, and that there are scattered people in our villages and in our rural districts, East and West, North and South, where there is no provision for taking care of the immortal souls of all, rich and poor, old and young. This being so, as is known and acknowledged on all hands, it follows that every professing Christian, every congregation, and every Church is under obligation to inquire how this evil is to be met, and CHRIST'S command be fulfilled to preach the Gospel to every creature.

In the plan of federation, it is to be understood that a minister's care is to be primarily over his own people, and he may visit them wherever they reside, and do good among them in every way sanctioned by Scripture. But surely his duty does not end there. Like his MASTER, he has to seek in order to save that which is lost. Let a convenient district be allotted to him of which he has special charge, say of five hundred or one thousand people, where his office is to secure that every person knows that a SAVIOUR has been provided for sinners. There need be no compulsion laid on ministers to undertake this work. Those who have the spirit of the SAVIOUR will offer themselves willingly, and will be glad to find that instead of being required to scatter their energies over an undefined region, there is a special field allotted to each. The minister should take charge of the whole machinery, but he will commonly call in to work with him all his Church agency,—his elders and deacons and deaconesses, his Sabbath School teachers, and all members who are willing to work; and where his congregation is large, he should have a paid agent, male or female, to visit daily among the people. In this way CHRIST'S message of mercy will be delivered to all,—to the forgotten and forlorn, to the deserted wife, to neglected children, to the bedridden, to those in sickness and in sorrow, to all who are looking forward to death, to the wanderer, the vagrant, the beggar, the outcast. As the most difficult work of all, prayers will be offered and opportunities watched, to discover a way in which the Gospel may find an entrance into the dwellings of the rich and proud who will not wait on the public ministrations of the Word.

This work may be begun by a few ministers agreeing to divide their district among them. As it advances, the country will come to be divided into districts, — let them be called parishes after the ancient usage, — and the whole land may be covered.

This plan is easily understood, and is perfectly practicable. It needs only a willingness on the part of ministers in order to carry it out. It interferes in no way with the rights and privileges of any Church or any individual minister. It secures one of the great advantages of the union of Churches, that CHRIST'S salvation be known to every one.

In unfolding this scheme I claim no originality, I take no credit to myself. The plan has occurred to hundreds, and has been carried out in a few places. What is needed now is to have it executed over the country. It was adopted by the early Church before it was divided into sects. It seems to me to be the only plan available in the present divided state of the Church. It has been continued in every country in Europe; let it be adopted in America. It can be started in any one district; it is capable of being spread over the whole country.

Being so long a parish minister with fourteen hundred communicants, I am prepared to enter into details. But my present desire is to have conferences where measures may be proposed and adopted for wisely carrying out the plan.

JAMES MCCOSH.

THE REV. JOHN HALL, D.D., LL.D. [PRESBYTERIAN], NEW YORK CITY.

EDITOR OF THE CHURCH REVIEW, SIR:

THE phrase "Christian Reunion" is, in one point of view, vague. Is a union like that of the Evangelical Alliance contemplated? In what sense is the proposed result a "reunion"? Is organic union contemplated?

To Article 1 of course there can be no objection. As to Article 2, explanation is needed as to the meaning of " the Apostles' Creed, as the Baptismal Symbol." The Nicene Creed I do not think a " sufficient statement of the Christian Faith " in our time. We are bound, I think, to have a creed that discriminates between great truths and current errors. We are bound, I think, to embody in our creeds a protest against mediæval substitutes for the truth, still urged over a part of Christendom.

So, as to Article 3, the question comes up: Can some administer the sacraments, teaching that their efficacy is dependent on the minister, while others in the same " Christian Reunion " teach that their efficacy does not depend on anything in them nor in him that doth administer them? This is, it seems to me, a vital matter, as is recognized within the Anglican Church at this day.

With regard to Article 4, the words " Historic Episcopate " do not define enough. One large denomination claims that the " bishops and deacons " of Philippi, the former being elders or presbyters without any superior, constitute the " Historic Episcopate." Is this claim admitted by the Lambeth Conference? Our Methodist brethren, in America, elect bishops. Does the Conference propose to regard them on the same foundation as the Anglican bishops? Are archbishops included in the " Historic Episcopate"? Again, the word " historic " is too vague for a definition so vital as is here involved. How much of time does " historic " include? There are many things for which " historic" claims could be set up, which as Protestant New Testament Churches we could not accept. There is need of greater definiteness of statement.

Once more: One cannot, however anxious for a fitting display of the relations of all believers to GOD in CHRIST, and to one another in Him, ignore the antagonizing views regarding the " Catholic Church," which must be settled. Does the " Catholic Church " consist of " the Church of Rome, the Greek Church, and the Anglican Church "? Are the outside " Protestant religious bodies sects, so called from a Latin word ' to cut off,'" and is it to be held that " they have cut themselves off from the full fellowship of the Catholic Church "? Does the Lambeth Conference deny all this, and favor the receiving of their ministers, for example, as ministerial brethren? Or must they be somehow taken back into the " Catholic Church," and if so, in what way? Are their orders to be recognized, or is there to be devised some way of giving orders, say to the Methodist Episcopal bishops? If they have " abandoned the Catholic ministry, sacraments, and Liturgy," how are they to be restored?

These are only specimens of many questions that must arise, requiring more explicitness than Article 4 involves. Are " bishops " of the " Catholic Church," as defined above, the only officers having the right to ordain? Do such bishops " keep up the Church " by consecrating their successors to the " Episcopate," etc.? In other words, is the tenet of " Apostolic Succession " involved in, or excluded from, the basis of the Lambeth Conference?

But I fear my questions and difficulties will take too much of your space. The statement of these gives me pain; but Christians are bound to be true to the truth of things, and any show of union not based on actual harmony of beliefs is, for all the purposes of a spiritual Church, of little value.

I am always glad to co-operate with my brethren of the various Protestant Churches, and I would rejoice in the removal of obstacles to closer fellowship. To exchange pulpits with the Congregationalists, Baptists, Methodists, and others, has been a pleasure, and has also been a manifestation of oneness in great common aims. All action consistent with fidelity to vital truth, and with frank openness in the profession of unity, I would welcome thankfully.

Yours most truly,

J. HALL.

THE REV. LYMAN ABBOTT, D.D., LL.D. [CONGREGATIONALIST], EDITOR OF THE *Christian Union*, NEW YORK.

EDITOR OF THE CHURCH REVIEW, SIR:

IT can hardly be necessary for me to say that I am very earnestly in favor of all practicable measures for Christian union in Christian work, since I have been for over ten years the Editor of a paper whose title thoroughly indicates this to be one of the fundamental principles which it has endeavored to inculcate. I welcomed, therefore, most cordially the basis for Christian Reunion proposed by the Lambeth Conference in

1888, not because that basis seemed to me a finality, but because in its definiteness and in its practicability it seemed a great advance on anything which had been before proposed by any Church.

While I have no objection to the Nicene Creed, I should be quite satisfied with, and on the whole should prefer, the Apostles' Creed as not only the Baptismal Symbol, but also as a sufficient statement of the Christian Faith.

If by the Historic Episcopate is meant, as I suppose, what is known as the doctrine of Apostolic Succession, I do not believe that a Christian reunion can be secured on that basis. There are many of us who have no desire to antagonize that doctrine, and yet who could not accept it and make it our own; for however much we may desire Christian reunion, we desire yet more to maintain absolute candor in the statement of our own convictions, and it is our conviction that the doctrine of Apostolic Succession finds no warrant in Scripture, as it is also the conviction of some men who are eminent in the Episcopal Communion.

May I be allowed to add one other suggestion? At present pulpit exchanges between Episcopalians and non-Episcopalians are unknown, and I suppose are not in accordance with your canons. Why should not such exchanges be allowed? I can understand why those who hold to the doctrine of Apostolic Succession must refuse to allow those whom they regard as unordained to pronounce absolution or to administer the Sacrament; but preaching is a prophetical, not a priestly office. If the Episcopal Church would recognize this fact and would admit to its pulpits men not Episcopally ordained; if, for example, Dr. Morgan Dix would invite Dr. John Hall to continue in Trinity Church the Lenten sermons so admirably initiated this year by Dr. Phillips Brooks, and Dr. John Hall would invite Dr. Morgan Dix to preach in the Fifth Avenue Presbyterian Church, — a sign of inter-denominational comity would be furnished, and a step toward the reunion of the dissevered Church would be taken, full of hope for those of us who recognize the fact that such a reunion must be a growth and the result of gradual and successive processes. For myself it was a great delight to me to have present at my recent installation in Plymouth Church two clergymen of the Episcopal Church, and to be permitted this Lenten season to give a

Lenten address in S. George's Church of this city, as it has been a pleasure and a profit to us in Plymouth Church to take some initiatory steps toward the recognition of Lent and Passion Week in special Church services.

Yours sincerely,
LYMAN ABBOTT.

THE REV. J. M. BUCKLEY, D. D. [METHODIST], NEW YORK CITY, EDITOR OF THE *Christian Advocate.*

EDITOR OF THE CHURCH REVIEW, SIR:

IN response to your courteous communication of March 10, I am willing to make a statement of my convictions upon the profoundly interesting topic of your communication. There are four points in the basis of the Christian Reunion proposed by the Lambeth Conference in 1888. The first, second, and third would be entirely satisfactory to Methodists. Upon the fourth I can with propriety give nothing more than my own views, adding, nevertheless, the statement of my belief that they are in accord with those of most ministers and laymen of the branch of Methodism with which I am connected.

I do not believe that what is known as the Historic Episcopate is enjoined in the Scriptures, or that it is necessary to constitute a true branch of the visible Church of JESUS CHRIST. Yet I highly approve the principle of Episcopal supervision, as contributing to unity, general uniformity, and efficiency in administration. It is not my belief that a Historic Episcopate, in the sense involving a separate Order in the ministry, can be demonstrated to be a continuous and unbroken chain from the Apostolic age to our own.

Therefore I could not unite in an ecclesiastical organization requiring as a matter of Faith, either expressly or by implication, a Scriptural or a historic basis for such an institution. It would, however, be possible to adopt it as expedient, to give it all the functions predicated of an Order, to conform to it and to require conformity to it by all the members of the said organization, provided it did not require a refusal to recognize the claims of ecclesiastical Communions orthodox in doctrine, which do not accept such an Episcopate and sacraments, to the possession of a valid ministry.

Methodists have no doubt as to their possession of both these, nor have they any doubt that the ministers of the Presbyterian, Baptist, Congregational, and Lutheran bodies are true ministers, not only of CHRIST, but of His visible Church. Entertaining no doubt of their own authority as ministers of the Gospel and of the visible Church, they do not feel the need of what is called the Historic Episcopate, nor would they under any circumstances or for any result place themselves in a position where an exchange with the ministers of other denominations would be a breach of propriety or of Church order; or where an invitation to the ministers of such Churches to administer the Holy Communion, or to perform any function, or exercise any prerogative, of the Christian ministry, would be a violation of the letter or the spirit of the laws of such an organization.

It is at this point that all the difficulties centre. If the "large freedom and variety on secondary points of doctrine, worship, and discipline, without interference with existing conditions of property and endowment," could be allowed, and the Historic Episcopate could be so held as not to put the intolerable burden of unchurching (a "vile word," but expressive of the thought) other Christian bodies, upon some such basis, "under GOD'S gracious providence, a reunited Church might rest."

Yours sincerely,

J. M. BUCKLEY.

THE REV. HOWARD CROSBY, D.D., LL.D. [PRESBYTERIAN], NEW YORK CITY.

EDITOR OF THE CHURCH REVIEW, SIR:

WILL you excuse me from preparing an elaborate opinion on the Basis of Christian Union proposed by the Lambeth Conference? I can put my views in a few words; they are these: —

1. The Lambeth propositions I believe to have sprung from the best of motives.

2. The external union of the whole Church of CHRIST under one government is not desirable. The endeavor to accomplish this end led to the frightful and bloody scenes of the fourth century; and when the end was gained, the Church became a political power of worldliness and tyranny.

3. The true union of the Church of CHRIST is spiritual, to be marked by brotherly love.

4. Bible doctrine and *local* government are the soul and body of the Church.

5. Externals should give way before spiritual life. Where the spirit of the LORD is, there is liberty.

6. The Apostles' (?) Creed and the Nicene Creed are man's creation long after the Apostles' day, and are imperfect statements. I deem the Apostles' Creed wrong in saying that our LORD *descended* into hell or hades. He went to *Paradise*, and when Paul went to Paradise, he was caught *up*. I believe that article of the Apostles' Creed was derived from a false interpretation of 1 Peter iii. 19, in the third century. I object to the Nicene Creed as entering into philosophical speculation, when it should have been content with the Scripture statement that "the Word is GOD." The Council of Nice was a disgraceful meeting in a corrupt age.

7. "The Historic Episcopate" is an ambiguous phrase. The Historic Episcopate of the first century was a parochial Episcopate. The Historic Episcopate afterward was Diocesan, Metropolitan, and Provincial, and finally Papal. Hence the ambiguity of the phrase.

8. All the Churches of CHRIST should recognize one another in all things and not allow mere external peculiarities to keep them in apparent hostility.

9. The blame for Christian schisms is with those who magnify externals and so bar off spiritual union.

10. There is no schism where there is mutual love and respect.

These ten propositions present my views of the subject better than I could give them in an essay.

Very truly yours, HOWARD CROSBY.

THE REV. TALBOT W. CHAMBERS, D.D. [DUTCH REFORMED], NEW YORK CITY.

EDITOR OF THE CHURCH REVIEW, SIR:

THE mutual recognition and fraternal co-operation of the existing Evangelical Communions would be a far better evidence of the oneness of the Church than any external bond of union such as is proposed.

2. The statement in regard to the Scriptures might be improved, but still may be accepted as it is.

3. The Nicene Creed is wholly inadequate as a statement of doctrine, because it makes no mention of the extent and nature of sin, or of the character of the atonement, or of the need of regeneration, or of the means of justification, or of the extent of future retribution. The varying views of Christians on these points would be a bar to any real or efficient union. "Can two walk together except they be agreed?"

4. Since the Nicene age GOD has led His Church to the development of a number of important truths contained in the Bible; to give up these truths formulated at such great cost, and confine one's self to the one formula of an infant period, would be simply folly.

5. The article respecting the Sacraments is unexceptionable.

6. The fourth point, the "Historic Episcopate," is too vague to serve its purpose. It might be interpreted to mean the Episcopate of the New Testament, or that of the age of Cyprian, or that of full-blown Romanism; or subsequent to the Reformation, it might mean that of the Anglican Church, or that of the Scandinavian, or that of the Moravian Brethren.

7. The Roman Church has unity in the sense which the present effort seeks to secure; but the results which have followed and are now following from the rigid outward clamp by which this unity is secured, do not commend it to favor, but rather the contrary.

TALBOT W. CHAMBERS.

THE REV. THOMAS S. HASTINGS, D.D., L.L.D. [PRESBYTERIAN], PRESIDENT OF THE UNION THEOLOGICAL SEMINARY, NEW YORK.

EDITOR OF THE CHURCH REVIEW, SIR:

THE action of the Lambeth Conference of 1888 I regard as an honest effort in the interest of higher Christian unity. As such it has a claim to general and earnest consideration. I do not understand that this action aims to absorb, but only to unify the different denominations, bringing them on common ground into closer Christian fellowship. With this aim I heartily sympathize.

The several branches of the Church should recognize their vital relations to one another as one in CHRIST JESUS, who alone gives life to all. To this end they should emphasize only what is essential and what is common to all who "hold the Head."

As to the four points in the proposed "basis for Christian Reunion," I would prefer that the first should state more strongly the *fact* of the Divine inspiration of the Holy Scriptures of the Old and New Testaments. I would leave room for differences of opinion as to the *theory* of inspiration; but I would assert the *fact* more distinctly.

The fourth point is not as clear as I could wish. It will bear an interpretation to which I would not object. "The Historic Episcopate," taking the words in their strict meaning, has possibilities of which we of our Church might avail ourselves to advantage, if thereby we could bring our own Churches closer together and at the same time come nearer to our brethren of the other branches of the one Church. But with the possibilities there are perils which cause us to hesitate to approve this fourth point, and to ask, Exactly what do you mean by "the Historic Episcopate"?

THOMAS S. HASTINGS.

THE REV. WILLIAM M. TAYLOR, D.D. [CONGREGATIONALIST], NEW YORK CITY.

EDITOR OF THE CHURCH REVIEW, SIR:

THE question of Christian Reunion has not a very great interest for me at this time. I do not regard it as, in the present state of things, a practical one; and I am not sure that I should regard a great aggregation of the different branches of the visible Church, on any basis, as very desirable.

So far as the first three articles of the basis proposed by the Lambeth Conference in 1888 are concerned, I can heartily accept them; but in the fourth the "Historic Episcopate" needs to be defined. I do not know what it means. If it denotes the Episcopate as at present existing in Episcopal Churches, I do not see any warrant for that in the New Testament Scriptures; while, if it signifies what I should call the Primitive Episcopate,

— that is, the government of each Church by a Board, the members of which are designated indifferently as Episcopoi or Presbuteroi, — that is Congregationalism, or in a sense, Presbyterianism; and the putting of it into the basis of reunion would imply either that we must all become Episcopalians or all Congregationalists, in order to be reunited. As a minister of a Congregational Church, I could not insist on other people becoming Congregationalists as an essential to reunion; and on the other hand, I could not think of becoming an Episcopalian for the purpose of helping on reunion.

Excuse me for my frankness in so stating my views, but in a matter of this kind, the truest brotherhood is manifested by the utmost frankness. Believe me,

Yours faithfully,

WILLIAM M. TAYLOR.

THE REV. EDWARD B. COE, D.D. [DUTCH REFORMED], NEW YORK CITY.

EDITOR OF THE CHURCH REVIEW, SIR:

I BEG you to accept my thanks for the invitation to contribute one of the articles on Christian Reunion. If it were possible for me to do this, it would give me great pleasure. The subject is one in which I take a very deep interest; and if I could do anything toward advancing the movement which now occupies so many earnest minds, I should esteem it a privilege. My own opinion is that the House of Bishops has laid an admirable basis for *discussion*, if not for ultimate reunion; and I greatly honor them for the catholic spirit in which their action was taken, and for the broad lines which they have drawn. It remains, however, as it seems to me, that these propositions (and particularly No. 4) should be *interpreted* as to their exact meaning. All that other bodies of Christians may rightfully claim seems at first sight to be conceded. But is this really so? I confess that I am in doubt; and I trust that the discussion in your REVIEW will lead to a more exact definition of that which is intended in these articles and would be acceptable to the Episcopal Church.

I regret that the state of my health, which has obliged me to suspend for a short time even my accustomed work, makes it quite impossible for me to prepare such a paper as you request; but I shall look with much interest for the series of articles when the next number of the REVIEW appears. I am

Very truly yours,

EDWARD B. COE.

THE

Church Review

VOLUME LIX. ✠ OCTOBER, 1890

Church Reunion.

Conference of Bishops of the Anglican Communion, holden at Lambeth Palace in July, 1888. Encyclical Letter from the Bishops, with Resolutions and Reports. London: Society for Promoting Christian Knowledge. New York: E. and J. B. Young and Company.
The Church Review, vol. lvii., April, 1890. New York: The Church Review Company.

Historic Presbyterians.

RIGHT REV. ARTHUR CLEVELAND COXE, D.D., LL.D.,
BISHOP OF WESTERN NEW YORK.

RELIGION in America has reached an alarming crisis, which cannot be neglected much longer by the patriot or the Christian. Disguise it as we may, American institutions are suffering a revolutionary change, if not a fatal subversion. Fatal it must be unless the American spirit can be roused to self-preservation; unless the salt of the earth can be rescued from losing its savor; unless the " ten righteous " in Sodom can be persuaded to join hands and hearts in common labors and intercessions for the thousands who desire not the knowledge of GOD, and choose none of His ways. A social revolution is needed to band together all the elements which are not solvent; and the only force which can organize the lovers of CHRIST and His Gospel for efficient operations must be a religious one. It was not a sentimental yearning for unity, therefore, which prompted the House of Bishops to present to their fellow-Christians a simple statement of first principles of elementary truths, essential to Church restoration. It was a practical movement, inspired by a sense of duty. Both friends and enemies have recognized the Anglican position as one of vantage for just such overtures as have been made; and at all events, the Bishops themselves understood their obligations and their opportunity at such a time as this. In humble trust, and in a hopeful spirit, they resolved to cast their bread upon the waters, with a holy confidence that it must be found productive " after many days." GOD has made their " word in season" apparently fruitful already, — fruitful, that is, in giving to discussion and inquiry a new direction, awakening a fraternal sympathy among Christians widely separated heretofore, and plucking the " root of bitterness " out of differences which have long been supposed incapable of any other treatment than such as perpetuates implacable hostilities, immedicable wounds, and putrefying sores. Even these have already been mollified as with ointment; and hopes are freely expressed that, after all, our worst evils are not beyond correction by the grace of GOD. He would be a bold man indeed who should say more of the actual situation than that it is not so desperate as has been supposed. The antagonisms and alienations of ages are not to be reconciled in a moment. The wide divergencies which exist among good men are fortified by habit, even where they are quite free from the venom of prejudice and the vanity of Pharisaic self-applause. Many who wish to meet their brethren halfway, or even more than halfway, are yet hindered by their inability to see any way whatever for making a start. Above all, there is the sturdy *vis inertiæ* of popular ignorance. Many things in which educated Christians are already agreed are scandals to the masses, whose dulness and misapprehensions we must take into account. Obviously a *process of assimilation* is the condition precedent to any practical solution of the great problem; and that this process is already begun is so evident that I find it a great encouragement to my honest belief that the HOLY SPIRIT is moving over our American chaos of strifes, heresies, and delusions, and that the dry land will certainly appear; nay, not merely dry land, but hills "with verdure clad," where the Good Shepherd may yet feed a united flock, and refresh them with living fountains of water.

To my own mind nothing in the spirit of recent discussions has presented features so promising as that which has been elicited from our Presbyterian brethren. This, indeed, is just what no superficial thinker could have anticipated. It reminds one of the *quod minime reris* of Virgil, of the prospect opened to pious Æneas from a quarter whence he had least right to look for it. Between Geneva and Canterbury how can any common foothold be established? Who can reconcile parity with prelacy? But he who has studied the origin of discord in this matter, and who is versed in scholastic efforts to prop the Papacy, by which the whole subject was artificially confused, knows very well that all the nobler spirits who found themselves originally arranged on opposite sides of the question were by no means implacable in their conflicts of opinion. In point of fact, the great expounder of Primitive Episcopacy, S. Cyprian, outlined a system which effectually meets the views of both parties, and frees the subject of all the subtleties by which it was found clogged at the epoch of the Reformation. As stated by the great Bishop of Carthage, the parity of all the chief pastors of Christendom is not so much asserted as assumed. It was the principle universally understood in Church legislation from the beginning. After this the position of presbyters (pastors, or "Bishops" of limited jurisdiction), and of the faithful laity as sharing in Church councils, is vindicated and insisted upon; so that, as will soon be seen, the Cyprianic system meets what Calvin himself considered Scriptural, and what Baxter and his contemporaries actually proposed as a formula of renewed conformity with the Church of England. Just here, then, let me linger for a moment, to note the historical base established by their co-religionists, which Presbyterians have a right to consider the only Presbyterianism to which they are actually committed, and that to which they may logically recur, in responding to the appeal of our Bishops, should they be so inclined.

It is surprising how generally Presbyterians have forgotten the fact that they largely co-operated with the Anglican Church in the restoration of the English constitutions, civil and ecclesiastical, in 1660. If their eminent spokesman and leader, Richard Baxter, could have persuaded the Anglicans to modify what was conceded to be of civil rather than of ecclesiastical import, a reunion might have been effected at that time. The Church of England, at this moment, concedes as much, when she recognizes our American Church Constitution as differing from her own in nothing of ecclesiastical importance. Her own polity is the product, in many respects, of her time-honored relations with the State, — relations which involve much to be deplored, but which few of her children are willing to see suddenly and rudely destroyed. We need not wonder, then, that after the civil strifes and the general overthrow of law and order under Cromwell, the restoration of the *ante-bellum* conditions appeared to be the only practical resolution of problems the most intricate, the only remedy for difficulties the most gigantic, and the mildest prescription for allaying the fierce resentments of the moment. It is very honorable to the Presbyterians, however, that they were able to unite upon proposals to the government, of which the substance is as follows: —

We are induced [they say] to insist upon the form of a synodical government conjunct with a fixt presidency *or Episcopacy*, for these reasons: (1) We have reason to believe that no other terms will be so generally agreed on; (2) It, being agreeable to Scripture and the primitive government, is likeliest to be the way of a more general concord, if ever the Churches on earth arrive at such a blessing; however, it will be acceptable to GOD and well-informed consciences; (3) It will produce the practice of discipline without discord, and promote order without hindering discipline and godliness; (4) And it is not to be silenced . . . that the Prelacy disclaimed in the late 'Covenant' was the engrossing, the sole power of ordination and jurisdiction, and exercising the whole discipline by Bishops themselves and their delegates, — excluding wholly the people of particular Churches from all share in it.[1]

Upon this the heavenly-minded Leighton cites Baxter's treatise of Church Government, as favoring " an Episcopacy for the reformation, preservation, and peace of the Churches." And why not? It was nothing new in Presbyterian statements of their *theoretical* position. In language too strong to be repeated, Calvin himself anathematized those who could refuse an Episcopate that recognizes CHRIST, and not the Papacy, for its Headship and its Lawgiver. " In my writings touching Church Government," says Beza, " I ever impugned the Romish hierarchy, but never intended to touch the Church of England." And Bucer, writing to Saravia, the bosom friend of Hooker, expresses himself thus forcibly: " If there be any, as you will not easily persuade me, who would reject the whole Order of

---

[1] *Two Papers of Proposals, humbly presented to his Majesty* by the Rev. MINISTERS OF THE PRESBYTERIAN PERSUASION. London, 1661.

Bishops, GOD forbid that any man in his senses should assent to their madness." It would be quite easy to multiply similar testimonies. At the Synod of Dort, its president welcomed the English Bishops in language that conceded the less fortunate condition of the Reformed in Holland, deprived as they were of the Episcopate. And later on, Diodati bewailed the same lack in the constitution of the Swiss Churches. Even then the most erudite and sagacious of the Presbyterians were of the same mind with Baxter; and what would they have said, had they fully foreseen the end to which they were drifting? A century later, Rousseau, and not Calvin, was the master of Geneva; and the Presbyterians of England had so generally lapsed into Socinianism, in the early years of this century, that it became necessary to enact a special law in behalf of three hundred congregations which had rejected the Faith of CHRIST. They were thus relieved from lawsuits which assumed that they had forfeited all right to their property by their acknowledged revolt from the principles of their original foundation.

But a rejection of Episcopacy was no part of those original principles, if we accept the testimony we have cited. In fact, the Presbyterians of England committed themselves to the acceptance of a primitive Episcopate almost identical with that defined by Chillingworth. He says: "If we abstract from Episcopal government all accidentals, and consider only what is essential and necessary to it, we shall find it no more but this: an appointment of one man of eminent sanctity and sufficiency to have the care of all the Churches within a certain precinct or Diocese, and furnishing him with authority, *not absolute or arbitrary, but regulated and bounded by laws, and moderated by joining to him a convenient number of assistants*, to the intent that all the Churches under him may be provided of good and able pastors; so that, both of pastors and people, conformity to laws and performance of their duties may be required, under penalties not left to discretion, but by law appointed."

Nor are these historic principles of the early Presbyterians a thing of the past. Again, *quod minime reris*, from Scotland come concessions to these principles far more emphatic than we have yet heard in America. In 1862, the "Moderator" of the great legislature of the Kirk of Scotland deplored the evils of separation, and broke out with this impassioned ejaculation: "Oh, that some great patriot of heaven-born thoughts, full of the wisdom of the holy Prophets, might arise in our land to show how this conjunction and consummation so devoutly to be wished for might be accomplished!" He admitted that increasing numbers in the Scottish establishment complained of the *bald and cold* nature of their worship, and he eulogized "the beautiful service" of the Church of England. In 1866, Dr. Campbell, Principal of the University of Aberdeen, thus referred to our own American Church: "The admirable constitution of which combines the advantages of Presbytery and Episcopacy, the lay element being represented and employed in a most wise and efficient manner in the councils of the Church." This spirit has grown and strengthened vastly in the course of twenty years. From many examples[1] of the kind take these words of the eminent Principal Tulloch: "Let the dead bury their dead; it is time to forget old conflicts which *all wise thinkers have abandoned.* Presbyterianism does not disown Episcopacy, and certainly does not denounce it; and there are few wise Presbyterians who do not see weaknesses in their own system arising from the disuse of it."

Essential Presbyterianism, then, only demands that "elders and brethren" shall have synodical place and privileges, *conjoint* with the superior order which is now known as the order of "Bishops," — a name which was once common alike to chief pastors and presbyters, just as in an army certain officers are "generals," though some generals are "brigadiers," and others commanders of the corps. The appeal of our House of Bishops, therefore, has come to Presbyterians from just such a Church as they are historically committed to acknowledge as Scriptural and as best fitted to reunite divided households in the family of CHRIST. In 1882, "the Moderator of the General Assembly" (Dr. Milligan) used this language: "There is much to draw us to the Episcopal Church of Scotland. . . . The earliest and best of our reformers had no objections to much that the Episcopal Church retains in *doctrine, worship, and government.* If in later times a spirit of mutual animosity prevailed, it was in no small degree because of temporary causes which have in great measure passed away, . . . deepened by that folly and sin, on both sides, which all parties now equally bewail."

When such language is heard and applauded in the great

---

[1] See these and others in a publication of Dr. Wordsworth, Bishop of S. Andrew's. — *Ecclesiastical Union between England and Scotland.* Edinburgh, 1888.

council of the Kirk, not once or twice, but again and again, year after year, one would think that "both parties" might embrace at once, and by uniting establish a power for good which the world itself must recognize as of immense import to mankind. Think of what it would mean for this American Republic if Presbyterians might unite with us on principles which their Scottish brethren have thus emphasized. But such a consummation is still a great way off, we may sadly suppose. The recent comments of eminent Presbyterians upon the proposals of our Bishops betray distrust. With suppressed feeling, and almost unanimously, they intimate a fear that there is something behind our theoretical statements,— something kept out of sight for the present, but which must become odious and irritating as soon as the matter is made practical. I think we ought not to give any ground for a suspicion that we are disposed to hide from our brethren what they are entitled to know, and hence I will not avoid the subject which with great delicacy they have approached in their candid and fraternal discussions. They have asked us to be precise in defining the "*Historical* Episcopate." In a word, they wish to know whether this means an Episcopate of which the "Apostolic Succession" is the criterion. This is the bugbear, apparently; but perhaps it may seem less terrible when we look at it in its actual bearings and divested of any desire on our part to subject learned and godly brethren to our convictions. The existence of an Episcopate which is historical is all that we have asserted. We present a fact, not a theory. By *historical* is meant something which has been recognized in the Churches of CHRIST from the beginning, — "always, everywhere, and by all;" something that has continuity of transmission under the original canons and constitutions from Apostolic or sub-Apostolic times. This fact and not any dogma concerning its origin is what we have defined. It is candid to remark that not Presbyterians only, but the Papists as well, have adopted theories touching this "Historic Episcopate" which we cannot accept. Practically, however, the Latins have not rejected the essentials of its identity and continuity, although their Papacy abhors the Cyprianic system in order to establish its own supremacy. If, then, we accept adhesion to the *fact* in behalf of the Latins, by the same law we must accept it elsewhere. No Roman Bishop is *Catholic* in his position, or has any claim to the Episcopal character, under the *theory* to which he subscribes as the condition of obtaining it.

The Moravian Episcopate is subject to similar objections; but if *in point of fact* the Historic Episcopate exists among these interesting Christians, it is our duty and privilege to recognize it as meeting our propositions of unity, at least so far forth.

What Presbyterians seem to scent with disrelish is a *subaudition* of reordination. None of them, however, is greater than Apollos, — that eloquent man of GOD, "mighty in the Scriptures," and pre-eminent as a successful preacher of CHRIST, who was yet so humble that he consented to learn "the way of GOD" *more perfectly* from a layman and even from a woman! He was even rebaptized without murmuring, in order to "fulfil all righteousness," as did CHRIST, his grand exemplar, who under that principle *demanded* a baptism of which He had no need at all. Now, whatever our learned brethren may object (and the Bishop of S. Andrew's has said it for them), I yet believe that, considering and studying this subject in its hierurgic and liturgic lights, they must come to the conclusion that they need to learn something of this "way of GOD" more perfectly.[1] The utter absence of any recognition of functions of the Christian Priesthood beyond that of *preaching*, in most of their expressions upon this subject, is remarkable. If the laity are also "a holy Priesthood," how must we account for this abnegation of all *priestly functions* in those set apart to be the special agents of the One Great High-Priest, in all things which He has commanded? I entreat dear brethren who have too little thought of this to examine the Greek of that remarkable text (Rom. xv. 15, 16), in which S. Paul asserts his *hierurgic* ministration of the Gospel, for which he had received the *charisma* of the HOLY SPIRIT. It is a passage which illustrates the grand hierurgy of the Epistle to the Hebrews, and connects it with Christian counterparts of the Levitical types.

I believe, then, that deep thought on this subject would persuade many that as Apollos did no dishonor to his former ministry, when he completed it, in this respect, so they might in like manner, *demand* a further gift. But we have not indiscreetly and unlovingly proposed this to our brethren. Our proposals are, in brief, that every organization of Christians, *throughout the world*, should recur to the requirements of the

[1] See *Apollos, or, The Way of God.* By Bishop Coxe, Lippincotts, Publishers.

Nicene Constitutions as to a common centre, and complete their organic form, by "setting in order the things that are wanting." This insures essential conformity with the constitution of the Historic Church before the Papacy existed, and so long as it was *visibly* "One, Holy, Catholic, and Apostolic." Such is what we require of ourselves; and wherever we ourselves can be proved to have suffered any loss, there we too are bound by our own terms to conform ourselves to the Nicene standard. We demand no less of arrogant and schismatical Rome; and we rejoice to see "the Old Catholics" restoring themselves to a pure Catholicity, on this principle. The "*Roman* Catholic Church," so called, is by that very name defined as *contra*-Nicene, and therefore non-Catholic. It is, in fact, not a Church, but an unlawful confederation of Western Churches, which are Catholic only in their individuality, and not in their confederacy. By this analysis only can we recognize them; even as CHRIST recognized severally each of the seven Churches of Asia, — types as they were of degenerate Churches of our own age. And what does he command them to do for their purification? In every instance, to "remember from what they have fallen; . . . to repent and do their first works." The fallen and corrupt Churches of antiquity, therefore, are still Apostolic Churches, — one a "Sardis," another a "Thyatira," perhaps, but still recognized by their only Supreme Head and Great High-Priest, who stands amid the golden candlesticks and holds their stars in His right hand. This is "the Catholic Church" even in its debasement, as viewed by its long-suffering LORD and MASTER. We may not be a "Smyrna," nor a "Philadelphia;" perhaps our Anglican Church is a "Laodicea." But our safeguard is this: we do not refuse to hear "what the SPIRIT saith to the Churches," and what we suppose to be the duty of others we prescribe rigorously, and first of all, to ourselves.

One difficulty which has thus far confused the discussion on the part of our Christian brethren generally has been the natural product of their position, or standpoint. Viewing us as they do, they have felt it somewhat presuming for us to state the case as we have done, because it seems to demand conformity to our standards, and a subjection of their organizations to ours. We, on the other hand, have hardly thought of our American Church at all; we have spoken *for the Universal*

Church of CHRIST, asking our brethren to conform themselves to its historic laws, and professing our readiness to do the same, in all respects, where we can be shown to have erred by Holy Scripture, interpreted by history and primitive constitutions.

They have therefore viewed our proposals as a local or national question, respecting chiefly the divided state of American Christianity, and reducing even this view of the case to divisions among those popularly known as " Evangelical." We, on the other hand, have been forced by our position to respect the entire common weal of Catholic Christendom; to enforce its organic laws as the common concern of all Christians; and to abate nothing from the requirements of those laws, whether in our own behalf or in behalf of others. We long to bear our part in healing local differences, and restoring Americans to Catholic, that is, Scriptural unity; but in order to do this, we must not forfeit anything that we retain in common with the Oriental Churches, — those great sources of liturgic formularies, those mother Churches of all Christendom. Our Anglican standpoint, even as the most embittered of our Roman enemies have been forced to allow, is " most precious." Yes, indeed! So says even that friend and ally of the Jesuits, the fanatical De Maistre. The inward convictions of the Roman Court itself find expression in what he has reluctantly admitted, influenced by a momentary hope to seduce England from a Catholic foothold, — down from the Nicene rock into the quagmire of Trent. " If ever Christians reunite," he says, " it would seem that the movement *must proceed from the Anglican Church*, which touches us on the one side and the Protestants on the other. . . . In this aspect she is *most precious*, and seems like those chemical *intermèdes*, which are capable of bringing together and combining elements in themselves the most dissocial." Yes, indeed! And this *precious* position we shall never forfeit. The time must come when the Roman immigration, or rather invasion, may produce its Döllinger, and will gladly listen to our *precious* testimony. We are the reserve force of Catholicity, and we bide our time. A glorious mission is ours, and we feel it. A fierce conflict menaces our country, between the aggressions of Romanism and all that is American. Marshalled, as it is, and wholly controlled, by the Jesuits, Ultramontane Romanism cannot maintain itself here. What all the Romanized States of Europe have expelled from their body politic, what even a

Pope abolished as intolerable to civilization, must sooner or later provoke a like retribution from a free republic. Our proposals to the Protestants of America were made in full view of this coming conflict. We urge our brethren to unity, partly because our divisions afford encouragement to the adversary, and wholly because the law of CHRIST ordains such unity. But, come what may, we cannot destroy our own Catholicity in behalf of a fictitious fusion, or rob ourselves of the high mission which awaits us in the near future, — our mission, that is, to co-operate with an "Old Catholic" movement that cannot long be delayed in these United States. Working with such allies, we are destined to save the nation itself from an alien hierarchy, intent upon making us what it has made of Mexico and Brazil. In this view our Church is "most precious."

Meantime, my own ideas of duty are these: To keep before our "Evangelical" brethren the common law of Christendom, and to aid them in conforming themselves thereto in their own way and in the LORD's good time, doing this in the fulness of fraternal love and social good-will. Responding to such overtures, let us suppose our Moravian brethren to awaken to the great importance of their relations to Presbyterians and others, assuming (what is *presumptively* the fact) that they possess the Historic Episcopate already. A *formal* though abnormal Episcopacy is maintained by our Methodist brethren; and we should rejoice to see the nobler Moravian character conferred upon Methodist Bishops by a movement which would prove greatly to the advantage of both. The maxims of John Wesley must sooner or later begin to operate upon that great American organization which justly glories in his beloved name; and if ever the Presbyterians, already renouncing Calvinism, should promote a fusion with Methodists, we may be sure that their learning and keen perceptions of truth must demand nothing less as a preliminary than a legitimation of Methodist Orders. The fusion that might thus come about would enable them to turn upon us and say, "See how great and strong we are, and how inconsiderable are you; come ye to us, for it is unreasonable on your part to expect us to come to you." And what must then be our reply? Brethren, you have made us one already; let us now operate together with "the Old Catholics" for the expulsion of Jesuitism and alienism from American Christianity, — for the restoration, that is to say, of Nicene unity,

Cyprianic unity, Ignatian unity; the unity ordained of CHRIST Himself; "one flock under one shepherd;" one house "built upon the foundation of Apostles and Prophets, JESUS CHRIST Himself being the chief Corner-stone."

Our fellow-Christians are more numerous than we are; we have not a particle of objection to see them thus organized into a majestic American Church, greater, richer, more Apostolic, and more loyal to CHRIST than we are. With such a Church we should be in full communion, and must soon coincide in a visible unity. The process thus fancifully outlined would involve temporary anomalies; but, as was demonstrated in the Donatist history, anomalies may be tolerated *in the process of reconstruction* which would be subversive of Catholicity if generated by the contrary spirit of schism.

To sum up all that has been said, and to clear the subject, let us note that what originated with the American Bishops was reaffirmed by the hundred and fifty Bishops at Lambeth, and is now presented to the Reformed, both in America and in Europe, in substance as follows: —

The Holy Scriptures, the Creeds, the Sacraments, and the Historic Episcopate are the ancient conditions of unity. They are the only imaginable conditions for its restoration. The Council of Nicæa has claims on all Christians, and whatever is subversive of the organized unity recognized by all the world when it bore its witness to CHRIST, is not Catholic but schismatical. We ask none of our fellow-Christians to come over to us; we say, "Let us all meet in old Nicæa." If we discover that we are deficient in any respect, when tried by that standard, let us, each for himself, seek to remedy his own defects. Let the spirit of fraternal love animate us in all our relations with others who cherish a similar spirit, however imperfectly they may seem to develop it. By prayer, and by the grace and providence of GOD, we shall be brought by converging lines to a common centre, in GOD'S good time. To some the process will be comparatively easy; the Moravians may find it much less of a task, for example, than the Baptists, though possibly the reverse may be practically true, for the Baptists practise, in administering baptism, what seems more in accordance with the spirit of all primitive antiquity. We, in turn, may be justly reproached for much that is inconsistent with our own professions; and we may not repel, we rather invite the rejoinder,

"Physician, heal thyself." In short, truth is to be sought and followed for its own sake; and he who accepts this as the law of his life, is already a Catholic at heart. "Ye shall know the truth, and the truth shall make you free." Such is the ennobling charter of the sons of GOD; and it includes a promise that should prompt all of us to effort for securing the result. It is something to believe in CHRIST'S promises and in the power of the HOLY GHOST to make them good to all believers. It is a great thing to make one's life a contribution to this end, though it may seem unattainable. And if, as the mathematicians inform us, there are lines that can never meet, though perpetually converging, let us be sure that even such lines are a parable, and intimate that it is well to move in the right direction at least, because there is a life eternal, where what is aimed at in this world is sure to be realized. For one, I do not think there is any probability of Catholic welding among us, save through the fiery trial of persecution, and under the hammer of tremendous visitations of Providence; but such trials *may be near at hand*. Irreligion and alien invasion are multiplying the perils of our common country. What happened in France a hundred years ago may warn us that we are not invulnerable. The uprising of wage-earners against the capitalist is but a token of what may be preparing in other complications. A general distrust of our politicians and governors forebodes a coming failure of all law, when the white heat of popular passion shall try every man's work. Our indifference to religion as it already exists may well remind us that the nation and people that will not serve GOD must perish by His judgments.

A. CLEVELAND COXE.

The Historic Episcopate.

RIGHT REV. WILLIAM CROSWELL DOANE, D D., LL.D.,
BISHOP OF ALBANY.

I PROPOSE to treat in this paper two questions,—*first*, "*What* we find about the Historic Episcopate;" and secondly, "Why we should naturally expect to find it." It is the case of an old friend, or to some people an old foe, with a new face. The long controversy has changed in many ways, prominently and particularly in terminology. The "Apostolic succession," which used to be ridiculed as a matter of magic and mummery, has got to be a question of history and fact; and the evidence of this is partly in the very change of terms. I may as well say that I firmly believe that CHRIST ordained the Historic Episcopate when He ordained the Apostolate; that the one included and involved the other; so that it does not seem to me to make an iota of difference *when* the Apostles set apart men for the carrying on of the work which CHRIST had assigned to them to do. The only question is, *whether* they did it; for it is incredible to me that they should have dared to invent, and intrude into the polity of the Church (that is to say, the government of the Kingdom of GOD on earth), anything of their own origination. And it being once granted that Bishops are found *in* the Apostolic age, *by* Apostolic appointment, and *with* Apostolic authority,—or, to put it more mildly, *without indignant Apostolic protest*,—it seems to me to follow inevitably that Bishops were of CHRIST'S own appointment. It is certainly a geological fact that in the earliest stratum of the most ancient earth the oldest fossil relic is the trilobite, which is a three-lobed or threefold thing. I believe it can be as thoroughly proven that in the most ancient stratum of the Holy Land— the oldest part and age, that is to say, of the Christian Church —the trilobite exists, in the threefold ministry of Bishops, Priests, and Deacons,—the first living organism of the Church.

This is the first point to be proved, or at any rate, that there existed an *Order* ($\beta\alpha\theta\mu\delta s$, S. Paul calls it, which we translate "degree," but by which the Eastern Church has always described the *Orders* of the ministry), — an *Order* of men, set apart for the two great acts of governing and perpetuating the ministry.

The statement which for a good many years has stood at the head of the English Ordinal is certainly a challenge, hitherto not successfully contested, of this truth. "It is evident unto all men diligently reading Holy Scripture and ancient authors that from the Apostles' time there have been these Orders of ministers in CHRIST's Church: Bishops, Priests, and Deacons." It looks a little bit as if the English Church meant by this to say that if people have not found these three Orders it is because they have either not read Holy Scripture and ancient authors *together*, or else they have not read them *diligently*. I am glad to say that Bishop Lightfoot has attained such an honorable reputation for thoroughness of research, and for impartiality of judgment, that one can safely appeal to him as an authority respected even by those who are not willing to accept or to act upon his conclusions. His vindication of the authenticity and authority of the Ignatian Epistles is one of the great masterpieces of honest and clear-headed criticism in the nineteenth century; and in his Commentaries to the Epistle to the Philippians he says: "The result of my investigation into the origin of the Christian ministry has been a confirmation of the statement in the English Ordinal." Over and over again he emphasizes this. For example: "The threefold ministry can be traced to Apostolic direction;" and again: "Unless we have recourse to a sweeping condemnation of received documents, it seems vain to deny that early in the second century the Episcopal office was firmly and widely established. Thus during the last three decades of the first century, and consequently during the lifetime of the last surviving Apostle, this change must have been brought about" (that is to say, from a Presbyterate governed by Apostles to a Diocesan Episcopacy). And still again: "The evidence for the early and wide extension of Episcopacy through proconsular Asia may be considered irrefragable." When you add to this the fact that proconsular Asia was the scene of S. John's life and labors to the end, there comes a very marked emphasis to the matter of our LORD's intention; for certainly the Apostle whom JESUS loved could not have suffered the existence and extension of an institution in the Church, which was not according to "the mind of CHRIST." We do not wonder that Lightfoot should add: "The prevalence of Episcopacy cannot be disassociated from the influence and sanction of the Apostles; and short of an express statement, we can possess no better assurance of a Divine appointment, or at least of a Divine sanction."

I desire to add, in connection with this same region of the world, what always seemed to me a very strong bit of historical evidence in the same direction. In the Acts of the Fourth General Council held at Chalcedon A. D. 451, in the course of a debate respecting the filling up of the Ephesian Bishopric which had been declared vacant, Leontius, Bishop of Magnesia, made the statement: "That from Timothy to the time then present, there had been twenty-seven Bishops of that See, all of whom had been ordained in Ephesus itself."[1]

I am quite well aware that this question of the Diocesan Episcopate, as illustrated by S. Timothy's appointment to Ephesus, is a somewhat mooted point, and that Bishop Lightfoot, from whom any one would hesitate to differ, considers his office "rather a movable than a localized Episcopate, so far as the Gentile Churches were concerned." But the localized or Diocesan Episcopate among the Hebrew Christians seems to me hardly to admit of a doubt, for S. James, who presided in the Council of Jerusalem, was either one of the twelve (which I do not believe),—and if he was, then we have certainly the case of an Apostle set apart as a Diocesan Bishop and presiding over a single See,—or else he was *not* an Apostle at all; in which case we have an instance of a Diocesan Bishop, in the time of the Apostles, presiding over them, their equal in order because he was a Bishop, and their superior in local dignity, because he was the Bishop of the See city in which the Council met.

Of course it is perfectly possible that Episcopacy grew "by way of development, as the needs of the extending Church demanded it." So did the Diaconate. But it does not follow from that, that it was not according to the polity of our LORD. Indeed, we must always use that word "development," not in the sense of the discovery and promulgation of something, without,

---

[1] Labbé, *Concilia* iv. p. 700; quoted by Bishop Charles Wordsworth in his invaluable treatise, *Outlines of the Christian Ministry*.

if not against, the original and Divine plan. A thing must be *enveloped* first, in order that it may be *developed* afterward. And there are various positive and important steps, recorded in the book of the Acts as taken by the Apostles not in a slow, doubtful, hesitating way, but positively and promptly, as men act who have been thoroughly trained and prepared for emergencies which arise. One of these I propose to speak of in detail, as answering the second question of the two which head this article; namely, why we should expect to find the Historic Episcopate. I mean the ordinance, certainly Sacramental in its character, which is called "the laying on of hands." The others will naturally suggest themselves, — the change from the seventh to the first day of the week; from the evening Passover to the morning Eucharist; the institution of the Diaconate; and the resort to a Council representing the whole Church as the method of settling any question of doctrine or order.

And now as to the holy ordinance known in Holy Scripture as "the laying on of hands," which has received, in the whole Western Church for nearly twelve centuries, the name of Confirmation; the Eastern Church calling it the Seal of the LORD, or the Unction. Our own name, venerable both for antiquity and for such authority as that of S. Ambrose and S. Gregory, is chiefly admirable because it is specific, — *laying on of hands* being of course used, not merely for confirming the grace and vow of the baptized, but for conveying Holy Orders, and indeed for any solemn act of benediction. My conviction and contention about this matter is, that if we can find it in Holy Scripture and ancient authors required, and confined, so far as its administration goes, to one Order of the ministry, it must mean that we shall also find the Order of the ministry authorized to administer it.

Let me begin by saying that the argument for the institution of the laying on of hands by CHRIST Himself, runs, as do so many arguments of a similar sort, in parallel lines of what in one way were parallel lives. The action of S. Peter (S. John being associated with him) in Samaria, immediately after the day of Pentecost, as illustrating the doctrine of S. Peter in the sermon preached on the day of Pentecost, is to be studied side by side with the action of S. Paul in the city of Ephesus, as illustrating the doctrine which I believe S. Paul taught to the Hebrew Christians, in the Epistle to the Hebrews, which I believe

S. Paul wrote. And before I proceed to put these four things side by side, I must urge the importance of remembering how absolutely independent S. Paul's testimony is. What he did and what he taught, he learned " neither from men nor by man," but by direct revelation from our LORD Himself. So that he was "no whit behind the chiefest Apostles" in his ability to say that he was teaching men " to observe whatsoever CHRIST had commanded him." And every witness of his, if I may so say, is therefore clear gain; so much extra light thrown on our LORD'S plan of teaching and work.

When S. Peter, in Samaria, preached the first Christian sermon in answer to that great question of the interested multitude, it always seemed to me that he told them to do *three* things and not *two;* that is to say, when he said, "*Repent and* be baptized, *and* ye shall receive the gift of the HOLY GHOST," I am quite sure he did not mean that the HOLY GHOST was to come to them in Holy Baptism.

Because, in the first place, when the news came to him of the conversion of the Samaritans, and of their baptism by Philip the Deacon, he and S. John went down immediately to Samaria, and " laid their hands on them, and they received the HOLY GHOST;" and S. Luke adds, by way of emphasis and explanation, " for as yet he was fallen upon none of them, *only* they were baptized." It seems to me an irresistible conclusion, therefore, that we have doctrine and practice side by side in S. Peter's sermon, " Ye *shall* receive the HOLY GHOST," and in S. Peter's act in the confirmation of the baptized Samaritans. And that this was not local, isolated, or temporary, one gathers from the fact that in speaking of the duty of receiving the HOLY GHOST, S. Peter says, " The promise to you *and* to your children, *and* to all that are afar off, even as many as the LORD our GOD shall call." I do not go into any argument, because it is needless, and out of place here, to prove that this laying on of hands was not for the conveyance of miraculous gifts alone. There are three things to be noted in such a transaction,—the gift, the sign, and the result. And they are all different. The gift is the HOLY GHOST; the sign is the laying on of hands; the result may be, or may not be, miraculous. Certainly, if one gathers anything from what S. Paul writes to the Corinthians (and nobody knew better than he the value of miraculous gifts), the manifestation of the SPIRIT is various; and the word of wisdom, the word of knowledge and faith, are put in the same catalogue with, and *put before*, healing and miracles and divers kinds of tongues.

Now take the other case. S. Paul, writing to the Hebrew Christians a description of what he calls the "principles of the *doctrine of* CHRIST," includes among the six, and as the fourth, the laying on of hands. What did he mean by it? Let him answer the question himself, and explain his teaching, as S. Peter explained his, by his practice. He went down to Ephesus, and finding twelve men there, believers so far as they had knowledge of the truth, he first taught them the doctrine of baptisms by his practice; that is, he showed them the difference between the merely formal and external rite of S. John the Baptist, and the spiritual and interior baptism which he gave them. And then *also* by his practice he taught them the doctrine of the laying on of hands, for he proceeded to confirm them, as we would say, just as S. Peter did at Jerusalem, and "they received the HOLY GHOST."

I go back now to the point from which I started. S. Paul calls this "a principle of the *doctrine of* CHRIST." He could only have known of it from CHRIST Himself. In like manner, S. Peter, as one of those who also "had the mind of CHRIST," acts in this matter, not *proprio motu*, but according to the teachings which he and the other Apostles had received during the years of intimate association before our LORD'S death, and during the great forty days which our LORD spent with the Apostles, principally "teaching them the things concerning the Kingdom of GOD;" and then by the motion of the HOLY SPIRIT, who was sent to "call to their remembrance" the things that CHRIST had taught them, in order that they might be both guarded and guided to fulfil the great commission; to teach baptized people "to observe all things whatsoever He had commanded them." Who shall presume to say that "this laying on of hands" was not one of the things which they were commanded to teach all baptized people to observe? If anybody objects to this that it makes Confirmation a Sacrament, I have only to say that this is no objection. The only objection would be for us as Churchmen, if we put it on a level with the two *great* Sacraments. For it is mere carelessness of speech not to remember that the only thing which this Church teaches is that CHRIST has ordained *only* two Sacraments as "generally *necessary* to salvation," which proves, *not* that Confirmation is *not* a Sacrament, but only that it is *not* necessary to salvation.

Under this presentation of the case, it does not seem to me that any words of mine are needed to bring the argument to the focal point of its application. If Confirmation is "a principle of the doctrine of CHRIST," and if its administration, by historical evidence, was confined to the Apostles, it stands to reason that the office appointed to administer it must necessarily be continued in the Church of CHRIST; and this is why we should expect to find what for convenience' sake is called the Historic Episcopate, perpetuated in the Church.

WILLIAM CROSWELL DOANE.

What is meant by the "Historic Episcopate" in the Resolutions of the House of Bishops in 1886, and the Lambeth Conference of 1888.

Right Rev. William Stevens Perry, D.D., LL.D., D.C.L. Bishop of Iowa and Historiographer of the American Church.

THE general acquiescence of Christian bodies and individuals in the first, second, and third resolutions proposed by the Lambeth Conference of 1888 as the basis of Christian reunion, leaves the fourth resolution as the one around which the controversy centres. What is the meaning of the Historic Episcopate referred to by the Bishops assembled at Lambeth, and earlier by the Bishops gathered at Chicago? It would seem from the various interpretations given to this phrase that it requires explanation and authoritative definition to remove ambiguity and emphasize its true meaning.

It is claimed that Churchmen themselves are not agreed as to the nature of the Historic Episcopate. It is said that "the Greek Church will not agree with the Roman" as to the Historic Episcopate, and that "neither of these will agree with the Anglican." In view of "this discord," it is asserted that the "Bishops, differing among themselves in their theory of the Episcopate, could not lay down a basis for the reunion of Christendom that would involve any particular theory of the Episcopate." It is further urged that "they could only mean that which was essential to the Historic Episcopate, — that to which divines like Hatch, Lightfoot, and Gore could agree."

The able and accomplished controversialist whose words we have cited, the Rev. Dr. Charles A. Briggs, of the Union Theological Seminary of the city of New York, adds to his deductions the following words: —

> The view that I have taken of the meaning of the Historic Episcopate as proposed by the House of Bishops and the Lambeth Conference as

the fourth term of union is confirmed by one who seems to speak with authority. Dr. Vincent, the Assistant-Bishop of Southern Ohio, tells us plainly, —

> Nothing is said here of Episcopacy as of Divine institution or necessity, nothing of 'Apostolic succession,' nothing of a Scriptural origin or a doctrinal nature in the institution. It is expressly proposed here only in its 'historical character' and as 'locally adapted to the varying needs of GOD'S people.' All else, unless it be its Scripturalness, is matter of opinion to which this Church has never formally committed herself. Her position here is the same broad and generous one taken in the Preface to her Ordinal. That phrase 'the Historic Episcopate,' was deliberately chosen as declaring not a doctrine, but a fact, and as being general enough to include all variants [1] [*An Address on Christian Unity*, p. 29].

"This platform," proceeds Dr. Briggs, "thus interpreted, is broad enough and strong enough for the feet of Presbyterians; and it contains nothing to which they can rightly object."

In other words, the non-Episcopal Churches are willing to consider and accept the Historic Episcopate, if it is regarded not as existing *jure divino*, but simply as *jure humano*, and as not essential to the existence of the Church, though as important for its well-being.

Elsewhere in the able and temperate article from which we have quoted, Dr. Briggs seems to consider the Historic Episcopate as related solely to the government and discipline of the Church; and he evidently regards the language of the Assistant-Bishop of Southern Ohio as conceding that the Historic Episcopate, as understood by the House of Bishops at Chicago and the Lambeth Conference, is to be regarded simply as being *jure humano*, and as "not essential to the existence of the Church," though "important for its well-being." He proceeds further to eliminate from the idea of the Historic Episcopate all claim to the existence of a threefold ministry, and all pretence that "Bishops had any exclusive Divine right or historic right to transmit the Episcopal Order." The Bishops of this Historic Episcopate are to "be simply the executive officers of the Church, chosen by the presbyteries." In other words, when the Historic Episcopate is made un-historic and un-Episcopal; when the term becomes synonymous with, and means no more than, the phrase of Dr. Briggs' coinage or adoption, "the Historic Presbyter," — then there will be Chris-

---

[1] It must be borne in mind that the Assistant-Bishop of Ohio was not a member of the House of Bishops in 1886, nor in attendance upon the Lambeth Conference of 1888.

tian union; for then *all will be Presbyterians*, a consummation, in the Professor's view, doubtless devoutly to be wished for.

We turn from such a *reductio ad absurdum* to the well-considered, and in our view unambiguous, words of the Lambeth resolution, reaffirming the language of the House of Bishops at Chicago: —

The Historic Episcopate, locally adapted in the methods of its administration to the varying needs of the nations and peoples called of GOD *into the unity of His Church.*

As present, and voting for this proposition, both in Chicago and at Lambeth, I am confident that I comprehend the nature of the resolution as it was understood by the great body of the Bishops in 1886; while from my clear recollections of the debates in 1888 at Lambeth, and from notes made at the time, as well as from the closest scrutiny of all that has subsequently appeared in print respecting this momentous discussion, about which more has been revealed than with regard to any other action of the Conference, I am confident that I can correctly represent and report what the Bishops at Lambeth said and did and meant.

That any theory or definition of the Historic Episcopate was intended by the American Bishops inconsistent with the call of GOD to all nations and peoples to *the unity of His Church*, is certainly untenable. That there was a Church — the Church of CHRIST, existing, visible, militant, upon the earth — was the belief of the great majority of the Bishops assembled at Chicago, if it was not the conviction of every member of this body. That the Historic Episcopate existed in direct, continuous succession from the Apostles' times; that the existence of the threefold ministry, Bishops, Priests, and Deacons, was to be traced to Apostolic days; and that as Lightfoot claimed, this " threefold ministry" can be traced to Apostolic direction, and, to quote the same great authority, that " short of an express statement, we can possess no better assurance of a Divine appointment, or at least a Divine sanction," [1] — was indisputably the conviction of every Bishop at Chicago and, we are confident, of every Bishop at Lambeth, with possibly two or three exceptions. That to this Church thus constituted, thus " built upon the foundation of the Apostles and Prophets, JESUS CHRIST Himself being the

---

[1] Lightfoot's *Dissertation on the Christian Ministry*, p. 265.

chief corner-stone," was promised the presence of its LORD and MASTER for all time to come, and "that from the Apostles' time there have been these Orders of Ministers in CHRIST'S Church, Bishops, Priests, and Deacons,"—we believe to be the conviction of every Bishop in the world. That for the return to unity of those long separated and estranged,—schismatics in fact, though often not in intent or even in guilt,—the Historic Episcopate, confessedly flexible in its administration, might be adapted to varied circumstances, even to the provision of a Bishop for every large centre of population—if this return to what Professor Briggs styles the "parochial Bishops" is desired; if this adaptation or accommodation of the Historic Episcopate might effect the longed-for return to unity,—this was the wish, the purpose, the prayer of the great body of the Chicago and the Lambeth Bishops. Views inconsistent with this understanding of the proposition were not even breathed by any Bishop at Chicago. If the words then adopted in the mind of any Bishop committed, or seemed to commit, the Church to the *jure humano* theory of the Historic Episcopate and the threefold ministry, it is a matter of history that such a conception was rigorously repressed. No one of the Bishops uttered, no one urged such a view of the Historic Episcopate as that deduced by Dr. Briggs from the language of the Lambeth resolution or as this resolution is interpreted by the Assistant-Bishop of Southern Ohio. Such a view of the Historic Episcopate would certainly have stultified our very position as Bishops of the Church of GOD, and would have committed the House to a revolutionary scheme at variance not alone with history, with precedent, with fact, but with the Constitution of the American Church, with our Ordinal, with our constant canonical practice of reordaining all applicants for Holy Orders not already Episcopally ordained, and with our consecration vows. Nor this alone. Action predicated on such a view of the Historic Episcopate as is deduced by Dr. Briggs from the Chicago-Lambeth resolution would widen the breach now existing between the Reformed Churches of the Anglican Communion claiming the Episcopal succession and inviting the fullest investigation as to the validity of their claim,—a claim in these latest days of historical research put forth by Lightfoot and admitted by Von Dollinger, and the Churches of Latin Christendom as well as those of the East. The comprehension of the Greek and Latin Churches into this unity of GOD's Church seems in no way a matter of concern to Dr. Briggs. In his desire to minimize the conception of the Historic Episcopate, to make it practically another form of Presbyterianism, Dr. Briggs would commit the Bishops to a concession that the Church's position on this point has been for years more than a blunder, practically a sin. Nor is this all. Were terms of union such as Dr. Briggs deduces from the Lambeth resolution seriously entertained by the Anglican Bishops, the non-Episcopal Christian organizations would lose the only possible means of ever comprehending in the united, the Catholic, the universal Church of CHRIST the communion of all saints everywhere in the world, that vast majority of Christians who recognize Episcopacy as a fact, and therefore as a rule. Even in the United States, which seems to bound the horizon of Dr. Briggs' vision, with the adoption of Presbyterianism, the reduction of the historic Bishop to a simple presbyter, the rejection of the Apostolical succession, the disuse of the threefold ministry, the denial of the grace of Orders, the sundering of the tie binding the Bishop, Priest, and Deacon to the Shepherd and Bishop of souls, — to Him who was also an Elder, to Him who came as a Deacon to minister, — the strife with Rome would be ended, but ended in an ignominious surrender of that which alone, even in the view of intelligent Romanists themselves, makes the Anglican Church and its American daughter the possible ground for the reunion of all Christendom. Nor would union with the great body of Latin Christianity alone be impossible. The Greek Church, which has drawn nearer and nearer to us of late, the Old Catholics, the Jansenists, and all the Churches of the East with whom Episcopacy is both a law and a fact, would be repelled from us forever.

So far from conceding to Dr. Briggs that the *jure divino* theory has been "slain by historical criticism," and that the New Testament affords no proof of the three Orders of the ministry, we affirm quite the opposite opinion. We submit in defence of our position the well-considered words of the late Bishop of Durham, Dr. Lightfoot, whose position Dr. Briggs seems unable to comprehend. Starting with this great scholar's statement that " history seems to show decisively that before the middle of the second century each Church, or organized Christian community, had its three Orders of ministers, — its Bishops, its Presbyters, and its Deacons," — and emphasizing his further assertion that " on this point there cannot reasonably be two opinions," it is easy, with Lightfoot as our guide, to reconstruct the *jure divino* claim for the Historic Episcopate, as including the threefold ministry and the Apostolical succession. Commenting on the position occupied by S. James, the brother of the LORD, in the Church of Jerusalem, Bishop Lightfoot states his conviction that " he was not one of the twelve," and proceeds to assert that " the Episcopal office thus existed in the Mother Church of Jerusalem from very early days, at least in a rudimentary form ; " while the government of the Gentile Churches, though presenting, in the Bishop's view, no distinct traces of a similar organization, exhibits " stages of development tending in this direction." Nor is this all. The same great authority assumes that the position occupied by Timothy and Titus, whom he characterizes as " Apostolic-delegates," and whom Gore regards as " Apostolic men," " fairly " — we are citing Lightfoot's conclusions — " represents the functions of the Bishop early in the second century." Even admitting with Lightfoot — whose scrupulous anxiety " not to overstate the evidence in any case " led him (to quote his own words) to use " partial and qualifying statements prompted by this anxiety," which, as he expressly states, " assumes undue proportions in the minds of some," even " to the neglect of the general drift of the essay "[1] — that " James, the LORD'S brother, alone within the period compassed by Apostolic writings can claim to be regarded as a Bishop in the later and more special sense of the term," it is evident that he regards this instance of the exercise of the Episcopal office in " very early days," even in the New Testament period, as unquestionable. Conceding with Lightfoot that " as late, therefore, as the year 70 no distinct signs of Episcopal government have appeared in Gentile Christendom," we must acknowledge, in the language of the same authority, that " unless we have recourse to a sweeping condemnation of received documents, it seems vain to deny that early in the second century the Episcopal office was firmly and widely established. . . . *Thus during the last three decades of the first century, and consequently during the lifetime of the latest surviving Apostles, this change must have been brought about.*" And again: " These notices, besides establishing the general prevalence of Episcopacy, . . . establish this

[1] *Dissertation on the Christian Ministry.*

result clearly, that its maturer forms are seen first in those regions where the latest surviving Apostles, more especially S. John, fixed their abode, and at a time when its prevalence cannot be dissociated from their influence and sanction." With this cumulative presentation of the proofs of the Historic Episcopate from the writings of the leading scholar of the age, we may well cite his summing up of the whole matter in these pregnant words: "If the preceding investigation is substantially correct, the threefold ministry can be traced to Apostolic direction; and short of an express statement, we can possess no better assurance of a Divine appointment, or at least a Divine sanction." To these words the same great scholar, not long before his lamented death, added the further assertion in his sermon before the Wolverhampton Church Congress that the Church of England (and consequently the American Church) has "retained a form of Church government which has been handed down in unbroken continuity from the Apostles' times." That this view of the Historic Episcopate, the threefold ministry, and the Church, was and is the view of the major part of the Anglican Episcopate may be inferred from the fact that it is in accord with the language of the Ordinal, with the requirement of Episcopal ordination found in the Prayer-Book and in the Canons, and especially with the action of the Lambeth Conference, which, so far from approving the proposal of the late Metropolitan of Sydney, Dr. Barry, now Suffragan of Rochester, speaking for the Bishop of S. Andrew's, Dr. Charles Wordsworth, to admit temporarily and with a view to the promotion of Christian union the validity of non-Episcopal Orders, refused by a decisive vote even to receive the report containing this revolutionary suggestion. It is not too much to assert that the scheme of recognition — even for a time, and that too with a view to the speedy subsequent discontinuance of all distinctively Presbyterian or non-Episcopal ordination whatever — of any other ordination than that received at the hands of Bishops would, had it obtained the votes of the Conference, have tended to the immediate disruption of the Church. Such is the outspoken assertion of a writer, presumably the learned Bishop of Edinburgh, Dr. Dowden, in an able article on this subject in the *(English) Church Quarterly Review*. It is certain that it would have occasioned the immediate withdrawal from the Conference of a large number of the assembled Bishops, and those too the most noted for general learning, for labors for the cause and Church of CHRIST, and for theological acumen and lore. None present, it has been said, will forget the flashing of the brilliant eyes, the contemptuous curl of the lips, the indignant scorn of expression, and the eager gesture of dissent, with which the proposal of this recognition of non-Episcopal Orders by a side wind, and the historical illustrations with which it was attempted to bolster up this plan, were impatiently listened to by the one man of vast historical learning, and the one chief authority for the constitutional history of England, and of the English Church, which the Conference contained.[1] It was in this connection, and during the debate on this report, that the Bishop of Durham, showing in his voice and manner that the hand of death was already upon him, took occasion in his expression of unqualified opposition to this scheme to " disclaim wholly the interpretation which the Bishop of S. Andrew's " had " put upon his words," as well as " the interpretation given them by Presbyterian controversialists." The Bishop proceeded to say, and no one who was present can forget the impressiveness of his words: " It is sometimes convenient to extract one sentence from a long essay, all of which is meant to hinge together, and to use that sentence for a purpose." It was a testimony to the threefold ministry and the Historic Episcopate then and there solemnly pronounced which but a few days later this distinguished scholar and prelate reiterated in his address at the reopening of the historic S. Peter's Chapel at Auckland Castle. The American Bishops, with but a single exception, spoke or voted against the reception of this report. And the testimony of the young and heroic Bickersteth of Japan as to the " fatal effects " of such action " on the work in the mission fields; " his further warning, " If you want vigorous self-sacrifice for the Church abroad, you must not shake the foundations of the Church at home;" and his prophetic words, " It will have no influence; it will be of no avail ; the converts from heathenism claim validity and regularity," — added to the almost unanimous verdict of the Conference against this measure. So strongly was this the conviction of the Conference that it felt called upon to vary its ordinary mode of procedure, and ordered the report to be recommitted with what was practically a direction to excise the

---

[1] The then Bishop of Chester, Dr. William Stubbs, since translated to Oxford. VIDE *Church Quarterly Review*.

proposition for this temporary recognition of non-Episcopal Orders, originating from the Bishop of S. Andrew's, and supported by the present Suffragan of Rochester.

The verdict of Von Döllinger on this episode in the proceedings of the Conference is thus expressed: —

Even the unfortunate attempt to unsettle so fundamental a principle as the indispensableness of the Episcopate to the transmission of the ministerial character and commission, by its complete failure supplied a useful illustration of the general temper of the Conference. It was the passing shadow which enabled us the better to do justice to the landscape.

The absolute and peremptory refusal by an overwhelming majority even so much as to entertain a proposition that seemed to set at nought such an essential characteristic of the Church's Apostolic organization as the Historic Episcopate, in the fullest sense and meaning, must be considered as affording sufficient answer to such unwarranted interpretations of the Lambeth resolution as are stated by Dr. Briggs and supported by the authority of the Assistant-Bishop of Southern Ohio. Our longings for union must not lead us to the surrender of the great trust committed to us as an integral part of the Church Catholic of CHRIST. Concessions involving disloyalty to revealed truths, to Apostolic practice, and to primitive belief, are out of the question. It is not to be expected that the great and overwhelming majority of Christians now living on the earth should abandon the form of Church government which has been theirs "from the Apostles' time," and which they believe to be *jure divino*, with a view of comprehending in their Communion a few most excellent and devoted Christian bodies or individuals who practically recognize no visible Church, who deny the existence of the threefold ministry, who refuse to admit the claims of the Historic Episcopate, and who will not concede the grace of Holy Orders. Thus abandoning the Church's vantage ground, we might, indeed, add to our numbers a small gain, but we should lose the greater possibilities which may GOD, in His good time, enable us to realize in the reunion of Christendom, — the bringing together of all Christian men and peoples in the unity of GOD'S Church.

WILLIAM STEVENS PERRY.

The Historic Episcopate.

Right Rev. George Franklin Seymour, D.D., LL.D.,
Bishop of Springfield.

It is evident unto all men diligently reading Holy Scripture, and ancient Authors, that from the Apostles' time there have been these Orders of Ministers in CHRIST's Church, — Bishops, Priests, and Deacons. Which Offices were evermore had in such reverend Estimation, that no man might presume to execute any of them, except he were first called, tried, examined, and known to have such qualities as are requisite for the same; and also by public Prayer, with Imposition of Hands, were approved and admitted thereunto by lawful Authority. And therefore, to the intent that these Orders may be continued, and reverently used and esteemed in this Church, no man shall be accounted or taken to be a lawful Bishop, Priest, or Deacon in this Church, or suffered to execute any of the said Functions, except he be called, tried, examined, and admitted thereunto, according to the Form hereafter following, or hath had Episcopal Consecration or Ordination. — *Preface to the Ordinal of the Book of Common Prayer.*

Extract from the Canons.

Title 1. Canon 14. No Minister in charge of any Congregation of this Church, or, in case of vacancy or absence, no Churchwardens, Vestrymen, or Trustees of the Congregation, shall permit any person to officiate therein, without sufficient evidence of his being duly licensed, or ordained to minister in this Church: *Provided,* that nothing herein shall be so construed as to forbid communicants of the Church to act as Lay Readers.

I IMAGINE myself surrounded by at least fifty gentlemen, representing as many different Churches, and each and all claiming that their Churches are respectively the most excellent way, if not exclusively the only way, of salvation, so far as we know, opened and prepared by CHRIST. These gentlemen have spoken at greater or less length on the subject of Christian unity, and have spoken well, and in excellent spirit and temper; and now the floor is conceded to me for a brief space, and I am called upon to address the assembly present, and through them an immense concourse beyond, of Christian brethren of every shade and variety of opinion.

I feel the weight of the responsibility which rests upon me as the champion of what I believe to be the truth; and I am anxious to improve my opportunity to the best advantage to my brethren.

I would, therefore, as far as I can, at the outset, remove prejudice and conciliate kind attention and consideration. Of course I am speaking for myself alone, although I am convinced I express the mind of the Church at whose altars I serve, as the humblest of her ministers, and to whose lawful judgment in this discussion, as in all similar matters, I meekly submit myself.

Again, I must be very brief upon a subject immense in itself, upon which hundreds of books have been written, and which, beside its general interest, is in certain aspects of its relation to Christian unity pressed upon our notice at the present time with great ability by those who have preceded me. I can hope therefore to do little more than write what the lawyers would call "a brief," and my brethren who preach, "sermon notes." I am the more willing to be reconciled to this, to me at least, unsatisfactory presentation of my case in this "symposium," to which we have been so courteously and hospitably invited by the CHURCH REVIEW, because I can respectfully ask my brethren one and all, as I now do, to listen to me at much greater length in a paper prepared at the request of the Church Unity Society, and published and circulated by their liberality.

Addressing myself then at once to the subject-matter before us, and with a view to clear the ground of that prejudice which arises in most cases, I am persuaded, from misapprehension, I would state that I am convinced that Holy Scripture and ancient authors and the universal practice of Christendom for fifteen hundred years, interpreting that Scripture, teach that CHRIST left an *official ministry to represent Him* until He shall come again at the end of the world to judge the quick and the dead; and further that He accredits this ministry to mankind after it has once been instituted and established, not by miraculous attestation at every fresh appointment, but by the only other method by which an office can be perpetuated when intrusted to creatures who must die; namely, by the *principle* of *succession*. This is the way in which all human governments of whatever kind are continued while they last in this world. I make this general statement now, because it explains at once my relation to my fifty brethren around me, and the scores outside who stand on the same ground with them, in refusing the Episcopate as the channel through which official authority and power pass. The moment I place the ministry of CHRIST on this basis, — namely, of official relation, — no rational or sane man can complain that he is slighted, or treated with disrespect, because he is not asked to perform, or to attempt to perform, the functions of office to which he can lay no claim. I may be in error as regards my conviction of the character of the Christian ministry, — that is an entirely different question, and my brethren may be able to show me my mistake; but while I conscientiously believe as I do, I cannot be justly charged with presumption or exclusiveness or narrowness or disrespect, because I do not invite my brethren to attempt to do what I am persuaded they have no right to do if they could, and am satisfied they cannot do if they would.

Would any one feel aggrieved if he were the guest of the Governor of the State, and was not asked to put his signature to pardons, or Acts of the Legislature? Would he in such a case consider that a slight was put upon his penmanship? Could any one with justice cry out, "Narrow, bigoted, exclusive!" if he, without being invested with the office, were to insist upon discharging the duties of any department of the civil service of our country, and in consequence was not allowed to do so? Would such prohibition raise any question as to his social standing, his learning, his excellence in character and morals? Could any one in reason take offence at the Governor or the Mayor or any other official person neglecting, or declining to do what he could not lawfully do? This is precisely in my judgment our relation to our brethren who refuse from whatever cause Episcopal ordination. The Preface to our Ordinal formulates the doctrine, and our Canons enjoin the practice.

I assure our brethren that this refusal to permit them to minister at our altars and officiate in our Churches is with me and such as agree with me, — and we are persuaded that whoever will read our Ordinal and our Canons will be convinced that we represent the mind of the Church, — this refusal is no question of comity or good-breeding; *it is simply a question of principle.* It cannot possibly be construed, if the Church's position be understood, as reflecting in any way upon our brethren, save and excepting as regards their lack of official character. We are ready to concede to them everything, — intelligence, learning, culture, piety, good works, the Christian graces; but we cannot allow, as we read GOD'S Word, and are instructed by GOD'S Church, — we cannot allow that they have received and hold the office which qualifies them to represent GOD, act in GOD'S stead. In this conviction we may be mistaken; but while we remain thus convinced, we plead that our Church and we are guilty of no incivility in not compromising our principles and stultifying ourselves before GOD and our fellow-men.

Suppose we drop from this position, and say, as some do, that Episcopacy is not of the essence of the ministry, that it is merely a preferred form out of many, and that all are good, but that this is the best, — then I admit on this assumption that our non-Episcopal brethren can make good their charge that it is an impertinence and an affront for us to decline to exchange with their ministers on terms of perfect equality. For those who take this ground, I have no plea to make; their attitude toward our brethren without is, as it seems to me, most offensive, as it makes non-recognition a mere caprice of human legislation, *and rests it upon no principle whatsoever.* Their attitude toward their own Communion is worse than offensive; it is insulting, since it virtually proclaims that they are better than their own Church, of which by voluntary act they became sworn servants, pledging themselves by solemn vow to do her bidding and obey her laws. Let us hope that such — we trust that they are very few — are so carried away by the desire to be liberal and broad and popular that they become blind to the effect of their own conduct, and can no longer see themselves as others see them. I entreat our brethren to be convinced that our Ordinal and our Canons place the matter on its true basis, — *that of principle,* — and that we mean no more offence to them in declining to ask them to officiate in our Churches than the President of the United States does in failing to ask, or if requested so to do, in refusing to allow others to share with him in the discharge of the duties of the executive mansion. It is no discourtesy; it is no incivility; it is simply an impossibility.

In reference to "the Historic Episcopate," which I represent, it is my duty, as it is my pleasure, to say to my fifty or one hundred or two hundred brethren, representing as many different systems of doctrine or practice, each claiming to be the best, as it ought, if not the only system for the religious training of man, — it is my duty and my pleasure to say to them: " Gentlemen, brethren, as we stand here before the world the busy world, absorbed in the present, ignorant of the past, we are antecedently, before a word is uttered by any of us in our own behalf, *all on an equality* No one of us can claim precedence over his companions by virtue of self-assertion, which will be for one moment listened to by the public. Can we find a test, then, which will be alike fair to all, and which can be at once understood and appreciated by all? I think we can. Certainly, if our ecclesiastical systems are, as we think, the ecclesiastical systems established by CHRIST and vindicated as His by Holy Scripture and the practice of His Apostles, then they ought to have clear, distinct, and unmistakable organic connection through the ages all along with CHRIST and His Apostles. For we cannot conceive that our LORD'S pledge and promise would fail; and we have His express word that 'the gates of hell shall not prevail against His Church.' We cannot conceive that His Church, organized and established by Himself, would soon disappear, like a subterranean stream, and remain hidden from human eye and human knowledge for fifteen hundred years, and then reappear to gladden mankind with its presence. We cannot believe that the golden chain of ministry, sacrament, and practice, forged and constructed by the Divine hand, was attached to the staple, CHRIST, and then, after a few links were added, was suddenly broken off and dropped, and disappeared to sight and sense for ages, and then was found, or was claimed to be found, by one and another, each in his own way, and on the responsibility of his own unsupported assertion. We cannot believe this, and can scarcely comprehend how any one else can believe it; hence I propose as a test to my brethren that we shall all in the sight of the great public embark in the ship 'History,' and sail away from the present moment back into the distant past; that our haven shall be the Mount of the Ascension, and our risen LORD, standing there in our glorified humanity, ready to enter heaven and occupy the throne of GOD; that we shall sail thither, if we can, that we may attach what we each severally claim to be the golden chain of CHRIST'S Church to His Divine Person, and vindicate its authenticity and unbroken continuity in the sight of the world, since all can watch our voyage, as we recede from the shore and pass through the waves of years and centuries to the august hour when the great Head of the Church gave His charter to His deputies, to act under Him and on His behalf, and made provision for the continuance of their office until He should come again at the end of the world. Of course, as we go back, and come to the date when our respective systems first appear, we necessarily leave the ship; we cannot claim to be passengers before we were born." If this test be accepted, and I cannot see why it is not perfectly just, then we must all present ourselves upon the deck, a great crowd, in the sight of those now living, and bid them good-by, as we take our departure, and start upon our voyage into the past. The test begins to operate forthwith, and thin out our goodly company. It is surprising that the first to disappear is one whom we would scarcely have expected to go so soon; it is no less a Communion than the Church of Rome. She is the latest sect of any importance among the divisions of Christendom. She broke away from her own past and Catholic polity in the year 1870. Then by formal act she disowned CHRIST'S charter, which vests the government of His Church in a *corporation*, and superseded it by a charter of human invention, her own, which converts His government into *a monarchy*. This is *revolution*, — a new departure and a novel invention. It changes a branch of the Catholic Church into a sect, as it violates and practically repeals the fundamental organic law of that Church, the Body of CHRIST. It is not development in any sense of that term; it is revolution, pure and simple. I am well aware that the *pious opinions*, as they were called, concerning the supremacy and infallibility of the Pope, had grown to be almost universal in the Roman Communion prior to 1870, but they were not required as of faith. Then at that date these pious opinions were formulated into dogmas, added to an already enlarged Creed, and enjoined upon the faithful to be believed under pain of excommunication. From that moment the Church of Rome, I claim, broke with *her own past*, and with the polity of the co-ordinate Apostolate, continued in the co-ordinate Episcopate as established by our LORD, and became *a sect*. She is therefore the first to leave us. In succession others must follow, sometimes singly, sometimes in companies of two and three, until at length the decks are deserted, and in A. D. 1500, those who own " the Historic Episcopate " are left alone upon the ship.

We reach, as I firmly believe, our haven, the Mount of the Ascension, and our object, CHRIST. In our presence, — that is, in the presence of the eleven Apostles, whom we succeed and represent, — we hear Him proclaim and enjoin His charter, as of perpetual obligation, in these words preserved for us by the HOLY GHOST: "All power is given unto Me in heaven and in earth; go ye therefore, and teach all nations, baptizing them in the NAME of the FATHER, and of the SON, and of the HOLY GHOST; teaching them to observe all things whatsoever I have commanded you: and lo, I am with you alway, even unto the end of the world" [S. Matt. xxviii. 18–20]. Here we have clearly brought out into bold relief: (a) *The source and channel of the power;* namely, from the GODHEAD through our perfected humanity in the person of the eternal SON. (b) *The extent of the power*, its plenitude, "all power in heaven and in earth." (c) *The form of government*, the *politeia*, under which the delegated power was to be exercised, — a corporation, not a monarchy; eleven men, not one; all the Apostles, not S. Peter; no one before the others, but all abreast, on an equality, in co-ordination; they are addressed throughout, without any distinction or difference, in the *plural number*. (d) *The extent of the jurisdiction of the government*, thus vested in a corporaration, *as to space*, the whole earth, "all nations." (e) *Its duration* as to time, "always, unto the end of the world." (f) *The purposes* of the government, the ministry of the Word and Sacraments, teaching in its widest sense, baptism, and "the breaking of the bread," for this was one of the things which JESUS commanded. (g) *The limitations* under which these delegated powers of government were to be exercised, *first*, in dependence upon the Divine Head, — "lo, I am with you alway, even unto the end of the world." *Second*, in mutual dependence upon each other, they are not to go off on their own individual lines, each by himself; they are to act in co-ordination. They received from their Divine Master *jointly;* and they and their successors are always to hold and exercise and hand on what they received *jointly*. *Third*, they were restrained as to what they were to teach and do. They must keep within the bounds of CHRIST'S prescription, "teaching them," He says, "to observe all things *whatsoever I have commanded you.*" Not what they pleased, but what He willed; not their own inventions, but His commands. (h) And finally this corporation, thus created, *was official*, not personal in its character, since our Blessed LORD expressly pledges Himself that He will shelter it with His presence forever: "Lo, I am with you alway, even unto the end of the world."

That CHRIST intended an office to be understood by His words is clearly shown by the action and language of these very Apostles who heard Him utter them. Within ten days afterward they filled the vacancy of Judas by the choice of S. Matthias; and in doing so, they contemplate a vacant office and quote the Blessed SPIRIT, speaking by the prophet, as a witness of the fact. S. Peter says, referring to Judas, "He was numbered with us, and had obtained *part of this ministry*" [Acts i. 17]. And still further, as the reason for choosing S. Matthias: "For it is written in the book of Psalms, Let his habitation be desolate, and let no man dwell therein; and his bishoprick [margin, — *office*, or *charge*] let another take" [Acts i. 20]. Here, then, we have the co-ordinate Apostolate, the highest and as yet the only Order in the Christian ministry, if we may anticipate the use of the phrase before the Church was born, waiting for the day of Pentecost to exercise their office, as soon as by Divine permission, in the reception of the HOLY SPIRIT, " the promise of the FATHER," they had the sign from above that they were allowed to act. The Church began her career with the *highest* Order of the ministry, the Apostles, who possessed *all the powers* necessary for the government and administration of CHRIST'S flock. After a time there came development, but it *was downward, not upward*. This statement needs to be repeated, because there are few points upon which there has arisen greater misconception than there has upon this. We are told that the Church started out with parity of Orders, and that in the time of Tertullian we have the *summus sacerdos*, and a little later the Cyprianic Bishop; and so human ambition manifests itself in developing the ministry *upward* until it reaches prelacy. Now all this, except the original parity of Orders, is purely imaginary; it is directly contrary to the recorded facts. It is true the ministry, as CHRIST left the earth, and as the day of Pentecost found it, was in *one Order*, but it was the *highest, and not the lowest*, and was endowed with all the powers necessary for the government and administration of the Church until the return of the Divine Head at the last great day. There came development very soon under the direction and at the hands of the highest Order, the Apostles. It was a development *downward* in the Deacon and the Elder or Presbyter or Bishop. These *three Orders* complete the Christian ministry in its fully developed form, and as such, I believe, it was intended to represent, and does represent, CHRIST officially, — CHRIST in His *three* offices of Prophet, Priest, and King.

Equally fallacious is the theory that at first we have parochial Episcopacy, or parity of Orders, or Presbyterian Church government, and then without the survival of any protest, we have this alleged original primitive Divine system supplanted by Diocesan Episcopacy; and then this passes by the law of development into *Popery*. I must demur to this sketch of a supposed transition upward from parity to Popery by remarking that it is contrary to GOD'S Word, that it makes Presbyterianism responsible not only for prelacy, but also for Popery, since it will be observed that Episcopacy is simply a stage of transition through which the seeds of error and abuse inherent in Presbyterianism pass in their growth to their flower and fruit in Romanism. Now I am willing to allow that the system of John Calvin is responsible for a great deal which had far better never have been; but I must insist that it is innocent of this alleged offence. The parity of Orders provided by CHRIST for His Church before she was born, protects her by Divine metes and bounds against this process of centralization reaching its culmination in placing all authority and power *in one*. CHRIST reserves that place and that dignity for Himself alone. He blocks the way against such an impious and sacrilegious invasion of the prerogatives of His throne on high by interposing His Apostolate, — a corporation of eleven men, passing officially into the Historic Episcopate as the nearest permitted approach to Him on earth and in time in His offices. The Apostolate, and its official equivalent, the Episcopate, is the great invincible foe of Rome. She has no place in her present polity for either, save as a name, the shadow of a reality, which she has expelled from her system.

The demand is often made by our brethren to show them Diocesan Episcopacy in the New Testament. This demand, I am confident, is urged without reflection. Diocesan Episcopacy presents for our contemplation an essential thing, with its accidents. The office, Episcopacy, is the *essential thing;* Diocesan embraces the *accidents*. I am not contending for the accidents, but for the essential thing. The Church was not born on the day of Pentecost clad with her beautiful garments, with a numerous laity ready for organization, with buildings prepared for occupancy, and all the instruments of public worship waiting to be used. All that she possessed in the way of equipment for work by direct Divine appointment and gift were the old economy, soon to vanish away, as a witness, in spite of the Jews, of the truth of the new economy of CHRIST, the Old Testament Scriptures, testifying of JESUS and His Body the Church, and the Apostolate, His deputies, viceroys representing Him to the fullest extent that He vouchsafed to be represented on earth and in time, and whose seed was in itself to perpetuate itself and develop itself under the guidance of the HOLY GHOST in inferior Orders of Presbyter and Deacon. This was what was supplied to the Church at her birth for the work which she was given to do. It was the business of her duly accredited Apostolate and the ministries which they called into being to create a laity by preaching and the administration of the Sacraments, to govern them and organize them ultimately into a normal ecclesiastical system, to provide a statement of doctrine as a security against fundamental error, and to complete or superintend the completion of the records of revelation in the addition of the New Testament to the Old. Diocesan Episcopacy came afterward, or if it began to exist in the Apostles' time, it was in exceptional cases, where the circumstances were favorable for a settled order of things, as in Jerusalem and Ephesus. The Apostles were never Diocesan Bishops in our modern sense of the term. Their jurisdiction and work bring them more nearly to our pioneer missionary Bishops, such as Selwyn in New Zealand, and the heroic men who are taking in charge at the present time vast tracts of savage Africa. The Apostles, it is often said, can have no successors, and hence Bishops cannot inherit from them. In their personal relations to our LORD as chosen by Him, as living with Him during His ministry, as witnesses of His death and resurrection, this is perfectly true; and no one, except possibly the Irvingites, would be, so far as I know, disposed to deny it. But aside from their *personal* relation to our LORD, the Apostles were invested by Him with an office; and this office He tells us with the last words which He uttered on earth He saw passing down the ages, and so seeing it, He promised to be with it to the end of the world. In reference to this office our contention is that the Apostles have successors. George Washington in his *personal* relation to these United States, as the Commander-in-chief of the army during our Revolutionary struggle, who under GOD brought the war to a successful termination,—George Washington, "the Father of his Country," can have no successors; but George Washington in his *official* relation to this Republic, thank GOD, has successors. He was not only the Father of his Country, but he was also the President of the United States. It is the office which passes, not the personality.

But I hear the murmur, "The name 'episcopos,' bishop, was in the New Testament applied to *the second Order*, who served under the Apostles, and were also called Elders, Presbyters;" and hence I am told, "The nomenclature of the New Testament is against you, and the allegation for which you stand,—that the Historic Episcopate carries on the Apostolic office, and brings it down to us." My contention is not about words, but about things. I freely admit that the name "episcopos" was used at first to describe an Elder. But am I to tell my brethren, as an unheard-of thing, that in the course of time words have been known to change their meaning and their applications? That "parish," for example, and "diocese" in ecclesiastical language mean very different things to our ears from what they did to S. Basil. What I maintain is that the Divine records plainly show us that the Apostles had co-laborers working with them in the same office, and that under them and their colleagues there were, besides, two distinct Orders of Divine appointment as created by them, who acted by direction of the HOLY GHOST; and that then writers who were contemporaries with the Apostles supplement the teaching of Holy Scripture by showing us that universally the Church in their day put the practical interpretation upon GOD'S Word that its meaning was that the sacred ministry was constituted in three Orders,—those, namely, of Bishop, Presbyter, and Deacon,—and that the ministry was continued by succession at the hands of the *first* or *highest Order*.

This gives me a living Church, bound together in time as one by a network of innumerable strands, crossing and recrossing one another until thought is confused in contemplating the greatness of the security which Apostolic and Nicene Canons give us to guard the continuity of Holy Orders. The succession is not the succession of links in a chain, to be counted one by one, nor as our lineal descent to be reckoned back by a multiple of two, but beyond this, the succession brings in at each remove an increase multiplied by three. But then there comes the cry, "Tactual succession!" It is not a murmur; it is a derisive cry, "Tactual succession, can that convey grace?" I answer yes, if GOD so wills; and I am fully convinced that He does so will, because He rules the New Dispensation, our Christian system, by the law of the *Incarnation*,— the law, namely, that GOD in the person of His Eternal SON comes to us through *the agency of matter*,— and hence I would anticipate, as I find verified in the event, that all subordinate blessings, so far as I know, in His Kingdom, and all other blessings, are subordinate to the gift of JESUS CHRIST, are conveyed to me through *the instrumentality of matter*. Indeed, I will venture to ask my friends who seem to be so shocked at the idea of tactual succession conveying spiritual gifts,— I will ask them to name to me a single blessing which they have ever possessed in the spheres of body, mind, or spirit, which has been bestowed upon them without the intervention of matter. I frankly state that, so far as I am concerned, I know of none. The Historic Episcopate, I am told, includes in its roll of countless names many bad men, and the Church which they represent has been at times and for long periods depraved and vile. Alas! the charge is only too sadly true. But what is that supposed to prove? Surely not that the wicked rulers and bad people destroy GOD'S Church; if so, then under the old covenant GOD'S Church must have come to nought many times; but not so, it survived the profanity of Aaron's and Eli's sons, the degeneracy of the days of Elijah, and the awful impiety of the epoch of the captivity. Such reasoning is fallacious and misleading, and must not be listened to for one moment. The Prophets refute it, and our Blessed LORD settles the matter, when He draws the distinction between the office and the persons who hold it, and demands respect and obedience for the one, and solemnly warns against the other. Addressing the multitude and His disciples, JESUS says, "The scribes and the Pharisees sit in Moses' seat: all therefore whatsoever they bid you observe, that observe and do; but do not ye after their works: for they say and do not " [S. Matt. xxiii. 2, 3]. Elsewhere He draws the character of these same scribes and Pharisees in the darkest colors, and denounces them with the severest maledictions. The same observation applies to all that the Church hands on and down to us,— the imperfections, nay, the monstrous sins of individual members, or even of large portions of the flock, do not necessarily vitiate and destroy the heritage thus transmitted. The Nicene Creed is not in the least degree affected by the disgraceful character and conduct of some members of the Council of Nice and the corruption of the fourth century. It is not without its purpose for persons who insist that the channel through which Divine gifts come to us must be as pure as the gifts themselves, to study the genealogy of our Blessed LORD as presented by S. Matthew, and find, as they will, that "Judas begat Phares and Zara of Thamar," and farther on, that "Salmon begat Booz of Rachab." It would not be unprofitable for such persons to reflect that their logic, if they are consistent, will compel them to affix their signatures to the dogma of the Immaculate Conception of the Blessed Virgin Mary.

While speaking of the Creeds, another matter presses: I find that some of my brethren object to the Apostles' Creed, *first*, on the ground that in its present form it is of later date than the Apostles; *second*, that it is an imperfect or incomplete statement of Divine truth; and *third*, that it contains the article, "He descended into hell," which some of them tell us they do not believe, because when our LORD went to hell, or hades, He went *up*, not *down*. To remove these difficulties, if possible, let me suggest that the Divine records prove that the Apostles at the very outset must have formulated their teaching into some condensed form which could be easily recited and retained in memory, since we learn [Acts ii. 42] that the believers baptized on the day of Pentecost "continued in the Apostles' *doctrine*." It is not pretended that the Apostles' Creed as we have it now is precisely in so many words the same form which the Apostles prepared and taught to their converts; but it is substantially the same, and their name is very properly given to the Creed, because it represents the essentials of their teaching. This practice is so common that it scarcely needs illustration; "Ciceronian Latin," "the Athanasian Creed," "the Monroe Doctrine," will serve as examples in as many different spheres of human affairs, — literature, religion, and politics.

That the Apostles' Creed is incomplete as a protection against heresy is shown by the presence of the Nicene, and in some branches of the Church of the Athanasian Creed. These together formulate the doctrine relative to the Blessed Trinity, the person and natures of CHRIST, the Divinity and personality of the HOLY SPIRIT, the Church and her notes, and the necessary things which the Incarnation secures for mankind, — the forgiveness of sins, the resurrection of the body, and the life everlasting. The purpose of the Creeds was to keep the essentials of the Faith ever present in the memories and ever fresh upon the lips of believers; and hence they were incorporated into the offices of Matins and Evensong and into the Divine Liturgy. They were made a part of public worship. Their recitation aloud secured that confession with the mouth which GOD expects, nay, demands from those who believe with the heart. The Creeds are incomplete, as setting forth schemes of theology, or as some would express it, bodies of divinity. They were never designed to do this; but as it is, they teach vastly more than the superficial Christian imagines, and they imply vastly more than they teach.

The illustration of this last remark brings me to what some of our friends very seriously and earnestly object to; the article, namely, "He descended into hell." A very distinguished member of the company whom I am primarily addressing, uses this to me most astounding language: "I deem the Apostles' Creed wrong in saying that our LORD *descended* into hell, or hades. He went to *Paradise;* and when Paul went to Paradise, he was caught *up*. I believe that article of the Apostles' Creed was derived from a false interpretation of 1 S. Peter iii. 19 in the third century." The words under consideration — "He descended into hell" — undoubtedly do not appear in the earlier forms of the Apostles' Creed, and it may be that the passage from S. Peter may have been employed to prove the truth of the fact alleged; but their introduction came from a natural expansion of the article, "He was buried," — for the burial of a man means more than the burial of a brute; it includes in the thought of a Christian the return of the body to the dust and of the spirit to the GOD who gave it. This was true of our LORD, as S. Peter expressly tells us in the first Christian sermon which he preached on the day of Pentecost [Acts ii. 31]. He quotes from the Sixteenth Psalm, and makes the following comment: David, he says, "being a prophet and knowing that GOD had sworn with an oath to him that of the fruit of his loins, according to the flesh, He would raise up CHRIST to sit on his throne; He seeing this before spake of the resurrection of CHRIST, that His soul was not left in hell, neither His flesh did see corruption." Here

S. Peter expressly distinguishes between the flesh and the soul of our Blessed LORD; and he rests his distinction upon the authority of the HOLY GHOST, and upon the same authority he affirms that our Blessed LORD'S soul went to hell, or hades, but was not left there, but returned to His body, and He rose from the dead. The article, therefore, " He descended into hell," is inevitably implied in its predecessor, " He was buried," because the Creed is speaking of *the man* CHRIST JESUS. It was drawn out and added, doubtless to refute a heresy which was spreading, which denied that our LORD had a reasonable soul, alleging that the Divine Personality supplied the place of the human soul. To withdraw the article, " He descended into hell," therefore, from the Apostles' Creed now is to obscure, if it be not to deny the perfect humanity of CHRIST. As to the expressions, " He descended, or ascended," they are, we all know, accommodations to our present condition, and not absolute terms. S. Paul [Eph. iv 9, 10], speaking of CHRIST, says, " Now that He ascended, what is it but that He also descended first into the lower parts of the earth? He that descended is the same also that ascended up far above all heavens, that He might fill all things." Such language then is used of CHRIST by the HOLY SPIRIT; and let the interpretation of " the lower parts of the earth " be what it may, the Incarnation, the burial, or the descent into hell, or hades, it serves my purpose just as well, since we learn from them that our LORD did descend; and after He was risen from the dead we learn on His own authority that He had not yet *gone up*, for He says to Mary Magdalene on the morning of His resurrection [S. John xx. 17]: " Touch me not; for I am not yet ascended to my FATHER: but go to my brethren, and say unto them, I ascend unto my FATHER and your FATHER, and to my GOD and your GOD." My very learned friend had not his Greek Testament at hand when he in an incautious moment built an argument, or rather rested his rejection of the article of the Apostles' Creed, " He descended into hell, or hades," upon the statement of S. Paul that he was caught *up* into Paradise as it appears in our English Version. S. Paul does not say that he was caught *up*; the "up" is an interpretation of our translators. S. Paul says simply that he was *caught, snatched* into Paradise.

One word about the Nicene Creed. It is objected that it enters into philosophical speculation, and that we should be content with the Scripture statement that "the Word is GOD." The primitive Church was content with Scripture statements to embody the truth, but alas! man finds out many inventions. He invented a subtle philosophy to deprave and destroy the truth; and this philosophy assailed the truth of truths in the plan of human redemption, the corner-stone of the Catholic Faith, the Divinity of JESUS CHRIST. No Scripture phrase could be found which the champions of that heresy would not accept and evade. They must be met and vanquished on their own ground; and the single word, "*homoousion*," was the weapon whose thrust they could not parry; it proved to be a barrier which they could not pass. There is here no more philosophy than is needed to shut out the most destructive heresy which ever invaded the fold of CHRIST.

Surely there is not so much philosophy involved in the argument of the homoousion that this age and my learned brethren need fear that they or their people will be bewildered in its mazes. This word simply asserts of the SON that He is of the same essence or substance with the FATHER; and as the attributes of any essence or substance must go with that essence or substance wherever it is found, it follows of necessity that if the SON be of the same substance with the FATHER, He must have the attributes of the FATHER. One of these attributes is eternal. The FATHER is eternal; hence the SON must be eternal. This was the point in dispute. The Arian denied the eternity of CHRIST's being; and this denial carried with it everything, — the Trinity, the atonement, the merits of our LORD's death. It left man where the Fall left him, stripped, naked, wounded, cast down, defenceless, helpless. Homoousion shut out this heresy and barred the way forever against its return. Is there too much philosophy in this? Not for me. Thank GOD for the Nicene Creed! Thank GOD for the Catholic Church, which with her living voice has rung out this Creed from age to age to guard our heritage of redemption through a Saviour, who is CHRIST our GOD! Thank GOD for the Historic Episcopate, the spinal cord of the Catholic Church, which carries down from the Divine Head — CHRIST our LORD, GOD over all in heaven — the gifts of the HOLY GHOST, and diffuses them through orders and sacraments and services, as nervous vitality permeates the body and fills it with life from the crown of the head to the sole of the foot! Thank GOD for the Historic Episcopate, which guards, as it has guarded, the sacred deposit which CHRIST committed to His Apostolate on the Mount of the Ascension, with the charge that they should keep it even to the end! The treasures are not for ourselves alone; they are a sacred trust for mankind. We hold them to guard them, not as hoarding them, but that we may have them in possession to share with our brethren if they will receive them at our hands. With joy unspeakable will we welcome them to our FATHER'S house, and give them freely and fully the best that is in that house; but we may not unroof the house and tear up its foundations that we may enjoy their society. If Holy Orders and Sacraments and Creed and Liturgy be gifts which come from the LORD, we may not, must not, compromise them or throw them away, since then we shall be faithless, disloyal stewards, and so far as we could do so will banish these gifts from the face of the earth and put it beyond the power of our brethren afterward, however much they may covet them, to obtain them.

My time is up, and I must stop and leave so many things unsaid which I fain would say that I feel as though I must go on; but necessity constrains, and I forbear with a parting word to my friends. Some of them have intimated, and others more plainly said, that if the cause of Christian unity requires them to surrender their position or take a step which reflects upon their ancestry in their specific belief and practice, and especially, where they have such, the great founders of their systems or Churches, they will not entertain the idea for one moment. Let me ask any man who values his reputation for fidelity to truth and principle whether in the sight of GOD and as responsible to his own conscience he dare occupy such a position. On these terms error would never be abandoned, truth would never be embraced. On these terms the heathen would never have forsaken their idols and become Christians; on these terms the Reformers would never have left what they believed to be the corruptions and abuses of their own age and country and gone forth on new lines and become the great leaders whom our friends delight to follow, and whose persons they hold in most sincere admiration. Let me point my brethren to these Reformers as examples in this respect of our duty. At all events, they shall be mine. For me, nothing must count in preference to truth.

GEORGE F. SEYMOUR.

The Holy Scriptures as the Basis of Church Unity.

REV. WILLIAM D. WILSON, D.D., LL.D., L.H.D., DEAN OF
S. ANDREW'S DIVINITY SCHOOL.

AS I am to write of the Holy Scriptures as the Basis of Church Unity, it would seem proper to preface what I have to say by a brief consideration of the problems and difficulties to be met, bearing always in mind the existing evils and the end to be accomplished.

Leaving out of account for the present the Oriental Church, including as it does nearly one third of the professing Christians of the world, we have around us three distinct bodies or classes of persons to be considered.

1. We have those who adhere to and advocate the supremacy of the Bishop of Rome as essential to Church Unity; they hold that our LORD made S. Peter the Prince of the Apostles, and gave him not only presidency, but authority also over the others, and through them, over the whole Church of believers in Him; that S. Peter became Bishop of Rome and transmitted to his successors through all time the presidency and the supremacy which he had exercised. And recently his adherents have declared that he is infallible whenever he speaks authoritatively and in his official capacity; so that no one can have any reasonable hope of final salvation who does not accept and follow his decrees.

2. Then we have what are called ultra-Protestants, who hold that when our LORD spoke of building His Church [Matt. xvi. 18] He did not refer to any visible organized body of those that should believe in Him, but rather to an invisible number, known only to Himself; that He caused His Gospel to be preached, and finally to be committed to writing, leaving the believers to organize themselves into Churches, as many and as various in form and discipline as they might think most expedient and conducive to the welfare and final salvation of men. They do not regard "the Historic Episcopate" or any other form of a

ministry that has any visible or tactual connection with the Apostles, or the ministry our LORD ordained and sent to preach His Gospel, as at all necessary.

3. Then in the third place we have a class of Christians who claim to have "the Historic Episcopate" with an actual and a tactual line of descent from the Apostles. They hold that the Church spoken of by our LORD [Matt. xvi. 18; xviii. 17] and often referred to in the Acts and Epistles [Acts iii. 47; 1 Tim. iii. 15] was a visible and organized body.

In fact, this view is inevitably implied, if indeed it is not expressly stated in the Declaration of our House of Bishops [*General Convention*, 1886, p. 80]: " We do hereby affirm that the Christian Unity now so earnestly desired . . . can be restored only by a return of all Christian Communions to the principles of unity exemplified by the undivided Catholic Church during the first ages of its existence; which principles we believe to be the substantial deposit of Christian Faith and Order committed by CHRIST and His Apostles to the Church unto the end of the world, and therefore incapable of compromise or surrender by those who have been ordained to be its stewards and trustees for the common and equal benefit of all men."

But the views of the Holy Scriptures entertained by them (which is the subject now more especially before us) differ quite as much among these bodies or classes of Christians we have named, as they themselves do in regard to the Church which our LORD founded. And in fact this diversity of views in regard to the Scriptures is, if not fundamental, yet essential to the diversity of their views in regard to the Church itself.

The advocates of the Papal claims hold that besides what is contained in the Holy Scriptures, there are traditions outside of their teachings, and especially such as have received the approval and sanction of the Pope, that are as essential and as necessary to salvation as the things that are contained in the Scriptures themselves.

Then the extreme Protestants hold on the other hand that the Bible alone is the guide for Christian believers, — that each one is to take it, study it, and interpret it for himself as best he can, under the influence of prayer and the guidance of the HOLY GHOST. They scarcely hold to any " Church authority" in the proper sense of the word. They do indeed hold to and see the necessity of Church regulations, such as each pastor or congregation may make as a matter of expediency and as conducive to edification.

Then finally we have those holding a somewhat middle ground, — like that of the Protestant Episcopalians, who, as it will be remembered, proposed the four conditions of union, one of which we are considering. They hold and expressly declare (Art. VI.) that "the Holy Scriptures contain all things necessary to salvation." But they also hold that there are many things spoken of or alluded to in the Holy Scriptures which are essential, in some one form or another, to any Church organization, to the preaching of the Gospel, and to the administration of the Sacraments, which are not expressly stated in the Scriptures. And they hold that the safest and most proper guide to a right understanding and observance of these things is what may be called tradition; that is, the records that have come down to us outside of the Scriptures, — such as notes of usages, canons, and opinions of early Fathers.

If we turn our attention to the Old Testament Scriptures we find that although, as it now appears, there may have been portions of the earlier books in existence before the time of Moses, yet that the books, from first to last, from Genesis to Malachi, with the possible exception of the book of Job, were written in the Jewish Church, by members of the Church, and after its organization by Moses in the wilderness, and after the priests and Levites had been set apart not only for the administration of the worship in the Tabernacle, but also to be the instructors and guides of the people in matters that pertain to their Faith and religion as well as in regard to their duties as men and citizens; and that all these books, with, as before said, the possible exception of Job, were written for their instruction and guidance in their responsible and arduous duties as priests and ministers.

If now we turn our attention to the New Testament Scriptures, we find very much the same result. We find that our LORD declared, some time before He died, His intention to build His Church on the confession of His Divine Nature which S. Peter had just made. He soon after, as it appears from S. Matthew's record, gave to His Apostles extensive power, not only of legislation, but of discipline as well, subordinate of course to any instruction He had given them or might thereafter give them [Matt. xvi. and xviii. 15–21]. Then in Acts [ii. 47] we find the Church spoken of as already existing and established, so that "the LORD added to the Church daily such as should be saved," — or were being saved.

The Apostles went forth and preached the Gospel as they were commanded; and it was not until some twenty years at least after their mission that any part of the Holy Scriptures of the New Testament as we now have them were written.

Our LORD, so far as we have any record of the words He uttered, never gave them any charge to *write* anything. They were to preach and proclaim by word of mouth the Gospel, make disciples of the people among all the nations or races of people on the earth, baptizing and thus bringing into the Church those that should believe the Gospel as they were to preach and to teach it; and the promise was, "Whosoever believeth and *is baptized* shall be saved."

But the earliest attempt to reduce the Gospel to writing, that the Church of the believers might have the benefit of reading it for themselves, did not occur for some twenty years or more after the Gospel had been preached, and Churches — that is, local Churches, as branches of the one Church which our LORD founded and which S. Paul declares to be the pillar and ground, stay or support, "of the truth" [1 Tim. iii. 15] — had been established in nearly all parts of the earth.

It is commonly supposed that the very first to be written of the books we now have in our Canon, or collection of Holy Scriptures of the New Testament, was the first of S. Paul's Epistles to the Thessalonians, about A. D. 52, nineteen years after the Crucifixion. The Gospels as we now have them were not written until somewhat later. It is sometimes claimed, indeed, that S. Matthew wrote, for the converts from Judaism who lived in Palestine, a Gospel in the Hebrew language, or what was called Hebrew at the time. But we have not that Gospel as he wrote it, if ever he wrote one; and what we have is of a later date, say about A. D. 60. And the other Gospels were written later on, until perhaps that of S. John sometime in the last decade of the first century, perhaps A. D. 92.

I think we have satisfactory evidence that there was at a

much earlier date than even the earliest of the Epistles, both a stated form of words for use in the administration of the Holy Supper, and also a "form of sound words" [2 Tim. i. 13], which was used in baptism at least, if not in the Holy Eucharist, and commonly accepted both as an expression and as a test of the faith of those who were to be received and retained in the holy fellowship of the Apostolic Church; dissent from which was "heresy" in the technical sense, while divisions and contentions among those who were still retained in the Church was called schism; and S. John speaks of some who "went out from" that fellowship as being in some sense "anti-CHRIST" [1 John ii. 18].

But the Scriptures that have come down to us were all of them, or at least nearly all of them, written for a local — I will not say a temporary — purpose. Thus S. Matthew is commonly held to have written primarily and chiefly for the Christian converts from Judaism who lived in Palestine. S. Mark, though with less unanimity of agreement, is said to have written under the immediate guidance of S. Peter, and at Alexandria for the Christians who were living in that part of Africa; while S. Luke's Gospel is said to have been written at Rome under the special guidance of S. Paul. S. Paul's Epistles, as is well known, and is also manifest from the Epistles themselves, were written to local Churches, — as that at Rome, that at Corinth, etc., — and were more or less intended for the discussion and settlement of questions which, if not of a temporary nature, were yet specially interesting and important for those to whom the letters were addressed. This remark applies with special force to the Epistles to Timothy, to Titus, and to Philemon.

Yet doubtless what these holy and inspired men wrote was (for the most part shall I say? 1 Cor. vii. 40) dictated by the HOLY SPIRIT, and remains as of inestimable value as indicating what was "the substantial deposit of Christian Faith and Order committed by CHRIST and His Apostles to the Church unto the end of the world," to quote again the declarations of our House of Bishops on this subject. But the fact was and is, that the Gospel was preached for many years before it was written and committed to writing as Holy Scripture at all; and the Church was founded and organized in some form or another, and more or less completely in all the larger cities and countries of the Roman Empire, which then included pretty much the whole world.

The controlling fact is that the Apostles and the ministry themselves were not only to preach the Gospel, but they were also to organize the Church, or local branches of it, one in each city or province. When the writers of the Holy Scriptures speak of this matter at all, it is either by way of allusion to what had been done, or by way of instruction to some one who had been ordained, and received authority for the work of organizing Churches, selecting and ordaining Elders and Deacons, as well as giving directions for their professions of the Faith, — for their worship and the principles of the godly life which they were to observe and enforce.

Herein we have the reason why there is to be found in the New Testament no express or full description of the Church, its organization, and its methods. The people for whom the Scriptures were written, with the exception of the two or three books I have just mentioned, had nothing to do with organizing the Church. It was not their work or duty. They could not do it. It was done for them by the Apostles whom our LORD had chosen for that purpose, and to whom He gave the command to go and teach all nations to observe whatsoever he had commanded them. And as in the cases of Timothy and Titus at least, we find that the Apostles gave like authority to others, uninspired men whom they chose for the work.

The several books of the New Testament Scriptures, thus written, began at a very early date to be collected into a whole, in several at least of the great centres of Christian population, as Antioch, Alexandria, and Carthage. But we have no definite information in regard to this collection. We have indeed a few hints in the Holy Scriptures themselves in regard to the circulation of these Scriptures, the desire to get them, and the anxiety to read and understand them [Col. iv. 16; Luke i. 1-5; Acts i.; 2 Peter iii. 16].

But it is most natural that the Christians in any one city should be extremely anxious as soon as they had heard of any writing by one of the Apostles, or perhaps by any one so intimately associated with any one of them as to be specially valuable as a teacher, to get a copy of the work, epistle, or gospel, as the case might be. And thus, as we know, collections began to be made in a large number of places; these collections, at the earliest date at which we can get any certain information concerning them, differed in some less important details from one another. And in some few cases, books not now received into our Canon, as the Epistles of Clement and of Barnabas, were received and read in the public worship; while others that we do now receive had not been received, or at least adopted as part of their sacred Scriptures in some few of the early collections that we know of.

We have, indeed, early lists of the books received, and there were two or three attempts by local and provincial synods to define the Canon. But there was no such action by any one of the General Councils of the Universal Church.

And yet the Church in the most important sense, though not acting in any synod, or in its organic capacity, was the judge, and did decide what books should be received. And in this it seems to have been guided by its religious instincts, shall we say? or shall we call it rather that HOLY SPIRIT which was promised to be in the Church and its guide through all time?

If now we turn to the use which the early Christians made of these Scriptures, we have three points to consider.

1. The use they made of them in their public worship. Of course they had no printed copies, as we have, that could be put into every man's hands. Copies were expensive, made only by transcription by the hand. But in the very earliest stage it appears that they were accustomed to read them in their weekly and daily assemblies with the greatest reverence and deference, — very much as we now read Bishops' charges and the pastoral letters of our House of Bishops. Reuss [*History of the Canon*, pp. 32, 138] says that the book of Revelation, which he supposes to have been written earlier than the Gospel by S. John, say A. D. 65–68, was the first of the books now included in our New Testament Canon that was read in public worship as part of Holy Scriptures. Soon, however, the Church began to read from them all, as second lessons in the services, as we do now, and as they were at first accustomed to do from the Prophets of the Old Testament.

2. In the next place, I refer to the early Christian writers who wrote in defence of Christianity, and for the most part against its avowed enemies, Jews and Gentiles, who did not profess to have received Christianity at all in any form or under any name,

—the Apologists, as they are called. Of these we have the names of some twelve or fifteen that have come down to us, although by far the larger part of their writings is lost. In the East we have Julian, Tatian, Athenagoras, Theophilus of Antioch, Clement of Alexandria, and Origen. In Africa and the West we have Tertullian, Minucius Felix, Cyprian, Arnobius, Lactantius, and Irenæus. Of these, two — namely, Irenæus and Tertullian — wrote in defence of the Faith against the early heretics and separatists.

Of those who wrote against the enemies of Christianity, — that is, the unconverted Jews and the heathen, — and in fact, of all of them when writing against these adversaries of Christianity, we must note the fact that although they quote the genuine Scriptures with the utmost reverence and deference, always accepting their statements, whether of fact or of doctrine, as in no way liable to dispute or distrust, they cannot be expected to quote them as they would have done if they were writing to professing Christians of whatever name. Nor yet of course can we expect them to show us very definitely how the Scriptures themselves were regarded by the Church or its members. Their writings are valuable for the purpose now before us, chiefly as showing what books were received and regarded as of authority in the Church; and in this respect they are most invaluable.

3. Turning now to those who wrote against the heresies of those who called themselves and claimed to be Christians, we have especially the two already named, Irenæus and Tertullian.

Irenæus was born and trained in the East, Asia Minor. He had seen, as he says, Polycarp, who was Bishop of Smyrna, and who had been a pupil and personal friend of the Apostle S. John. He became Bishop of Lyons about A. D. 178. The heretics against whom he contends were chiefly those that are now known as Gnostics, — not Agnostics, — who claimed to understand all the doctrines of revelation, and to have a philosophy which taught them many things not to be found in the Holy Scriptures; and they also claimed to interpret the Scriptures and deduce from them many doctrines not generally held in the Church. And while there were many who were either of this number, or inclined to their views, and were thus both heretics and schismatics remaining in the Church, there were also many who, as Irenæus says, " being more anxious to be sophists of

Holy Scriptures as the Basis of Church Unity. 199

words than disciples of the Truth," separated themselves from the Church, and "assembled themselves in unauthorized meetings" [book iii. c. iii. § 2] of their own and by themselves.

S. Irenæus constantly quotes the Holy Scriptures as unquestionably true and authentic. He also shows how these errorists pervert its true meaning, and attribute to mere incidents of phrase, and even of the letters used, significations and an importance which they do not deserve. He also shows the absurdity and evil tendency of their claims that the Apostles knew and held the views which they teach, but refrained from committing them to writing either in the Gospels or the Epistles which they wrote, because the people were not at that time sufficiently advanced in understanding to accept and appreciate them. They also claimed that these doctrines had been handed down to them by tradition, or revealed by special inspirations and revelations to Valentius and other founders and leaders of their various sects.

S. Irenæus does indeed constantly quote the New Testament Scriptures with the utmost reverence and deference to their authority and their very words; yet he does so in a manner that shows that he regards them — the written word — as subordinate to the Faith as it was delivered to the Church by the Apostles before the Scriptures were written, and handed down to his times, one and the same in each and every one of the Churches, — that is, provincial Churches, which had been founded in the chief or capital city of each province. He writes [book i. c. x. § 1] the Apostles' Creed as we now have it in substance, though not in the exact words. In fact, De Barron has shown in his work, *The Greek Origin of the Apostles' Creed*, that the early Christians never stated the Creed in the exact words in which it was used in the Church and by the initiated, and gives the reason for it [p. 40]. He claims that it was first written in its exact form of words by Marcellus, Bishop of Ancyra, about A. D. 341.

But S. Irenæus, as I have said, recites the Creed in substance as we now have it, some one hundred and fifty years before the time of Marcellus. This Creed, he says, " the Church, though dispersed throughout the whole world, even to the ends of the earth, has received from the Apostles and their disciples." This " Faith," he says [§ 2], "the Church, although scattered throughout the whole world, has received, as if occupying but one and the same house, and carefully preserves it. . . . She believes these points of doctrine, and proclaims them as if she had but one soul, and one and the same heart; and she teaches and hands them down with perfect harmony, as if she had but one mouth; for although the languages are different, yet the tradition in its meaning and import is one and the same. For the Churches which have been planted in Germany, in Spain, in France, in the East, in Egypt, in Libya, or even those that have been established in the central regions of the world, do not differ in the Faith they hold, the Creed they profess. . . . Nor will any one of the rulers of the Churches, however highly gifted he may be in point of eloquence, teach any different doctrine; nor on the other hand, will he who is deficient in power of expression inflict any injury on the tradition." But among the "heretics" and Dissenters, he says, " there are as many schemes of redemption as there are teachers of their opinions " [book i. c. xxi. § 1].

This is a favorite topic with this author, and he frequently recurs to it. Thus, in book iii. [c. i. § 2], he says, " When we refer them to the tradition that originated with the Apostles and is preserved by means of a succession in the ministry in the Churches, they object to tradition. . . . It is in the power of all, therefore [c. iii. § 1], in every Church, who may wish to see the truth, to contemplate clearly the tradition of the Apostles manifested throughout the whole world; and we are in a position to reckon up those who were by the Apostles instituted Bishops in the Churches, and to demonstrate the succession of these men to our own times. . . . Since, however, it would be very tedious to reckon up the succession in all the Churches, we put to confusion . . . those who assemble in unauthorized meetings, by indicating " several of the ancient Churches. And among these as most conspicuous and as being in some sense the centre of the world, he mentions Rome, giving a list of their Bishops from Linus to his own time. (S. Peter is *not* one of the list.) But he mentions also several others, more especially those in the East.

Now, as this idea constantly recurs in the somewhat long essay of Irenæus and pervades his whole discussion, I will cite one or two more passages [book iv. c. xxvi. § 2] : " Wherefore it is incumbent to obey the ministry of the Church,—those who, as I have shown, possess the succession from the Apostles, those who together with the succession of the Episcopate have received the certain gift of truth, according to the good pleasure of the FATHER. But it is incumbent on us also to hold in suspicion all others who depart from the primitive succession and assemble themselves together" in other places, in " meetings of their own."

Again [book v. c. xx. § 1]: "Now all these heretics are of much later date than the Bishops to whom the Apostles committed the Churches, which fact I have taken all pains to demonstrate in the third book. . . . But the path of duty of those belonging to the Church circumscribes the whole world as possessing the sure tradition from the Apostles, and enables us to see that the Faith of all is one and the same, . . . since all are cognizant of the same spirit, conversant with the same commandments, and preserve the same form of ecclesiastical constitution, and expect the one advent of the LORD, and await the same salvation of the complete man,— that is, of soul and body."

Tertullian fell into some of the errors of the Montanists, though it is generally held that he never separated himself from the communion of the Church. He had been trained a lawyer, and shows the results of that training in the tract of his on *The Prescriptions of Heretics*, from which only I shall make citations. He agrees in general with the views I have cited from Irenæus, though it is most likely that the two men had no personal knowledge of each other's existence, — the one living in Lyons in Gaul, and the other in the north of Africa, at about the same time; that is, the latter part of the second century.

Tertullian takes the same view as Irenæus with regard to the first preaching of Christianity, — the tradition or handing down of the Faith in each of the Churches that had been founded by the Apostles or their immediate successors; but he does not undertake to show to the heretics that the views held by them were contrary to the Scriptures. He takes the ground, on the contrary, that they have no right to appeal to the Scriptures. The Scriptures were written in the Church by members of the Church, and for the use of the disciples that were in the Church and remained in its communion and fellowship, so that they that had left the Church not only had no right to claim to justify or defend their views by argument and texts derived from it, but that they had no right to use the Scriptures at all; it was no Holy Scriptures for them; their use of it was like that of a citizen of one country, — these United States, for example, — who should cite from and claim as his authority and vindication the laws of another country, as Turkey, Russia, or Germany.

It will be remembered that Tertullian had been a lawyer; and his idea was that heretics who had left the Church should be thrown out of court as having no status, or standing, or right to be heard there [§§ 15–21].

It is indeed quite true that Tertullian does claim that the Scriptures themselves do not teach the doctrines which these heretics hold, and that they are without foundation in the Scriptures themselves when rightly understood. But his main line of argument is that they have no right to exist as Churches or use the Scriptures.

Tertullian gives substantially, though not verbally, the Apostles' Creed as given by S. Irenæus, and makes it, in fact, as he calls it, "The Rule of Faith," by which all doctrines and teachings should be tested.

He says: "Immediately therefore the Apostles, . . . having chosen by lot a twelfth, . . . having throughout Judea borne witness to the Faith, went forth into the world and preached the same doctrine of the same Faith to the nations, and forthwith founded Churches in every city from whom the other Churches thenceforward borrowed the tradition of the Faith and the seeds of doctrine, and are daily deriving them that they may become Churches. Indeed, it is on this account only that they will be able to consider themselves Apostolic, as being the offspring of Apostolic Churches; . . . therefore the Churches, although they are so many and so great, constitute but the one primitive Church founded by the Apostles" [§ 20].

But "if there be any heretics that are bold enough to plant themselves in the midst of the Apostolic age, . . . let them produce the original records of their Churches; let them unfold the roll of their Bishops, extending down in due succession from the beginning in such manner that their first Bishop will be able to show for his ordainer and predecessor some one of the Apostles or of Apostolic men who continued stedfast with the Apostles. For in this manner do all the Apostolic Churches keep their registers; as the Church of Smyrna, . . . the Church of Rome. In the same way the other Churches exhibit the names of those whom, having been appointed to their Episcopal places by Apostles, they regard as transmitters of Apostolic seed." He mentions several others besides Smyrna and Rome, and says, as Irenæus has done, that there is no one who is not near enough to some one of these centres to consult its Bishop and find out from him what was "the Faith once delivered to the saints," which all Churches must keep and teach as the condition of their remaining in the communion of the One Holy, Apostolic, and Catholic Church.

Tertullian never indeed intimates or hints that this Faith could be any other, or different, from what was and is taught in the Holy Scriptures. But in his view, as in that of Irenæus, the Faith, the tradition, the doctrine, handed down in these Churches by all and everywhere, was the test, the thing first to be consulted, and the Scriptures later, and in a sense subordinate to the Faith thus once delivered and perpetually handed down from the Apostles by the succession of Bishops.

Of course, besides these two Fathers and the others that wrote apologetically and controversially, whether against heathen or heretics, there were many others whose writings have come down to us and are very valuable as showing what views were then entertained on the three great questions, — what constituted the Canon, of what authority they were as binding on the consciences of Christians, and what were the true or allowable principles of interpretation. On these points they are clear and instructive. The authority of the Scriptures was held to be supreme, or at least in no sense inferior and subordinate as a matter of authority to the Creeds and Church usages, or organization and discipline which have been handed down from the Apostles or their times, as shown by universal consent and observance.

Not only did these writers discuss the questions that had arisen in their times, or had occurred to their own minds as they studied the books and compared them one with another, but they compiled synopses, — contrasting and comparing the Gospels, explaining as best they could the apparent discrepancies, and suggesting what appeared to them to be the best modes of interpreting and explaining difficult and unintelligible passages.

How far these principles and modes of interpretation are

obligatory on us in this nineteenth century, and will be so on the centuries to come, is another and an entirely different question. But I suppose that the Church in its plan for unity, and in its practical application after that unity shall have been effected, and to the extent to which at any time it may have been effected, will feel bound to tolerate the modes and principles that were then in use.

But undoubtedly, on the other hand, the altered state of things will demand and produce some changes in this respect.

In fact, every legitimate branch of the Church claims, and has [Matt. xviii. 18] the right to interpret the Scriptures for itself and its own members. [See also the English Articles, xxi. and xxxiv.]

We have, then, the Holy Scriptures with these three characteristics: (1) Revelation from GOD of truths and facts that are beyond human insight or discovery; (2) Attested by miracles such as no man can work except GOD be with him; and (3) Committed to a ministry of Divine appointment.

Our LORD speaks of the miracles He wrought as attesting His word and the Divinity of His nature, on several occasions and in different ways, thus, S. John [xv. 24]: "If I had not done among them the works which none other man did, they had not had sin; but now have they both seen and hated both me and my FATHER."

And not only do our LORD'S words in appointing His ministry imply a perpetual continuance, "always, even unto the end of the world," but S. Paul, in two places at least, speaks of this ministry collectively in a way that implies its perpetuity; thus, in 1 Cor. xii. 28: "And GOD hath set some in the Church, first, apostles; secondarily, prophets; and thirdly, teachers," etc. Here are three Orders expressly mentioned and denoted by words that express this fact; and whatever we may think of the names, there can be no doubt of their threefoldness. Again [Eph. iv. 11], the same Apostle speaks of several Orders which our LORD "gave," or appointed; and he also speaks of the object of their appointment,—"for the perfecting of the saints, for the work of the ministry, for the edifying of the Body of CHRIST" (the Church), "till we all come in the unity of the Faith, and of the knowledge of the SON OF GOD, unto a perfect man" (the perfection of manhood), "unto the measure of the stature of the fulness of CHRIST."

Surely nothing more can be necessary either in the line and character of the work to be done, or in the constitution and continuity of the Orders of the ministry, than is thus clearly described and indicated. And this ministry is expressly declared to have been " given," " set," and appointed by our LORD Himself, and for the work and the only work which He would have anybody do or attempt to do in His name, and for the promotion of the cause for which He came into the world and took upon Himself our nature, and died on Calvary.

Now, of the three classes of professing Christians of whom I spoke at the beginning of this essay, the first one that I named — the adherents of the Papal Supremacy — accept these three elements, — the Scriptures, as containing a revelation; miracles as proofs of the fact of a revelation; and a ministry or priesthood of perpetual obligation, and without which there can be no true Church, or legitimate branch of the Church of our LORD JESUS CHRIST.

But they, as I have said, make the Church, or at least its ministry, and especially its visible head, the Pope, coequal in point of authority with the Scriptures themselves. Hence we cannot, in accordance with the terms of our Declaration or Proposal, unite on the Holy Scriptures in their sense, and in the use they propose to make of them. For in their sense, though they may be regarded and accepted as " the revealed Word of GOD," they cannot be regarded as containing all that it is necessary for one to believe as a Christian, or to teach as one of the Divinely appointed ministry; nor do they apparently regard them as a standard that may not be departed from.

The next class that I mentioned — the extreme Protestants — also hold a view of the nature, position, and functions of the Holy Scriptures that is equally fatal to their serving as any basis of Church unity, or Church existence, in fact, in any proper sense of the word.

The persons I am now speaking of do indeed hold to the first two elements spoken of, — namely, revelation and miracles, — as attesting it; and in this respect Christianity in their views differs essentially and *toto cœlo* from any of the heathen religions. But in rejecting as they do the third element, — the Church, and a permanent ministry or priesthood, as of Divine appointment, with power to interpret and teach the Scriptures, with a perpetual succession in what our Declaration calls " the

Historic Episcopate," — they reduce the Gospel of CHRIST to the same level, and subject it to the same fate, as has befallen the great heathen religions, — the Chinese, the Hindu, the Buddhist, and such like.

In this view we have the Scriptures indeed, and they are of inestimable value; and they and their contents are attested in the most satisfactory manner by miracles. But who is to teach the doctrines contained in the Scriptures? Who, in fact, is to say, who has any authority to say, what are the Scriptures and what are the doctrines they teach? Who may say whether this, that, or the other form of confessing or professing one's belief, amounts to a profession of the Christian Faith? For surely there is such a thing, and we are warned against the danger of it, — a form of confession or profession which does not amount to the Christian Faith, does not fit one for Holy Baptism, nor qualify him to receive the Holy Supper, " rightly discerning the LORD'S Body " [1 Cor. xi. 29]. Who, in fact, may decide what is that confession of faith that makes one a Christian?

And there is no escape from this issue. Either every one must judge for himself, and interpret the Scriptures for himself as best he can, or he must follow the guidance of some one else. If he decides for himself, we have abundantly seen that there is no doctrine so absurd but that it may be held, and no duty so sacred but that it may be explained away and neglected. If he chooses for himself who shall be his guides and teachers, the case is not much better; but if he seeks out and accepts those that the LORD has appointed, there must be something of submission, docility, and obedience, as well as a profession or confession of faith before men.

Every Church, whether of human origin or Divine, must claim and exercise some authority over its members, so far at least as to exclude those who do not believe what it regards as essential in doctrine, or live a godly life according to its notions of what constitutes godliness.

Doubtless our LORD gave to His immediate Apostles authority for this purpose; and we find also that even those who had no special inspiration to guide them, as in the case of Timothy and Titus, had express instructions implying authority, not only to select and ordain for the people Elders and Deacons, but also to see to the soundness of their Faith, to direct their worship, and to explain and enforce the rules and principles of a godly life.

What gives this point the greater importance is the fact that in the Holy Scriptures we are often and again warned against "false teachers," that would come and lead away disciples after them [Matt. vii. 15; xxix. 11; 2 Tim. iv. 3].

Now I know of but two ways, as indicated in Holy Scriptures, by the one or the other of which alone can we determine whom we may regard as Divinely appointed, and to whom we may safely trust ourselves in these most sacred and most important concerns. The one is Apostolic descent by actual, visible, tactual succession from those whom our LORD appointed; and the other is miracles performed by those who claim to speak in GOD's name and be His ministers.

We have in the Old Testament two classes of Divine teachers clearly distinguished from each other in this way, — Priests and Prophets, though of course the same individual may have in some cases been both a Priest and a Prophet.

But the Priesthood, including High-Priest, Priests, and Levites, came to their office by descent from Levi, Aaron, etc., and needed no other testimony or vindication of their right to perform the duties and claim the privileges and prerogatives of their office. But the Prophets who were not in the priestly line vindicated their claim to speak from GOD, and in His name, by miracles, as in the case of Elijah, Elisha, and Isaiah, to name no others.

It would seem, therefore, that there are and can be but the two classes, each with its appropriate sign and verification of authority, — lineal descent from those who were at first Divinely appointed, and miracles.

But this is not all. The position which this view of the last named of the elements furnished for us in the Holy Scriptures puts Christianity itself on a level with the heathen religions already named. The founders of those religions did not found or build a Church, and they instituted no ministry or priesthood, who should take their writings or verbal messages, preach them to the world, explain and expound them for all who might desire information and guidance, and preserve, protect, and appeal to those sacred writings forever, to the end of the world.

Hence when degeneracy came, as it was sure to come, and when diversities of opinion should arise among honest and sincere inquirers, or be suggested by ambitious aspirants, which were no less sure to come in the order of time and events, — should arise and plead some one or another of the doctrines of the founder of their religion more distinctly or emphatically than the rest, — there was no one to decide, no one to whom it was a duty to refer, no one having any special authority, any more than any other who might happen to be as intelligent and have as much confidence in himself, — perhaps I ought to say as much spiritual pride and conceit, — to whom appeal could be made; there was no Divinely appointed Church, ministry, or priesthood, and the result was a division, — the rising of a new sect. Possibly the new sect was an improvement upon the state of things that existed before it arose, so far as mere purity of doctrine was concerned, and possibly it was not.

But there was no help for it. There was no adequate basis or bond of unity; and the followers and disciples of the old religion formed as numerous sects, and became as diverse from one another as our modern Christian denominations. There was no help for it, and nothing that could be done, except for each of these persons to start off, get as many followers as he could, and make a sect, — a Church of his and their own.

The only remedy for this evil is "the Church idea," the doctrine and belief that the Author and Giver of our Salvation instituted a Church and appointed a ministry whom believers must receive, if they would receive Him [Matt. x. 46; Mark ix. 37; John xiii. 20], — the ministry of Whom we read in the Acts and Epistles as actually doing the work He had appointed them to do, and with whom He promised to be "always, even unto the end of the world."

But from the days when the Bishop of Rome began to claim the supremacy, the idea of the Church began to disappear and be lost and swallowed up in that of the Papacy, so that now the Pope is all in all; and at the reaction that began to prevail during the Reformation, the idea came into vogue that Church authority was little or nothing, and doctrine was the one essential thing, and the individual became the all in all, each one for himself.

There remain three topics on which it seems desirable to say a few words before we close: (1) The Canon, and what is to be regarded as constituting "the Holy Scriptures;" (2) In what sense they are to be regarded as inspired, or "the revealed

Word of GOD;" and (3) In what way and by what rules of interpretation they are to be expounded and insisted upon in proving doctrines, or in teaching the way and the duties of a holy life.

We have seen, as has been well said in the vigorous words of Bishop Temple, the present Bishop of London, that "it must always be remembered that although the Bible is a good text-book of religious instruction, our LORD did not first have the Bible written, and then send forth His Apostles to lecture upon it. He first sent them forth, and then supplied them with the New Testament, as the great instrument by which they were to convert the world; the Church which He created was the agent for using that instrument."

I have said something of a slight diversity of opinion among the early Christians with regard to a few of the books that we now receive; and it is not at all likely that our Bishops intended to preclude discussion of these subjects or a diversity of opinion concerning them.

Yet even now, as in early times, nearly every dissenter from the Church professes to disregard and reject some of the books that are generally received. Luther despised the Epistle of S. James. Calvin had his preferences and partialities. And as Reuss [*History of the Canon*, c. xvi.] and Westcott [*The Bible in the Church*, c. x.] have shown, there has been scarcely a new sect founded, or the founder of a new sect, that did not either invent some new Scriptures, or find reasons for rejecting some parts of those that the Church held.

Our Declaration says, "the revealed Word of GOD;" that is, a revelation from GOD.

In what sense a revelation? We often use the words "inspiration" and "revelation" in a subordinate sense, as in fact implying thoughts and truths which are not regarded as from GOD, in any special sense, — in any sense, in fact, higher and more especial than that in which all truth is regarded as from Him. In this view there is no real distinction between discovery and revelation, — between the truths that are discovered whether by explorations into the records of the past, or by penetration into the nature and relations of the facts of the present order and course of Nature.

But I think the Church means to be understood as holding, and intends to adhere to and enforce, a higher sense than this; for in this sense all religions are based on revelations, and given by inspiration. But I think that our Church intends something more: thus, if the account which Moses gives of the several stages of creation be true, and in accordance with facts, it must have been given by a higher inspiration, — for there was no human being present to see them, and it had not been discovered at that time by men of science. The expression is "the revealed Word of GOD." So in our Constitution no one can be ordained in our Branch of the Anglican Communion without making in the most solemn manner a declaration that he "believes the Holy Scriptures of the Old and New Testaments to be the Word of GOD."

It is to be noted that the expression in both cases is in the singular number, — "the Word of GOD," not "the Words of GOD," as if it were intended to indicate and teach a doctrine of plenary inspiration. The men who wrote the books were inspired to write and say just what GOD for the occasion would have them to say. And I think that we must be on our guard against a very prevalent opinion, — that because these men were inspired and spoke as they were moved by the HOLY GHOST, therefore what they said must be taken in accordance with the Englishman's oath, "The truth, the whole truth, and nothing but the truth." Of course I do not mean to say or to imply that anything that is thus said when rightly understood — that is, when understood as they understood it and intended it should be understood — is untrue. But what I mean to say is that GOD left them, for the most part, to express what was really His truth in their own way, and as best suited their personal usages and tastes, and was best calculated to produce the effect that was intended on the people of the time.

Nearly all the language and forms of expression we use have grown out of past theories, many of which are no longer held. We do not suppose that a man denies the Copernican theory because he uses the expression, "the sun rises."

The fact that a man uses words that imply a theory of things is no certain proof that he holds that theory unless he so uses his words as to show that he intended to affirm it. This would seem to be the only safe rule.

In discussing and criticising the statements of others, it is but fair and candid — doing by others as we would like to be done by -- to suppose that they knew what they were talking about and understood the facts which they undertook to assert.

Thus, when a man is professedly teaching astronomy, it is but fair to take his words literally in reference to the point directly before him, and to suppose he intended to teach, and ascribe to him the views, that his words imply or express when taken literally. And so with every other subject; but in discussing or speaking of any subject a man must of necessity use the language of his time, and such as is understood or will be best understood by those for whom it was intended. And of course the subject will sometimes be one that is beyond their comprehension; then, of course, he must resort to parable, figures of speech, and similes, such as will in his judgment best effect the purpose he had before him.

Hence it is very often the case in dispute that both parties are right if they will only understand each other. Moses said, "GOD created the heaven and the earth," and specifies the successive stages. Modern scientists have discovered that this was really the order and the successive stages; and they call it evolution. Well, they may both of them be right. There could hardly be creation without a method, and with successive stages and progress; nor can there be evolution without something to work upon, and something or somebody — a person — to work upon it. Evolution may be only GOD'S way and method in creation.

It has been said of one of the wags of our day that he once remarked that he would not give "five cents to know what Ingersoll thinks of the mistakes of Moses, but he would give many dollars to know what Moses thinks of the mistakes of Ingersoll."

Now, as Moses was one of the meekest of men, we may imagine him saying, "My friend, I expected wiser and more considerate and candid men to study and interpret my writings. You do not seem to have the slightest idea of what I was writing about, or what I was trying to accomplish. Put yourself in my place, and you would say about what I did, and perhaps a good deal better."

We have, then, these three: (1) The Church with its ministry; (2) The Holy Scriptures; (3) The godly life. Of the three the Church was first in the order of time. But the last, personal holiness, is first in the order of importance, and that for which the other two were instituted. Man needs light and guidance; and somewhere along in the course of his life there must come the element of faith, docility,— the walking by faith under the guidance of those who have the right to teach and guide him, — if he is ever to rise above the mere natural life which ends and ever must end in spiritual death, the eternal death of the soul.

The word "Church" is used in the New Testament in three ways: (1) In the singular, to denote the one Body that our LORD founded, as in Matt. xvi. 16, "I will build my Church;" S. Paul, when he speaks of the Church as the Body of CHRIST (or of Christians) or "the Pillar and Ground of the Truth" [Eph. i. 23; Col. i. 24; 1 Tim. iii. 15]; (2) When it denotes the body of baptized believers or disciples in any one city or locality, as the Church at Jerusalem, the Church at Antioch, etc.; (3) In the plural, when it is always accompanied by some geographical designation denoting not now a city or any one community, but a province, which, like the States of our Union, had many cities; as the Churches of Judea, the Churches of Samaria, the Churches of Galilee, the Churches of Asia, etc.

But the idea of many Churches, or bodies of recognized believers, in the same city or community, never occurs. And in fact, the existence of such a state of things is precluded by the way in which the New Testament Scriptures speak of: (1) Heresy [1 Cor. xi. 19; Tit. iii. 10]; (2) Schisms [1 Cor. i. 10–iii. 4] or divisions among Christians, who, though in a state of insubordination, were still in the Church as its recognized members; (3) Those who had seceded, "gone out," from the Church, and yet claimed to be Christians with a rule or standard of Faith of their own, different from that in the Church. They were called anti-CHRIST [1 John ii. 18, 19]. The word "Church" is also used to denote the place or building in which Christians met for worship [Rom. xvi. 5; Acts xix. 37].

But when the word is used in the singular number to denote a body of believers, it is used as above described, (1) and (2), and never otherwise.

The parochial system as we now have it did not come in until later. When the believers in any one city became too numerous or lived too far apart to assemble for worship in one place, they built more places of worship, sometimes as many as thirty or forty. But there was always one Bishop, or chief pastor, with as many Elders and Deacons to assist him as were necessary for the work to be done; but for some one or two hundred years there was no division into organized parishes, as we have now in every large city in all denominations. The first question to be settled, then, would seem to be not one that relates to Church organization or modes of worship, and possibly not even to the details of doctrine; but it is rather the question of historic continuity, of Church identity, of visible connection, as a Branch with the Vine, the members with the one Body.

Of these branches we have unquestionably four: (1) That in the East, which was early brought under Mahometan domination; (2) That in Russia, where Mahometanism never prevailed; (3) That in the West, which was brought and still remains under the Papacy; and (4) The Anglican in England, America, and the colonies, a part of which, the English Church, was once included partly under the domination of the Bishop of Rome, but threw off that domination in the sixteenth century at what is called the Reformation; the rest never acknowledged his claims.

The Churches in Africa and the East were early divided by heresies and schisms and endless contentions, until the Mahometan conquest put a stop to them. In the West there were fewer heresies and much less speculation, indeed, the rise of the Papacy put a stop to what there were, and also served a most invaluable purpose in preserving the Church and Christianity itself during the Middle Ages.

Our LORD said not only that He would build His Church on the Faith in Him which S. Peter had confessed, but He said also that "the gates of hell should not prevail against it" [Matt. xvi. 18]. Doubtless this implies and declares that the Church should never become extinct; but does it not imply and declare also that no one soul that trusts to its teaching and instructions is in any danger of losing his soul? And I think if it has an application like this to the individual believer, it must be understood as applying to each one to his Church; that is, the city or provincial Church that has jurisdiction in the city or province where he lives.

The one great central thought of the Old Dispensation was the unity, the oneness, the oneliness of GOD, — the GOD whom the Jews were to worship, adore, and obey; and the one great sin that they were disposed to, and which for them was the parent of all sins, even if it did not in the sight of God involve them all in its one act, was the worship of other gods.

It seems to have been about as difficult under the New

Dispensation to make people believe in and understand the oneness and the oneliness of the Church which our LORD founded to be, on earth, the means of training those that believe in Him, while they are living here, for His Kingdom above.

But just as under the Old Dispensation, so soon as the idea of the oneness of GOD had passed out of mind, the idea of His majesty and the majesty of His law began to fade until it entirely disappeared, and lost all its force of restraint upon the evil tendencies of the human heart. So if we have diverse Churches in the same community, no one of them nor all of them together can exert so much influence for good, as if any one of them spoke with one voice, proclaiming the doctrines of the Gospel and the duties of the Christian life even in the lowest and worst forms in which they ever have been presented.

Naturally men are disinclined to the restraints and discipline that religion imposes; and when theologians begin to dispute about any of its doctrines, men naturally come to the conclusion that that doctrine is either unimportant or not so clearly revealed as to be obligatory. And it would seem that if this is to go on under the influences that are now at work, we shall soon come to a stage in which there will be a denial of miracles and of any revelation in the proper sense of the word, and we shall be left to the mere truths of natural religion, calling them Christianity, a Christianity without CHRIST.

Nor can we expect to stop here; the tendency to a philosophy which denies the possibility of any knowledge of anything above the mere facts and objects of Nature seems to be prevailing in most influential quarters. And if this prevails, we shall have mere agnosticism, body without a soul, a universe without GOD, and a life that is not worth living. Those that are naturally and by instinct inclined to be good will observe the principles of morality and decency as a matter of taste and of choice; but those of a different natural constitution, having nothing to restrain them, no belief in GOD or immortality, will abandon themselves to the base instincts and inclinations of their bad natures.

Men naturally ask why, if there is but one GOD, He should have many Churches in the same community, each teaching a different doctrine, each with a different mode of worship and different mode of life as the way of gaining His favor; and the question is pertinent and forcible. It is sometimes said that the object is to have doctrines and worship to suit the various tastes and characters of the different kinds of people.

But Christianity, though in a most important sense adapted to the wants and needs of man, was not intended to be adapted to his pleasures and preferences; it was rather intended to work a change in him, change his tastes and his habits so that instead of pleasing himself, he should come to love that which pleases GOD, — in short, to regenerate him and make him fit for and able to enjoy the pleasures and delights of heaven.

The great mass of men continue through life to be pretty much what they were brought up to be. Nor is this all. Everybody, I suppose, will assent to the notion that of all the ideas and influences that can be brought to bear on the youthful mind during all the days of its early training, and while it is adopting its principles and forming the habits which are to be its character in after-life, there is no one so powerful as the idea of an Overruling and All-Powerful Being who loves righteousness and will reward those that love and obey Him; this with the corresponding idea of one Perfect Man, His only SON, whom He has sent into the world to be our pattern and the example for our imitation, is of all others the most powerful and effective.

And if the progress of science and the results of observation and experience have taught us any one thing, it is the fact that all men, and especially while they are children, must have the stimulus of some motive that is higher and more powerful than any understanding, foresight, or appreciation of the natural consequence of their acts of which they are now capable, if they are to lead lives that are much above their natural instincts.

The first question, then, is, Who are they that "sit in Moses' seat," and whose teachings we are to follow? It is written also, and for Christians, after the full establishment of the Church, "Remember them which have the rule over you, who have spoken unto you the Word of GOD: whose faith follow. . . . Obey them that have the rule over you, . . . submit yourselves: for they watch for your souls" [Heb. xiii. 7, 17].

As we have seen and said, the Romanists make the Bible not only subordinate to the Church, and to their special branch of the Church, but also to the one man who is recognized as the head of that Church, — the Bishop of Rome. Hence they are not inclined to encourage, or even to allow, the free use of the Bible by their own people, — by the very class of people to whom and for whom, as we have seen, the several books of the New Testament, with very few exceptions, were written.

In the extreme Protestant view, on the other hand, whatever may be held or inculcated in theory, the Bible comes to be regarded, in fact and in practical results, as plenarily inspired; that is, all that is received as part of the Word of GOD, and inspired at all, is regarded for all practical results as being not only the very words of GOD, but each sentence by itself as the whole truth that relates to that subject. Hence each one fixes upon some favorite passage or text, and insists upon that as the truth and the whole truth, and makes all the other parts of the Scriptures that he accepts, or has ever read, conform to that one. Hence we have Baptists, Calvinists, Methodists, Unitarians, Universalists, etc., according as these students of the Bible fix upon one or another text and make this central or controlling fact or text as the foundation and controlling element of the system of theology or the Church they adopt.

From these considerations it would appear that if we are to have a Church unity, on the basis of the Holy Scriptures as the revealed Word of GOD, we must also have a Church that, in teaching the people, will take care to rightly " divide the Word of Truth," giving to each one a portion in due season. And here comes in the fact and the doctrine of the supremacy of the Holy Scriptures; this was the Jewish law. " To the Law and to the Testimony " [Isa. viii. 20]. Not even a Prophet, though he could perform miracles, was expected or allowed to teach anything contrary to the law as given by Moses. And so with the early Christians. They had no thought that the Church could teach anything that was contrary to the teachings of the New Testament. And as a matter of fact, the writers of the Holy Scriptures themselves never seem to contemplate or anticipate the fact that any of the duly authorized ministry in any province or nation can so far depart from that Faith in their teachings as to endanger the souls of those that are duly subject to them, or to justify us in rejecting them or departing from their ministrations.

From this it would appear that it is as important at least, if not more so, that we should in the first place ascertain and know who it is that has the right to teach us — who sit in Moses' seat — as it is to know what they teach. And yet there is doubtless a " form of sound words," a " faith once delivered to the saints," to which we are to "hold fast," whatever any man or Church may teach.

I think we must admit that each of the great denominations around us arose from the fact and to remedy an evil, that some one of the great doctrines of Christianity which the Church ought to have taught was not held forth and presented as it ought to have been by the Church and the clergy of the day and of the country when and where it arose. On the other hand, there can be no doubt that the adherents of the Papacy, in our country at least, do insist upon certain points of order and discipline which are conducive to that "obedience to the Faith" of which the Holy Scriptures speak, and are, for many persons at least, a part of, if not necessary to, that preparation for heaven which the Church itself was instituted to promote. And not only so, but each of the great denominations around us reaches and gets hold of and brings under some measure and kind of religious influence many persons, which is for the persons thus reached, and for the community at large, what neither the Protestant Episcopal Church, nor any of the denominations, could in the present state of things reach. These denominations, each and all of them, appeal to and develop, however imperfectly, the religious sentiment. They do also inculcate a higher idea of morality than would otherwise prevail. To this remark I make no exceptions, — not even of the most widely diverse religionists among us. And that is really the substance and the ground of our hope. These denominations do all of them reach a portion of the people that probably would not be brought under any religious influence if the denominations were not so many and so diverse. They do all develop and cultivate the religious sentiment, and they do all teach people to look up and forward to something higher than this world, — something holier than self to live for.

But more than this we need not acknowledgment and profession only, we need worship also, — public worship, — to educate the religious sentiment and the fear of GOD. And to accomplish its end this worship must be adapted to the wants and conditions of the people, each nation, age, and era by itself, and doubtless different in some respects in all of them.

It would appear also that not only the fact, but also the character of the public worship is of great importance. Perhaps the character and mode of worship does quite as much toward forming the character of the people as the doctrinal teaching. I think we can see this in the difference among the members of the different denominations around us.

But who shall prescribe the form of worship? It is not fully described in the New Testament any more than the mode and form of the organization of the Church, and apparently for the same reason. We do, however, find the Apostles giving directions about the worship, and giving authority to others, as Timothy and Titus, to regulate it for the people.

But on what terms shall we unite? Will the Romanists consent to restore the " Historic Episcopate " to its original dignity and independence of Papal control? Will the Protestants consent to have Bishops exercising the control over their people, including their Elders and Deacons, that Timothy and Titus exercised, one at Ephesus and the other at Crete? Shall we concede to either of them what our forefathers did not feel at liberty to concede? Will they, as organized bodies, abandon and renounce the points for which their forefathers seceded and went into a state of schismatic insubordination or anti-Christian opposition?

But I fear that we shall have no real Church unity until views of the Christian life itself come to be entertained quite different from those that we see now prevailing around us. It is not the Scriptures only, nor yet the Church only, with regard to which such widely different views as we have been considering are entertained by the members of the various sects and denominations that are found in our country. But their views of what constitutes piety — the real Christian life — are quite as widely variant as their views on either of the other subjects. No two of them agree or speak in the same terms on that most important subject.

The one essential thing in the truly religious and godly life is doubtless the doing or intending to do the will of GOD. Genuine conversion for the natural man is the turning from doing our own will and pleasure to the habitual doing of the will of GOD. Mistakes, in fact, are easily overlooked by man, and as we may believe, by GOD, the Final Judge, also. But if a man does not try or care to ascertain and do the will of GOD, he is none of His; he has not the root of the matter in him. Whatever he may do for the sake of outward appearance is but shallow, perhaps only mere hypocrisy and false pretence. But doing the will of GOD, even when it implies self-denial, and especially when it implies self-denial, is the essential thing.

"Obedient to the Faith." These seem to be the words that are used in Holy Scripture to characterize the Christian life. S. Luke uses them in speaking of the converts from among the Jews [Acts vi. 7]; S. Paul uses them to characterize his work "among all nations" [Rom. i. 5; xvi. 26]. The Romanists, on the one hand, insist on the first element, — "obedience," — and subject all to the Bishop of Rome; the extreme Protestants, on the other hand, rejecting Church authority, insist on the second element, — "the Faith." But for any substantial or permanent and harmonious unity, we must have the two united, — "Obedience to the Faith," — as, each in its due proportion, what GOD has united, and no man hath any right to put asunder.

The first sin and the beginning of all sin on earth was an act of disobedience. Our first parents lacked faith. They did not believe that GOD meant what He said and would do what He had threatened. When He warned them against eating the forbidden fruit, they thought that they would be much wiser and happier for having their way. And with the end of disobedience and a hearty and entire return to "the obedience to the Faith," we shall see what S. Paul predicted as the final end and aim of the Incarnation, the establishing of the Church and the preaching of the Gospel; namely, "Then cometh the end, when He shall have put all enemies under His feet, and He shall have delivered up the kingdom to GOD; even the FATHER, and GOD will be all in all" [1 Cor. xv. 24–29]. Then right and righteousness will everywhere prevail.

But whatever we may do and whatever may come, we must see to it that we unite on Church grounds; that in any union or confederation with others, we bring them into the Church, and not cast ourselves out of it; that we bring them under the jurisdiction of the "Historic Episcopate," and not, leaving that, invent one of our own, forsaking and forfeiting all possibility of recognition by those branches of the Church which are unquestionably of Apostolic origin, and which, whatever they may have lost or invented, have retained the Holy Scriptures, the Creeds, and the Sacraments, and have also preserved in its unbroken succession the one "Historic Episcopate."

W. D. WILSON.

"The Faith which was once for all Delivered."

JOSEPH F. GARRISON, D.D., PROFESSOR OF LITURGICS AND
CANON LAW IN THE PHILADELPHIA DIVINITY SCHOOL.

FOR more than a thousand years the external unity of the Church of CHRIST has been broken up.

Temporary ruptures between the East and West had occurred at times from a very early period in the history of the Church, but finally their disputes became so bitter that they separated entirely. Intercommunion between them ceased. Each tolerated only its own adherents; and so far as organic or visible unity is concerned, the Greek, or Eastern, and the Western, or Latin, Communions have remained disunited to the present day.

At the Reformation in the sixteenth century divisions arose in the Church in the West. Its differing portions became separated from each other, and numerous breaks were thus made in " the corporate unity" of this part of Christendom.

Upon the continent, besides the Romanists, who still retained their allegiance to the Papal throne, there were the Lutheran communities of Germany, Sweden, Denmark, and Norway. Some of these preserved the Episcopate, as they claim, in a perfectly valid and historic form; while with others this was lacking, apparently rather from circumstances than any special desire to have it so.

Scotland and Holland had in like manner assumed independent positions, and had adopted for their national Churches the mode of organization favored by Calvin, — a system maintained also by the heroic Huguenots of France, and the republic of Geneva; while the Church of England, although it also was separated from external communion with Rome, had yet carefully retained in their integrity all the elements which the Church of the Apostles had regarded as essential, in either its Faith or its organization.

But these larger and historical divisions of " the corporate unity" of the Church are not the only ones with which we are concerned; there have been, since the Reformation, a considerable number of religious bodies separated from the English Church, which are now independent Communions. Each of these has its own creed, ministry, and discipline, and is organized according to the circumstances or convictions in which it had its origin.

Among the more prominent of these are the Presbyterians, Methodists, Baptists, Congregationalists, and others with them, too numerous to mention; we must take all these into account in any scheme designed to promote the reunion of Christendom. The principles which are to be "the basis for the restoration of the corporate unity" of the whole Church, must apply equally — though in very different ways — to the comparatively recent separations of the followers of George Fox and John Wesley, and to the problem of the ancient disunion between the Churches of the East and the Communion of Rome. But though the question of reunion, taken in its whole extent, thus concerns the entire Church, and reaches far back into its history, we are called upon here, by the terms of the Lambeth Encyclical, to deal chiefly with the Christian bodies once of our own Communion, but now separated from us by "the unhappy divisions" which so sorrowfully rend and weaken our Protestant Christianity.

These should certainly have the first place in our interest and affection. Their founders were in most cases members, in some ministers, of the Church of England. The separation of some of them from that Church might have been easily prevented by a larger measure of wisdom and charity on the part of its authorities. They have now grown to vast institutions which are daily preaching the Gospel to multitudes, and showing "by their fruits" that the spirit of the MASTER is with them in much they do.

No one having in him the true spirit of CHRIST can read the reports of the immense work for good, "casting out devils in the name of CHRIST," wrought by the great Protestant Churches, without thanks to GOD that such Divine work, and so blessed, is being done, — even though it be by those who in certain things "follow not us" [Mark ix. 38], or without a corresponding sense of loss and grief that we cannot join hand in hand with them in every element of Church activity, and manifest that we are brethren, not only in that "unity of the spirit" which binds us all to CHRIST, but also in the offices of that ministry which was given to the Church "once for all" by its founders, and which, with its Holy Scriptures, its Faith, and Sacraments, it was charged to hand down to the end of the ages.

It was especially our relations with these divisions from our branch of the Church, and a deep conviction of the evils of their continuance, that led the Bishops in the General Convention, and in the Lambeth Conference, to prepare and issue their earnest appeals upon the subject of Church unity and to state the conditions which they deemed essential to any basis for the reunion of Christendom.

It is with the general principles involved in these propositions, and some practical thoughts on the course of the Church in this matter, that the following paper will chiefly be occupied.

The word "reunion" expresses, in my mind, the real essence of the whole movement. It indicates, in its simple meaning, a return of some kind and in some way to "a unity" which had once existed, but at present is interrupted. The original unity of Christendom was the Church as established primarily on principles derived from the Apostles, and agreeing in all its parts in certain essential elements; namely, the one Faith, the Holy Scriptures, the Sacraments of CHRIST, the Orders of the Ministry, and the means for its continuance and government; and where there have been divisions which rejected or perverted any of these, the only way to a true reunion is by a return to, and acceptance again, of all the principles which were regarded as essential to the original unity.

This conformity to the essential elements of the primitive Church as the only basis for Christian reunion is not the device or invention of any branch of the Church of to-day, nor was it struck out by any Convention of Bishops as a plausible theory to commend the Episcopate; upon the contrary, the principle on which it rests — the assumption that the great outlines of Church faith and Church order were to be preserved in their substance through all after-time — pervades all the writings of the ante-Nicene period, and is in strict accord with all that the New Testament teaches of the nature and continuance of the Church.

Many scout at all such obligations, on the ground that CHRIST gave no command as to any mode of the organization or transmission of the Church. Neither, however, did He give any command that the four Gospels should be written, nor do these Gospels declare by whom, or when, or under what authority they were composed; the chief *external* evidence on which we receive them is that they form an integral part of the constitution of the primitive Church. Hence we believe that the Faith, Sacraments, and Orders which were also accepted by this Church as essential in its organization, were likewise to be preserved in their principles through all the after-history of the Church.

It is contended by some that the conditions of the primitive Church cannot be reproduced in our day, hence that it is absurd to imagine that these principles of the Apostolic age can be applied in the Church of the present time. It is undoubtedly true that the needs of the changing centuries require corresponding modifications in the *workings* of every institution, the Church among the rest; the modes of *interpreting* even articles of the Creed will vary; the "Historic Episcopate" must "be adapted in its administration" to the changed conditions of different times and peoples. But there is no reason to believe that there will be any period when the principles which were deemed fundamental in all the early centuries of the Church should not be held equally so in every succeeding age of that same Church. Nay, more, if the Church be, as we hold, a Divine institution, it is eminently rational that the Faith, Sacraments, Holy Scriptures, and Ministerial Orders which were regarded as essential from its beginning, should have been given to it "once for all," and should therefore be retained as living elements in all the future of the Church.

It is just these fundamental elements of the Church of the Apostolic ages which the Bishops set forth as a basis for the reunion of Christendom.

This was not issued as a sort of Protocol for future negotiation, but as a clear and definite statement by the Bishops of the great Anglican Communion that the only and true basis for a restoration of the unity of all the parts of the Church, whether Greek, Roman, Anglican, or Protestant, is the acceptance by all alike of the principles on which the Church was originally founded, and their adoption, unperverted and unmutilated, as the necessary conditions of reunion of the Churches in the future. Nothing of vital import can be added, nothing of fundamental value cast away.

The position above taken implies that the basis which is proposed must be regarded *as a whole ;* its several parts are linked together and form a coherent system ; all of them were essential in the Church's primal unity; no one of them can be discarded from the conditions of reunion in our day; and further yet, when taken separately, and apart from the living whole of which they are the elements, no one of them can by itself meet the very ends for which it was intended in its association with the others.

Take, for example, the acceptance of the two Creeds, — the Apostles' and that called the Nicene — as " a sufficient statement of the Christian Faith."

In the Church of the first three hundred years the only and " all-sufficient statement of the Faith " was a summary substantially the same in its essential features as that which has been known for centuries as " The Apostles' Creed."

This Creed now occupies well-nigh the same position in the Churches of England and America as the analogous but simpler form did in the ante-Nicene age ; in connection with its expansion in the Creed of Nicæa, it is the only " Confession of Faith " which they require from all their members. The *Church* does not need to require any more.

This is due mainly to the fact that in the Church the *Creed does not stand alone,* but is an integral part of a system. It is an introduction to a large and connected whole; in this its fitting place it is associated with other agencies which present the Church's teaching on duties and doctrines that are not embodied in the Creed, and yet are necessary to the full and right development of the Christian life. Hence, as these means of supplying all the necessities of the spiritual life are thus provided, the Church does not need any other obligatory standard of Faith than this which has come down to us from the earliest ages.

While, however, the Creed is satisfactory in its place as " The Creed of the CHURCH," its position is very different when considered as the sole basis of unity, or the sole body of doctrine for a denomination.

On the one hand, as the denominations do not possess the complete system by which the Creeds are accompanied in the

Church, they find it necessary in some way to meet this want. Hence the more thoughtful of them embody their leading principles in "Confessions," which their people often find complex and burdensome, but which at the same time they feel it to be equally difficult to revise or to do without.

Upon the other hand, the bare adoption of the Creeds, with no other authorized teaching on doctrine or on morals than is expressed in them, would be but a slim safeguard against the intrusion into the Church of certain bodies which might profess a formal symbol of belief and yet maintain opinions and allow practices wholly foreign to the spirit of the Gospel. Communities such as these are by no means unknown phenomena in the history of the past.

Hence the Creeds, when taken alone, are incompetent to serve as a basis on which we can ever build a reunited Christendom. What is true in this respect of the Creeds is likewise true of the other parts of the basis we are discussing, whether taken singly or with some portions only of their number to the exclusion of the others. Regarded in their connection, and as a whole, they form the original conditions of the unity of the early Church; but considered separately, no portion of them without *all the others* can offer a practical, or even plausible, ground on which a theory of reunion could be reasonably based.

There have been since the present awakening of the Christian world to the importance of reunion many plans suggested for bringing about some mode of mutual interchange of ministry without an adoption of the original system of the Church as this is embodied in the papers of the Bishops.

One of the most popular of these is that known in general as "A Federation of the Churches."

As indicated by the term, the leading idea seems to be to establish some sort of an arrangement between such of the Christian denominations as may unite in the agreement by which each of those in the association shall preserve its own "corporate" existence, teach its own special doctrines, have its own Creed, — excepting only in such points as may have been adopted as the conditions of their Federation, — while at the same time the ministry of each shall be allowed free interchange in preaching, and in other offices of the Church, with all the others.

Apart from any principles concerning the nature of the Church, the practical difficulties of any such scheme would be insuperable.

How should the basis of their association be prepared? Should a consultation of certain denominations lay down the conditions and ask the others to adopt them? What reason have we to think that the acts of any such self-constituted body would be accepted by the other parts of Christendom? Can any sane man imagine that a universal conference of the innumerable sects of Protestantism could be had, or, if it should be attempted, that it could possibly agree on any terms which would allow that each should interchange its pulpits and its Sacraments with all the others? And without such universal agreement the divisions of Protestantism, even outside the Church, would be no nearer a unity than they are to-day.

This brings us to the consideration of the much-vexed question of the refusal of the Church to allow the ministers of other denominations to preach in its pulpits or to take part in its public offices.

This is not, as some seem to think, an exhibition of the insolence of caste on the part of our clergy; still less is it an expression of their sense of individual merit or personal superiority. GOD forbid that any one belonging to the ministry of the Church of CHRIST should have these feelings, or feelings in any manner akin to them! This were, indeed, not only un-Christian, but unchurchly and unwarranted upon any ground. There are numbers in the ministry of the Communions of which we speak, at whose feet I have willingly sat as an humble learner in many of the deep truths of theology and the spiritual experiences of the Christian life; the question in no sense concerns the individual members of their ministry, or the personal excellence of the men to whom the work of their ministrations is committed. The Church holds itself to be "a witness and keeper" of the fundamental elements of the Church's organization and order as well as of the Holy Scriptures and the Faith; and when it declares in the Ordinal that "no man shall be suffered to execute any of the functions" of the ministry "in this Church except he have had Episcopal ordination," this is simply an application of one of the principles which was universally accepted in the Church of the Apostles, and from which no portion of the historic Church has ever departed.

There is also another consideration arising from the relation of the Episcopate to the other elements of the primitive Church that may be noted here. The existence and successions of Bishops do not stand alone in the constitution of the primitive Church, any more than its accepted Creed. No one of its original elements can be discarded from this Church without imminent peril to the preservation of the others.

The Episcopate and the requirement of Episcopal ordination, like the others, are integral parts of an organic whole; the same "ancient authors," in the same argument, often in the same passage or page, in which they refer to the existence and teachings of the Scriptures of the New Testament, will also assert the Apostolic origin and the succession of the Bishops as facts equally undoubted and universal in every portion of the Church. If we refuse to accept their testimony, when they witness to facts so patent as the connection of the Bishops with the Church, or to allow full weight to their authority when they assume "an unbroken line of the Episcopate" as a reality which no one would question, can we rely upon them as trustworthy evidence in the far more difficult and subtle discussions on the authorship and divineness of the books of the New Testament? It would prove, soon or late, a disastrous experiment to disparage their testimony as to the position and character of the Episcopal Order, and then expect to have them received as chief witnesses in support of the canonicity of Holy Scripture.

"The Historic Episcopate" is thus to be accepted, with the other principles of the original form of the Church, as one of the essential parts of that Church, and as such it cannot be rejected from any proper basis of reunion.

Whether there shall ever be a reunion of Christendom, or how it can be effected, lies only in the mind of the "All-knowing."

That the great Protestant Communions shall, as organized bodies, be willing to agree with us on any such basis as will produce a real or corporate union, is, in my opinion, most unlikely ever to happen. Both the circumstances of their several origins, and the position they now occupy, render any such fusion in mass almost impossible.

If there should ever be a return of Christendom to its original and intended unity, it will not, in all human probability, come from resolutions or proceedings of any assembly or conference or convention, but from a wide-spread conviction among Christian people as to what really constitutes a Church, and a consequent flowing of the multitudes into the Communion which shall have proved itself by its truth, spirit, and works, as well as its Orders, to be the true Church. Should the Church which claims to be Apostolic ever thus win "the hearts and minds" of the bulk of the Christian community, the unity of Christendom would then be attained by the gathering of its people into its one Church.

The practical interest of the Anglo-American Church in this matter of reunion is chiefly concerned, as we have already stated, with the position of the various Protestant Communions among whom we are.

There is a feeling, far too common, on the part of many Churchmen, that the fault of these separations from the Church of England was all upon one side; that these organizations had gone into schism without any reason, and being in schism, had but one thing to do, — this was to confess their error, and return at once to the bosom of the Church.

But there is a far deeper significance in the origin and continuance of these separations than can be thus easily disposed of; and the Church can never deal wisely with the questions now presented to her without realizing that there is a philosophy in *sectism*, and a profound meaning in the existence of sects, which she is called on to understand and to apply.

The reasons for the separation of many of the Dissenters from the Church of England rest largely with the Church itself; and a correct appreciation of some of these reasons may furnish lessons of no slight importance to the future of the Church.

The source of several of the more important of these divisions lay in a condition of the Church at the period of their occurrence by which some great truth or duty which belonged to her had been neglected or repressed. Earnest men, feeling that their spiritual nature demanded a fuller recognition of this than the Church would then permit, gathered themselves into associations to supply this special lack. These gradually shaped themselves into complete organizations, which after a time became wholly independent Communions, and were entirely severed from the Church.

It was an impulse of this kind which resulted in the formation of the Quaker Society, and the establishment of John Wesley's Methodism.

In the former case the strife of parties had well-nigh silenced the Church's voice on the vital doctrine of the inner personal testimony of the HOLY SPIRIT to the soul; and the fervid, though often wild and misdirected zeal of George Fox embodied this great truth in a sect which called the thoughts of many who had no sympathy with his society to realize their need of a personal communion with the SPIRIT far more vividly than they would otherwise have done.

So again, had the Church of England been at all awake in the time of Wesley to the necessity of zealous preaching to the poor and destitute, and of an individual awakening to the need of their conversion to a Christian life, he would have been able to keep his followers and converts, as he always desired to do, in the Communion of the Church; and the Church would thus at the same time have profited by his zeal, and have added to her numbers multitudes who were her rightful children.

There were also separations which grew out of oppressions and hardships, — from the harsh actions of Ecclesiastical Commissions, and sometimes the personal severity of Bishops. And those who might have been kept in the Church by a measure of consideration and Christian charity, upon the part of its authorities, were largely through these means driven off into new organizations that have transmitted to their members feelings of bitterness which long generations have not yet effaced.

Viewed in this connection with their causes, the existence of these separated Communions has an intended meaning for the Church, and one of great practical significance in our day.

It teaches very clearly that we should seek in each of these denominations what is that feature or aspect of the Christian life which has been its distinguishing characteristic and its chief power for good in actual practice, and should endeavor ourselves to do that thing by the Church more wisely and more effectively than it has been done by its special advocates. Live more closely in the communion of the SPIRIT than the followers of Fox. Be more eager in the work of saving souls than even Wesley was. Study to be more powerful in preaching than the Presbyterians; and so of all the rest.

Considered thus, the continuance and success of these denominations are constant and urgent calls to the Church that it should learn what there is in each of them that we may profit by and use as a means to aid us in ministering through the Church to these same spiritual needs of men.

There is no one of the causes that led to these divisions that may not now be remedied. There is no one of their special lines of Christian labor that we may not carry on more effectively in the Church than they can do without it.

Here, in my view, is a large responsibility resting on the Church in this matter of reunion. Let her in every form of Christian usefulness show herself more zealous and more effective than any of "the Churches." Let her make good her Apostolic character by act and spirit, as well as by claim and argument, however well grounded these may be. Let her demonstrate, by fulfilling the high duties laid upon her, that there is no need for any other agency than the Church of CHRIST to do the work of CHRIST.

When she presents in some adequate degree these evidences that she is entitled to be in fact, as she is in right, the centre of the unity of Christendom, multitudes, who before have stood apart, will come to her, because in her they will find the fullest and most effective means of satisfying the spiritual needs of both the individual man and the whole community.

Time, zeal, great labor, and self-sacrifice must all be given, and in abundant measure, before any such result can be attained. But if there ever shall be any reunion of Christendom, it only can be, I believe, upon essentially the principles which have been outlined here.

J. F. GARRISON.

The Holy Eucharist the Lord's Eirenicon.

Prof. John J. Elmendorf, D.D., Western Theological Seminary, Chicago.

I HAVE been asked to write a contribution to the great subject of union among the followers of Christ, and the special topic assigned to me is the Holy Eucharist. If the dogmatic, or the controversial, or the historical treatment of the subject were in question, I should feel obliged to decline the invitation so kindly extended to me. Centuries of controversy and very numerous dogmatical, historical, and liturgical treatises have already presented all that can be said upon the subject. A résumé of these is not now, perhaps, demanded. But the letter of the Bishops which has called out such copious correspondence seems to be an Eirenicon; and the Holy Eucharist is the Lord's own Eirenicon, — not only the bond of love and union between Him and the faithful, but also the Sacrament of love and union throughout the members of His Mystical Body.

So viewed, my writing in haste will not be thinking hurriedly. Since I have no authority to speak for any other than myself, my words must, of course, seem to be merely individual opinion. But being what some call an "extreme High Churchman," or, what some of us claim to be, an Anglo-Catholic Christian, I will endeavor to present an Eirenicon from their point of view, not controversially, nor even offering proofs or references, but simply as a part of the call to unity in the bond of peace and Christian fellowship.

If the Saviour of the world preserves us in union with Himself through this holy and blessed Sacrament, it should surely be the sign and seal of unity, as it is the source of unity among all believers. And if the history of Christendom in its later ages tells us another story, the fault is in us, not in Him or in the means which He has instituted.

Let us, in the first place, agree to say nothing of abuses or perversions on one side or the other. If high doctrine respecting the Holy Eucharist is to be held responsible for the superstitions with which sensual or degraded souls have ever overlaid it, the retort, " Tu quoque," is close at hand. Profanation and blasphemy which spared not the adorable REDEEMER Himself have been the protest of other sensual or degraded souls. Let us lay aside arguments from abuses. Politics of the baser sort employs that kind of argument; let us leave it there. One politician is accused of malfeasance in office. If the accusation is but too glaringly true, our " leading newspapers " retort, " You 're another; " and, it seems, with fair success. But the union of Christendom is not to be promoted by the use of such weapons.

I seek only to call attention to certain facts which in these days may be sometimes overlooked, and to try to make some necessary inferences from those facts.

When, in past days, the Holy Eucharist has seemed to be an occasion of discord, the true cause of that must have been the lack of charity or the lack of faith in us. There have been grave misunderstandings also. Even such a comparatively minor point as kneeling at the reception of the gift has been called idolatry, on one side; the refusal to do so, profanity, on the other. Philosophy, Christian philosophy, if it please any one to call it so, has undertaken to give a rational account of the LORD'S mysterious words in instituting this Sacrament. And rationalism, substituted for simple faith, has asked the old question, " How can this Man give us His Flesh to eat? " I do not write for or against either of these. But addressing myself to those, whatever their Christian name may be, who desire to give all faith and love to the SAVIOUR of the world, I ask them whether the perpetual testimony to the everlasting love of JESUS needs to be counted among the barriers which separate us in these last days.

If we may make our inference from the articles that appeared in the April number of the CHURCH REVIEW, the question is easily answered. Only one of the twenty found serious difficulty in this direction [p. 80], and objection was made in that reply, not to the Bishops' Eirenicon, but, first, to those features of our Liturgy which it shares with all Liturgies throughout Christendom, at least until the Reformation, and, secondly, to the seeming disregard of a part of the Christian Faith. A possible answer to these objections will, I humbly hope, be found in the course of this article.

The Bishops who issued the invitation to union among Christians are the only authority which can explain their words respecting the Holy Eucharist. But it may be permitted to me to suggest that they have distinguished between *Sacramental* necessity and what may be called *moral* necessity. Some things are necessary for a valid Sacrament. Other things are necessary for decency and reverence, for suitable action toward GOD, and for a proper expression of faith and love.

I. SACRAMENTAL REQUISITES.

These are what the Bishops specified. Without them there can be no Sacrament, no Sacramental union among " those who profess and call themselves Christians." Those requisites are three in number.

1. There must be a lawful minister of the Sacrament. Since this commemoration is the outward as well as inward act of the united family of GOD, it needs a leader who may speak for all, the mouth-piece of all who are the " spiritual Priesthood, ordained to offer up spiritual sacrifices, acceptable to GOD through JESUS CHRIST." Viewed in this light alone, it may seem that the Holy Eucharist finds the authority of its minister only in the choice of those whom he represents.

But acting also in CHRIST'S stead as the medium through which the loving gift of JESUS is bestowed, he must have received also from his LORD special authority and commission for that purpose. If any one assert that no special gift is bestowed on a worthy recipient of the Sacrament, or that however that may be, the only requisites for a valid administration and a lawful ministry are election by the brethren and an inward call (a call which none can attest but him to whom it is given), if any one assert that any Christian man, woman, or child has like authority to break bread and bless wine to be drunk in memory of the LORD'S death, our way to union with him is barred. We have no common ground on which this Eirenicon can stand. I suppose that the Bishops imply, and the twenty respondents admit this first requisite for a valid Sacrament. The difficulty of the latter is found where I have no occasion to follow them; to wit, the deciding what constitutes a valid ordination of a minister of this Sacrament.

2. There must be the Divinely appointed action, the words

uttered, the material which the LORD blesses, and the outward act which employs and unites the word and the matter. There is no Sacrament without the bread and the wine, the words of Institution which the LORD employed, and the action of the minister which unites these. This also the Bishops implied, and the respondents accepted.

3. There must be a general intention on the part of those engaged to do what the LORD ordained. A mock celebration would be empty and blasphemous profanity, not a Sacrament. And I say a general intention, because it will not, I think, be maintained that a full understanding and agreement respecting what is done, is requisite. For who of us understands all that we say even when we utter the LORD'S prayer? And our child who understands less still, may say a truer prayer than we ourselves. So is it also with the Creed in which we profess our faith. As we move upward toward the Divine Light, many things grow clearer; but the clearest insight vouchsafed to an earthly saint does not pierce to the centre of the Divine mysteries. Therefore it appears that only a general intention on the part of minister or communicant is requisite, and not a full comprehension, provided only that he does not, in self-willed obstinacy, pride, unbelief, or hardness of heart, close his eyes to such light of truth as has been given to him. Even in that case it is not to be supposed that the sinfulness of the minister hinders whatever the love of JESUS may be ready to bestow. But I do not touch any mooted point respecting the secret intention of the minister of the Sacrament. I have in mind only the general intention of the family of GOD to obey their LORD'S command.

This leads us to the great question of the Christian Faith respecting the Holy Eucharist; but let it be deferred while we consider what have been called the moral requisites of a true celebration of this august Sacrament.

II. MORAL REQUISITES.

The Divine injunction that all "things be done decently and in order" unites with all due feelings of reverence and devotion to make that celebration the most solemn, the most august religious act of our holy religion. At the very lowest, and in what we Catholic Christians consider to be the most imperfect view, it is our nearest approach to our SAVIOUR and to His Cross, on the one side, to His present glory on the other.

From this moral necessity has arisen the use of Liturgies dating from primitive ages, and special orders provided by the various Protestant bodies in modern times. Our Protestant brethren must not misunderstand our use of the word "Liturgy." Popularly employed for all forms of Christian worship which are not extemporary, it is used by us in its strict and narrower signification, as the ordered formula of the one perpetual and always obligatory service of Christian people, the appointed commemoration of the LORD'S sacrificial death. Around the three Sacramental requisites have clustered other words and acts, suited to express Christian love and faith, and intended for compliance with the command to "glorify GOD with our bodies and our souls, both of which are GOD'S."

Granting, as we freely do, that the Apostles and those whom they ordained for this purpose, preserved only the three Sacramental requisites as an invariable norm, and expressed their devotion in words spontaneously arising or Divinely inspired for the occasion, we think that no impartial inquirer will deny that certain forms became at once associated with Eucharistic worship. Among such forms are, the LORD'S Prayer, Eucharistic hymns like the *Sanctus*, an oblation of the elements previously to their being blessed as the Sacrament, and other such ritual observances. These were the germs of the Liturgy of S. James, of S. Mark, or some other primitive form. The preservation of what are essentially the same forms among the oldest sects of Oriental heretics, and the agreement between Churches so widely separated as those of Gaul and Egypt, Ephesus, Africa, and Spain, are conclusive respecting the primitive, we might venture to say the Apostolic origin of the chief features of the Liturgy. The external evidence is, to say the very least, as strong as that for the Canon of the New Testament. We think it to be a note of the Historic Church that in so important a matter the primitive path is still pursued. And I will venture to add that the internal evidence of the spiritual power of the Divine Liturgy is quite as great as that of the Books of the Kings, the Song of Solomon, or the Epistle of S. James.

But this letter is not a dissertation on Liturgies, and therefore its author is not called on to specify the points of agreement which indicate the common source in Apostolic days of the chief primitive Liturgies. We are ready to show, if necessary, that the Liturgy of the Anglo-Catholic Church is one with those primitive norms, but that is not now in question.

In the Bishops' invitation to union, and in the twenty articles of reply, there was entire reticence respecting what I have called the "moral requisites." The Bishops, it is to be supposed, understood that the outward expressions of faith and love vary according as all human institutions are variable. If sitting at the reception of the Holy Communion means a wilful denial of what the Catholic Church is obliged to teach, then sitting would be condemned by her, along with the unbelief from which it springs. But in this year of the LORD 1890 it is possible that a penitent, loving, faithful Christian may approach his GOD, and have His SAVIOUR make special approach to him, while he is sitting and not kneeling, having never learned or practised any other gesture. He removes his hat, he closes his eyes, he has his own ritual observances, and will have them until his day for ritual observances is past; and he rests in hope of a joyful resurrection. On that day of the LORD'S return and the rising again in glorified humanity of all his people, he will make no objection to the "extreme ritual" which S. John saw in vision, and he will see in reality. But at present the Bishops seemed to admit that, so far as we are concerned, a company of faithful people might be duly observing the Sacramental requisites, might be one with us, without those moral requisites which the customs of the Catholic Church have preserved.

III. SACRAMENTAL INTENTION.

It is not what Christians *believe* which divides them; it is their doubt, their denial of what is affirmed. But it is not doubt or denial which is the work of faith; it is not that which unites them to their LORD and SAVIOUR. Suppose, then, that the three Sacramental requisites are duly observed, what will their faith and love attest? The LORD may be for them, He may do for them far more than their hearts conceive; but what will they *intend?*

1. All Christian people desire to commemorate the Sacrifice of JESUS, which was consummated on His Cross. All desire to adore Him as their LORD, King and Priest forever, ever living to make intercession for them through the merits of

His Cross and Passion. They believe that He is now presenting Himself, in His glorified human nature, Priest and Victim, Victim once slain, now glorified through shameful death and transfigured Resurrection.

2. All Christians believe that they are "a holy Priesthood" before GOD, permitted and enjoined to plead the merits of their once slain REDEEMER, and to have their prayers for themselves and their intercessions for one another presented by their great High-Priest, with whom, by whom, and in whom, they approach their gracious GOD. There is but one meritorious sacrifice continually offered. He "ever liveth to make intercession" for them. This is the one spiritual sacrifice to which they unite the oblation of themselves, "presenting their souls and bodies a living sacrifice," acceptable in the Beloved.

3. All Christians believe that in this action some spiritual gift is bestowed on them so far as their penitence, faith, and love have qualified them to receive it. Just what that gift may be, what are the means which the LORD employs for their salvation, they may not clearly understand. The result of it is what has all their attention; to wit, their union with their LORD, and their growth in His likeness through their union with Him.

Whatever more is true, these three things are true, and he must have a very contracted soul who can fancy that those who endeavor faithfully to observe all that their LORD commanded, and have all that is sacramentally requisite, are rejected by Him because of their limited knowledge, and the consequent imperfection of their faith.

4. But another is more fully instructed, and has gone farther in knowledge of the mystery of Redemption. The special gift bestowed in Holy Communion, the special means employed for his salvation, is a participation of what the LORD of glory took to Himself, when "for us men and for our salvation, He came down from heaven, and was Incarnate by the HOLY GHOST of the Virgin Mary." He is "the living bread which came down from heaven." The fruits of this Christian's fuller faith may be no more than those of the imperfect faith of his brother. And yet his fuller faith is a good gift, and should have yielded more abundant fruit.

5. Another calls to mind the spiritualized and glorified nature of his REDEEMER, and remembers His Sacramental words,

"This," which I break, "is my Body." And he believes, not understanding "how this Man can give us His Flesh to eat." But he adores his SAVIOUR, who has found out earthly means to come so near, ever since He was incarnate for us. The fruits of his faith may be less than his brother's are, though they ought to be more, since his faith is more truly adapted to all the length and breadth of his compound humanity.

6. Finally, another remembers that the LORD appointed an outward and visible Sacramental action; that He said, not merely, "Eat this in remembrance of Me," but, "This do for My memorial;" that He appointed a certain action, — the taking into the hands and breaking, with benediction and giving of thanks, the doing all that from which the Sacrament obtains its name of Holy Eucharist. This is seen to require a duly commissioned representative of CHRIST, as well as a representative of the brethren, one whose authority comes from above, and not merely from the spiritual Priesthood of the faithful people. Such an office is, outwardly, what all inwardly possess and exercise. If theirs is a spiritual Priesthood, his is an outward and visible one, representing the other, which is only such because of union with the one true "Priest forever." What the faithful do inwardly, through CHRIST, in CHRIST, and with Him, that is done outwardly and visibly, in an outward and visible Sacrament, for them and with them, by their representative, who is also their SAVIOUR'S representative, in, through, and by the one Mediator between GOD and man, the Man CHRIST JESUS.

Such a fuller faith believes that all this is true whether all the brethren have it in mind or not. But who has such authority and outward Priesthood, and how such authority is conferred by the LORD in these last days, are not questions now before us. They belong to that fourth condition of union among Christians of which the respondents to the Bishops have had much to say.

I will only add that when the Divine Liturgy is used, all these six points of intention are clearly expressed, whether they are fully in the mind of the celebrant or not. But since the use of it is not a Sacramental necessity, and since a full understanding of it is not requisite, but only a general intention to do what the LORD commanded, it would seem that those may be united on earth as they are joined in the LORD, whose faith, not rejecting any light which it has received, is yet not wholly upon what we regard as the highest plane of supernatural truth.

IV. THE LITURGY AND FREE PRAYER.

It is a question sometimes asked, Are Christians to be tied down to an unvarying form of prayer, while their needs are varying from day to day? Have they not the privilege of going to their FATHER, and saying to Him their special desires and needs, according as their own hearts may prompt them? And is this liberty, if they have it, confined to their own private devotions?

But the answer readily appears. The Liturgy is, indeed, an unvarying form in which the Mystical Body of CHRIST appears with Him before the FATHER'S throne. But it has a place for what is one of its moral requisites, intercessions for the living and the departed members of the LORD. Nothing hinders their being named personally. That is a matter of custom and convenience. But I have heard them named in a "ritualistic" Church, and have used the same privilege myself, under suitable circumstances.

Restore, also, the unvarying norm of worship, the Liturgy, — and what Christian can find it in his heart to object to it? — and then, at other times, Church order allows, or may allow, varied prayers. The Daily Morning and Evening Prayer of the Prayer-Book are pretty well understood to be the regular offices of the clergy and Church institutions, providing for their use the regular reciting of the Christian's inspired Hymnal, the Bible Psalms, and regular reading in course of the Sacred Scriptures.

Outside of these, loyal and faithful Christians may receive license for other prayers, more specially adapted to the special occasion, and the Bishops, within their own jurisdiction, more and more frequently give such license. And this, if I am not mistaken, is most freely done where the Divine Liturgy is most frequently and regularly used. If I may be allowed to use personal illustration, it was in a Cathedral where it is daily used, that while holding a mission there, I had the Bishop's permission to use special prayers for that special occasion.

Whenever the Holy Eucharist shall become what the LORD made it, His own Eirenicon among Christians, there will surely be no difficulty respecting free prayer, which some Christian societies may approve, while others more carefully restrict it.

V. WHAT SHALL THE CHURCH TEACH RESPECTING THE HOLY EUCHARIST?

As Anglo-Catholics, we answer to ourselves, "What the Church has always taught in and through the Liturgy, which is her perpetually living voice." This is an unvarying, living voice, louder, clearer, and more authoritative than all the sermons, Papal Bulls, Confessions, Articles of Religion, or what not, which may issue from any man or any part of the Christian Church, for the instruction and guidance of the faithful.

But one of the twenty respondents finds a difficulty respecting teaching [p. 80], and asks, "On the one hand, why, by such a proposition do they (the Bishops) allow the addition to the words of Institution of those prayers and ceremonies by which the Holy Communion is presented as a sacrifice for sin, an offering for the living and the dead? And, on the other hand, are they able to ignore the historical faith of the Church in the Real Presence of our LORD in the Holy Sacrament? Is not this of faith too, and can we, dare we intimate that it is of secondary importance?"

The first question, I beg the writer of the article to notice, is not a reply to the Bishops' Eirenicon, because they said nothing at all of the use of any of the ancient or modern liturgies as a condition of union. Therefore the writer was objecting to our usage, to that of the Greek and Latin Churches, to that of every Church which from Apostolic times has used the Liturgy of S. James, of S. Mark, or any other. He was not called upon to accept such use for himself and his brethren. The question proposed to him was whether or not he could be in outward communion with those who did accept and use such a Liturgy.

Our reply to the second question is, that those very Liturgies are the chief witnesses, after the Word of GOD, to the "historical faith of the Church in the Real Presence of our LORD in the Holy Sacrament." There is no one of them in which it is not as clearly expressed as in that which the Bishops use. Viewed simply as a commentary on the LORD'S own Eucharistic words, they show the clearest, the most unanimous agreement.

It is most emphatically denied that those ancient Liturgies, or that of the Anglican Church, which is derived from them and follows them in all important particulars, present the Holy Eucharist as a repetition of the one sacrifice forever offered for the remission of sins. Pretending to repeat that, is blasphemy against CHRIST; but to be allowed to join ourselves in what He is doing forever at the right hand of GOD, is the most precious privilege of His earthly Body, the "Spiritual Priesthood." And that is what the Liturgy enables us to do in the most reverent, solemn, and august manner.

In asserting this we are, under compulsion, defending ourselves, not the Bishops' Eirenicon.

Let us, then, take it up again. Our last topic is before us, the objection, "What, then, shall the Church teach respecting the Holy Eucharist?" Has the spiritual Body of CHRIST, has the "Ecclesia docens," any teaching to give the contrite, believing, loving soul? If she "ignores" any part of the Faith, or "makes it of secondary importance," is she complying with her SAVIOUR'S command to teach all her people whatever He revealed and commanded? If Eucharistic faith is believed to be anywhere imperfect among the followers of the LORD, is she not bound to lead all onward and upward to a higher and truer faith?

1. In this form, the objection of our Lutheran brother, which, he may well understand, is equally objection on the part of Anglo-Catholics, is not to the teaching of Liturgy and Catechism, but to what he regards, and must regard, as the imperfect teaching of our Protestant friends. We might well leave the answer to those who issued the Eirenicon, and are answerable for the teaching of that part of the Church which is committed to their care. But we might ask our Lutheran friends whether they are thus shut out from union with other Protestants. Or do they admit that others may have a gift beyond what they know, expect, or believe? Would union cause Lutheran Christians to renounce or lose their higher faith and the teaching of it?

2. I am regarding the question from another's point of view. But from our own we see what does not appear to be familiar to our Protestant friends. With them the individual preacher may stand on a higher platform, checked by the Bible, which each hearer interprets according to his best ability. A

Church which has the continual use of the Liturgy in the mother-tongue, and an open Bible daily read in her courts, is teaching with that living voice which our Roman brethren seem to think can only be found in an infallible earthly head. Bible and Liturgy are the infallible earthly voice of the DIVINE SPIRIT speaking outwardly and inwardly to the faithful. It is higher than all the preachers, more authoritative than all the Bishops; it speaks clearly and continuously age after age; it is older than Confessions and Articles, but it is always new and freshly applied to the difficulties of the time and the needs of each individual soul. The Holy Word is spoken as the LORD and His Apostles spoke it; but it is applied and interpreted in being turned into prayer and adoration. The *lex orandi* is the *lex credendi* and the *lex docendi*.

How far authority in the Christian Church is bound to follow the oral teaching of each minister of Sacraments, and require a strict conformity to the law of prayer, belief, and teaching, is a question of Church discipline on which I would rather not touch. But it is plain that the louder, clearer, and more authoritative voice of the whole Church is approving or rejecting his poor murmur and echo of some part of the unchangeable deposit, whenever he ceases to preach and begins to utter the obligatory words of the Liturgy.

3. It must be plain to all that the Bishops did not propose that they or the Church over which they preside should cease to use the Liturgy at all times when the Holy Eucharist is celebrated, or should leave its use optional with any one whom they ordained. They could not make such a proposition, and certainly the Church for which they spoke would not sanction their action if they did.

The only practical question, therefore, was of restoration of outward and visible communion, on the basis of the three Sacramental requisites, with those who have discarded, or have never used the Liturgy. Each individual Christian man, each congregation of Christian men, and each organized association of believers will, I suppose, consider, accept, or reject, as GOD shall give them light to consider and to judge. But, be that as it may, the Church for which the Bishops speak will continue to teach, as she has received, the unalterable Creed, to use the unalterable Liturgy, and to leave open the door to all that will enter.

Her constitutional law, which is practically unalterable, a law just renewed in this country in Prayer-Book revision, says that "there shall none be admitted to Holy Communion until such time as he be confirmed, or ready and desirous to be confirmed." This implies that if so confirmed, and if there be no moral obstacle which Church discipline is bound to consider, he shall be so admitted. Hence the door is open, and, so far as lies in us, there is intercommunion through the length and breadth of those three ancient Churches of Christendom, the Greek, Latin, and Anglican. For our law without question admits to Holy Eucharist any Christian man from any of these Churches, or any other Christian who is "ready and desirous to be confirmed."

That confirmation, on the part of each and every one who receives it, carries with it a recognition of the "Historic Episcopate." And it hardly seems credible that any Christian who gives such recognition would refuse the "laying on of hands."

This is fundamental law in the Greek, Latin, and Anglican Churches. The Bishops said nothing of it in their overtures to our Protestant brethren; so one might infer that they did not regard this form of recognition of their Divine office as an essential to intercommunion with themselves. But they are the sole interpreters of their own words. The writer of this article has quoted no authorities for his statements, and would have added none, if the Editor of the CHURCH REVIEW had not intimated something of this kind. Among familiar and easily accessible works which confirm his chief statements may be mentioned, Daniel's *Codex Liturgicus*, Neale's *Tetralogia Liturgica*, Bright's *Annotated Book of Common Prayer*, Forbes A. Corse's *Eirenicon*, or, latest and excellent, Swainson's *Greek Liturgies*, London, 1884.

J. J. ELMENDORF.

WESTERN THEOLOGICAL SEMINARY,
    CHICAGO.

The Validity of Non-Episcopal Ordination.

PROF. THOMAS F. GAILOR, M. A., VICE-CHANCELLOR OF THE UNIVERSITY OF THE SOUTH.

The Validity of Non-Episcopal Ordination. The Dudleian Lecture delivered in the Chapel of Harvard University, on Oct. 28, 1888, by GEORGE PARK FISHER, D.D., LL.D. New York: Charles Scribner's Sons. 1888.

IT is interesting from time to time to examine the arguments of able men against the Church's theory of the ministry, in order that we may not deceive ourselves by any blind reliance upon the security of our own position. In the pamphlet before us we have quite the most learned statement on "the other side" which has appeared in America for many years; for Professor Fisher's lecture is important as presenting in a very ingenious and complicated manner the whole argument against Episcopacy, and also as indicating conclusively the real question at issue in this well-worn debate. Its ostensible object is to disprove the claims of Episcopacy. Its real object is to deny the existence of any authorized ministry at all. And yet so cautiously, so delicately are the two things blended together in the lecture that it is difficult upon the first reading to determine with any precision the several divisions of the argument. Everything of positive or negative value that has ever been suggested against the superiority of Bishops is ingeniously brought in from time to time, and is reinforced by the underlying assumption of the absence of any authorized organization, until the reader is apt to consider the argument as strong against Episcopacy without realizing fully its ulterior object. The following extracts from different portions of the lecture may serve to clear the ground.

The real object to be proved is stated as follows: —

We desire to guard against the Sacerdotal theory of the ministry, which separates the clergy as a distinct, self-perpetuating body in the Church, — as a close corporation, — from the laity. Against this theory the Reformers in all Protestant lands uttered an emphatic protest. They asserted for the congregation, the general company of Christian people, the right to call their ministers, and to provide for their induction into office [p. 20].

The purpose of the ministry was to perform acts which the flock, according to the principles of the Gospel, was empowered to perform, but which, from the nature of the case, it must perform through agents and instruments [p. 22].

The theory of a clerical society, independent of the laity in virtue of its power to shut out from the ministry whom it will, and having in its hands the exclusive authority to dispense the Sacrament, is good Romanism, but not sound Protestantism [p. 22].

The true theory, then, according to the lecturer, is that all Christians are equally authorized to " dispense the Sacrament " and govern the Church; the performance of these offices is intrusted to certain men by the congregation; there is no separate class of men who can be called clergy in the sense that they have any special Divine authority in what they do distinct from laymen. In other words, the visible Church is an accident of human association, and its organization as a society was the result of natural circumstances, but not antecedently necessary for the progress of the Gospel.

Thus we are enabled to understand the positiveness, otherwise extraordinary, of the following description of the organization of the early Church; namely, —

Organization was a gradual thing. There was from the outset a profession of faith in JESUS as the CHRIST; there was baptism, initiating the convert into the company, scattered far and wide, of His followers. These followers were associated in fraternities in the several towns where they lived. Certain offices after models furnished by Jewish synagogues, and partly, it would seem, by Gentile societies, both universal and private, grew up one after another as necessity called for them, and Deacons and Deaconesses to look after the poor; . . . Pastors to whom is given a kind of oversight, . . . the title Bishop and Elder applied to them indiscriminately.

This, then, is the great result of all S. Paul's words about the Church, of all his claims to authority: this poor, weak, uncertainly organized " association of fraternities " is the actual realization of that kingdom which occupies so large a share of the LORD'S teaching, — which was founded upon a rock and against which the gates of hell should not prevail; this is "the Church of the Living GOD, the pillar and ground of the truth," "the Body of CHRIST," in which, according to the Apostle, GOD, and not man, had established differences of office and function, and had set " first some Apostles, secondarily Prophets, thirdly teachers " [1 Cor. xii. 28]. This theory of "municipal offices" and "Gentile societies" is something for which we should be glad to see some positive evidence. (Professor Fisher does not accept Hatch's imagination about "Episcopal Almoners.") It accords well with the theory of no Church and no ministry, and would be an interesting question, provided that there were no such documents as the New Testament writings, and no such thing as Church history.

Quite consistently we are told that the terms denoting ordination were the same as those which signified election or appointment to civil office; and "the laying on of hands is not enumerated in several passages of ancient authorities, — for example, in one passage in the *Apostolic Constitutions*,[1] where the essentials of ordination are set down as included among them."

To be sure, there is an awkward passage in S. Paul's II. Epistle to Timothy [i. 6], where he says, "Stir up the gift of GOD which is in thee, by means of the laying on of my hands" [c. v. 14], but this is easily disposed of with the remark, "The gift of Timothy was his fitness for the work to which he was appointed. It rested, like all the various gifts of the SPIRIT [1 Cor. xii.], on native qualities, the basis of a vocation from above, but further quickened and guided by the SPIRIT of grace. Prayer with the imposition of hands was a supplication for the SPIRIT'S influence" [p. 9].

This elaborate explanation, though rather subtle, is highly interesting, but seems quite unnecessary to those who are satisfied with the universally received practice and teaching of the Church in late years, and are therefore under no necessity to explain

---

[1] It would hardly be inferred from this statement that the *Apostolical Constitutions* distinctly declare that Bishops and Priests and Deacons must all be ordained by the imposition of hands, and yet this is unquestionably the fact [viii. 46]. The lecturer (misled by Hatch) has found a short chapter, one page long, concerning the ordination of Bishops, where the phrase "laying on of hands" does not occur, but only the word *cheirotonein*, and therefore argues that there was no "laying on of hands;" when a few chapters farther on "laying on of hands" is almost necessarily included by the bearing of the context *in cheirotonein*. The use of S. Augustine's name against the effect of imposition of hands is positively amazing. No man ever used stronger language about the Sacramental character of ordination [for example, *De Bon. Conj.* xxiv.].

away Timothy's *charisma*, or to doubt that when he was instructed to lay hands on other men for the work of the ministry, he intended to convey to them the gift which he in the same manner had himself received.

But the discussion of the manner and effect of ordination forms only a part of a wider argument, or rather statement of the non-Sacerdotal character of the ministry; namely, —

> This early Episcopacy was not Sacerdotal, but governmental. We find that in the second century Christian ministers were not clothed with the attributes of a Priesthood. To Irenæus and the other Fathers down to the period of Cyprian, or the middle of the third century, Bishops were not looked upon as Priests. Even the germs of such a view are not to be discerned until near the end of the second century [p. 7].

In this passage the ominous word is of course "Sacerdotal," and Bishops are synonymous with Presbyters, that being the point assumed immediately before. What then is this "Sacerdotalism," of which not even "the germs" appear "until near the end of the second century"? We have a definition of it given on page 22; namely, —

> The theory of a clerical society, independent of the laity in virtue of its power to shut out from the ministry whom it will, and having in its hands the exclusive authority to dispense the Sacrament, —

or in other words, the theory taught in the Preface to the Ordinal in the Book of Common Prayer, that no man shall be accounted a lawful minister except he have been ordained by one having authority. This is a true Sacerdotalism, we admit; but we are afraid that we cannot accept the statement that "even the germs of it do not appear until near the end of the second century." If Sacerdotalism mean that a man must be appointed by one already in authority before he can minister in the Church, then S. Paul was a Sacerdotalist, and so were Timothy and Titus; for they all exercised authority which was distinctly conferred on them from above and not from the people. Against these unquestioned positive examples of authority derived from above, no one ever yet has produced an instance of a minister exercising authority in the early Church who derived that authority from the congregation. Indeed, Clement of Rome, the first of the Apostolic Fathers, as early as A. D. 95 seems to be a Sacerdotalist [for example, *Ep. ad Cor.* ch. xl., xli., xlii.]. (The Edinburgh translation.)

These therefore being manifest to us, and since we look into the depths of the Divine knowledge, it behooves us to do all things in their proper order which the LORD has commanded us to perform at stated times. He has enjoined offerings to be presented, and service to be performed to Him, and that not thoughtlessly or irregularly, but at the appointed times and hours. Where and by whom He desires these things to be done, He Himself has fixed by His own supreme will, in order that all things, being piously done according to His good pleasure, may be acceptable unto Him. Those, therefore, who present their offerings at the appointed times are accepted and blessed, for inasmuch as they follow the laws of the LORD, they sin not. For His own peculiar services are assigned to the High-Priest, and their own proper place is prescribed to the Priests, and their own special ministrations devolve on the Levites. The layman is bound by the laws that pertain to laymen. Let every one of you, brethren. give thanks (*eucharisteito*, make his Eucharist) to GOD in his own order, living in all good conscience, with becoming gravity, and not going beyond the rule of the ministry prescribed to him. . . . The Apostles have preached the Gospel to us from the LORD JESUS CHRIST; JESUS CHRIST from GOD. CHRIST therefore was sent forth by GOD, and the Apostles by CHRIST. Both these appointments, then, were made in an orderly way, according to the will of GOD. Having therefore received their orders, and being fully assured by the resurrection of our LORD JESUS CHRIST and established in the Word of GOD, with full assurance of the HOLY GHOST, they went forth proclaiming that the Kingdom of GOD was at hand. And thus preaching through countries and cities, they appointed the first-fruits of their labors, having first proved them by the SPIRIT, to be Bishops and Deacons of those who should afterward believe. . . . And what wonder is it if those in CHRIST who were intrusted with such a duty by GOD, appointed those (ministers) before mentioned, when the blessed Moses also, 'a faithful servant in all his house,' noted down in the sacred books all the injunctions which were given him? . . . For when rivalry arose concerning the Priesthood, and the tribes were contending among themselves as to which of them should be adorned with that glorious title, he commanded the twelve princes of the tribes to bring him their rods, etc. . . . Did not Moses know beforehand that this would happen? . . . Our Apostles also knew, through our LORD JESUS CHRIST, that there would be strife on account of the office of the Episcopate. For this reason, therefore, inasmuch as they had obtained a perfect foreknowledge of this, they appointed those (ministers) already mentioned, and afterwards gave instructions that when these should fall asleep other approved men should succeed them in the ministry. We are of opinion therefore that those appointed by them (the Apostles) or afterwards by other eminent men, with the consent of the whole Church, and who have blamelessly served, etc., cannot justly be dismissed from the ministry.

It is hard to escape the conclusion that in S. Clement's mind the ministry derived its authority by delegation from the Apostles, and the Apostles from CHRIST; and that to question their special right to the office was to sin with Korah and his company. Leaving out of view for the present the suggestion of the three Orders by the mention of High-Priest,[1] Priest, and Levite, in connection with an instruction on the Christian ministry, and minimizing or secularizing the phraseology as much as possible, it does seem (remembering our definition of real "Sacerdotalism") that we have here a "germ" sufficiently potential to account for the strong doctrine of Ignatius,[2] twenty years afterward. As already said above, it is quite easy to assume that there was no authorized ministry, and that one Christian had as much authority to "dispense the Sacrament" as another; and it is interesting to note how a great mind can make this theory fit in with the facts, but we should like to have one single positive fragment of evidence to support it. It certainly cannot be found in the New Testament. There the line was clearly drawn between the laity and those who were "over them in the LORD" [1 Thess. v. 12], just as it had been by the Jews before. There were men who had authority to rebuke, to exhort, to warn, and to whose care the people were committed as a flock to the Shepherd [Acts xx. 28]. There were "Apostles" and "Elders" as well as "brethren," and the perpetuity of the system was provided for in the in-

[1] The word "high-priest" (*archiereus*) occurs in the *Didache* [A. D. 90] as the designation of an officer in the Christian Church superior to Bishops and Deacons [xiii. 3]. Dr. Schaff calls this the "first intimation of the 'Sacerdotal view'" [p. 206 n.].

[2] Ignatius [A. D. 110] says: "In like manner let all men respect the Deacons as JESUS CHRIST, even as they should respect the Bishops as being a type of the FATHER and the Presbyters as the council of GOD and as the college of Apostles. Apart from these there is not even the name of a Church" [*Ep. ad Tral.* 3]. "He that is within the sanctuary (*thusiasterion*) is clean; but he that is without the sanctuary is not clean, — that is, he that doeth aught without the Bishop and Presbytery and Deacons, this man is not clean in his conscience" [*Ibid.* 7]. Ignatius is so intent on the authority of the Bishops that he does not stop their succession with the Apostles, but traces it back to CHRIST Himself. And so the lecture makes a point and gravely informs us [p. 13] that Ignatius "deems the Bishops to be successors, not of the Apostles, but of CHRIST."

structions to Timothy and Titus, to "commit the traditions to faithful men who shall teach others" also, and "to ordain Elders in every city." In the only ordination of officers recorded, the people elected, but the authorized ministry ordained [cf. Article "Laity" in Smith's *Dict. Chris. Antiq.*]. It is no reply to this to say that the government under the Apostles was extraordinary; for the very fact that it was "extraordinary" — not only "extraordinary," but inspired — might guarantee the conclusion that their constitutional distinctions were of a necessary and permanent character. If a regular minister was deemed necessary at a time when miraculous gifts were common, how much more when miracles had ceased! It is a notorious fact that, three generations afterward, the whole Church, insisting upon the integrity of its traditions, did so regard them; and yet we are asked to assume, without positive evidence, that two revolutions took place in the mean time, — first, a reversal of the constitution which obtained under the Apostles, and a substitution of another copied from Jewish and Gentile models, and second, a revolution returning again to the original constitution.

For this is the all-important question: Was the authority exercised by the Christian ministry delegated to them by those in authority before them, or were they only accidental and provisional officers who were appointed by the people as imitations of Jewish and Gentile civil and municipal officers? If the latter view is true, then we ignore the inspiration in any special sense of the New Testament,[1] and we are to suppose that in one hundred years the Christian Church had completely revolutionized the primitive teaching and practice, and we have an instance of something evolved by natural process out of nothing. Then we shall say that the word or words used to describe "ordination" meant nothing more to the Christians than they did when used to describe the heathen appointments to civil offices. Why not go on and say that baptism, being a Greek

---

[1] Dr. Hatch, upon whose *Bampton Lectures* this view, as stated in the lecture, is based, frankly admits that he is treating the question of ecclesiastical organization without regard to the New Testament evidence [p. 20], and assuming that the origin of the Christian Church can be accounted for like any fact in civil history, "without any special interposition of that mysterious and extraordinary action of the Divine volition which, for want of a better term, we speak of as 'supernatural'" [p. 18]. This sounds like the title which the Deist Toland gave to his work, "Christianity not mysterious."

word meaning washing, can have no special Christian signification? So with Eucharist and Ecclesia, — had they no special meaning as used, for example, by S. Paul? Is it not true, as Prof. A. V. G. Allen [*Continuity, etc.*, p. 224] says, that the question is deeper than that of the ministry, — that the real point is whether there is a supernatural as distinguished from a natural order, and that the moment you admit that there is, then you open the way for a Sacerdotal conception of the Church with ministry and sacraments? But let us do away with the idea that ordination means anything, or that the Church means anything, then we shall fall back upon a most seductive but most destructive Pantheism which leaves no room for sin or sacrament, for ministry or Churches, or for the Incarnation itself.

It is evident that if it be assumed that there is no authorized ministry at all, any discussion of the origin of Episcopacy is superfluous. Therefore this fundamental question has received a longer notice, although the greater part of Professor Fisher's lecture is taken up with a discussion of Episcopacy. He admits that there was no period when the Presbyters and Deacons did not have a superior officer over them. He also admits that the position of S. James at Jerusalem, and of Timothy and Titus in Ephesus and Crete, was practically that of modern Bishops [pp. 10 and 14]. He also sees in the tradition which ascribes the Episcopal organization in Asia Minor to the Apostle John "a kernel of truth" [p. 14]. We might ask what more could be desired? But we are met by the reply that the Episcopacy which succeeded the New Testament period was not "roving" nor "Diocesan," but "parochial." But we reply that makes no real difference, for if you admit that there was one officer associated with a number of Presbyters and having superior authority, the *principle* of Episcopacy is proved, whether they were roving or confined to one city, or to one parish, or to one room. It is not a question of names nor of places, but of an office and authority. The language of the lecture is as follows; namely, —

If Diocesan Episcopacy had followed these, the work fulfilled by the Evangelists (Timothy and Titus) might plausibly be considered the beginning of it, and later Bishops might be thought to be their lineal successors. But the office of the early Bishops, when they became distinguished from other Presbyters, was not at all a roving Episcopate. It was a local or parochial Episcopate or superintendence, — as completely so as the office of any Presbyterian or Congregational pastor at the present day.

In other words, the assumption of "no authorized ministry," which underlies the whole lecture, takes the force out of all admissions in favor of Episcopacy. This "parochial Episcopate" means simply the charge of a congregation by one pastor, himself authorized by the people, and assisted (!) by a company of Elders, who themselves have no ministerial functions or authority. This the lecture admits was not the kind of Episcopacy exercised by Timothy and Titus; therefore there was no precedent for it. It was not the Episcopate known to Irenæus in A. D. 175, therefore it was not continued in the Church. And just why it should be imagined here without one line of positive evidence is hard to see.

Yet it renders the further discussion of Episcopacy practically useless, for if we are allowed to assume every time that Episcopacy is mentioned by an early writer that it refers to a single pastor with lay Elders in charge of his flock, then any theory can be established. Ignatius, for example (whose date, by the way, is "determined" with sufficient "positiveness" to place it between 108 and 112 A. D.,— cf. Lightfoot *Ap. F.* I. 30), is disposed of with the remark that "his Bishops are local or parochial," which is true only in the sense that perhaps his Bishops did not exercise their jurisdictions over areas as large as modern Dioceses. It is pure assumption to say that Ignatius' Bishops were "parochial" in any other sense.

Again, it is impossible to discuss the question fairly when the mind is confused by inaccurate conceptions of what the real point at issue is. Churchmen hold that there are two facts which raise a strong presumption in favor of the principle of Episcopal government; namely, the fact that the whole Church after S. Cyprian [250 A. D.], to take a late date, maintained the principle not only as historically true but as essential,[1] and sec-

---

[1] Eusebius, "the Father of Ecclesiastical History," wrote his history of the Church in 340 A. D., and by the authority of the Emperor had access to all the records. He made faithful use of the libraries in Cæsarea and Jerusalem, and has preserved fragments of many valuable documents which have since been lost. A detailed account of his sources of information, sixty in number, has been given by Flugge. [Cf. Schaff. *Ap. Ch.* p. 52.] Eusebius gives in his history, as a matter of course, the succession of Bishops from the Apostles in Jerusalem, Antioch, Alexandria, Rome, and Cæsarea. Episcopal government is evidently the only kind of Church government that he ever heard of.

ondly, the fact that the *principle* is clearly indicated in the New Testament, and this is even a stronger presumption than that for the Canon of Scripture. Against this, admitting all that may be said about the unfixedness of nomenclature in a formative period, no positive evidence can be adduced, however much inferences may be drawn from the silence of two or three documents whose negative value vanishes before the positive statements of contemporaries. Yet the lecture informs us that the question is whether we can find any Apostolic decree on this subject [p. 10], and this is repeated two or three times. We might as well look for an "Apostolic decree" on the subject of the Divinity of CHRIST or the Canon of Scripture.

Why should nearly two pages of the lecture be taken up with the possible significance of the silence of the Epistle of Clement to the Corinthians, and of Polycarp to the Philippians, when we have positive evidence of considerable value that both Clement and Polycarp were themselves Bishops? [Iren. *Cont. Her.* iii. 3, 3, Ignatius *Ad Polyc. Martyrdom of Polycarp.*] No just inference against its Episcopal character can be drawn from the absence of Bishops in the American Church during the period before the Revolution. Negative arguments are of small value, especially when opposed to positive evidence and when urged in defence of a case which has the burden of proof to bear. However, without recounting the clear evidence of Hegesippus [150], Polycrates [175], and Tertullian [200], Churchmen may safely rest their case on the testimony of Irenæus. As Bishop Lightfoot has said concerning the Canon of Scripture: —

> It is high time that fascinating speculations should be shaken off, and that Englishmen (or Americans?) should learn to exercise their judicial faculty independently. Any one who will take the pains to read Irenæus through carefully, endeavoring to enter into his historical position in all its bearings, striving to realize what he and his contemporaries actually thought about the writings of the New Testament, and what grounds they had for thinking it, and *above all, resisting the temptation to read in modern theories between the lines*, will be in a more favorable position for judging rightly of the early history of the Canon than if he had studied all the monographs which have issued from the German press during the last half-century [*Essay on Sup. Rel.* p. 141].

What is true of the Canon is equally true of the Episcopate; for the life of Irenaeus extends over the period from about 120

A. D. to 175 A. D. He represented three Churches at least, situated in different quarters of the world; namely, Asia Minor, Rome, and Gaul,— having been brought up in Asia Minor, having frequently visited Rome, and being himself Bishop of Lyons in Gaul. He was a pupil of S. John's disciple, Polycarp, and he lived for years in daily companionship with Potheinus, who must have been, from the evidence, ten years old when S. John died. Irenæus' testimony to the succession of the Episcopate occurs incidentally (all the stronger for that) in his work against Heresies [iii. 3, 1],[1] and is contained in the well-known passage:

The tradition, therefore, of the Apostles, made manifest in all the world, all may look back upon, who wish to see things truly. And we are able to recount those whom the Apostles appointed to be Bishops in the Churches, and their successors quite down to our time, who neither taught nor knew any such thing as they fondly devise. Yet surely if the Apostles had known any hidden mysteries, which they used to teach the perfect, apart and unknown to the rest, they would deliver it to those even more than others to whom they were intrusting the Churches themselves. For very perfect and blameless in all things would they have them to be whom they were leaving to be their actual successors, committing to them their own place of presidency, whose correct dealing would be a great advantage, their failure again an extreme calamity. But because it were very long in such a work as this to reckon up the successions in all the Churches, there is one very great and most ancient and known to all the Church founded at Rome, etc.

He then gives the names of the Roman Bishops; namely, Linus, Anencletus, Clement, Evarestus, Alexander, Xystus, Telesphorus, Hyginus, etc.

In other places Irenæus sometimes applies the word "presbyters" to the Bishops, very justly too, because a general must be

[1] Traditionem itaque Apostolorum in toto mundo manifestatam in omni ecclesia adest respicere omnibus qui vera velint videre; et habemus annumerare eos qui ab Apostolis instituti sunt episcopi in ecclesiis et successores eorum usque ad nos qui nihil tale docuerunt neque cognoverunt quale ab his deliratur. Etenim si recondita mysteria scissent Apostoli, quæ seorsim et latenter ab reliquis perfectos docebant, his vel maxime traderent ea quibus etiam ipsas ecclesias committebant. Valde enim perfectos et irreprehensibiles in omnibus eos volebant esse, quos et successores relinquebant, suum ipsorum locum magisterii tradentes; quibus emendati agentibus fieret magna utilitas lapsis autem summa calamitas. Sed quoniam valde longum est in hoc tali volumine omnium ecclesiarum enumerare successiones, maximæ et antiquissimæ et omnibus cognitæ, a gloriosissimis duobus Apostolis Petro et Paulo Romæ fundatæ, etc. [iii. 3, 1].

a soldier, and a Bishop is nothing if not a Priest. But from this fact we have the extraordinary inference [p. 14] that Irenæus "held to no essential distinction between the respective functions of 'bishop' and 'presbyter,'" which hardly tallies with a previous remarkable statement [p. 13] that

> Irenæus plainly falls into the mistake of regarding the Ephesian Elders who met the Apostle Paul at Miletus as 'the Bishops and Presbyters which were of Ephesus and of other towns in the neighborhood,' which demonstrates that he antedated the origin of the Episcopal system.

In short, Irenæus is so wedded to Episcopacy that he ignores the fact that in the New Testament "bishop" and "presbyter" are sometimes interchangeable terms; and yet he is charged with holding no essential distinction between Bishops and Presbyters! Bishop Lightfoot has a few words on this subject which are weighty and to the point; namely, —

> A Bishop may be called *presbyteros*, but a Presbyter is not called conversely *episcopos*. In Irenæus, for instance, *presbyteros* has a very wide significance, being used of antiquity or of old age, as well as of office. In this wider sense the *presbyteroi*, the 'elders,' are the primitive Fathers (irrespective of office), whose views of Christian doctrine and practice are especially valuable by reason of their proximity to the Apostles. *On the other hand, he always employs 'episcopos' with precision of the Episcopal office alone* [*Ap. Fath.* I. 378, n.].

Again: —

> The view of Irenæus respecting the subject before us is unmistakable. The Episcopate, as distinct from the Presbyterate, is the only Episcopate which comes within the range, not only of his personal acquaintance, but even of his intellectual and historical cognizance [*Ibid.* 378].

These words of that distinguished scholar, who is quoted more than once in the lecture, are even more significant when taken in connection with his judgment about Ignatius; namely, —

> If the evidence of its extension (that is, of the Episcopate) in the regions east of the Ægean at this epoch [that is, A. D. 110] be resisted, I am at a loss to understand what single fact relating to the history of the Christian Church during the first half of the second century can be regarded as established; for the testimony in favor of this spread of the Episcopate is more abundant and more varied than for any other institution or event during this period so far as I recollect [*Ibid.* p. 377].

So much for the fact [1] of Episcopacy. Its full meaning and significance are arrived at not only by historical investigation, but by logical deduction. Some minds, like that of S. Cyprian, cannot allow facts to jostle one another, so to speak, in their memories without unifying and accounting for them in a coherent, philosophical system. Thus the Catholic Church for at least fifteen centuries, in spite of the contradiction of the Papacy [Counc. Trent, sess. 22], has held not only to the Episcopate as an historic fact, but to the Apostolical succession as the only intelligible and defensible philosophy of that series of sacraments and mysteries which CHRIST established, and His ministry has perpetuated. But on the lowest grounds, judged merely as a question of historical interest, thinking only of the truth and not of the consequences, can any man with all the evidence before him refuse to accept Bishop Lightfoot's very cautious and sifted statement, that *the form of the ministry has been handed down from Apostolic times, and may well be presumed to have a Divine sanction?* [*Christian Ministry*, p. 145.]

As for the doctrine of the Church of England on this subject at the time of the Reformation, the "argument from silence" is again strongly urged by the lecturer. Individual Churchmen, during those terrible years between 1559 and 1589, when the world was divided by the sword between Papalists and anti-Papalists, did refrain from denouncing the want of Episcopal organization among their fellow-reformers, thinking, as Bramhall says, that it was "charity to think well of our neighbors and good divinity to look well to ourselves" [vol. iii. *Serp. Salve*, p. 475]. It is true that Hooker, while maintaining that "the institution of Bishops was from heaven, was even of GOD, the HOLY GHOST was the author of it" [vi. 5, 10], did admit an ordination without Bishops in case a man was "raised up by GOD" and his "calling ratified by manifest signs and tokens from heaven," or in case there was an "exigence of necessity" where "the Church must needs have some ordained, and neither hath nor *can have possibly* a Bishop to ordain" [vii. 14,

---

[1] It has not been thought necessary here to discuss the opinions of S. Jerome [410 A. D.], although the lecture lays great stress upon them, because (1) Jerome is too late by at least three hundred years to give us any new evidence; (2) There is really nothing in his writings which materially affects the argument; (3) His views on the ministry have been discussed at great length by many writers, notably by Mr. Gore in his *Church and the Ministry* [pp. 137, 380].

11]. It may even be that there were isolated cases of men who officiated in the English Church in violation of the law, without having received Episcopal ordination, although the two instances mentioned by the Puritan Neale are instances of men who were tried and condemned for that very offence. Yet the fact remains that the law of the Church of England never wavered for an instant. The Preface to the Ordinal in the Book of Common Prayer, indorsed by the Articles, distinctly taught Episcopacy as a principle and a fact. It makes no difference whether Cranmer got his catechism from Justus Jonas or not. The language of that document was adopted as his language, and must be interpreted according to the laws of language. It was published moreover just at the time that the Preface to the Ordinal was written, and therefore explains it. Cranmer's words (*Sermon on Keys*), are as follows; namely, —

After CHRIST's ascension the Apostles gave authority to other godly and holy men to minister GOD's Word, and chiefly in those places where there were Christian men already, which lacked preachers, and the Apostles themselves could no longer abide with them. For the Apostles did walk abroad into divers parts of the world, and did study to plant the Gospel in many places. Wherefore when they found godly men and meet to preach GOD's Word, they laid their hands upon them and gave them the HOLY GHOST, as they themselves received of CHRIST the same HOLY GHOST, to execute this office. And they that were so ordained, were indeed, and also were called, the ministers of GOD, as the Apostles themselves were. And so the ministration of GOD's Word (which our LORD JESUS CHRIST Himself did first institute) was derived from the Apostles unto others after them, by imposition of hands and giving of the HOLY GHOST from the Apostles' time to our days. And this was the consecration, orders, and unction of the Apostles, whereby they at the beginning made Bishops and Priests; and this shall continue in the Church, even to the world's end. And whatsoever rite or ceremony hath been added more than this, cometh of man's ordinance and policy, and is not commanded by GOD's Word.

It would indeed be a triumph of genius to show that when Cranmer used those words he rejected the Apostolical succession and held to the equal right of all Christians to administer the Sacraments and preach the Word in the congregation. More might be said about the almost unanimous recognition on the part of the Continental Reformers (for example, Melancthon, Bucer, Beza, Calvin, — the Augsburg Confession itself) of the historic fact of Episcopacy. In reply to the statement that "Apostolical succession" means Romanism [p. 30], attention might be drawn to the fact urged by Burnet, Pearson, Bramhall, and others, that the Papal theory has ever been against the doctrine of the "Divine right of Bishops;" that the Council of Trent for that reason refused to state the doctrine; and that it was not until Popery had dethroned Episcopacy that Protestantism took courage to dethrone it also. For, as Burnet says [*Ref.* I. 347], the theory of parity of Orders is "the very dregs of Popery."

But enough has been said to vindicate at least the very moderate proposal of the Bishops in their plea for unity, and to show that the Historic Episcopate as a principle of Church government is the very least that could be insisted upon consistently with a belief in a supernatural revelation illustrated by the evidence of antiquity and the history of the Christian Church.

THOMAS F. GAILOR.

The Voice of the Church of England on Episcopal Ordination.

Rev. Arthur Lowndes.

THIS article is written in answer to the request of the Editor of the CHURCH REVIEW that I should state what view the Church of England has held on the Historic Episcopate during the period covered by the years 1534 to 1589, and that this paper should be as far as possible an abstract of the various articles on *The Voice of the Church of England* contained in the CHURCH REVIEW since April, 1887. Those two dates, 1534 and 1589, have been chosen for the reason that before the abolition of the Papal supremacy in England in 1534, and the preaching of Bancroft's sermon in 1589, no one has called in question the teaching of the Church of England on the matter at issue.

It is admitted that before 1534 the validity of the Sacraments was connected with the Episcopal succession, and that the exclusive validity of Episcopal ordination was the sole view taught and tolerated in the Church of England.

But it is claimed that this view concerning ordination and the Sacraments was rejected by the Church at the Reformation, and that the very first time it was broached again in England was on the occasion of Bancroft's sermon at S. Paul's Cross on Feb. 9, 1589.

The task before us is then to show what the Church officially taught and enjoined during the years 1534 and 1589.

We have too much regard for the sincerity of purpose of the prominent Protestant ministers who discussed from their standpoint the Lambeth Proposals in the CHURCH REVIEW for April last to bring into the discussion the personal views and predilections of individual Churchmen, no matter how eminent. It would be but waste of time, and not advance the question one whit. The retort would be, "These views are no doubt interesting and suggestive, but we want an official explanation of the Church herself as to what she meant by the Episcopate, — in other words, what was the 'Historic Episcopate' during the years 1534 and 1589 in England."

We thoroughly agree with one of the writers, who says it lies with the Anglican Bishops to show what they mean by the term "Historic Episcopate." It is not for persons to whom a proposal is made to define its terms, but for the makers of the proposal. It is for the Anglican Bishops only to define what they meant by that very vague term; still by an appeal to any portion of history we may be able to find out the voice of the Church during that period. And if we find that the Church during those very critical years of her history that have been selected held a certain definite and pronounced view on the matter, then the Church of the present day will be obliged, if she wishes not to break her "historic" continuity, to uphold that same view.

At the outset it will be well to reproduce here two passages from the contributions to the April CHURCH REVIEW, one by a Methodist, the other by a Presbyterian minister, as showing the importance logical thinkers outside the Church attach to the period under review.

If we mistake not, there were a hundred years during which, in the language of an eminent clergyman of that Communion, 'no one in the Church of England thought of calling in question the validity of the Orders and Sacraments of the Reformed Churches,' which was presbyterial in ordination and government, and from which ministers and members were received to immediate and equal standing in the Church of England [*William V. Kelley*, p. 110].

It is only since the days of Charles I. and his Prime Minister Laud, that the Episcopal denomination has refused to recognize the validity of other ordinations besides its own [*Henry J. Van Dyke*, p. 122].

We reserve our comments on these two extracts till we have seen what history has to tell us on the subject.

Let us precise some dates for further reference: —
    Papal supremacy abolished in England in 1534.
    Accession of Edward VI., Jan. 28,[1] 1547.
    Accession of Mary, July 6, 1553.
    Accession of Elizabeth, Nov. 17, 1558.
    Bancroft's sermon, Feb. 9, 1589.

If reference is made to the King's Articles of 1535, to the *Declaration of the Functions and Divine Institution of Bishops*

---

[1] Some tables give the 29. At any rate he was proclaimed on the 31.

and Priests of 1537, embodied in the *Institution of a Christian Man*, to the *De Ordine et Ministerio Sacerdotum et Episcoporum* of 1538, to the *Necessary Doctrines and Erudition for a Christian Man* of 1543, or to other such public documents asserting the ministerial powers of dispensing the Sacraments, of conveying absolution, of binding and loosing, — in one word, the whole Sacramental system, — the answer will be that the Reformed Church had not yet had time to clear herself from the defilement of Popery in the Eighth Henry's reign.

With only one reference to the reign of Edward VI., for fear of a like charge, we will pass on to the reign of Elizabeth, — Cranmer's *Catechism*, 1548, compiled by Justus Jonas, but deliberately adopted and translated by the Archbishop, and constantly referred to by him as his own.

And so the ministration of GOD's word, which our LORD JESUS CHRIST did first institute, was derived from the Apostles unto others after them by imposition of hands, and giving the HOLY GHOST, from the Apostles' time to our days. And this was the consecration, Orders, and Unction of the Apostles, whereby they at the beginning made Bishops and Priests, and this shall continue in the Church even to the world's end, . . . wherefore, good children, you shall give due reverence and honor to the ministers of the Church . . . you shall take them for GOD's ministers. and the messengers of our LORD JESUS CHRIST. For CHRIST himself saith in the Gospel, he that heareth you. heareth Me, and he that despiseth you, despiseth Me. Wherefore, good children, you shall steadfastly believe all those things which such ministers shall speak to you from the mouth, and by the Commandment of our LORD JESUS CHRIST. And whatsoever they do to you, as when they baptise you, when they give you absolution, and distribute to you the Body and Blood of our LORD JESUS CHRIST, these you shall so esteem, as if CHRIST himself, in His own Person, did speak and minister unto you. For CHRIST hath commanded His ministers to do this unto you, and He Himself (although you see Him not with your bodily eyes) is present with His ministers. and worketh by the HOLY GHOST in the administration of His Sacraments. And on the other side, you shall take good heed, and beware of false and privy preachers, which privily creep into cities, and preach in corners, having none authority, nor being called to this office. For CHRIST is not present with such preachers, and therefore doth not the HOLY GHOST work by their preaching, but their word is without fruit or profit, and they do great hurt in commonwealths. For such as be not called of GOD, they no doubt of it, do err, and sow abroad heresy and naughty doctrine [*Sermon on the Keys* in Cranmer's *Catechism*, pp. 193 *seq.* Oxford, 1829].

What an outcry there would be nowadays of want of charity, exclusiveness, and unchurching other Churches, if the Archbishop of Canterbury or the Presiding Bishop were to put forth such a manual with such plain teaching on the Apostolical succession and the validity of the Sacraments and Absolution in connection therewith!

What a commentary on the English Ordinal by the very man who, it is said, wrote the Preface as it stood in the year 1588!

And even if Cranmer did not himself compose the Preface, he was the head of the commission which gave us the Ordinal of 1550.

In 1552 the Ordinal was revised, and several ceremonies and practices were omitted in the vain hope of conciliating the extreme wing; but no material alteration was made in the wording of the service, and no change made in the Preface.

It cannot, therefore, even be said that Cranmer had not the chance given him of qualifying the Ordinal or its Preface.

We come now to Elizabeth's reign, which commenced on Nov. 17, 1558.

In Elizabeth's reign we will take the different links of our chain of historical facts in their chronological order.

I. THE CONFERENCE IN WESTMINSTER ABBEY.

The lower House of Convocation had passed a resolution which they requested the Bishops to present to Parliament, in favor of the maintenance of the unreformed system, which had not yet been legally set aside. The Bishops were therefore the Marian Bishops. In answer to this petition, a conference was ordered to be held between the Romanists and the clergy of the Church as reformed under Edward VI. There were five articles brought forward in the petition,— the first three concerning Transubstantiation, the fourth the Papal Supremacy, the fifth the inherent authority of the clergy to settle matters of Faith, Sacraments, and discipline apart from the laity.

The Conference opened on March 31, 1559. Into the details of it we need not enter. The discussion on the mystery of the Holy Communion does not concern us at present. Under the fourth head, the Papal Supremacy, the paper which Dr. Horne read in the name of his party, and which, therefore, is the official declaration of the Reformed clergy, the following proposition is laid down as self-evident: —

Farther: the Apostles' Authority is derived upon after ages, and conveyed to the bishops, their successors. This must be granted by the Roman Catholics; with what color else can they press obedience to the Pope's decrees? And S. Jerome is full for the point. And S. Cyprian makes no scruple to affirm that the Apostles were all equal to S. Peter by their commission. From whence it follows that all bishops have the same authority for ordering things to edification [Collier, vol. ii. p. 418].

The argument then goes on with the authority of each national Church to deal with matters of rites and ceremonies. The Conference broke up, owing to the refusal of the Romanists to continue the discussion on the lines agreed upon.

The above proposition covers the whole ground of the position of the Church of England on the Apostolic succession.

The Episcopal authority is not to be swallowed up by one Bishop, as the Romanists would have it; nor is it to be so disparaged as to belong to all Orders of the clergy, as the Precisians, Puritans, Presbyterians, from that day to this would assert.

The clergy selected to represent the Reformed Church of England were Richard Cox (afterward Bishop of Ely), Robert Horne (afterward Bishop of Winchester), Edward Grindal (successively Bishop of London and Archbishop of York and Canterbury), Edmund Guest (successively Bishop of Rochester and Salisbury), John Aylmer (afterward Bishop of London), John Jewel (afterward Bishop of Salisbury), a Mr. Whitehead,[1] and John Scorey, Bishop of Chichester under Edward VI., and afterward Bishop of Hereford.

These were the men who were chosen to represent the doctrines of the Reformed Church, and who chose Horne to read out on their behalf the paper from which we have quoted. Here, then, we have the doctrine of Apostolical succession laid down as one taken for granted at the very outset of Elizabeth's reign, and before the Act of Uniformity was passed.

"*The Apostles' authority is derived upon after ages, and conveyed to the Bishops, their successors.*"

II. ACT OF UNIFORMITY.

Elizabeth's first Parliament met for business on Jan. 25, 1559, and passed, on April 28, the Act of Uniformity, which

---

[1] The writer is unable with the means at his command to trace what preferment Mr. Whitehead obtained, if any.

ordered the Prayer-Book (suppressed, of course, in Mary's reign) to be again taken into regular use "from and after the feast of the Natiuitie of Sainct John Baptist" (June 24).

The Act of Uniformity was bound up with the Prayer-Book, not as a supplement, but as part of it, as can be seen by the table of contents: —

"The Contents of this book.
" 1. An Act for the Uniformity of Common Prayer.
" 2. A Preface."
And so on to 21, which is the Commination Service.

III. THE ELEVEN ARTICLES OF 1559.

These Articles, which, according to their heading, were to be read out by all the clergy "at first entry into their cures, and also after that yearly, at two several times," are entitled: —

A Declaration of certain principal Articles of Religion set out by the order of both the Archbishops Metropolitans, and the rest of the Bishops; for the Unity of Doctrines to be *taught* and *holden* of all Parsons, Vicars, and Curates, as well as in testification of their common consent in the said doctrine, etc.

Of these the fourth and seventh are the only ones that concern us.

IV. Moreover I confess that it is not lawful for any man to take upon him any office or ministry either ecclesiastical or secular, but such only as are *lawfully thereunto called* by their high authorities, according to the *Ordinances of this realm.*

VII. Furthermore. I do grant and confess that the Book of Common Prayer and Administration of the Holy Sacraments, set forth by authority of Parliament, is agreeable to the Scriptures, and that it is Catholic, Apostolic, and meet for the advancing of GOD's glory, etc.

Taking, then, the Act of Uniformity enjoining the Book of Common Prayer and the Eleven Articles set forth by the Bishops together, what do we find the voice of the Church to be in 1559?

That every clergyman had, on entry to his cure, and twice a year thereafter, to declare openly his belief in the Scriptural, Catholic, and Apostolic character of the Prayer-Book, and Administration of the Sacraments, and further, that *only those who* were lawfully called according to the Ordinances of the realm could take upon themselves any ecclesiastical ministry.

If the seventh Article was aimed at the Romanists, the fourth was directed against the Puritans; yet both together proclaimed that the Church of England was Catholic and Apostolic, and admitted none within her ministry but those who were lawfully called thereunto.

The questions then arise, What was set forth by authority of Parliament? What were "the Ordinances of the realm" by which a man could know if he were lawfully called to office or ministry?

The "authority of Parliament" was the Act of Uniformity which made Elizabeth's Prayer-Book of 1559 a legal ordinance. If a man wanted to ascertain the law as to who were at that time the legal ministers in England, he would have to turn to the Ordinal, which bore on its titlepage these words: —

"The fourme and maner of making and consecratyng bishops, priestes and deacons Anno Domini 1559" [*Liturgical Services.* Queen Elizabeth. Parker Society, 1847, p. 272 *et seq.*], and the Preface, differing slightly from that of the present Ordinal; both Prefaces are given side by side.

The Preface of 1559: —

It is evident unto all men, diligently reading holy Scripture, and ancient authors. *that from the Apostles' time there hath been these Orders* of Ministers in CHRIST's Church, Bishops, Priests, and Deacons: which Offices were evermore had in such reverent estimation, that no man, by his own private authority, might presume to execute any of them, except he were first called, tried, examined, and known to have such qualities as were requisite for the same. And also, by public prayer, with imposition of hands, approved and admitted thereunto.

And therefore, to the intent these orders should be continued and reverently used and esteemed in this Church of England: it is requisite *that no man (not being at this present Bishop, Priest, nor Deacon)* shall execute any of them, *except he be* called, tried, and examined, and *admitted according to the form hereafter* following. And none shall be admitted a deacon except he be xxi years of age at least. And every man which is to be admitted a Priest shall be full xxiv years old. And every man which is to be consecrated a Bishop shall be full thirty years old. And the Bishop, knowing either by himself, or by sufficient testimony, any person to be a man of virtuous conversation and without crime, and after examination and trial, finding him learned in the Latin tongue, and sufficiently instructed in Holy Scripture, may upon a Sunday or Holy Day, in the face of the Church, admit him a deacon, in such manner and form as hereafter followeth.

Present Preface as revised in 1662: —

It is evident unto all men diligently reading the holy Scripture and ancient Authors, that from the Apostles' time there have been these Orders of Ministers in Christ's Church; Bishops, Priests, and Deacons. Which offices were evermore had in such reverend Estimation, that no man might presume to execute any of them, except he were first called, tried, examined, and known to have such qualities as are requisite for the same; and also by publick Prayer, with Imposition of Hands, were approved and admitted thereunto by lawful Authority. And therefore, to the intent that these Orders may be continued, and reverently used and esteemed, in the United Church of England and Ireland; no man shall be accounted or taken to be a lawful Bishop, Priest, or Deacon in the United Church of England and Ireland, or suffered to execute any of the said Functions, except he be called, tried, examined, and admitted thereunto, according to the Form hereafter following, or hath had formerly Episcopal Consecration, or Ordination.

And none shall be admitted a Deacon, except he be Twenty-three years of age, unless he have a Faculty. And every man which is to be admitted a Priest shall be full Four-and-twenty years old. And every man which is to be ordained or consecrated Bishop shall be fully Thirty years of age.

And the Bishop, knowing either by himself, or by sufficient testimony, any Person to be a man of virtuous conversation, and without crime; and, after examination and trial, finding him learned in the Latin Tongue, and sufficiently instructed in holy Scripture, may at the times appointed in the Canon, or else, on urgent occasion, upon some other Sunday or Holy-day, in the face of the Church, admit him a Deacon, in such manner and form as hereafter followeth. ·

The last words of the Preface of 1662, "or hath had formerly Episcopal Consecration, or Ordination," were added because the words in parentheses of that of 1559 were omitted ("not being at this present Bishop, Priest, nor Deacon"). "At this present" applied exactly to the circumstances of the present time in 1559, when most of the clergy had been ordained under the Sarum, or other Ordinals; but in 1662 "at this present" would strike every one as incongruous and absurd. There could be then living no man who had been ordained under the ancient Ordinals. Whichever Preface is taken, there is no loophole for a non-Episcopally ordained man to creep into the sacred ministry. He must either have been a Bishop, Priest, or Deacon according to the unreformed Ordinals or the Edwardian; else he must be admitted "according to the form hereafter following," to satisfy the Preface of 1559.

He must be admitted "according to the form hereafter following," if he has not already received Episcopal ordination to fulfil the requirements of the Preface of 1662.

What was "the form hereafter following" in 1559?

For a Deacon, after the candidate has declared that he believes that he has been inwardly called to enter the sacred ministry, and has been outwardly called according to the will of our LORD JESUS CHRIST, and the due order of this realm, to the ministry of the Church, the Bishop lays his hand upon him, saying, —

"Take thou authority to execute the office of a Deacon," and thus the Deacon receives his mission.

For the Priesthood, the question as to the inward call is omitted, the candidate having already entered the sacred ministry; but the question is asked as to whether the candidate believes himself to have received the outward call, —

"According to the will of our LORD JESUS CHRIST and the Order of this Church of England to the ministry of Priesthood?"

The terms of the question for the Diaconate are general, but for the Priesthood they become precise.

The Bishop and the Priests present lay their hands on the candidate, the Bishop saying, —

"*Receive the Holy Ghost:* Whose sins thou dost forgive they are forgiven: and whose sins thou dost retain they are retained."[1]

"*Take* thou authority to preach the word of GOD," etc.

Here, then, first his spiritual power is given him in the selfsame words the Apostles received theirs from CHRIST; and secondly, his mission.

In the office for the consecration of a Bishop, the rubric, following the primitive Canons, insists on the presence of two Bishops besides the officiating Bishop. This shows the anxiety of the Reformers to guard against any possible break in the

---

[1] The reader will notice the difference in this form from that in the present Prayer-Book, which is word for word the same as the first form in the American Prayer-Book. It is doubtful if the older form is not the stronger.

continuation of the Apostolical succession. The consecration of a Bishop by only one Bishop might be valid, but is uncanonical, since the primitive Church had, in order to be sure of the succession, laid down the rule, and constantly reaffirmed it, that, —

"Let a Bishop be ordained by two or three Bishops."

"Let a Priest or Deacon and the other clergy[1] be ordained by one Bishop." — *Canons 1 and 2 of the Apostolical Canons.*[2]

The reformers enjoined the presence of three Bishops at least at every consecration, while one was sufficient for the ordaining of a Priest or Deacon.

Could a Church have done more to insure the Apostolical succession? Yet we are told the Church of England is indifferent on the subject.

Again, in the address to him that is to be consecrated Bishop the Archbishop is to say, —

"Brother, forasmuch as Holy Scripture, *and the old canons*, commandeth that we should not be hasty in *laying on hands* and *admitting* of any person to the government of the congregation of CHRIST," etc.

And at the consecration, —

"*Take* the HOLY GHOST and remember thou stir up the grace of GOD which is in thee by *imposition of hands*," etc.

In the Confirmation service the Bishop claims to be the successor of the Apostles in their Apostolic functions : —

"Upon whom (after the example of thy Holy Apostles) we have laid our hands," etc.

Throughout the most solemn parts of her service, wherever any Sacramental grace is to be given, the Church directs, beyond the possibility of any person quibbling as to the generic term "minister," that a Priest or Bishop shall perform the

---

[1] That is, the minor clergy, including readers, sub-deacons, etc.

[2] The Apostolical Canons belong to no later date than the end of the second or the very commencement of the third century.

Canon 4 of the Council of Nice, A. D. 325, rules, —

"A Bishop ought to be constituted by all the Bishops of the Province, and should this be impracticable on account of urgent necessity, or because of distance, three at least should meet together," etc.

And so Canon 19 of Antioch, A. D. 341, — a Bishop not to be obtained without a Synod and the presence of the Metropolitan of the Province.

The African code, A. D. 418, collected out of sixteen councils at Carthage, etc., rules in Canon 13, "Three Bishops may consecrate another Bishop with leave of the Primate."

act, as in Holy Communion, in the Visitation of the Sick, and Confirmation.

And wherever she refers to her Orders, she ever refers to them as a *Divine institution.*

Almighty God, which by *the* [1] *Divine providence* hadst *appointed diverse orders of ministers in the Church;* and didst *inspire* thine Holy Apostles to choose unto *this order of Deacons* the first martyr S. Stephen, with others: mercifully behold these thy servants now called to the like office and administration, etc.

In the prayer for Priests the language is, as we should expect, still stronger.

Almighty God, giver of all good things, which by *thy Holy Spirit* hast appointed diverse orders of Ministers in thy Church, mercifully behold these thy servants, now called to the office of Priesthood, etc.

In the exhortation following, the Church institutes a direct comparison between her Priests and the Apostles. One of the Gospels appointed to be read is chapter xx. of S. John, ending with the words of our LORD, "And (He) said unto them: Receive ye the HOLY GHOST. Whose soever sins ye remit, they are remitted unto them, and whose soever sins ye retain they are retained."

In the prayer before the imposition of hands, the Bishop prays for the candidates: "Thou hast vouchsafed to call these thy servants here present to the same office and ministry" as thy "Apostles, Prophets, Evangelists," etc. Then follow the words of imposition, when the Bishop, standing in the place of CHRIST,[2] repeats the selfsame words as the Head of the Church, —

"Receive the HOLY GHOST: whose sins thou dost forgive they are forgiven; and whose sins thou dost retain they are retained."

And when under that Commission the Priest absolves individual penitents, the Church provides the form, —

Our LORD JESUS CHRIST, who hath left power to his Church to absolve all sinners which truly repent and believe in Him; of his great mercy

---

[1] Misprint for "thy." All these quotations are taken from the Elizabethan Prayer-Book, as given in *Liturgies and Occasional Forms of Prayer set forth in the Reign of Queen Elizabeth.* Parker Society, 1847.

[2] "Those that fill the room of CHRIST" is the term applied to the Bishops in the Homilies.

forgive thee thine offences: and by his authority committed to me, I absolve thee from all thy sins, in the name of the Father, and of the Son, and of the Holy Ghost.

Well has it been said: —

Orders, then, in the view of the Church of England, are (historically) an Apostolical Ordinance, but one both in itself necessary to the Church, and in its origin a direct appointment of CHRIST Himself by His Holy Spirit, with no less an end than the salvation of men's souls, and with no less a power than that of administering Sacraments and conveying instrumentally GOD's gift of the forgiveness of sins, and those orders, of course, are asserted to be so, and none others, that are set forth in the Ordinal itself, viz., Bishops, Priests, and Deacons, with their several powers as thus distinguished and declared — powers certainly in their own nature such as none but Almighty GOD can give, and which, therefore, only the authority of Almighty GOD can ever excuse, much less sanction, men in claiming to bestow. Beyond all power of gloss, our services are either rank and fearful blasphemy, or they rest upon the doctrine here laid down.[1]

To this we can only say a solemn Amen.

The Church recognized in 1559 (and recognizes now) as her ministers only those who had Episcopal ordination, and were willing to conform to the doctrines as embodied in the Prayer-Book, or those who were ordained by Bishops according to the form she set forth, and emphatically declares "that no man being at this present [1559] Bishop, Priest, nor Deacon" shall execute any ministerial office.

The State by the Act of Uniformity of 1559 imposes this law of the Church as the law of the realm, therefore when the "Ordinances of the realm" are invoked in behalf of the Eleven Articles which the Church, through her Archbishops and Bishops, demands all her ministers to assent to, the Church invokes her own ordinances.

If a man appealed to the ordinances of the realm, the appeal lay to the Ordinal.

If a man appealed to the ordinances of the Church, the appeal lay likewise to the Ordinal.

There was thus a twofold encircling of the law.

---

[1] Haddan's *Apostolical Succession in the Church of England.* Rivingtons, 1869, p. 143.

IV. A PURITAN VOICE.

It may, however, be said that to take the words of the Prayer-Book, the Ordinal, or its Preface, " in such just and favorable construction as in common equity ought to be allowed to all human writings " [present Preface to the Book of Common Prayer], and to state that the " Priest " of the Prayer-Book means only the legal Priest, — that is, the one ordained according to the Ordinal (or according to the Roman Ordinal and willing to conform), — is to take a view only taken by those having " the Church idea." It may, therefore, not be out of place to quote from a rare and curious publication entitled,—

" *Certaine Considerations drawne from the Canons of the last Sinod, and other the Kings Ecclesiastical and Statute law,*" etc., published, as such productions mostly were, without the name of author or printer, in 1605.

Under the section devoted to "Considerations against subscription to the booke of the forme and manner of making and consecrating Bishops, Priests, and Deacons," the writer argues against subscription[1] to the Prayer-Book being compulsory on all the clergy, and endeavors to arouse the King's jealousy as to his supremacy, and so accordingly [on pages 48, 49] proceeds, —

So that by subscription to allow that provinciall and Diocesan Bishops be Scripturely Bishops, and that their jurisdiction and power is a Scripturely jurisdiction and power, is to deny that their jurisdiction and power dependeth upon the King's jurisdiction and power, or that by the King's gift and authoritie they be made Bishops.

But how doeth subscription (you will say) to the booke of Ordination approve the orders and degrees of provinciall and diocesan Bishops to be by Divine right rather than by humane ordinance? How? Why thus : It is evident (saith the preface of that booke) to all men diligently reading holy Scripture and ancient authors, that from the Apostles' times, there have been these orders of ministers in CHRIST's Church, Bishops, Priests, and Deacons. Yea, and by the whole order of prayer and of scripture read, and used in the forme of consecrating of an Archbishop or Bishop, it is apparent that the order of an Archbishop or Bishop, consecrated by that booke, is reputed and taken to be of Divine institution. And therefore seeing the names of those orders of ministers must necessarily be taken and understood of such orders of ministers as be

---

[1] When we come to examine the Articles later on, it will be seen that the terms of subscription do not affect the present argument.

sett forth and described in the body of that booke, it must needes be intended, that the ministers by their subscription should approve the orders of ministers mencioned in that booke, to be of Divine institution, and consequently that provinciall and diocesan ministers or Bishops, have not their essence and being from the nomination, gift and authoritie of the King.[1]

Besides if we should understand by the word (Bishop) him that hath the ministrie of the word and Sacraments, as the pastor and teacher; and by the word (Priest) the Presbyter, that is, the governing elder; and by the word (Deacon) the provider for the poore, then for the ministers to subscribe to the booke of Ordination would no way justifie those offices, or degrees of ministers which are described in that booke, but would indeed utterly subvert and overthrow them.

Because the orders and degrees of a provinciall, and diocesan Bishop, of a Priest and Deacon, mentioned in that booke, be of a farr differing nature from those orders, and degrees of ministers which are mentioned in the Scriptures, because they only agree in name, and not in nature.

Quite so. Is the voice of the Church so very uncertain? Our friend Master Anon., and his co-peers, Precisian, Puritan, or Presbyterian, think it only too certain, and groan that the Preface is not open to a double interpretation. The Divine right of Episcopacy was no " open question," as far as the Church of England was concerned, in the eyes of these men.

Not believing in the Divine institution of Episcopacy, and recognizing that wherever, in the Book of Common Prayer, the Orders of the ministry are referred to, only those Orders of ministry are allowed by the Church that are ordained according to her Ordinal, Anonymous and his friends say: " We cannot subscribe to such a book. We believe in Orders, — yea, but Orders not of Divine institution; and while, if you like, we will retain the names of Bishops, Priests, and Deacons, those names must not represent the Orders, having the nature of the Orders mentioned in the Book of Ordination of the Church of England, but must represent Pastors, Elders, and Providers for the poor."

The Puritan testimony has been introduced at this point because, although not published in the period under review at

[1] What the King thought of this Erastian appeal, we have already seen in his address to Spotswood, Hamilton, and Lamb, on the eve of their consecration as Bishops for Scotland, where he said he never would presume on such authority, and " that such authority belonged to none but our Blessed SAVIOUR and those commissioned by Him."

present, it yet voices the reasons for the continual fight against subscription to the Prayer-Book and Ordinal.

Without staying any further to reflect on these "considerations," though they are wonderfully suggestive, we pass on to the next link in the historical chain of evidence as to what the realm and the Church considered lawful ministers before the year 1588.

V. VISITATION ARTICLES.

The Act of Uniformity of 1559 was, as we have seen, not only statute law, but ecclesiastical law, being part of the Book of Common Prayer. One of its provisions is as follows:—

Provided always, and be it ordained and enacted by the authority aforesaid, that all and singular Archbishops and Bishops, and every of their Chancellors, Commissaries, Archdeacons, and other Ordinaries having any peculiar ecclesiastical jurisdiction, shall have full power and authority, by virtue of this act, as well to inquire in their visitation, Synods, and elsewhere within their jurisdiction, or any other time and place, to take accusation and information of all and every the things above mentioned, done, committed, or perpetrated within the limits of their jurisdictions and authority, and to punish the same by admonition, excommunication, sequestration, or deprivation and other censures and processes in like form as heretofore hath been used in like cases by the Queen's ecclesiastical laws.

We must also remember that a Bishop's visitation is *a lawful court*, and clerks not appearing are liable to punishments and costs [Phillimore's *Ecclesiastical Law*, p. 1346].

Let us now see what were the interrogatories addressed at sundry visitations.

I. *Interrogatories in the injunctions of Parkhurst, Bishop of Norwich*, 1561.

17. Whether there be any laye or temporall men not being within orders, or children that hath or enjoyeth any benefice or spiritual promotion.

II. *Parker, Archbishop of Canterbury*, 1563.

6. Item. Whether there be any Parsons that intrude themselves and presume to exercise any kind of ministry in the Church of GOD without imposition of hands and Ordinary [1] authority.

---

[1] That is, authority of the Ordinary, the Bishop of the Diocese.

III. *Parkhurst, Bishop of Norwich,* 1569.

16. Item. Whether ye know any parson or vicar that sel their benefice to meare laymen.

IV. *Cox, Bishop of Ely (about* 1570–1574).

Item. Whether there be any Parsons that intrude themselves and presume to exercise any kinde of ministrie in the Churche of God without imposition of hands and ordinarie authoritie [see note on p. 139].

V. *Grindal, Archbishop of York,* 1571.

36. Whether there be any lay or temporall man not being within orders or any childe that hath or enjoyeth any benefice or spirituall promotion.

VI. *Grindal, Archbishop of Canterbury,* 1575.

Whether any person or persons not being ordered at least for a Deacon, or licensed by the ordinary do say Common Prayer openly in your Church or Chapel.

Whether any Priest or Minister be come into this Diocese out of any other Diocese to serve any cure here without letters testimonial of the ordinary from whence he came, under his authentic seal and hand to testify the cause of his departing from thence, and of his behaviour there.

VII. *Aylmer, Bishop of London,* 1577.

10. Whether any person, or persons, not being ordered at least for a Deacon, or licenced by the ordinarie, doe say Common-Prayer openly in your Church or chappell, or any not being at the least a Deacon doe solemnise matrimony or administer the Sacraments of Baptisme, or deliuer vnto the communicants the Lordes cuppe at the celebration of the Holy Communion, and what he or they be that doe so.

55. Whether any new presbiteries [1] or elderships be lately among you erected, and by them any ministers appointed with [2] [*sic*] orders taking of the Byshop doe baptise, minister the communion, or deall in any function ecclesiastical, or gather any priuate conuenticles whereby the people be drawn from the Church.

VIII. *Sandys, Archbishop of York,* 1578.

4. Whether any Person, or persons, not being ordered at the least for a Deacon, lycensed by the Ordinary, do saye Common-Prayer openly in your Church or Chappell, or any not being at least a Deacon, do sol-

---

[1] We shall see farther on that such a "presbiterie" had been established about five years previously at Wandsworth.

[2] Evident misprint for "without."

emnise matrimonie or administer the Sacrament of Baptisme or deliuer vnto the communicants the Lord's cup at the celebration of the Holy Communion, and what he or they be that do so.

IX. *Whitgift, Archbishop of Canterbury*, 1588.

Whether doth any take on them to read lectures or preach, being mere lay persons, or not ordered according to the laws of this realm.

X. *Aylmer, Bishop of London*, 1586.

4. Whether any Parson or Parsons not being ordered at the least for a Deacon do saye Common Prayer openly in your Church Chappell, or any not being at the least a Deacon do solemnise matrimony, or administer the Sacramentes of Baptisme, or deliuer to the Communicantes the Lord's cup at the celebration of the holye communion, and what be their names that do so.[1]

Here, then, we have a series of Visitation Articles, commencing within two years of the passing of the Act of Uniformity and the restoration of the Prayer-Book, and down to two years before the date of 1588, when we are told that the doctrine of the exclusive claim of Episcopacy as a Church government and its connection with the validity of the Sacraments *was first publicly set forth* or *first broached!*

There were two classes of intruders that the Church had to guard against,—the men non-Episcopally ordained and minors holding the temporalities of the Church. It is a matter unfortunately too notorious that in the Roman Communion children had been preferred to benefices, and also to dignities in the Church. Pope Leo was abbot of two monasteries at the age of seven, and at thirteen was a Cardinal. Another Pope, that of Geneva, Calvin, though a layman, possessed two places of preferment in France. He afterward sold one of them.

Against such abuses was the question aimed, " Whether there be any childe that hath or enjoyeth any benefice."

This class of abuses may be said to belong to the old order of things, while that of men not lawfully ordained belonged to the new order.

---

[1] All these Visitation interrogatories are taken from the *Second Report of the Commissioners appointed to inquire into the Rubrics, Orders, and Directories for regulating the Course and Conduct of Public Worship*, etc., according to the Use of the United Church of England and Ireland, etc., 1868, with the exception of Grindal's, for 1575, and Whitgift's, for 1585, which are taken from Cardwell's *Doc. Ann.*, vol. i. p. 404-407: vol. ii. p. 4.

It would not, therefore, have been surprising had there been no interrogatories aimed against this new class of intruders. Silence would, however, have given no sanction. Does the Church recognize the Methodist Episcopal "Bishops" because she nowhere condemns them by name?

That some of the Bishops from 1559 to 1588 may not have been very desirous of enforcing the law of the Church and realm, and that they would have preferred to connive at the intrusion of men not ordained according to those laws, may be perfectly true, but even if such could be proved [1] beyond the shadow of a doubt, such proof would not affect the law of the Church. A judge may wink or connive at an offence; but that would not make the offence the less an offence. Nay, more, when called upon to act against the offender the judge, no matter how he may dislike the law, has to pass sentence according to the law of the land.

In some States there are laws against the selling of liquors. Such laws are notoriously broken; and if rumor speaks correctly, with the knowledge of the magistrates. Yet the moment the law is set in motion, a judge, although he had himself been buying liquor from the offender, would have to pass on him the sentence provided by the law. Nor is non-user a repeal of a law. In the above Visitation Articles, however, we see clearly beyond the possibility of a cavil that there was a widespread desire to enforce the law. And it is curious to note the similarity of language employed; the Interrogatory of the Archbishop of York, of 1578, is almost word for word the same as that of the Bishop of London, of 1586. It would really seem as if the Bishops had concerted a united plan of defence against these new intruders.

The Roman Orders the Church acknowledged, and has always acknowledged as valid, and the law of the realm has also always done so, on the ground of their having the *Apostolical succession*, as we have seen Lord Brougham so decide [CHURCH REVIEW for April, 1887, p. 441].

The words in parentheses in the Preface to the Ordinal of 1559 ("not being at this present Bishop, Priest, nor Deacon") certainly left it open to a Roman clergyman to hold a cure legally without any further authority than the Ordinal gave him. In this there was a source of danger, for while the Church recognized the validity of his Orders, she did not desire a Roman Priest to

---

[1] No *proof* of such cases has yet been given.

minister at her altars without first having some guarantee that he would abide by her reformed standard of doctrine and worship.

To effect this an Act was passed in the thirteenth year of Elizabeth's reign. And now we come to the sixth link in our chain of historical facts,— the *Act* 13 *Eliz. c.* 12, and the *Articles*.

It would be impossible to understand the bearings of the provisions of the *Act* 13 *Eliz. c.* 12 without a somewhat detailed review of the various Articles to which subscription was enforced prior to the date of 1588 or 1589, which limits our inquiries. The object before us is to prove what was the voice of the Church of England on Episcopal ordination prior to the delivery of Bancroft's sermon on Feb. 9, 1589. It is not our concern to show whether Presbyterianism be right or wrong, but simply to prove what the Church of England has said on the subject up to Feb. 9, 1589. It is not our concern either to show what the English Reformers, or individual members of the Church, thought on the subject, but plainly to prove that the Church of England, as a Church, never accepted as in any way valid the ministrations of one not ordained or consecrated by a Bishop.

In tracing the history of subscription to Articles back to their first origin, it is to Geneva and not to Rome that we find the clergy owe enforcement of subscription to Articles of Religion. The Puritan and Presbyterian party who so bitterly railed against subscription to the successive Articles have to thank that foreign prince and potentate, that "busy intermeddler in foreign Churches," that "infallible arbiter in controversy," John Calvin, for its introduction into England.

It was Calvin who, as Collier says of him, "thought himself wiser than the Ancient Church, and fit to dictate Religion to all countries in Christendom," who wrote to Protector Somerset in 1548 to inform him as to his will and pleasure concerning Church and State in England. After commending the Protector for the zeal and resolution[1] he had shown in retrieving

---

[1] Doubtless referring to his "zeal and resolution" in endeavoring to pull down Westminster Abbey wherewith to build himself a palace; or to his unabated "zeal and resolution" in tearing down a stately cloister, two chapels, three Bishop's houses, and two Churches, for his palace, when bought off by the Dean with half the revenues of the Abbey.

religion, he unfolds his plan, which may be summed up as follows: —

1. A form of Common Prayer to be enforced on all subjects by the State.

2. Articles of Religion to which all Bishops and Parish Priests should be forced to subscribe, and that no person should be admitted to any ecclesiastical function without giving solemn consent to the doctrines received.

3. Both Papists and Gospellers [1] to be coerced by the sword.

Here, then, is the germ of all subscription and test acts.

Hooper, Calvin's apt pupil, when he had so sufficiently overcome his scruples as to enable him to accept the See of Gloucester, followed his master's injunctions, set forth a series of Articles of his own, and took very kindly to enforcing them on his clergy.

Hardwick, in his Appendix III., has collated the XXXIX. Articles of 1562, with the preceding formularies, and also with these Articles issued by Hooper to his clergy.

We now come to the sixth head of our argument.

VI. THE ARTICLES.

The following table may help us to distinguish between these numerous formularies, and to understand their connection:

I. The Articles of 1548.
II. The XLV. Articles of 1551–52.
III. The XLII. Articles of 1553.
IV. The XI. Articles of 1559.
V. The XXXIX. Articles assented to by Convocation, Jan. 31, 1562.
VI. The Advertisements of 1564.
VII. Canons passed by Convocation of April and May, 1571.
VIII. Act of 13 Elizabeth, cap. 12, passed April or May, 1571.
IX. Subscription to the XXXIX. Articles enforced by Parliament by said Act.
X. Order of Ecclesiastical Commissioners, June 7, 1571.
XI. Parker's Three Articles, June, 1571.

---

[1] That is, the Puritan party, who were then also nicknamed "Pseudo-evangelicals."

XII. Queen's Proclamation, Oct. 20, 1573.
XIII. The XV. Articles passed by Convocation in March, 1576.
XIV. Whitgift's Three Articles, April 15, 1584.
XV. The XXIV. Articles, May, 1584.

§ I. *The Articles of* 1548.

What these were, or how many they were, we cannot say. But that subscription was enforced to a set of Articles as early at least as the second year of the reign of Edward VI. is beyond doubt, and possibly in the very first year.

Hooper, under date of Feb. 27, 1549, writes, —

He (*i. e.* Archbishop Cranmer) has some Articles of Religion to which all preachers and lecturers in divinity are required to subscribe or else a licence for teaching is not granted them [Hardwick on the *Articles*, London, 1881, p. 72].

Archbishop Whitgift, writing to Burghley, July 15, 1584, says, —

But I have altered my first course of dealing with them for not subscribing only (justifiable by law, and in common practice in the time of King Edward, and from the beginning of her Majesty's reign to this day), and chosen this to satisfy your lordship [Whitgift's *Works*, Parker Society, 1853, vol. iii. p. 607].

Complaining of the rigorous way in which subscription had been enforced, a Marian Bishop, in a sermon Nov. 12, 1553, at S. Paul's Cross, indignantly asks: —

Hathe there been anye spiritual promotion and dignitie, ye or almoste anye meane liuyng of the Churche, *bestowed these few years paste*, but vppon such onely, as would ernestly set furth (either by preaching, *either by subscribing*) al the erronious doctrine, falsi termed the Kinges procedinges? [Hardwick, p. 222, note.]

If, however, we are unable to give either the precise wording or the number of these Articles, we do know that three at least of them concerned *the Prayer-Book, the Ordinal, and the Sacraments*, because it was to these three that Hooper objected in May, 1550, when nominated to the See of Gloucester [Hardwick, p. 92].

The Prayer-Book and Ordinal being of course that of 1549, the First of Edward VI., Hooper could not have objected to these Articles on account of their Puritanism, for he was the leading exponent of the Calvinistic school in England, and the determined foe of the Ordinal and Prayer-Book.

Here, then, at the very outset, we have a manifestation of the Puritan opposition to subscription to the Articles on account of the *Prayer-Book and Ordinal*. And we have also from the very beginning of the Reformation the determination of the Church that those seeking Orders within her fold should bind themselves to uphold her teaching as formulated in her Prayer-Book, and the form of Episcopal ordination as laid down in her Ordinal.

So Hooper, notwithstanding his objections, found himself obliged to subscribe to them in 1551 before he could be consecrated Bishop, which proves that there must have been authority for these Articles, else Hooper, anxious as he was to evade subscription to them, could have met the demand to subscribe by a point-blank refusal on the simple plea that they were unauthorized.

Hooper may be said to have been the first to throw down the gauntlet in the lists against the Church, on behalf of Puritanism, Presbyterianism, and the Parity-men, and summon her to open her gates wide to them.

From 1550 to the present day there have not been wanting men to re-echo that challenge.

But what has been the action of the Church in reply?

Has she altered her Prayer-Book or her Ordinal?

Has she relaxed her formularies of subscription to such a degree as to admit as her accredited ministers any non-Episcopally ordained?

Let the following brief survey of the successive series of Articles to those of 1548 answer these questions.

§ II. *The XLV. Articles of* 1551-52.

These XLV. Articles may be found in Latin, taken from the State papers *Domestic*, Edward VI. vol. xv. No. 28, signed by six royal chaplains, in Hardwick, p. 279 *seq*.

The Privy Council appear to have directed, in the year 1551, that they should be set forth by public authority. Some delay seems to have occurred in doing this; and consequently we find the Council writing, on May 2, 1552, to Archbishop Cranmer about the delay, and requesting that a copy of the Articles be forwarded to the Council.

Having made some alterations and additions, the Archbishop forwards a copy of the Articles, in September, 1552, to the Council. Finally a copy is submitted to the King with the request that the Articles be enforced as a test.

Six royal chaplains are thereupon directed to report on the Articles, and these chaplains, — Harley, Bill, Horne, Perne, Grindal, and Knoks, — having signed a copy, in token of their assent, the Formulary is then sent, on November 20, to the Archbishop for the "last corrections of his judgment and pen." Four days after, they are returned to the Council, accompanied by a request from Cranmer that all Bishops may have authority from the King " to cause all their preachers, archdeacons, deans, prebendaries, parsons, vicars, curates, with all their clergy, to subscribe to the said Articles."

On June 19, 1553, in compliance with the Archbishop's wish, the royal order was issued that the new Formulary be publicly subscribed. The number of the Articles had, however, been reduced to forty-two since November, 1552.

As the XXXVIII. of these XLV. Articles is the parent of all "the subscription Articles" objected to by those who fought against Episcopal ordination, it is important to reproduce it here.

XXXVIII. De libro Ceremonarium Ecclesiæ Anglicanæ. Liber qui nuperrime authoritate Regis et Parlamenti ecclesiæ Anglicanæ traditus est, continens modum et formam orandi et sacramenta administrandi in Ecclesia Anglicana: similiter et libellus ille, eadem authoritate æditus, de ordinatione Ministrorum ecclesiæ, quoad doctrinæ veritatem pii sunt, et quoad ceremoniarum rationem salutari Evangelii libertati, si ex sua natura ceremoniæ illæ æstimentur, in nullo repugnant, sed probe congruunt, et eandem in complurimis inprimis promovent, atque ideo ab omnibus ecclesiæ Anglicanæ fidelibus membris, et maxime a ministris verbi, cum omni promptitudine animorum et gratiarum actione recipiendi, approbandi, et populo Dei sunt commendandi.

Now the English of the above is as follows (making use of, so far as it goes, the translation of the thirty-fifth of the XLII. Articles as set forth in 1553).

XXXVIII. Of the Book of Ceremonies of the Church of England.

The Book which of very late time was given to the Church of England by the King's authority, and the Parliament, containing the manner and form of praying and ministering the Sacraments in the Church of England, likewise also that book of ordering ministers of the Church, set forth by the foresaid authority, are godly with respect to the truth of their doctrine; and with respect to the matter of ceremonies, if these ceremonies are estimated from their nature, are in no point repugnant to the wholesome doctrine of the Gospel, but are excellently agreeable thereunto, and further the same not a little; and therefore by all the faithful members of the Church of England, and chiefly of ministers of the Word, they ought to be received and allowed with all readiness of mind and thanksgiving, and to be commended to the people of GOD.

It is quite true that these XLV. Articles do not appear to have been actually enforced; but their existence proves that even thus early the most moderate of Churchmen were pressed to defend the Prayer-Book and Ordinal against the attacks of those who would have neither the Catholic doctrine nor the threefold ministry.

This attitude of the Reformers is well depicted in the words of Cranmer, as quoted by Hardwick, p. 68.

Lest any man should think that I feign anything of mine own head, without any other ground or authority, you shall hear by GOD's grace, as well the errors of the papist confuted as the Catholic truth defended both by GOD's sacred Word, and also by the most approved authors and martyrs of CHRIST's Church.

§ III. *The XLII. Articles of* 1553.

We have seen in the preceding section that the XLV. Articles, having been reduced by three, were by royal order of June 19, 1553, ordered to be publicly subscribed. The weight of authority is in favor of these Articles having been agreed to in Convocation prior to the issue of the King's order. The burning of the records of Convocation in the fire of 1666 makes proof in such things a matter of long and tedious research; but the complaints of both Papists and Puritans prove that they were enforced. There is very little alteration between this Formulary and the XLV. Articles.

The thirty-eighth, which we have already given at length, becomes the thirty-fifth of the XLII. Articles; and as both a Latin and English version was set forth, we will content ourselves with giving the English.

XXXV. Of the booke of Praiers, and Ceremonies of the Churche of Englande.

The Booke whiche of very late time was geuen to the Churche of England by the Kinges Aucthoritie, and the Parlamente, conteining the maner and fourme of praiyng, and ministring the sacramentes in the Churche of Englande, likewise also the booke of ordring ministers of the Churche, set foorth by the forsaied aucthoritie, are godlie, and in no poincte repugnant to the holsome doctrine of the Gospel, but agreeable thereunto, ferthering and beautifying the same not a litle, and therefore of al faithful membres of the Churche of Englande, and chieflie of the ministers of the Worde, thei ought to be receiued and allowed with all readinesse of mind, and thankes geuing, and to bee commended to the people of GOD [Hardwick, p. 340].

If the opponents of the Church and Church government were dissatisfied with the thirty-eighth of the XLV. Articles, they would not have less reason for dissatisfaction when this thirty-fifth Article was set forth, for if anything it is stronger than the former one. Nor would such persons derive much comfort from the thirty-third and thirty-fourth, which are identical with the thirty-sixth and thirty-seventh of the XLV. Articles; the former, on the Traditions of the Church, censures those who of their *private judgment willingly and purposely break the traditions and ceremonies* of the Church; the latter, on the Homilies, declares them to be " godlie and holsome, conteining doctrine to be received of all menne."

§ IV. *The Eleven Articles of* 1559.

When we were considering the Act of Uniformity (on p. 130 *et seq.*) we saw what these Articles enjoined. Since the XLV. and XLII. Articles, Cranmer had perished in the flames, and the authority of the Pope had had a brief sway. It would not have been strange to find that when fresh Articles were issued in Elizabeth's reign, they had been set forth with a view to greater strictness against the Papists and with more leniency to the Puritans.

Now, if ever, following the inevitable law of reaction, there ought to have been hopes for the minimizers of the Catholic Faith and levellers of the Apostolic ministry. It is instructive to find that the Church authorities preserved the same calm and judicious attitude which is such an eminent characteristic of the Church of England. The Articles of Edward VI. had not been repealed by any express statute in Mary's reign, but they had nevertheless been considered as abrogated by the restoration of

Popery, and in this view Queen Elizabeth and Archbishop Parker seem to have concurred. Not waiting for the readoption of so elaborate a series of Articles as the XLII. of Edward's reign, though such a series was being actually under consideration, and was soon to be published as the XXXIX. Articles of 1562, there issued from the royal press, "by order of both Archbishops, Metropolitans, and the rest of the Bishops," the Eleven Articles of 1559.

Insisting that the Papist should grant that the Prayer-Book was "Catholic and Apostolic," it provided in more emphatic terms that the Puritan should confess that it was not lawful for him to take any ecclesiastical ministry upon himself until called thereto in accordance with the laws of the realm.

What the laws of the realm were we have seen, when dealing with these Eleven Articles (on p. 136). To quote our own words: —

If a man appealed to the ordinances of the realm, the appeal lay to the Ordinal.

If a man appealed to the ordinances of the Church, the appeal lay likewise to the Ordinal.

The Eleven Articles were, as we have already observed, to be read in public by all the clergy at their first entry into their cures, *and twice a year thereafter*. They thus concerned the *continual practice and teaching of the clergy ;* and moreover, while the subscription of any Formulary was effected only between a minister and his Ordinary, the public reading in Church of a declaration worded throughout in the first person singular and ending with this exhortation, "I exhort you all of whom I have cure, heartily and obediently to embrace and receive the same," could not fail to act as a check on the clergy, since the laity could easily perceive whether the daily teaching of the minister was the same as that embodied in the confession made under the "Eleven Articles."

§ V. *The XXXIX. Articles of* 1562.

Of these Articles nothing need here be said, as we have not to deal with their doctrinal significance, but only with their enforcement by subscription. Subscription was not enforced till 1571, on reaching which date we will see what these Articles have to tell us on the matter in hand. (See § IX. p. 157.)

It may, however, be as well to note here that all Church authorities — Archbishops, Bishops, Convocation, or Ecclesiastical Commissioners — in their references to these Articles always refer to them as the Articles of 1562; and never even when enforcing subscription do they refer to the Statute Act of 1571, which by Parliamentary law made subscription compulsory on all the clergy, but always to the Articles as passed by the Convocation of 1562. The reasons of this silence we will examine later on, under § IX., so as to keep the whole subject-matter under one head.

According to Soames, these Articles were passed on January 31, the Bishops seem to have subscribed to them on January 29, and the principal members of Convocation on Feb. 5, 1562–63.

§ VI. *The Advertisements of* 1564.

In the year 1563, and before the same Convocation that passed the Articles commonly called the Articles of 1562, there were submitted seven Articles for adoption by the Lower House.

Number 1 was against responsive singing, or reading, of the Psalms, and against all musical instruments. 2. Against lay Baptism and the sign of the Cross. 3. Against kneeling at the Holy Eucharist. 4. That the copes and surplices be laid aside, and that the habit of the desk and the pulpit be the same. 5. Against gowns and caps. 6. That the clause in Article 33 of the Articles of 1552 against breaking the traditions and ceremonies be considerably softened down. 7. Against Saints' days. [See Collier's *Ecclesiastical History*, vol. ii. p. 486.]

Although after considerable debate these Articles were much modified, and reduced to six, yet they did not succeed in passing. The Puritan party, notwithstanding their defeat in Convocation, continued to set the law at defiance in their ministrations, and to uphold their conduct in the pulpit. Consequently the Queen, on Jan. 25, 1564, wrote to the Primate, as head of the Ecclesiastical Commissioners, complaining of these irregularities " as tending to breed some schism or deformity in the Church." As the immediate consequence of that letter the Advertisements were issued in March. The chief provisions of these Advertisements were, so far as they concern our inquiry: —

That all preachers should be " examined for their conformity in unity of doctrine."

That all licenses issued prior to the first of March be void, but be renewed to meet persons.

That the celebrant, gospeller, and epistoler use copes, the surplice to be used in other ministrations.

That no ministers be " admitted to serve without testimonye of the diocesan from whence they come."

Concerning these Advertisements, Cardwell rightly states that the point at issue was not the necessity of wearing the same apparel that was used by the Romanists, " but the real point at issue being, and soon afterwards showing itself to be, the right principle of Church government" [*Doc. Ann.* vol. i. p. 321].

It is for that reason that a survey, no matter how brief, of the contest of the Puritans against the Ordinal would be incomplete without some reference to the Advertisements. By recalling the licenses, and examining the applicants as to their doctrine before granting fresh ones, it was hoped to silence the depravers of the Prayer-Book and Ordinal.

§ VII. *The Canons of* 1571.

The Convocation of 1571 which sat between April 3 and May 30 passed a book of Canons in April. The date of April can be fixed by means of the Canon on Bishops. One of the enactments of that Canon was that all licenses should be recalled before the September following. In other words, all licenses issued before the passing of the Canon were to be considered void. Now, the order issued by the Ecclesiastical Commissioners on June 7, 1571, in consequence of these Canons, instructs church-wardens to see that the minister " be such as is licensed to preach after the first of May last," hence the Canons must have been passed before the first of May, 1571.

The instructions of the Bishop of Ely to his Chancellor, under date of August 28, 1571, are to the same effect.

It was further ordained that all preachers having licenses to preach at any time before the last day of April last must render up the old license unto the Bishop of the Diocese, etc. [Strype's *Parker*, vol. ii. p. 61].

Before the applicant could obtain a fresh license he had to subscribe to the XXXIX. Articles of 1562 and promise to maintain and defend the doctrine in them contained, as being most agreeable to the Word of GOD.

Besides this clause ordering the recall of licenses so that doctrine inclining to Rome or Geneva might not be taught in the pulpit, there were two other injunctions laid on Bishops in this Canon *De Episcopis* which need mention.

The Bishops were not to lay hands on any that were brought up in husbandry, or some other mean trade or calling, but all the candidates should well understand the Latin tongue, and be conversant in the Scriptures.

That they should suffer none who by an idle name called themselves readers, *and received not imposition of hands* in the ministry of the Church.

Episcopus neminem, qui se otioso nomine lectorem vocet, et manus impositionem non acceperit, in ecclesiæ ministerio versari patietur.

These provisions were aimed against the Puritans and those who denied the exclusive validity of Episcopal ordination. The country was being filled with ignorant men who, as the Archbishop had said, " sought under cover of reformation the ruin and subversion both of learning and religion."

Tailors, bricklayers, and such like set themselves up as blind leaders of the blind, and justified their conduct by the text *Spiritus ubi vult spirat*.[1]

Nor was any person to be received into the ministry of the Church in any Diocese, without dimissory letters from the Bishop of the Diocese he was leaving. This clause would not only serve the purpose of preventing excommunicated, deposed, or suspended clerics from entering a Diocese as clerks in good standing, but would enable the Bishop of the Diocese he sought to enter to ascertain not only as to the moral fitness of the applicant, but also as to his orthodoxy in doctrine and conformity to the Prayer-Book and Ordinal. What perhaps was still more important, it would be a means of discovering such men as had forged letters of Orders.

At the end of the Canon, " Ædituus ecclesiarum et alii selecti viri," mention is made of the celebrated *Book of Advertisements*, about which there has of late years been so considerable a dis-

---

[1] "A bricklaer taken upon him the office of preachyng, affirmed he might lawfully do it, though he were not called thereonto by ye Church. For *Spiritus ubi vult spirat*." Huggard's *Displaying of the Protestantes*, sign B. iii. as quoted by Hardwick, p. 102, note.

One of the Kentish ministers cited before Archbishop Whitgift in 1583 has against his name, " No graduate, lately a tailor."

cussion, and of which we made a cursory survey in the last section.

By this and other Synods, as Cardwell rightly states, the Advertisements were always considered as having the most perfect authority. The Advertisements, like these Canons of 1571, were not formally sanctioned by the Queen. When dealing with the enforced subscription to the Articles under Section IX., we will recur to this apparent lack of royal sanction.

The Canons of 1571 were issued in Latin, unnumbered, but with a heading containing the subject-matter. An edition in English was also shortly put out; as, however, the Latin seems to have been the only authoritative edition, or at any rate appears to have been the only form in which they were passed by Convocation, the Canon on preachers is given in full in Latin.

CONCIONATORES.

Imprimis vero videbunt, ne quid unquam doceant pro concione quod a populo religiose teneri et credi velint, nisi quod consentaneum sit doctrinæ veteris aut novi Testamenti, quodque ex illa ipsa doctrina Catholici patres, et veteres Episcopi collegerint, et quoniam articuli illi religionis Christianæ in quos consensum est ab Episcopis in legitima et Sancta Synodo, jussa atque authoritate serenissimæ Principis Elizabethæ convocata et celebrata, haud dubie collecti sunt ex sacris libris veteris et novi Testamenti, et cum cœlesti doctrina, quæ in illis continetur, per omnia congruunt; quoniam etiam liber publicarum precum, et liber de inauguratione Archiepiscoporum, Episcoporum, Presbyterorum, et Diaconorum, nihil continent ab illâ ipsâ doctrina alienum; quicunque mittentur ad docendum populum, illorum articulorum authoritatem et fidem, non tantum concionibus suis sed etiam subscriptione confirmabunt. Qui secus fecerit, et contrariâ doctrinâ populum turbaverit excommunicabitur [Cardwell's *Synodalia*, Oxford, 1842, vol. i. p. 126].

Or in English: —

PREACHERS.

First. however, they shall take care not to teach anything for a sermon, which they wish the people religiously to hold and believe, except what is agreeable to the doctrine of the old, or new Testament, and which the Catholic Fathers and ancient Bishops have gathered from that very doctrine; and since these Articles of the Christian Religion, to which the Bishops agreed in a lawful and holy Synod which by command and authority of the most serene Lady Elizabeth was convoked and held, were undoubtedly gathered from the Sacred books of the old and new Testament, and agree throughout with the Heavenly doctrine contained in those Testaments: Since, moreover, *the Book of Common Prayer, and the Book of the Ordination of Bishops, Priests, and Deacons contain nothing at variance with this very doctrine,* whoever shall be sent to teach the people shall confirm the authority and truth of these Articles, *not only in their Sermons, but also by subscription.*

He who shall have done otherwise, and who shall have disturbed the people by contrary teaching, shall be excommunicated.

Here, again, the Canon on Preachers runs contrary to the cry of the Puritans, who maintained that the Book of Common Prayer, *and especially the Ordinal,* was contrary to the doctrine of the Old and New Testaments.

§ VIII. *Act* 13 *Elizabeth, c.* 12.

Under this Act, which received the royal assent May 29, 1571, it was required that —

' Every one under the degree of a Bishop, which doth or shall pretend to be a priest or minister of GOD's holy Word and Sacraments by reason of any other form of institution, consecration, or ordering than the form set forth by Parliament in the time of the late King of most worthy memory, King Edward Sixth, or now used in the reign of our most gracious Sovereign lady, before the feast of the Nativity of CHRIST, next following. shall in the presence of the Bishop, or guardian of the spiritualities of some one Diocese, where he hath, or shall have Ecclesiastical living. declare his assent, and subscribe to all the Articles of Religion, which only concern the confession of the true Christian faith, and the Doctrine of the Sacraments comprised in a book entitled —

and here follows the title of the XXXIX. Articles of 1562.

This Act, therefore, barred Roman Priests and Deacons from holding a cure without first assenting to the XXXIX. Articles; since the only Priests or Ministers or Deacons who could pretend to have received any form of legal institution, consecrating, or ordering than that set forth under Edward VI. or Elizabeth were those who had been so ordained under the reign of Mary, and who of course under that reign were the *only* legal Priests or Ministers or Deacons.

Henceforth, then, the two side avenues to the Church's cures were barred, the Roman and the Puritan.

Even this very *Act* 13 *Eliz. c.* 12, further enacted that:

No person now permitted by any dispensation or otherwise, shall retain any Benefice with Cure, being under the age of one and twenty years, or not being a Deacon at least, and none shall be made Minister, or admitted to preach or administer the Sacraments, being under the age of twenty-four years. nor unless he bring the Bishop of the Diocese testimonial of his regular life and of his professing the Doctrine expressed in the said Articles. . . . And lastly all Admissions to Benefices, Institutions, and Inductions contrary to the form and provision of this Act, and all Tolerations, Dispensations, Qualifications, and Licenses whatsoever to be made to the contrary hereof shall be void in Law.

The Puritans, who were ever on the watch how to avoid sanctioning the Ordinal, seized hold on one word in the first part of this Act, the word "only," and under cover of that word refused to sign the XXXIX. Articles. Their plea was that they had merely to sign those Articles "which *only* concern the true Christian Faith and the Doctrine of the Sacraments," and that therefore by this limitation all of the XXXIX. Articles which related to the Homilies (which they detested, owing to their strong doctrine), to the Ordinal, and to the Authority of the Church, were not to be included in the Articles presented them for their subscription [Collier, p. 530].

The word "only" in the text of the Act of course referred to all the Articles, and was used in an apologetic or explanatory sense of the contents of the whole of these Articles, and was in that first section of the Act, which, as we have seen, was aimed at the Roman Catholics. It was as much as to say, "We do not want you to declare your Orders to be invalid, or to make any other Confession of Faith in signing these XXXIX. Articles, for after all, they only contain a Confession of the Christian Faith, and the Doctrine of the Holy Sacraments."

By raising a quibble as to the meaning of the word "only," and maintaining that the law did not require them to do so, the Puritans refused to subscribe to all the XXXIX. Articles, thus appealing from one Act to another Act.

As a conclusion to these remarks on this statute the words of Sir Edward Coke, as quoted by Collier [p. 536], are singularly appropriate.

And that this (*i. e.* Subscription to all the Articles without exception) was the meaning of the Legislature is further made good by Sir Edward Coke's authority. who positively affirms, That the Subscription required by the Clergy takes in all the Nine and thirty Articles. And that by this Statute the Delinquent is disabled and deprived, *ipso facto.* He adds further : —

'That when one Smith subscribed the Nine and thirty Articles with this addition (so far forth as the same were agreeable to the word of God) 't was resolved by Sir Christopher Wray, Chief Justice in the King's Bench, and all the Judges of England, that this subscription was not according to the Statute of 13 Elizabeth, cap. 12 [Coke's *Reports*, liber 6, fol. 29, Green's case].

Because the Statute required an absolute Subscription, whereas this Subscription made it conditional. And further, this Act was made for avoiding Diversity of Opinions, &c. But by this qualification or addition, the party might by his own private opinion take some of the Articles to be against the Word of God; and so by this means diversity of opinions would not be avoided. And thus the scope of the Statute and the very Act itself made touching Subscription would be of none effect. Thus far Sir Edward Coke [*Institutes*, part iv. fol. 323, 324].

From the days of Elizabeth to those of Victoria the Puritans have always, possibly owing to what Archbishop Parker called their "Germanical natures," shown a singularly convenient inability to understand plain English.

§ IX. *Subscription to the XXXIX. Articles enforced by Parliament*, 1571.

By the *Act* 13 *Eliz. c.* 12, subscription to the XXXIX. Articles as passed by Convocation in 1562 was, as we have just seen, made by Parliament compulsory on all the clergy.

There is little need to say much here concerning these Articles. Convocation in 1553 had passed XLII. Articles, as we have seen, which were reduced to XXXIX. by the Convocation of 1562, and now in 1571 Parliament enforces subscription to them. The XXXIX. Articles are thus made not only the law of the Church, but the law of the realm. They are not a creed, but partake more of the nature of a declaration of principles affecting the chief matters of controversy then existing. The popular conception of them is certainly very curious. They have been called by some outside of the Church the Creed of the Church; whereas, of course, the Church of England recognizes but the Three Creeds.

Protestants of all stripes have in latter times spoken of the XXXIX. Articles as if they were so many mysterious charms by which the "Protestant religion" could alone be saved.

They seem to have derived as much comfort from the XXXIX. Articles as the old woman did from the repetition of "that there soothing word 'Mesopotamia'" in her parson's sermons. They appear to have looked upon them as the only comforting words between the covers of the Prayer-Book. Their ancestors knew better; for the Low Church party in the Church of England is *the only party which has ever endeavored to get rid of the XXXIX. Articles!* Not once, but repeatedly.

Another misconception is that the Articles contain the highest form of Calvinism, whereas the truth is that the Articles which did contain Calvinistic doctrine were what are called "the Lambeth Articles," and that notwithstanding the repeated attempts, especially the two determined ones of 1595 and 1603, to foist them on the Church, the Church utterly repudiated them.

The clause in Article XX., "The Church hath power to decree Rites or Ceremonies, and authority in controversies of Faith," which the Puritans, Presbyterians, etc., so strongly objected to, does not appear in some of the copies of the Articles issued between 1563 and 1571. This was one of those Articles which they endeavored to shirk, on the quibble already noticed, that it "only concerned the confession of the true Christian Faith and the Doctrine of the Sacraments."

To us there seems very little doubt that the Puritans resorted to one of their favorite weapons, — falsification, — and that it was they who caused copies of the Articles to be printed with the omission of the Article they detested.

Archbishop Laud did not scruple, when absurdly accused of having added the clause, to retort the charge of falsification on the Puritan party.

"I do openly here in the Star Chamber charge upon that pure Sect this foul corruption of falsifying the Articles of the Church of England. Let them take it off as they can" [as quoted by Collier, vol. ii. p. 487].

Heylin, in *History of Presbyterianism* [p. 283], gives another instance of falsification which occurred about the same date. Since editions of the Prayer-Book were issued in which two services opposed by the Puritans, the order for private baptism and confirmation of children —

was quite omitted, which grand omissions were designed to no other purpose, but by degrees to bring the Church of England into some conformity to the desired orders of Geneva.

The opinion of the patient and erudite Strype is also against the Puritans in the matter of the omitted clause.

So that at length an edition that appeared abroad in the same year, printed by John Day, wanting the clause, hath been judged, and that upon good grounds, to be spurious; and the rasure of the Church's power and authority, to be owing to the interest and cunning of a faction that then prevailed much, and had not a few favourers at court, which indeed we see abundantly in this present history, and by the labours and troubles our Archbishop[1] continually underwent on that account [Strype's *Life of Parker*, vol. ii. p. 56. Oxford, 1821].

Parallel with this is the constant endeavor, past and present, to prove the seven letters of S. Ignatius and the Epistles to Saints Timothy and Titus forgeries, on account of their uncomfortable teaching on Apostolical succession.

Before leaving these XXXIX. Articles a word must be said why the Church authorities have so unanimously passed over the Parliamentary Statute of 1571, which is always cited as having given legality to the enforcement of subscription to those Articles. This silence on the part of Church authorities appears so strange to many writers that all kinds of explanations for it have been given, some of them very far-fetched. To discuss the whole matter fully would require a whole article in the CHURCH REVIEW, nor would it be an unprofitable task, as there seems to be so much misconception on the point. Briefly, however, the reason seems to be that the Church authorities considered the *Act* 13 *Eliz. c.* 12 superfluous, so far as it gave legality to subscription to the Articles. They considered that they had legal power inherent in themselves to enjoin and enforce subscription to whatever Articles they chose to put forward, without asking "by your leave" of the Parliament. This appears to the writer the simple reason, and the true one.

Accordingly, when the Convocation of 1571 met, although the Parliamentary Statute was not then passed, the Primate ordered every member of Convocation, on penalty of exclusion, there and then to sign the Articles of 1562. The Articles were thereupon read out aloud, and every member of both houses subscribed to them.

The Canons of 1571, enjoining subscription to the Book of Articles of 1562, as we have seen, contain no allusion to the statute then being passed through Parliament.

Parker's Three Articles of June, 1571, enjoined subscription to the Book of Articles of 1562; no reference again to the

---

[1] That is, Archbishop Parker.

statute just passed, and assented to by the Queen. The XV. Articles passed by Convocation in 1576 likewise enjoin subscription to the Articles of 1562, with no reference to the statute; and so Whitgift's Three Articles, the XXIV. Articles of 1584, and Canon 36 of the Canons of 1604, in force till 1865, all require subscription to the Articles of the Convocation of 1562, and never allude to the Statute of 1571.

The same reason actuated the Queen in refusing her formal sanction to the Advertisements of 1564, to the Canons of 1571, and to the successive steps which the Bishops or Ecclesiastical Commissioners took for the enforcement of conformity to the Prayer-Book or Ordinal. However keen the Queen might be after money, and however scandalously she may have acted in appropriating Church revenues, she was not so Erastian as even some of the Bishops. The title "Head of the Church" was distasteful to her, as arrogating an honor due to CHRIST alone. She considered that whatever Convocation did touching doctrine, or the discipline of the clergy, Parliament had no inherent right to meddle with, either by sanctioning by a special Act, or by disannulling. She even went farther, and considered that each successive step which the Bishops might consider necessary to take to enforce conformity did not require direct and fresh sanction at their hands; *that they had the authority inherent in their office.*

It is perfectly true that some of the Bishops, and even Parker, were anxious to obtain the Queen's formal sanction or the authority of Parliament for what they did; but the reason for this was probably on Parker's side, that he might "level up" the Puritan Bishops and give them no excuse to avoid enforcing conformity, and on the part of the Bishops generally that they might overawe the boldness of the Puritan leaders by representing them as disloyal subjects to the State, as well as to the Church.

If this view of Elizabeth's conduct be the correct one, as we submit it is, then we have the key to what seems so unnecessarily puzzling to many writers in the fact that Church documents were issued, and their provisions acted upon and enforced, although, as they complain, without royal authority; and the silence of these or similar documents on the Statute of 1571 is likewise accounted for.

The same general principle governs the whole: —

The inherent right of the Church to rule herself, either by her voice expressed in Convocation, or by the Bishops speaking on behalf of Convocation.

§ X. *Order of the Ecclesiastical Commissioners, June* 7, 1571.

The Parliament which had met on April 2 was prorogued on May 29, and Convocation, which had assembled on April 3, broke up on May 30.

As a result of the Canons passed by Convocation, the Ecclesiastical Commissioners lost no time in issuing an order headed: "The Commissioners Ecclesiastical to all Church wardens concerning the Puritan Ministers," and omitting the preamble, the charge is as follows: —

We wil and require you, and in the Queen's Majesties name straitly charge and command you, and every of you, that in no wise ye suffer any person or minister to minister any sacrament, or say any publick prayers, in any your churches, chappels, or other places appointed for common prayers, in any other order, maner, or sort, than only according to the prescription in the Book of Common Prayer, and the Queen's Majesties law published in that behalf.

And that in no wise you suffer any person publicly or privatly to teach, read, or preach, in any the said churches, parishes, chappels, private houses, or other places, unles such be licenced to preach, read, or teach, by the Queen's Highnes authority, the Archbishop of Canterbury his licence, or by the licence of the Bishop of the dioces: and that he be such a minister as is licensed to preach after the first of May last. and not removed from the ministry by us, or any other lawful authority [Strype's *Parker*, Appendix, Number LXII. vol. iii. p. 183].

§ XI. *Parker's Three Articles, passed in June,* 1571.

In the history of the conflict of the Church with the Puritans, Precisians, and Parity-men, *et hoc genus omne*, there are no more important Articles than the Three Articles which Parker insisted on the clergy subscribing, and which we have named Parker's *Three Articles.*

We know of no writer that has given them that prominence they deserve. A few have an incidental notice of them, or relegate an obscure allusion to them in a foot-note. Many seem to have confounded them with Whitgift's Three Articles. They seem to have escaped the notice of even the painstaking Hardwick, for there is not a stray allusion to them in his book on the Articles.

The references by Whitgift, in his *Defence of the Answer to the Admonition*, to Three Articles to which Cartwright and his compeers strongly objected, make it evident that there must have been in force before the publication of the *Admonition* in 1571 Three Articles directed against the Puritans. The remarks, therefore, that follow on these *Three Articles* do not profess in any way to be a summary of what has already been said by others on the subject, but are the result of such researches as can at best be but very limited on this continent. Enough, however, will, it is hoped, be said to show the extreme importance of these Articles, while at the same time it must be borne in mind that much more might be said on further research.

The Convocation, as we have seen, passed canons regulating the action of Bishops and preachers so as to prevent the intrusion of unworthy, unlearned, or unauthorized ministers. One of the means of effecting this was the plan of recalling all licenses, and enjoining that the applicants should subscribe to the XXXIX. Articles as approved by the Synod in 1562, and that they would defend the doctrine therein contained. We saw what injunctions the Ecclesiastical Commissioners issued in the Advertisements of 1564, and also the order they issued after the passage of these Canons, on June 7, 1571, to the church-wardens; incidentally we have also noticed the instructions given by the Bishop of Ely to his Chancellor, on August 28.

How to carry out effectually the wishes of Convocation, as expressed in the Canons referred to under Section VII., was the task the Archbishop now set before himself. Grindal, Archbishop of York, was lukewarm, and so was Parkhurst of Norwich and Sandys of London. On the other hand, Jewel of Sarum promised to stand by the Archbishop, and so did Horne of Winchester, Cox of Ely, Ballingham of Worcester, and Curteis of Chichester.

Parker determined to strike an effectual blow at the Puritans by dealing with their principal leaders. These were accordingly cited to appear at Lambeth, to answer for their erroneous doctrine and for their non-conformity to the Prayer-Book. Some were merely admonished; others had to resign their benefices.

This occurred on June 6, as appears from a document signed by Deringe, one of the leading Puritans. On the very next day, June 7, the order to the church-wardens was issued; this dealt with the Puritans in the country as well as in London.

Whether Archbishop Parker had already, prior to June 6, framed the *Three Articles* or not, the writer is unable to ascertain; the probabilities are that they were not, but that finding the Puritans evaded the injunctions of the Commissioners, or possibly did not appear when cited, the Archbishop determined to devise more effectual means to obtain conformity. If the *Three Articles* had been framed prior to the issue of the order to the church-wardens, they would most likely have been mentioned. Be that as it may, they certainly were not only framed, but actually tendered for subscription before July 4. For we read in a petition of Robert Johnson, domestic chaplain to Lord Bacon, to the Ecclesiastical Commissioners, dated August 14, 1571, —

That whereas the 4th of July last, being before their Lordships to answer to their three articles, he did forbear to subscribe to the first of them, etc. [See Strype's *Parker*, vol. ii. p. 70.]

Historically speaking, then, the Canons of 1571 were the origin of Parker's *Three Articles*, although they derived their legal authority from being issued by Parker, as head of the Ecclesiastical Commissioners appointed by the Queen.

The strong authority claimed by the Commissioners comes out very forcibly in the letter of remonstrance which the Commissioners addressed to the Duke of Norfolk, who had endeavored to shield the notorious Robert Brown [1] from the reach of the Commissioners by claiming that as his domestic chaplain, Brown was in a place of privilege.

Our Commission (so reply the Commissioners) extendeth to all places as well exempt, as not exempt, within Her Majesty's dominions, and before this time never by any called into question. . . . We would be loath to use other means to bring him (*i. e.* Brown) to his answer, as we must be forced to do if your grace will not like hereof [quoted by Strype's *Parker*, vol. ii. p. 68].

---

[1] Brown became the founder of the "Brownists," the ancestors of the Independents and Congregationalists. After eighteen years' schismatical preaching Brown conformed; but, as Strype says, "he still continued very freakish."

When the Commissioners addressed a personage of the standing of the Duke of Norfolk thus, and, as we shall see, attacked the chaplain of the Lord Keeper Bacon, they could not have had much doubt of their legal authority, although, as will be noticed, they studiously ignore the Parliamentary Statute, 13 *Eliz. c.* 12, just passed.

Having therefore shown the approximate date of the issue of these Articles, the second week in June, 1571, and their historical origin, the Canons of 1571, and their legal authority, the Queen's Ecclesiastical Commissioners, there remains but to give the wording of the Articles.

By the help of Whitgift's *Defence of the Answer to the Admonition*, and the letter of complaint of the Puritan Johnson, we are able to give their very terms, *for the first time since the Reformation.*

PARKER'S THREE ARTICLES.

I. That the book, commonly called the Book of Common Prayer for the Church of England, authorized by Parliament, and all and every contents therein be such as are not repugnant to the word of GOD [Whitgift's *Works*, vol. iii. p. 326].

II. That the manner and order appointed by Public Authority about the Administration of the Sacraments, and Common Prayers, and that the apparel by sufficient authority appointed for the ministers within the Church of England, be not wicked, nor against the Word of GOD, but tolerable, and being commanded for order and obedience' sake are to be used [*Ibid.* p. 458].

III. That the Articles of Religion which only concern the true Christian Faith and the Doctrine of the Sacraments comprised in a book imprinted: *Articles whereupon it was agreed by both Archbishops, and Bishops of both Provinces, and the whole clergy in the Convocation holden at London, in the year of our Lord* 1562, *according to the computation of the Church of England,* and every of them contained true and godly Christian doctrine.

Articles I. and II. speak for themselves. The words " repugnant to the Word of GOD " were brought in because that was the pet Puritan phrase against the Prayer-Book, just as " wicked and anti-Christian " was brought in, in the Canons of 1604, because that was the stock phrase of the Presbyterians against the doctrine and government of the Church.

Article III. enjoins subscription to the XXXIX. Articles of 1562. There is a material point to be noticed bearing on the quibble raised afterward by the Puritans on the word "only," as referred to already under Section VIII. The very preamble of the *Act* 13 *Eliz. c.* 12 is used, "which only concern the true Christian Faith," etc., but there is added at the end of the title the words, "and every of them." The addition of these four words, added as they are in an unstudied manner, and *before the quibble* was raised, show quite clearly what was meant by the Act within a month of its being passed, and by the persons whom it intimately concerned.

When Robert Johnson wrote to the Ecclesiastical Commissioners on August 14 on the subject of these Three Articles he says that as to Article I. he would put up with the Prayer-Book, and was ready to declare the contents

> were not defective, nor expressly contrary or against the Word of GOD, and that the imperfections thereof might for unity and charity sake be suffered till GOD grant a time of perfect reformation.

To the second he submits in the following terms: —

> To the Second, That the minister's apparel as it was not wicked, and directly against the Word of God, being by the Prince appointed only for policy, obedience, and order sake, might be used; yet not generally expedient nor edifying.

He thus submits, ungraciously and grudgingly perhaps, still he submits to the first two Articles. To the third, which he repeats *in extenso*, and has thus preserved for us, he submits without a murmur; he does not raise a single objection.

Let it be noted that Robert Johnson[1] was a leading man, that he was chaplain to Lord Bacon, that he dates his letter from Bacon's house at Gorhambury, beside S. Albans, and sends it

---

[1] This Robert Johnson, like Brown, afterward conformed. Johnson appears, however, to have conformed with more heart than Brown, for Strype mentions a sermon of his on Sept. 3, 1609, where he blamed the laity "for refusing their own parish churches, and to hear their own pastors were they never so well learned or well habited in speech because they wore a surplice, or made a cross upon a child, and would run after and get them a heap of teachers, that spake evil of them that were in authority — that would rail against Bishops," etc.; and in another sermon he spoke of "schismatical spirits who, under color of zeal, etc., would, if they could, banish those Bishops which CHRIST and His apostles appointed, and would turn all discipline and government upside down, churches into chambers, Bishops into Syndics," etc.

All very good and true, but the pity is that he had not followed his own advice years before.

in all human probability after having submitted it to the keen and almost unrivalled intellect of his patron. What becomes, then of the quibble on the word "only"? If Parliament had intended to limit the subscription to some of the Articles, clumsily and ungrammatically as they would have expressed such an intention in the wording of the Act, yet Bacon would have known of that intention, and have quickly pointed out to his *protégé* a legal, and therefore effective, means of defying the Ecclesiastical Commissioners.

These articles are important as adding another convincing proof, if one were needed, that Chief-Justice Coke's ruling was the right one. They are, however, still more important as having been the immediate cause of the publication of the celebrated *Admonition* to Parliament by the Puritans before May, 1572, which led to Whitgift's *Answer to the Admonition*, which in turn brought out Cartwright's *Reply to the Answer*, to which succeeded Whitgift's *Defence of the Answer to the Admonition*, followed by Cartwright's *Second Reply*.

The importance of Parker's *Three Articles* are historically, therefore, very great. When dealing with the *Admonition* controversy later on, we shall refer to them again; for the present we pass on to the next section.

§ XII. *The Queen's Proclamation of Oct.* 20, 1573.

The heading of this proclamation is: "A proclamation against the despisers or breakers of the Orders prescribed in the Book of Common Prayer."

This proclamation was one of the results of the *Admonition* controversy alluded to in the last section. The following clause instructing magistrates and others is all that we need give:

If any person shall by public preaching, writing, or printing contemn, despise, or dispraise the orders contained in the said book (*i. e.* Book of Common Prayer), they shall immediately apprehend him, and cause him to be imprisoned until he have answered to the law, &c. [Strype's *Documentary Annals*, vol. vi. p. 385].

Comment is unnecessary.

§ XIII. *The XV. Articles passed by Convocation in March*, 1576.

Parker died May 17, 1575, and Grindal was not appointed Archbishop till Feb. 15, 1576.

Of these Articles only the substance of those which concern our inquiry need be given.

I. Subscription to the XXXIX. Articles of 1562 enjoined on all candidates for ordination, who were to be ordained only on Sundays or Holy days and according to the form prescribed in the Ordinal.

III. Unlearned ministers formerly ordained not to be admitted to any cure or function.

IV. and V. enjoin diligent inquiry in each Diocese for the discovery of such as have counterfeited letters of Orders.

IX. None under a Deacon to be allowed to preach.

These Articles again afford no loophole for any one to enter the ministry except according to the form of Episcopal ordination provided in the Ordinal. They also go farther. They show a strong desire on the part of Convocation to weed out the unlearned men who at all times smuggle themselves in, despite all regulations; and what is still more remarkable, the provisions of the IV. and V. Articles point to a scandal, which must have been caused by the Puritans only because the Papist had no need to forge letters of Orders, since his own Orders were never called into question.

The IX. was a blow struck at the gospellers, or readers. If a layman could not preach, *a fortiori*, a layman could not administer the Sacrament.

So far, then, as the year 1576 there are no signs discoverable on the part of Convocation to admit anything but the exclusive validity of Episcopal ordination.

It must also be borne in mind that the Puritans had not been without influence in this very Convocation, for it was through them that the last four were passed. The XII., which allowed none but "a lawful Minister or Deacon" to baptize privately, was a concession on lay baptism against which the Puritans were always reviling. The XIII. and XIV. related to commutations of penance and matters of discipline. The XV. provided for the solemnization of matrimony at *all* times of the year,— in other words, allowing marriages in Lent.

The Queen refused to sanction the XII. and XV., hence these Articles are sometimes known as the XIII. Articles of 1576. But Convocation passed the whole fifteen, although when the Articles were printed only thirteen were given.

Strong, therefore, as Puritan influence was in the Convocation of 1576, there was no tampering with the Ordinal, or any relaxation in subscription to the Articles allowed.

§ XIV. *Whitgift's Three Articles of April*, 1584.

These Articles have been very inaccurately stated to be the same as Parker's *Three Articles*, or, rather, Parker's *Three Articles* have been passed over because they were considered to be the same as Whitgift's *Three Articles*. Even in the Preface to the *Liturgical Services, Queen Elizabeth*, edited by the Parker Society, this mistake is made of confounding these two sets of Articles. We have seen what Parker's Articles really were. The following are those issued by Whitgift: —

I. That Her Majesty, under GOD, hath, and ought to have, the sovereignty and rule over all manner of persons born within her realms, and dominions, and countries, of what estate ecclesiastical or temporal soever they be. And that none other foreign power, prelate, state, or potentate hath, or ought to have, any jurisdiction, power, superiority, or preëminence, or authority ecclesiastical or temporal, within Her Majesty's said realms, dominions, or countries.

II. That the Book of Common Prayer, and of ordering Bishops, Priests, and Deacons, containeth nothing in it contrary to the Word of GOD. And that the same may be lawfully used; and that he himself will use the form of the said book prescribed, in public prayer, and administration of the Sacraments, and none other.

III. That he alloweth the book of Articles of religion, agreed upon by the Archbishops and Bishops of both provinces, and the Clergy in Convocation holden at London, in the year of our LORD, 1562, and set forth by Her Majesty's authority. And that he believeth all the Articles therein contained to be agreeable to the Word of GOD [Strype's *Whitgift*, vol. 1. p. 230].

None were permitted to "preach, read, catechise, minister the Sacraments, or to execute any other ecclesiastical function, by what authority soever he be admitted thereunto, unless he first consent and subscribe to these Articles, before the Ordinary of the Diocese wherein he preacheth, readeth, catechiseth, or ministereth the Sacraments."

The enforcement of subscription to these Three Articles gave great offence to the "maintainers of the discipline of GOD," as the Puritans and Parity-men called themselves. "They struggled with all their might to have them vacated or thrown aside," as Strype expresses it, and the country swarmed with pamphlets against the Bishops for "depriving many faithful ministers of the Gospel for not subscribing."

Of course the second was the great rock of offence, *because it enjoined subscription to the Prayer-Book and Ordinal.* To use Strype's forcible expression, —

> The second of which, viz., the approbation of the Common Prayer Book, and the form of Ordering Ministers, to be agreeable to the Word of God, *would not down with many that had offices and places in the Church* [Strype's *Whitgift*, vol. i. p. 241].

During Grindal's primacy, especially in the latter years, when he was growing blind, some men who did not believe in Episcopal ordination may have been admitted. Perhaps in some rare cases, men who had been "ordained" abroad in the Protestant communities at Antwerp or Geneva, had thrust themselves not into the ministry of the Church, for that they could not do so long as the Ordinal lay unrepealed, but into the cures or benefices of the Church, and thus like wolves in sheep's clothing appeared to be ministers of the Church. Perhaps there may have been such cases, although not a single authentic case has yet been brought forward of an un-Episcopally ordained man having been wittingly admitted. The Queen and the Archbishop were, however, determined to enforce the law of Church and State against Papists and Puritans alike.

If the second article was aimed against the Puritans, the first was against the Papists, and the third against both of them. The wording of the third Article, be it noted, leaves no room for even Puritan quibbling; he has to profess belief in "all the Articles."

The Bishops proceeded with their visitations, and everywhere enforced subscription to Whitgift's *Three Articles.* A list is given by Strype of non-subscribing ministers. Lord Burghley made some notes as to the opinions and doctrines of these men. They are all Puritanical objections, not one of them is a Roman objection, showing plainly, if proof were needed, the class of Non-Conformists against whom these articles were intended.

A few of these and other Puritan objections will show their opinions as to what the Ordinal taught, and will prove whether the voice of the Church of England was uncertain on the question of the exclusive validity of Episcopal ordination or not in their ears.

The Book allows to the clergy a superiority, and establisheth not the authority of the Elders. It is contrary to GOD's Word to order these degrees in the Church, — Bishops, Priests, and Deacons.

Bishops and Priests can give no reason of any calling they have out of the Word of GOD.

The whole government of the Church is declared to be, —

Thus, he that teacheth in doctrine, is *Doctor;* he that exhorteth in exhortation, is *Pastor;* he that distributeth in singleness, is *Deacon;* he that ruleth in diligence, is *Senior;* he that showeth mercy in cheerfulness, is *Widow.*

The people ought in every Church, by the Word of GOD, to choose their own Ministers. . . . Every Church, by the prescript rule of GOD'S Word, ought to have a perpetual government of Doctor, Pastor, Seniors, Deacons, etc., which ought to rule and govern the whole Church, and every member of the same.[1]

The Archbishop drew up the following three deductions that would follow from refusal to subscribe to the *Three Articles:*

I. If you subscribe not to the Article concerning the Book of Common Prayer, then by necessary consequence must follow, there is not the true service of God, and right administration of the Sacraments in the land.

II. If you subscribe not the book of Ordering Ministers, then it followeth your calling is unlawful, and the Papist argument is good: *No calling, no ministry, no Church,* etc.

III. If not to the last Article, then you deny true doctrine to be established in the churches of England, which is the main note of the Churches. And so I see no reason why I should persuade the Papists to our Religion, and to come to our Church, seeing we will not allow it ourselves [Strype's *Whitgift*, vol. i. p. 248].

When the Puritan party of the Privy Council complained to the Archbishop as to the rigor with which he was enforcing subscription to his *Three Articles* he, in the course of his reply, threw out this challenge: —

And here I do protest, and testify unto your Lordships (of the Privy Council), that the Three Articles, whereunto they (the non-conforming

---

[1] Taken from the answers in writing of Dudley Fenner. Strype's *Whitgift*, vol. i. p. 246. The following names are mentioned as having been given by this Fenner in baptism, — Joy Again, From Above, More Fruit, Dust.

ministers) are moved to subscribe, are such as I am ready by learning to defend in manner and form as they are set down, against all mislikers thereof in England or elsewhere [Strype's *Whitgift*, vol. i. p. 255].

No wonder "the Brethren," the "pseudo-evangelicals," the "Gospellers," the "Godly disciplinarians," and all their like-minded friends who had been so strenuously fighting for the "parity of ministers," called this year of grace 1584 "the woful year of subscription."

§ XV. *The Twenty-Four Articles of May*, 1584.

Whitgift succeeded Grindal in the Archbishopric on Sept. 23, 1583. Grindal, who had been lax both by inclination and through failing health, had not enforced the laws against the Puritans as rigidly as his predecessor. Whitgift determined to enforce conformity. With that object in view twenty-four Articles were drawn up by the Ecclesiastical Commissioners under authority of the Queen, in May, 1584.

These Articles were framed on a different model from all the previous ones. A man had simply to subscribe to the former formularies, or else be refused ordination, or compelled to resign his cure. Now the proceeding was different. The burden of proof that he was not guilty was thrown on the accused; as will be clearly seen by reciting any one of the Articles.

Take the eighth, for example.

8. *Item objicimus, ponimus, et articularum*, that for the space of theise three years, two yeres, one yere, half a yere, three, two, or one moneth last past, you haue at the tyme of communion, and at all or some other tymes in your ministration, vsed and worne onlly your ordinarie apparel and not the surplesse, as is required; declare how longe, how often, and for what cause, consideration. or entente youe haue so done, or refused so to doe. Et objicimus conjunctim de omnim, et divisi de quolibet.

This is pretty severe. It is presuming at the outset that the unfortunate accused is guilty, and forces him, at the edge of the sword, as it were, to prove his complete innocence. The whole series is directed against the Puritans, and is set in the same terms as the one quoted. The latter part of the twenty-second is the only portion of them directly affecting a Papist, as it is a declaration against any foreign power, prelate, potentate, etc.

By the first one the accused is summoned to declare —

that you are a Deacon, or Minister and Priest admitted, declare by whome, and what tyme you were ordered; and likewise that your orderinge was accordinge to the booke in that behalf by lawe of this land provided.

By the second, that he deemed "his ordering, admission, and calling into the ministrie to be lawfull and not repugnant to the Word of GOD." The third deals with canonical obedience; the fourth, fifth, sixth, and seventeenth and twentieth with "the virtuous and godly booke entituled *The Booke of Common Prayer, etc.;*" the eighth with the surplice, the ninth with the sign of the cross at baptism, the tenth and thirteenth with infant baptism, the eleventh with the ring at matrimony, the twelfth with objecting to use the form of thanksgiving for women, the fourteenth with the Litany, the fifteenth with changing the lesson for the day, the sixteenth with the Burial Service, the eighteenth with the Communion Service, the nineteenth with preaching against the Prayer-Book and assembling at conventicles, the twenty-first with former accusations, the twenty-second with subscription to the *Prayer-Book, Ordinal, and all the Articles of Religion*, the twenty-third, with preaching in houses or unlicensed places, and the twenty-fourth, that he has violated all the preceding twenty-three, wholly or in part. Familiar as Whitgift was with the Puritan contentions through his controversy with Cartwright, he dealt with them *omnia et singula* in these Articles. At the very outset the Puritan has to produce his letters of Orders, or give satisfactory proof of his Orders. If he cannot do that, — if he cannot prove that he is ordained "*according to the law of this land provided*," — it is useless to go on farther with the inquiry. He stands condemned.

Where is the uncertain voice in 1584?

The Puritans, on the issue of these Articles, used all their influence to have them mitigated, but in vain; nor were they more successful with the petition they succeeded in obtaining from the House of Commons to the Upper House. The main clauses of that petition were that the Bishops should restore such "godly preachers" as had been suspended for no other crime than their refusal to subscribe to the XXXIX. Articles, and that they should not be examined on the oath *ex officio* (meaning the proceedings under the XXIV. Articles), but that the Bishops should only act upon definite informations supplied. The Lords gave them no relief. The *legality* of the proceedings under these

XXIV. Articles was never once questioned, though their rigor was complained of.

Lord Burghley, who favored the Puritans, wrote to the Archbishop pleading for less "vehement proceedings." Whitgift, under date of July 3, 1584, defends the action of the Commissioners concerning these XXIV. Articles and incidentally asserts that they were "framed by the best learned in the laws," and ingenuously asks why any object to answer if innocent of the charges laid against them. "Qui male agit odit lucem," is the answer he gives to his own question.

To satisfy objectors the Archbishop drew up a paper of "Reasons" why culpable ministers should be examined on their oaths as set out in the XXIV. Articles. These "Reasons" are given at length in Strype's *Whitgift*, vol. i. p. 318. The eleventh is as follows: —

XI. The Article for examination whether these bee Deacon or Ministers ordered according to the lawes of this lande is most necessarie : First, For the grounding of the proceeding, least the breache of the Book bee objected to them, who are not bound to observe it : Secondly, To meet with such schismaticks (whereof there is sufficient experience), *which either thrust themselves into the ministrie, without any lawful calling at all, or ellse take orders at Antweorp, or ellswhere beyond the sea.*

The "lawful calling" is the calling according "to the lawes of this lande," and "the lawes of this lande" are, no calling is lawful which is not according to the Ordinal, which admits only of Episcopal ordination.

"Orders at Antweorp or ellswhere beyond the sea" were Presbyterian "Orders," and these are declared to be not "according to the lawes of this lande," as not being according to the Ordinal.

What becomes of the theory that the exclusive validity is not the sole view to be tolerated and taught in the Church of England?

We have seen, when examining into the history of Parker's *Three Articles*, that they were the immediate cause of the *Admonition to Parliament*. It will be well to turn back for a while to that half-forgotten chapter in Church history.

VII. THE ADMONITION CONTROVERSY.

The opponents of the Church drew up two pamphlets in 1572, setting forth their views as to Church government, replete with attacks on every point of the Church's doctrine, services, liturgy, worship, ritual, and government. This production derived its title from an ecclesiastical term,[1] and though addressed to Parliament, was never presented to that body, but was printed and sown broadcast over the kingdom before the prorogation of the Parliament of 1572.

Whitgift, then Dean of Lincoln, was chosen by Archbishop Parker to answer the *Admonition to Parliament*, which he accordingly did before the close of the year, in his *Answer to the Admonition*. Cartwright, one of the framers of the *Admonition*, produced under his initials, T. C., *A Reply to the Answer to the Admonition* in 1573. Whitgift thereupon wrote his *Defence of the Answer to the Admonition against the Reply of T. C.*, in 1574, in which he met Cartwright's objections paragraph by paragraph, point by point. This work, thus containing both sides, is not only conducted in the fairest method of controversy, but is a regular storehouse of the point at issue between the Church and her Puritan opponents. Cartwright published a *Second Reply*, in two parts, with an interval of two years between the parts, and can thus claim the distinction of having had the last word.

The Preface to the *Admonition* gives us a summary of the meaning of the *Admonition* itself: —

But in a few words to say what we mean. Either we must have a right ministry of GOD [Matt. ix. 37, 38; Eph. iv. 11, 12] and a right government of His Church [Matt. xviii. 15, 16, 17] according to the Scriptures set up (both which we lack); or else there can be no right religion, nor yet for contempt thereof can GOD's plagues [Prov. xxix. 18; Amos viii. 11, 12, etc.; Matt. xxi. 23, etc.; 1 Cor. xi. 30] be from us any while deferred [*Works of John Whitgift.* Parker Society, 1851, vol. i. p. 140].

Here, then, we see that the ministry of the Church, — that is, Bishops, Priests, and Deacons, — is the main object of the attack. The *Admonition* bears out the promise of the Preface, and is full of attacks on the ministry of the Church. The "Godly minis-

---

[1] Thomas Cartwright, chief of the Non-Conformists, presents the Parliament with a book called an *Admonition*, some members taking distaste at the title thereof. For seeing that *Admonition* is the lowest of ecclesiastical censures, and a preparative (if neglected) to suspension and excommunication, such suggested that if the Parliament complied not with this *Admonitor's* desires, his party (whereof he the speaker) would proceed to higher and louder fulminations [*Fuller*, p. 102, as quoted by Soame's *Elizabethan History*. London, 1839, p. 163, note].

try" is declared to be lacking, the "Godly ministry" being the same as that desired by the anonymous Puritan, in the *Certaine Considerations*, already referred to, and being pastors, governing elders, and providers for the poor. So we read in the *Admonition*: —

We in England are so far off from having a Church rightly reformed, according to the prescript of God's word, that as yet we are not come to the outward face of the same. . . . Touching the first, namely, the ministry of the Word, although it must be confessed that the substance of doctrine by many delivered is sound and good, yet herein it faileth, that neither the ministers thereof are according to God's Word, proved, elected, called, or ordained [*Works of Whitgift*, vol. i. p. 290].

Again, on p. 485, same volume: —

But now Bishops (to whom the right of ordering ministers doth at no hand appertain) do make sixty, eighty or one hundred at a clap, and send them abroad into the country like masterless men.

The *Admonition* grounds one of its main reasons against the Puritans signing Parker's *Three Articles* that —

This prescript form of service (as they call it) is full of corruptions, it maintaineth *an unlawful ministry* unable to execute that office [*Ibid.* vol. i. p 336].

Referring to Parker's Third Article, which required subscription to the XXXIX. Articles, they naively assert, —

For the Articles concerning the substance of doctrine, *using a Godly interpretation in a point or two*, which are either too sparely or else too darkly set down, we were, and are ready according to duty to subscribe unto them [*Ibid.* vol. iii. p. 461].

It is thus that the same party continue to subscribe to the same Articles, or to use the *Prayer-Book*. " *Using a Godly interpretation in a point or two,*" is certainly a very convenient method of interpretation.

Touching Deacons [the *Admonition* complains] though their names be remaining, yet is the office foully perverted and turned upside down. . . . Now, it is the first step to the ministry, nay, rather a mere order of priesthood [*Ibid.* vol. iii. p. 282].

It asks for the "assistance of Elders and other officers" [p. 132], claims that "Elders or seniors ought to be in the Church when bespeaking for a Seigniory or Government by Seniors" [p. 150].

Instead of chancellors, archdeacons, officials, commissaries, proctors, doctors, summoners, church-wardens, and such like, you have to place in every congregation a lawful and godly seigniory [*Ibid.* vol. iii. p. 153].

It laments that "concerning Seniors, not only their office, but their name also is out of the English Church utterly removed" [p. 156], and that instead of the Seniors the Church yet maintains " the lordship of one man over sundry Churches " [p. 161], and claims that the whole regiment of the Church ought to be committed to those three jointly; that is, Ministers, Seniors, and Deacons [p. 295]. Of Bishops, the *Admonition* complains, "They make ministers by themselves alone, and of their sole authority" [p. 246], and holds "that a Bishop at no hand hath authority to ordain ministers" [p. 502].

But if Deacons and Bishops are treated with scant respect, the virulence of abuse is reserved for the Priesthood. It has always been so in every attack on the Church. If the Deacon is exalted, it is that the Priest may be lowered. If the Bishop is lowered, it is because he is the source of the Priesthood. If the Sacraments are disparaged, it is to sap the very foundation of things Sacramental, which derive their being from the office of the Priest. If preaching is exalted, it is because by common consent of the Catholic Church a preacher need not be a Priest.

The *Admonition*, therefore, condemns in no measured terms the retention of the word "Priest." "We speak not of the name of Priest wherewith he defaceth the Minister of CHRIST" [vol. iii. p. 350]. It is noteworthy to observe that when Whitgift, in his *Answer to the Admonition*, says that the name of Priest should not be so odious to the Puritans since its derivation is from "Presbyter," Cartwright, in his reply, is not slow to attack the weakness of that defence, for after very justly observing that it matters not what the derivation of a word is, but rather what is meant by a word in the usual and common speech, he attacks the retention of the word "Priest" as follows: —

The case standeth in this, that, forsomuch as the common and usual speech of England is, to note by the word 'Priest,' not a minister of the Gospel, but a sacrificer, which the minister of the Gospel is not; therefore, we ought not to call the ministers of the Gospel 'Priests' [*Ibid.* vol. iii. p. 351].

The *Admonition* even denies the right of "popish Mass-mongers" to become ministers of the Gospel; in other words, it would not have the Church continue the Apostolical succession, or allow men ordained under the old Ordinal to serve in the Reformed Church. Not to overlay the text with too many quotations, let these two, taken from the conclusion of the *Admonition* where the argument is summed up, suffice:

... but CHRIST should be suffered to reign, *a true ministry according to the word instituted*, discipline exercised, Sacraments purely and sincerely ministered [*Ibid.* vol. iii. p. 461].

Neither is the controversy betwixt them and us as they would bear the world in hand, as for a cap, a tippet, or a surplice, but for great matters *concerning a true ministry*, and required of the Church according to the Word [*Ibid.* vol. iii. p. 459].

The writers of the *Admonition* have thus, in their conclusion, made good the words of their Preface, and shown that their whole object was the overthrow of the ministry *as continued in the Ordinal*. As an enemy will seize and lay hold of villages and hamlets, and small fortified places that cover the approach to the strong city, the fall of which terminates the campaign, and will even make feigned attacks on outlying points to divert the attention of the defenders, so did the whole host of Puritans, Precisians, Presbyterians, and Parity-men, attack and overthrow certain points of the Church's worship and ritual, and make feigned attacks on others, in order that they might the more easily destroy and utterly abolish the whole root of the Apostolic ministry.

To use the very words of the framers of the *Admonition* :

The way therefore, to avoid these inconveniences, and to reform these deformities, is this : Your wisdoms have to remove advowsons, patronages, impropriations, *and Bishops' authority claiming to themselves thereby right to ordain Ministers* [vol. iii. p. 8].

The point in the present controversy lies in a nutshell.

Has this authority and claim ever been removed? If so, let it be stated where, and *cadit quæstio*. If not, then the Church of England never denied the claim.

The appeal to Parliament was thus to legalize a ministry other than that then legal. It was not an appeal for liberty to worship GOD in their own way, but an appeal for the establishment of a government, regiment, or discipline, as they variously termed it, of Seigniory, which was in fact effected when the Puritan party got the upper hand under Cromwell's Protectorate.

In the year previous to the appearance of the *Admonition*, Cartwright had been deprived from his Margaret Professorship at Cambridge, and inhibited from preaching within the jurisdiction of the University, in consequence of the Six Propositions maintained by him. Briefly they were as follows: —

I. The names and functions of Archbishops and Archdeacons ought to be suppressed.

II. The name of lawful ministers in the Church, such as Bishops and Deacons, when abstracted from the Office described in Holy Scripture are likewise to be rejected, and the whole brought back to the Apostolical Institution. And thus the Bishop's functions ought to be limited to praying and preaching, and the Deacon's to taking care of the poor.

III. The government of the Church ought . . . to be in the hands of the Minister and Elders of the same Church.

VI. That ministers ought not to be ordained on the sole authority of the Bishop, much less are they to receive Orders in a study, or such private place, but this Office ought to be conferred by a public choice of the congregation [Collier's *Ecclesiastical History*, 1714, p. 525].

Cartwright and his friends also drew up XIX. Articles embracing their demands. Almost all of them strike at the Episcopacy or Priesthood of the Church. It will be sufficient to mention the III., IV., and XVIII.

III. Preaching, prayers, and administering the Sacraments ought to be performed by the same person. From hence it follows that those who are not ministers of the Word, that is, those who can't preach, ought neither to pray publicly for the congregation nor administer the Sacraments.

IV. Popish priests have no authority to be ministers of the Gospel by virtue of their own ordinations.

XVIII. These words *receive the Holy Ghost*, at the Ordination of Ministers, is a ridiculous and wicked expression.

Here, again, we have the testimony of the enemies of the Church as to what the Church meant by her Ordinal and Ministry: —

Nowhere do we find that the Puritans claimed that the Church allowed any other ordination than that by Bishops.

Nowhere do we find that the Puritans claimed that the Church considered her Bishops on a parity with her Priests.

Nowhere do we find that the Puritans claimed that the Church meant nothing by her solemn forms in Ordination, Confirmation, Holy Communion.

If the opposite contention was a true one, that the Church maintained no exclusive claim for her ministers as being Episcopally ordained, then we ought to find abundant references to that false liberality. The Puritans would have exultantly spied this weakness out, and have exclaimed, —

You call your Elders Bishops, but you allow them to do just what we claim Elders ought to do, and no more. You call your Ministers Priests, and yet they do nothing more than the Ministers we wish to establish. All the forms and ceremonies of the Church are nothing, are idle, peevish, or popish, and your Book declares them so to be; why continue them?

This would have been their argument, for they were by no means devoid of reasoning, or slow to apprehend a point in their favor. But their cry is the very reverse of this. Substantially it is, —

You admit Popish Priests on account of their Episcopal Ordination, and reject us!

You maintain the three Orders and reject our 'Apostolic Institution of Elders and Pastors and Providers for the Poor'!

You stubbornly maintain imposition of hands in Ordination and Confirmation, which we reject!

Such and such-like was their wail. All of which proves the voice of the Church was, alas, too certain for them: Whitgift's *Answer to the Admonition* was naturally violently attacked by the Puritans. One Chark, in a sermon *ad clerum*, laid down these two conclusions: —

I. Episcopatus, Archiepiscopatus, Metropolitanatus, Patriarchatus, et Papatus, a Satana in Ecclesiam introducti sunt.

II. Inter Ministros ecclesiæ non debet alius alio esse Superior [Collier, vol. ii. p. 538].[1]

A certain Nicholas Brown, Fellow of Trinity College, Cambridge, declaimed in the pulpit against the —

---

[1] I. Bishops, Archbishops, Metropolitans, Patriarchs, and Popes, are by Satan introduced into the Church.
II. Among Ministers of the Church there ought not to be any one superior to the other.

English Ecclesiastical constitution, and pronounced the Orders received in the reigns of King Henry and Queen Mary of no significancy, and those who were then made priests ought not to officiate without a new ordination. Being called to account for these heterodoxies, he was at last prevailed to recant them [Collier, vol. ii. p. 538].

Despairing of reforming the Church to their model, or of getting Parliament to alter the legal status of a minister, the Puritans erected a Presbytery at Wandsworth. Among those concerned we need only note Travers and Chark. The preamble to their resolution establishing this Presbytery was: —

That forasmuch as divers books had been written, and sundry petitions exhibited to Her Majesty, the Parliament, and their Lordships to little purpose, every man should therefore labour by all means possible to bring the Reformation into the Church [Collier, vol. ii. p. 541].

When this open act of schism became known, the Puritans, notwithstanding their influential friends at court, were vigorously pressed. To gain time most likely, they proposed a public disputation. The challenge was accepted by Sandys, Bishop of London, but Burleigh was opposed to the idea, and instead of a conference several of the leading Puritans were brought before the Council and the Ecclesiastical Commissioners, and examined touching their opinions on Cartwright's *Reply to the Answer to the Admonition.*

The second and third questions were, Whether the *Prayer-Book* and the XXXIX. Articles were agreeable to GOD's Word or not? The fourth, "Whether we are obliged to follow the customs of the Primitive Church or not? The fifth, "Whether all Ecclesiastical Ministers ought to be of equal authority, both in Office and Jurisdiction?" After railing at being forced to subscribe in matters of religion, the malcontents now drew up a "Protestation" which reminds us of the recent words of the Bishop of Western New York, when speaking of the feeble title, "Protestant Episcopal." He says: "I call it feeble because a *protest* is the last resource of an unsuccessful cause. Men enter a *protest* when they give up a case they are not able to maintain."

This "Protestation" they obliged each member, on admittance to a congregation, to swear. Each of these "Protestants" had to make this "Protestation" singly and individually, as it is drawn up in the first person throughout. He begins his Protestation by having to declare, " I am escaped from the filthiness and pollution of these detestable Traditions." The doctrines of the Church are called " idolatrous trash," " marks of the Romish beast," and the Church nicknamed " The Church of the Traditioners." He undertakes that he will not attend the parish Church by the following pharisaical declaration : —

I will not beautify with my presence those filthy rags, which bring the heavenly Word of the Eternal our LORD GOD into bondage, subjection, and slavery [Collier, vol. ii. p. 544].

He finally declares, —

Moreover, I have now joined myself to the Church of CHRIST, wherein I have yielded myself subject to the Discipline of GOD'S Word. . . . For in the Church of the Traditioners there is no other Discipline than that which hath been maintained by the Antichristian Pope of Rome, etc.

The Church of England is then polluted, filthy, abominable, idolatrous, and Episcopal government declared " Antichristian," — the very term used by the Scotch Presbyterians.

The Wandsworth Presbytery was the first open act of schism, and these " Protestants " the first declared schismatics in England. Be it carefully noted that the cause of this schism was the refusal of Church and realm to tamper with the threefold ministry.

Our self-imposed task is concluded.

If any reader has followed us through these historic researches, we ask him, Is there the faintest doubt as to what the Church of England taught and proclaimed on the question of the exclusive validity of Episcopal ordination? Can any one lay his finger on any one official act of the Church which countenanced presbyterial ordination? It is most remarkable that almost every year between 1534 and 1589 there was some official pronouncement against any other than Episcopal ordination. The documents from which quotations have been given may be set forth thus:

1534. Abolition of the Papal Supremacy.
1535. King's Articles.
1537. Declaration of the Functions and Divine Institution of Bishops and Priests.
1538. De Ordine et Ministerio Sacerdotum et Episcoporum.
1543. Necessary Doctrines and Erudition for a Christian Man.
1548. The Articles of 1548.

1548. Justus Jonas Catechism.
1550. The Ordinal.
1551. The XLV. Articles.
1552. Revised Ordinal.
1553. The XLIII. Articles.
1553, July 6, to Nov. 17, 1558. Queen Mary's reign.
1559, March 31. Westminster Abbey Conference.
1559, April 28. Act of Uniformity. The Eleven Articles.
1561–1588. Visitation Articles.
1562. The XXXIX. Articles passed by Convocation.
1564. The Advertisements.
1571. The Canons of 1571.
1571. Act 13 Eliz. c. 12.
    Subscription to XXXIX. Articles enforced by Parliament.
    Order of Ecclesiastical Commissioners.
    Parker's Three Articles.
1572–1580. Admonition Controversy.
1573. Queen's Proclamation.
1576. The XV. Articles.
1584. Whitgift's Three Articles.
1584.[1] The XXIV. Articles.

If the above table is carefully examined it will be found that between the years 1534–1588 official declarations were being constantly made asserting the exclusive validity of Episcopal ordination in the Church of England, and condemning either directly or by implication every other kind of ordination. For any one to assert, as Dr. Kelley did, that " no one in the Church of England thought of calling in question the validity of the Orders and Sacraments of the Reformed Churches," or to state with Dr. H. J. Van Dyke that " it is only since the days of Charles I. and his prime minister, Laud, that the Episcopal de-

---

[1] It will be remembered that the years 1584–89 were those when England was distracted by Jesuits' intrigues culminating in the Armada. The attention of the Church during those five years was therefore directed more to its Roman than Genevan foe. Not that the Puritan party ceased its attacks against the Threefold Ministry during those years; on the contrary, the country was flooded with venomous libels culminating in 1588 in the Martin Marprelate libels, that year being unpatriotically chosen, as they boldly owned, that the Church — a nation then in fear of outward force — might neither deny nor discourage the Puritan pretensions. The uncompromising attitude of the Church on the question of Orders may be inferred from this very manner and time of attack.

nomination has refused to recognize the validity of other ordinations besides its own" is, in both cases, historically false.

As to the latter half of Dr. Kelley's statement, that from the Reformed Churches which were presbyterial in ordination and government, "ministers and members were received to immediate and equal standing in the Church of England," in the face of the foregoing official declarations of the Church of England, it needs no reply.

No one in the Church, Archbishop or Queen, had the power to receive an un-Episcopally ordained minister on equal standing with the Priests of the Church.

With much special pleading and after an infinitude of research, six names out of the tens of thousands of Priests of the Church during that troubled period are brought forward as having possibly been recognized as Priests of the Church without having had Episcopal ordination. These six are Cartwright, Travers, Whittingham, Morrison, Barrington, and Saravia.

To persons desirous of going into the details of the first four of these cases, I beg to refer them to my article in the number of this REVIEW for October, 1889. It will there be seen that Cartwright, being a Deacon, was allowed to preach, but forbidden the exercise of any priestly ministry; that Travers was deposed and silenced for being ordained only according to the foreign Reformed use, and not according to the English Ordinal; that Whittingham was arraigned and tried, but died before the trial was concluded; that as to Morrison, it is an open question still as to whether he was not Episcopally ordained, and that even if he was not, we have no record of any of his acts.

Barrington and Saravia I hope to treat at some length at a future time, as soon as I have all the necessary material at hand. I may, however, say thus much, that the only ground for supposing Saravia to have been un-Episcopally ordained is that no record of his ordination has been found, which is a very poor argument, since many a record of much greater importance has perished by accident or design during the last three centuries in England, and that to doubt of his ordination would logically be on a par with doubting the ordination of Haddan and Gore,— writers who have equally with Saravia defended the threefold ministry. I am ready to prove that Barrington has been mentioned entirely owing to a careless reference to an Index to a

State paper, and that he was involved in a lawsuit with Whitgift not about his ordination or lack of ordination, but simply about some lands.

Let sixty instead of six such shadowy cases be brought forward, — ay, or even sixty times six, — and what would it prove? Only this, — lax administration of the law. Murders are daily committed in the United States; does that prove there is no law against murder? Does it prove that there is a law favoring murder?

It is waste of time to discuss individual cases and airy hypotheses as to what the Church might have said, when we know so well, so indisputably, what the Church has said, what the Church has pronounced.

The law of the Church of England before 1534 maintained the exclusive validity of Episcopal ordination, and of the Sacraments in connection therewith.

The law of the Church since 1589 is admitted to be the same as before 1534.

During the period of 1534 and 1589, year by year, it has been proved from *official sources*, passing by all private opinions, that the exclusive validity of Episcopal ordination was the sole view taught and enforced by the Church of England. That gap in her history having been filled, it may be said without the slightest fear of contradiction that from the earliest planting of the Church till now, — that is, for eighteen centuries at least, — there has been on the question of Episcopal ordination no stuttering, stammering, or hesitancy in the voice of the Church of England.

ARTHUR LOWNDES.

Bishop Lightfoot on the Historic Episcopate.

BY THE REV. THOMAS F. GAILOR, M.A., S.T.B., VICE-CHANCELLOR OF THE UNIVERSITY OF THE SOUTH.

HISTORICALLY there are three theories as to the origin and nature of the Christian ministry. No one of them can be absolutely demonstrated from the fragmentary records of the sub-Apostolic age,[1] and therefore the discussion of them affords abundant and unusual opportunity for the influence of surroundings and prejudices, of associations and previous education. No mind is entirely free from this influence; and therefore, without great sacrifices of personal opinion, it cannot be hoped that there ever will be in Christendom an universal agreement upon a subject so important and yet so stimulative of new speculation.

I. The first and oldest of these theories may be called the theory of Cyprian, which is admitted to have been generally held in the middle of the third century. It is the first formulated statement of the doctrine of the Apostolical succession as distinguished from the fact of the succession which was emphatically appealed to by Irenæus nearly one hundred years before. Briefly stated, and omitting the necessary coloring of Cyprian's individuality, the theory is as follows, namely; The Incarnation is the foundation and the interpretation of the nature and the object of Christianity. The lesson of the Incarnation is the exercise and the conveyance of Divine supernatural authority

---

[1] It should be remembered in the discussion of all constitutional and doctrinal questions that the first generation of Christians had no *theory* or *philosophy* of Christianity. The *facts* of CHRIST'S Incarnation, Life, Death, Resurrection, and Ascension were enough for them. Therefore, in going to the earliest records in order to formulate a theory, we can choose either the theory which the Universal Church of the second and third generations drew from those facts, or else the theory which some modern scholar has invented. This consideration is more important when we remember that these Christians had no book called the New Testament to appeal to, that volume having been collected and the canon fixed not before the fourth century.

through and by means of human and material instrumentalities. The Church or Kingdom of CHRIST is the extension of the Incarnation in a vast sacramental system, wherein men are trained and prepared through the free development of their faculties for their salvation in body and soul in His everlasting Kingdom. This is S. Paul's argument in the Epistle to the Ephesians [ch. 4]. The delegated authority which our LORD Himself exercised as man on earth [cf. Luke v. 18] was by Him delegated in turn to His Apostles, " As My FATHER hath sent me, even so send I you." That ordinary official authority the Apostles exercised in their lifetime and transmitted to other men who succeeded them. James at Jerusalem, Timothy and Titus, and perhaps the " Angels of the Seven Churches " are examples of this succession. It is certainly neither impossible nor improbable that the name " Apostle " was gradually reserved for the " witnesses to the resurrection," and that the old Gentile designation " Bishop," was given to their successors in office. The collective Episcopate, thus originating, is the centre of the governing authority in the Church as against the later individualism of the Papacy and of the Protestant sects.

This theory of the ministry fits in with every fragment of early Christian literature; it satisfies the demands of the Incarnation as a supernatural revelation; it was the universal belief of the Church in her best age. It makes a philosophy of Christianity intelligible and consistent. The objections to it are: (1) That it is comparatively late. It was not formulated — at least the literature remaining to us does not formulate it — until the middle of the third century. To this it is replied that in this respect it is far earlier than the doctrine of the Trinity, which was not formulated for a hundred years afterward. (2) That it is sacerdotal; but this depends on what is meant by sacerdotal. If sacerdotalism is identified with the Hildebrandine conception of a separate caste of Priests and rulers in the Church, then it is not sacerdotal. The theory is quite consistent with the representative character of the Priesthood; indeed, it insists upon the fact that the Priesthood of the laity is impossible without the Priesthood of the clergy. (3) The third objection is that it "unchurches" other Christians, but this is a mistake. It unchurches not other Christians, but other Christian societies. It presumes not to judge men; but it has a right to judge systems and organizations, and that without just charge of narrowness or uncharitableness. (4) The final objection is that the theory is too simple. It is a plain expansion and application of the idea of the Incarnation, and affords too little opportunity for the exercise of metaphysical subtlety and discrimination. Yet the Incarnation itself is simple enough for the unlearned to realize, though it be too deep for the wisest to explore.

This is an imperfect outline of the first and oldest theory of the Christian ministry. It is referred to in order to clear the ground.

II. The second theory is the theory of the Continental Reformation. It has had many phases of development, and is too shifting to be easily formulated. It began with John Calvin, who, though a mere layman, undertook to preside over and to organize a Christian Church. He said, —

> These worthy men tell us that no molestation must be given to the successors of the Apostles. But a knowledge of the fact is to be ascertained by a discussion of doctrine.
>
> Prophets were raised up by the extraordinary inspiration of GOD. . . . What is said in Ezekiel and Jeremiah belongs to us not less than to the ancient people, — that GOD, to punish the iniquity of evil shepherds, will drive them away, and give good and faithful shepherds. For although GOD daily gives such by the calling of men, yet there is a singular species of giving, when the work of man ceases, and He Himself appoints those whom He sees to be necessary, though human judgments pass them by [*True Method*, pp. 297-298].
>
> That our discipline is not such as the Ancient Church professed, we do not deny [*Reply to Sadolet*, p. 39].
>
> The succession which they so haughtily arrogate to themselves, I have already rescued from them [*True Method*, p. 247].

Thus Calvin by " special inspiration " became a " steward of the mysteries of GOD." By ability and force of character he established the " Presbytery " and " the holy discipline " at Geneva, denying the validity of " prelatic " ordination; and this new government was introduced into England by the Puritans. Gradually, however, men saw that the essential point in this position was the assertion of the right of any man who felt the inward call, to minister in the congregation, irrespective of outward ordination, and that Calvin had no authority to fasten upon the Church a particular mode of government. Little by little the notion of any necessary fixed form of ecclesiastical organization faded away. Logically, the congregational theory had to be accepted; namely, no form of Church government can be said to have had the Divine sanction. Ministers are servants authorized by the congregation for convenience and order. They have no ordinary authority as distinct from laymen. The organization of the Church was completed by the Apostles, perhaps by S. John, as a matter of necessity, and they adopted the form which appeared most natural and effective to check the divisions and oppositions of the time. After all, it was only the Apostles who did it, not CHRIST; and their acts are not binding upon us. Besides, there is no formal ordinance extant which was issued by the Apostles on this subject. The true succession in the Church is the succession of sound doctrine; and the real authority of the minister is in the consciousness of his inward call and his appointment by the congregation.

There is a breadth and freedom and a certain consistency about this theory which attract many minds; but it repels others who fear that it ignores facts, and does not guard nor realize the Incarnation and the Sacraments. Calvin justified the theory on the ground that his doctrine was so pure that an extraordinary call was needed to preserve it; and multitudes now, suspecting that Calvin's presentation of the Gospel was not so pure after all, begin to question whether his "specially inspired" interruption of the ancient order must not fall to the ground with his doctrine.

III. Besides these two theories of the ministry, there is a third theory different from either, which has been advocated with great ability and learning by the late Bishop of Durham. It originated evidently from a keen desire to reconcile contending parties, and to commit the Church to no position which could not be fully justified by a close, cautious, and even sceptical investigation of the facts. Bishop Lightfoot's conception of the origin of the Episcopate differs from both the others mainly in this, that it is the result of an honest effort to reconcile all differences by the sympathetic admission of whatever can be said on the other side; and without prejudice, without any preconceived notions, to go back to the ascertained facts of early Christian history and make a guarded induction from them. The importance of such an investigation by such a scholar can hardly be over-estimated, for facts are the bone and sinew of any true philosophy, and what he gives us, though it be but a bare skeleton, will indicate the true form and nature. Yet it is easy to see that such an attempt to solve the problem of the origin of the Christian ministry will by many be misunderstood. To refer again to the doctrine of the Trinity, any scholar who should undertake to trace the growth of the philosophical statement of this doctrine up to its completion in the fourth century, with a sympathetic account of some of the crude statements of the earlier Fathers, would lay himself open to the charge of not believing in it himself, although he firmly held in his own mind the doctrine, the history of which in the interests of scholarship he had tried to analyze. This is eminently true of Bishop Lightfoot's account of the Christian ministry. Compared with the ordinary statement of the Apostolical succession, it seems at first to be against it. Compared with the ordinary congregational theory, it contradicts it at many points. It is certainly not inconsistent with the strongest churchmanship; and to say this is to say everything, for it does not purport to be a statement of the doctrine of the ministry so much as a scholar's investigation of the facts upon which that doctrine is to be based.

At the outset, he pricks the bubble of " no authorized ministry," and says, —

The Church could not fulfil the purpose for which she exists without rulers and teachers, without an order of men who may in some sense be designated a Priesthood [*Essay on C. M.*, p. 6.]

The real Episcopate of Timothy and Titus is asserted as something not to be questioned: —

The position of these Apostolic delegates fairly represents the functions of the Bishop early in the second century [p. 36].

Of S. James, he says, —

It seems vain to deny with Rothe that the position of S. James in the Mother Church furnished the precedent and the pattern of the later Episcopate.

More than once he insists upon the fact that the Episcopate was established by the Apostles, saying, for example, that " its prevalence cannot be dissociated from their influence or their sanction " [p. 81].

He therefore strongly urges the weight of this authority; for example, —

The Priest may be defined as one who represents GOD to man and man to GOD. It is moreover indispensable that he should be called by GOD, for no man ' taketh this honor to himself.' The Christian ministry satisfies both these conditions. Of the fulfilment of the latter, the only evidence within our cognizance is the fact that the minister is *called according to a Divinely appointed order*. If the preceding investigation be substantially correct, the threefold ministry can be traced to Apostolic direction; and short of an express statement, we *can possess no better assurance of a Divine appointment or at least a Divine sanction* [p. 144].

His exhaustive summary of the evidence for the widespread prevalence of the Episcopal government as early as 112 A. D. is given in the first volume of his *Apostolic Fathers*. He calls attention to the fact that Ignatius claims to get his exalted conception of the Episcopal office not from man, but from GOD [p. 376], and says, —

If the evidence on which its extension in the regions east of the Ægean at this epoch be resisted, I am at a loss to understand what single fact relating to the history of the Christian Church during the first half of the second century can be regarded as established, for the testimony in favor of this spread of the Episcopate is more abundant and more varied than for any other institution or event during this period, so far as I recollect [p. 377].

His treatment of the testimony of Irenæus is complete and unanswerable. He dwells upon the fact that Irenæus was the disciple of Polycarp and Polycarp of S. John.

Irenæus was probably the most learned Christian of his time. He had travelled far and wide. . . . He was in constant communication with foreign Churches on various subjects of ecclesiastical and theological interest. . . . *The Episcopate as distinct from the Presbyterate is the only Episcopate which comes within the range, not only of his personal acquaintance, but even of his intellectual and historical cognizance*. . . . To this Father it is an undisputed fact that the Bishops of his own age traced their succession back in an unbroken line to men appointed to the Episcopate by the Apostles themselves [p. 378].

Here, then, we have Bishop Lightfoot's strong assertion that from the most cautious review of all the evidence it is clear that the succession of the Episcopal authority from the Apostles was regarded as an undisputed fact in the second century, and his own conviction that the threefold ministry was established by Apostolic direction and is therefore to be regarded as "by Divine appointment, or at least by Divine sanction." What more can be asked? Upon what grounds has Bishop Lightfoot been quoted as in favor of the Presbyterian or Congregational theory of Church government? Controversialists seem to forget that the only real difference between Bishop Lightfoot's theory and the old theory of the Apostolical succession lies in the method used to reach the results and in his two points of variance as to the manner of the historical development. Those two points are well known; namely: (1) The Bishop says that the sacerdotal theory of the ministry does not appear until Cyprian, although the germs are found in the second century. He devotes a large portion of his essay to showing the development of the conception, — from Ignatius, who regarded the Episcopate as the centre of unity, to Irenæus, who appealed to it as the depositary of Apostolic tradition, and thence to Cyprian, who makes the Bishop the "absolute Vicegerent of CHRIST." This he calls "sacerdotalism" in the popular acceptation of the term, — sacerdotalism in which "the Bishop is regarded as exclusively the representative of GOD to the congregation, and hardly if at all as the representative of the congregation before GOD;" and "from being the act of the whole congregation, the sacrifice came to be regarded as the act of the minister who officiated on its behalf" [p. 138]. Such sacerdotalism appears in the later developed doctrine of Apostolical succession, and is not found in the earliest period. Clement of Rome, for example, in the first century, insists, Bishop Lightfoot says, upon the "Divinely appointed order," and not on any sacerdotal consecration. Bishop Lightfoot does admit a real "sacerdotalism," but it is that sacerdotalism which the Church of England has put into her Prayer-Book, and which is "in some sense involved in the appointment of a special ministry" [p. 112]. But the admission of this "special ministry" and "Divinely appointed order" is a gulf of variance from that individualism which protests against any authorized ministry and denounces as Romanism any theory of Church government which places in the hands of the rulers the perpetuation of the ministerial office. (2) The other peculiarity of Bishop Lightfoot's position which has led to misconception is his conjecture that the Bishops were not at the outset appointed by the Apostles to succeed them and originally placed over the council or college of Presbyters; but that the Episcopate was a "legitimate development" from the Presbyterate, immediately due to the felt necessity of unifying Christians and checking divisions. This development, however, was, in his opinion, by and with the sanction and direction of the Apostles; and "its maturer forms are seen first in those regions where the latest surviving Apostles (more especially S. John) fixed their abode" [p. 81]. Bishop Lightfoot believed that GOD'S creation of protoplasm was GOD'S creation of life, and if the Episcopate was, under Apostolic direction, the "legitimate development" out of the Presbyterate, it was CHRIST'S work just as really as the Creator of the germ is the Creator of the universe. To his mind the outpouring of the SPIRIT at Pentecost was real, and the Apostles "had the mind of CHRIST" in the upbuilding of His Church. Yet willing as a scholar to make every concession, he placed the Episcopate after the Presbyterate in order of time, and thus satisfied the objection as to the persistent application of the name "presbyter" to Bishops, and tried to show that the later sacerdotalism which we have referred to was not necessary to a loyal belief in the Divine claims of the Episcopate, the Priest having no authority and no priestly character to which "every individual Christian is not at least potentially entitled."

After all, we may ask ourselves what is the essential difference between the two positions. In one case we suppose that the Apostles, inspired and commissioned to organize the Church, appointed Presbyters to succeed them in the exercise of their ordinary authority; in the other case we suppose that gradually, on account of pressing needs, the importance of the Episcopal office forced itself upon the minds of the Apostles, and certain Presbyters were, by their sanction and direction, raised above their fellow-Presbyters. If we believe the Apostles to have been inspire by GOD, we need not greatly distress ourselves as to the exact mental process through which this inspiration operated. What we must insist upon as the key to the whole problem is that the authority to govern the Church came from above, from CHRIST, not from below, from the people.

And so long as we hold to the reality of the Incarnation, to the authority and Divine constitution of the Church, to the reality and efficacy of the Sacraments, we may safely differ as to the exact manner in which that form of the ministry arose in the first age, — a form which, whatever else may be said about it, has certainly, to quote Bishop Lightfoot's words, " been handed down from Apostolic times, and may well be presumed to have a Divine sanction."

Bishop Lightfoot has himself recognized in the prefaces to more recent works the unfairness with which his " Essay " has been interpreted; for example (Ignatian Epistles), —

While disclaiming any change in my opinions, I desire equally to disclaim the representations of those opinions which have been put forward in some quarters. The object of the essay was an investigation into the origin of the Christian ministry. The result has been a confirmation of the statement in the English Ordinal: 'It is evident unto all men diligently reading the Holy Scriptures and ancient authors that from the Apostles' time there have been three Orders of ministers in CHRIST'S Church, Bishops, Priests, and Deacons.' But I was scrupulously anxious not to overstate the evidence, in any case; and it would seem that partial and qualifying statements, prompted by this anxiety, have assumed undue proportions in the minds of some readers, who have emphasized them to the neglect of the general drift of the essay.

J. B. D.

September 9, 1886.

The following correspondence, which appeared in the *Church Guardian* of Montreal and was republished in the *Living Church*, explains itself: —

LOCKEPORT, N. S. March 1, 1887.

To the Editor of the Church Guardian:

SIR, — Having been shown a speech by a Presbyterian minister in which he claimed that Doctor Lightfoot, Bishop of Durham, acknowledged that Presbyterian order was the rule in Apostolic times, I wrote his Lordship and received from his chaplain the following reply, which may be of much service in refuting the views imputed to the great historian and commentator.

S. G.

AUCKLAND CASTLE.

THE REV. S. GIBBONS, SIR, — The Bishop of Durham finds to his great regret that owing to the great pressure of work by which he is surrounded, your letter respecting the Christian ministry has remained unanswered.

The Bishop desires me to say that so far from establishing as the fact that 'Presbyterianism was the first form of Church government,' his essay goes to prove that Deacons existed before Priests, and yet no one would contend that Church government by Deacons was the 'first form,' hence the writer's argument, based on priority of time, proves too much for his taste. It is, however, generally allowed that the names *Presbuteros* and *Episcopos* in the New Testament are *sometimes* synonymous [Acts xx. 17; 1 Peter v. 1, 2; 1 Tim. iii. 1–13, where the Apostle passes at once to Deacons from *Episcopos*, Titus i. 5, 7]; but even in the times covered by the New Testament writings, we see in the lifetime of the Apostles individuals singled out to preside over certain Churches and to exercise powers of ordination, government, presidency, etc., as Titus at Crete, James at Jerusalem, Timothy at Ephesus; and though the evidence is necessarily limited, we find in Asia Minor Episcopacy pure and simple, appointed and established (no doubt by the influence of S. John) at the date of the Ignatian Epistles, and its institution can be plainly traced as far back as the closing years of the first century.

We see the threefold ministry traced to Apostolic direction, and this bears out the truth of our Prayer-Book Preface to the Ordinal, and is the belief of the Anglican community.

I regret that in a brief letter so much must be passed over and so inadequate an account be given of so interesting and absorbing a subject.

But enough has been said to prove that the Presbyterian's deduction from the Bishop of Durham's article is not justified by the facts.

Yours faithfully,

J. R. HANNER,
Chaplain.

January 20, 1887.

There is no mistaking the ecclesiastical convictions and sympathies of a man who dedicated the second edition of his life-work, as "a tribute of admiration and affection" to so stalwart a Churchman as the late Dr. H. P. Liddon of S. Paul's.

THOMAS F. GAILOR.

The Nicene Creed as the Sufficient Statement of the Christian Faith.

PROF. FREDERICK W. DAVENPORT, S.T.D., PROFESSOR OF CANON LAW IN THE WESTERN THEOLOGICAL SEMINARY, CHICAGO.

THE title of this paper is the second of the four propositions submitted by the House of Bishops in 1886 " as essential to the restoration of unity among the divided branches of Christendom." So far the Historic Episcopate has been the central point in the discussion of the subject of Christian unity. This appears to be because the Historic Episcopate would call for more concessions by our non-Episcopal brethren of different Communions. Unless I have misinterpreted the many articles which it has been a privilege and pleasure to read and study, unity means to the vast majority of these writers only a unity of those bodies which, for lack of a better term, I may call non-Roman Churches. But the Bishops do not so limit their Declaration. They "affirm that the Christian unity now so earnestly desired by the memorialists can be restored *only* by the return of *all Christian Communions* to the *principles of unity* exemplified by the *undivided Catholic Church* during the first ages of its existence." These principles of unity they embody in four propositions. If these four principles were to be treated from the historical development of them solely, we should — in my opinion — reverse the order as given in the Declaration.

The body of Christian truth was given first to those who were called Apostles, the Sacraments were given by them, and the ministry ordained by them, to the faithful, and the Nicene Creed formulated and accepted prior to the final settlement of the Canon of Holy Scripture. In short, the earliest life of the Church of CHRIST was taught and nourished by personal teachers to whom a Divine trust was held to have been committed. But the Church Catholic won her way to the world's heart, led by the ministry, taught by them orally, fed sacramentally, and not as agreeing in a confession of faith modelled on a book not then completed as to the Canon of its contents. Hence the ministry would come first in the general treatment of Christian unity, and the other articles in reverse order. The early Church came as a Divine messenger to sorrowing, sin-laden souls, and she gave that message with its teaching of the MASTER'S love and death first, then formulated her Faith and finally her sacred books. It can, then, hardly compass the idea of the Bishops' Declaration to confine the discussion to any unity of merely the other non-Roman Communions and our own. In their view unity means the unity of all the "divided branches of Christendom." Hence that unity, to be possible, must base itself on truths existing and accepted prior to any division of the East and West. The area of such a basis of unity will. be therefore narrow, and hence the Bishops formulate the Declaration in only four points. These granted and acted upon, reunited Christendom may then give her answer to such questions as are truly questions of each age. But no answers to these "burning questions" will bring conviction to the thoughtful sceptic when he realizes that they, whatever such answers may be, are the replies of a yet divided Church. Is there, then, any formula of doctrine so a part of the life of the "undivided Catholic Church during the first ages of its existence" that its statements may form an adequate and hence the "sufficient statement of the Christian Faith" as a basis of doctrinal unity? The Bishops express their belief that the Nicene Creed is thus adequate, and hence sufficient.

The object to be sought would seem to be a body of doctrine about which there may be practical unanimity. Such we believe the Creed of Nicæa to be. Now, the objections to this Creed are either to its lack of completeness or its too great philosophic use of terms. But what is a creed? Is it a complete body of dogma? History does not show any such idea of a creed. The history of dogma and the history of law run parallel in this respect. In law there is a body of common-law and statute enactments in special cases. So is it in the history of dogma. There are a number of doctrines so inwrought into the life and consciousness of the Church that they are a body of common law of doctrine. Then there are the Creeds, as the Church's statute law of doctrine, — positive statements of the Faith as the *answer* of the *Church* to the *denials of heresy*. Among the unquestioned doctrines of the early Church were those of the

Inspiration of Holy Scripture, Regeneration, the Sacraments as *media* of Divine grace, the Eucharist as the great Christian pure offering or unbloody sacrifice, and the Atonement by the sacrifice of our Blessed LORD. These truths stand to the Creed very much as the idea of uniformity in Nature and the idea of cause and effect do to scientific thought. I have not herein included the doctrine of the Ministry, because it is now under discussion, though I have not the least doubt that it too belongs in the same category. It may be well to call attention here to the difference between the popular idea of the formation of a creed and the fact of history on such formation. In the popular idea a creed is the result of separate votes on the various articles. The history of the Councils shows, however, that the Creeds were simply a statement of certain dogmas as having been held by the Church "everywhere, always, and by all," and hence as dogma.

The Creed of Nicæa is then simply a set of facts witnessed to by various witnesses from widely separated regions of the world, and all the witnesses agree in the one teaching. The question at Nicæa was, What has been always and is now the teaching of the Church on the Divinity of CHRIST? The Council simply witnessed to a set of facts, but did not decree a confession of faith in the popular sense of the words. What is the truth as we have received it unchanged from Apostolic times? was the real question at Nicæa. The fact of there being such a body of continuous accepted truth was then proven by the witness of the Fathers of the Council. The continuity of truth there witnessed to gave the name of dogma, or received and accepted truth, to the science of theology as the permanent name for revealed truth as distinct from developed opinion. In my opinion this is the real reason for the Bishops naming the Nicene Creed as the doctrinal basis,—that it is in itself a statement of universally received truths as dogma, not as the result of any modern theory of development. And just here will be found to be the difficulty in its acceptance by the other Christian bodies of the non-Roman Churches. It may not be stated explicitly, but the actual obstacle to the acceptance of the Nicene Creed is in the *character* of its *contents as dogma*,— continuous and hence logically involving a continuous body holding it, and a continuous ministry teaching it as a deposit of truth handed down from Apostolic times. This idea of dogma is expressed exactly by the language of the

Fathers of the Council of Chalcedon, " This is the Faith of the Fathers. This is the Faith of the Apostles. We all assent to this. We all hold this." Again they speak of the Creed as coming from preceding Councils, as set forth "for the confirming of our Catholic and Apostolic Faith." [1]

The Nicene Creed, then, seems to meet the requirements of what the Bishops term " the sufficient statement of the Christian Faith" in that it accepts Christian truth as dogma delivered in continuous line of witness at a period when there were no divisions of Christendom as an organic body. The confessions of one kind and another, valuable as they are for the history of Christian opinion, cover an area of opinion so large, crowded with philosophical issues, and about which there has never been any substantial agreement of the vast majority of Christendom, that they cannot form a basis of mutual acceptance. The Nicene Creed, on the other hand, gives the universally held dogma on the Persons of the Holy Trinity, the Church as the Body of Christ, remission of sin, and eternal life as the crown of hope. Is there any more needed to meet the practical wants of any life seeking the full enrichment of its nature in the higher spiritual work of a Christian? There are, it is true, questions that emerge in the sphere of speculative and comparative theology which the Nicene Creed does not deal with; but these are not such as touch the heart of a sin-sick humanity which longs for a positive voice that shall echo the blessing of old to every home, — Peace be to this house! In every line of scientific thought to-day there may be seen a tendency to unity and the narrowing of the area of accepted scientific truth. We are told that the Christian thought of the age needs some restatement to meet the present needs. Let us then admit this need as seen in the idea of unity and a narrowing of the area of dogma. What, then, meets this dual idea as fully as the Nicene Creed? The Bishops do not say that this Creed is the perfection of complete statement of all possible speculative teaching. They affirm it to be the sufficient, that is, adequate, statement of the Christian Faith. Adequate or sufficient for what? For the daily and practical needs of all souls striving to deepen their spiritual life, until they come to realize, at least in a measure, the strength of the glowing words of S. Paul, " For to me to live is CHRIST." But there is a deeper objection to the Nicene

[1] *Hardouini Acta Conciliorum*, tom. ii. pp. 451, 456.

Creed, perhaps, in the minds of many who are not ready to accept it. The objection is not so stated in words, but I believe it a real fact in the thought of the day. It is to the truth of the Creed as objective and therefore positive. If the Nicene Creed be accepted as dogma, objective and positive truth, it will carry with it certain obligations and be *subject* to the *interpretation of the day in which it was set forth*. Let us be frank with our brethren of every Christian name. Better frank, open difference than to have half-hearted acceptance, a sort of armed neutrality, or *an acceptance* that *explains away the Creed itself*. There is an abundance of that kind of so-called acceptance already. There is a common expression, " I am not under any obligation to do this or that, for I do not accept such a truth or statement." The true under-lying premise of this statement is this, that only is true as the person accepts it, or in other words, truth is subjective, not objective, and being subjective, is open to constant revision. If this theory be true, the Nicene Creed cannot be accepted, for it is a statement of truth as positive, objective, and hence as dogma or received truth, a deposit of the Faith. The real issue is whether Christian truth is objective and hence continuous and delivered by authority, or subjective and hence constantly subject to revision and development. If the latter, then there can be no absolute and positive truth which can be traced as held by the early Church as a deposit of Faith once for all delivered. But is not all truth objective? In no other line of thought but that of Christian truth do men accept the idea that the obligation of acceptance is based upon personal reception or rejection. In physical science, law, and medicine we admit the existence of truth utterly independent of whether men accept it or not. Do we not admit the law of gravity or the law of the circulation of the blood as objective or existent independent of its reception or rejection by any one? Equally that truth which, in religion, is to be the motive-power to higher aspiration, nobler thought, and holier living should be objective and hence positive, therefore dogma. If, then, Christian truth is a body of teaching handed down, objective and therefore dogmatic, we ought to be able to find some body of such dogma so well attested and continuous in history that it may be a basis of doctrinal unity. Such a body of truth we hold the Nicene Creed to be. The development discussed by the early Fathers as admissible is that of the *method* of *statement*, *defence*, or *explanation* of *already accepted dogma*, *not* a development of the *body of dogma*. This idea of development is thus expressed by S. Vincent of Leims, " But the Church as a careful and cautious guardian of the *dogma deposited* in *her keeping* never changes anything, nought diminishes, adds nothing." " Finally, what else has she ever attempted by the decrees of Councils but that the *same thing* might afterward be more diligently believed which before was simply accepted?"[1] The Nicene Creed was the symbol of the Faith accepted by all parts of the Church as distinct from dogmas peculiar to any one part of the Church, — that is, as held by the vast majority of the Church as distinct from the views of any private doctor, or any school of thought in the Church, as held continuously in history as opposed to doctrine held during recent ages or for a limited period of time. A careful study of the *Commonitorium* of S. Vincent shows this, we believe, to be the true meaning of the famous " Quod ubique, quod semper, quod ab omnibus creditum est."

The admission of the Nicene Creed as the sufficient statement of the Christian Faith will, we firmly believe, mean the taking of a new point of view as to the character of what is held to be essential truth, and involve the recognition of its essentiality as consisting in its being positive, objective, continuous, and hence that it is dogma, not evolved opinion, whether that evolution be in and from the consciousness of the Church as the body of the believers or an evolution from the Holy Scriptures. If, then, the Nicene Creed be thus accepted, there will logically follow the question, To whom was such a body of truth committed and by whom handed down during the period of the " undivided Catholic Church "? Here will emerge the question of the Historic Episcopate as the witness to the Faith; and the article of the Nicene Creed, " One Holy, Catholic and Apostolic Church," will prove a grave question to our non-Episcopal brethren unless our Bishops are ready to interpret these words in an etymological sense rather than in the historical, which we do not suppose for a moment. If the Episcopate be, as Dr. Charles A. Briggs defines it, " the *executive head* of the *one Order* of *ministers*," then there will be no connection between the body of dogma and the witness of the Episcopate to such dogma. For in his view the Episcopate is an *office*, *not*

---

[1] *Commonitorium Vincentii Liv.* pp. 219, 220. Edition II. Hunter, S. J.

The Nicene Creed. 335

an Order. Three fourths of the Christian world has for centuries held, and still holds, that the Episcopate is an *Order, not merely* an *executive headship* or *office*, as may be seen by the Ordinals and Canons of the Greek, Roman, and Anglican Churches and the Old Catholic Church. The plain truth is that in the treatment of the Nicene Creed and its fuller discussion, it will be found that the Faith and the Episcopate are inseparably connected. And we believe that no less a conviction than that the two, Faith and Order, were thus connected underlies the statement of the Bishops' Declaration concerning the four points, " which principles [they say] we believe to be the substantial *deposit* of Christian *Faith and Order committed* by *Christ* and *His Apostles* to the *Church unto the end of the world*, and therefore incapable of *compromise* or *surrender* by those who have been *ordained to be* its *stewards and trustees* for the common and equal benefit of all men." This joining of Faith and Order by the Bishops is very significant of their conviction that the Episcopate is a *witness to the truth*, not merely an *executive office*. Still further is it significant that the Declaration of the Bishops passed unanimously, so far as the Journal shows. In the time at our disposal, snatched from pressing engagements, we cannot attempt to elaborate the further theological and canonical reasons for holding the Nicene Creed to be " the sufficient statement of the Christian Faith," hence we must rest the case on the four suggestions of this paper.

In our view the sufficiency of this Creed as a basis of doctrinal unity consists in its being the accepted voice of the whole body of historic Christianity, when passed, and therefore a basis for unity of all Christian bodies; in its character as positive, continuous truth, therefore dogma as opposed to modern developments, whether in the Roman or Protestant theories of development; in the narrow area of dogma to which assent is asked, thus leaving questions of speculative theology untouched; and finally in the fact that this Creed has the witness of that Historic Episcopate which appears in sixteen centuries of Canon Law as the highest Order of the ministry. Law is enacted upon the basis of the conviction of certain facts as true on the part of the sovereign body, and thus accepted by the persons for whom it was enacted. So far no Canon Law, accepted by the Church Catholic, has been found which fails to state the Episcopate as the highest Order and the ruling power, distinct in Order from the Presbyterate and Diaconate. The Faith and Holy Order are thus historically bound together, and as such to be accepted or rejected together. This paper will perhaps sound a note of discord in the harmony of present voices attuned to the hope of unity. But in view of the Declaration of the House of Bishops, the history of our Canon Law, and the actual practice of the Anglican Church, and in view of the relation of this Church to ancient Christianity as seen in " the undivided Catholic Church," no other presentment of the case would seem to me loyal to the Church whose servant I am, or fair and just to those who cannot yet accept the " Faith and Order committed by CHRIST and His Apostles to the Church unto the end of the world." In conclusion permit me to express the earnest conviction that mutual respect for honest differences between brethren of different Christian names is better than the surrender of any truth which we hold upon such authority as that on which the Faith and Order of the undivided Catholic Church rests. Unity won by minimizing the real force and meaning of hitherto vital doctrines will be valueless to all parties now discussing Christian unity. Perhaps one of the best results of this discussion may be found to be a clearer idea of the exact reasons why unity is not a very present probability, and an opportunity of seeing with what grasp and conviction of certitude different religious bodies hold to-day what they have for the past called essential truths.

F. P. DAVENPORT.

"Three Points."[1]

An Essay. Read before the Associate Alumni of the General Theological Seminary in the Seminary Chapel, New York, May 31, 1887, by the Rev. JOHN HENRY HOPKINS, S. T. D.

FOR many years three points of importance have presented themselves to my mind with great force, in considering the relations of different parts of Christendom to one another; and yet I do not remember having ever seen that attention paid to them which they seem to me to deserve. Nor shall I be able to do them justice now. The full consideration of them would require far more of time and of books than a country parson can command, and far more of opportunity to listen than our brief annual meeting could afford. All I can do, therefore, is to set before you a few sketch-like hints, which, perhaps, some one having more leisure and learning may work up hereafter in a manner not now possible to me.

I. The first of these three points is in regard to the loss of Apostolic order in the Reformation movement on the Continent, — the chief point of organic difference between the Anglican Reformation and the others. It is commonly said that this loss was a matter of *necessity,* — that they *had* to do without Bishops on the Continent, because none of the Bishops would take part with the Reformers. The point I would make is, that historically *this is not true.* There *were* Bishops enough to have preserved the Apostolic succession for them, if they had cared to do it; and the neglect was therefore due to other causes.

The full proof of this can hardly be given without a minute search of the more diffuse records of the times; for our general

---

[1] These "Three Points" strike me as being of such value in themselves, as hints to historical students, that I have ventured to depart from our usual custom, and instead of confining their consideration to the members of the Associate Alumni of the General Theological Seminary, I ask for them the wider circulation of the CHURCH REVIEW. One who was present at the delivery of this paper, and had been for many years an able Professor of Ecclesiastical History, assured me that each of the "Three Points" was new to him. — J. H. H.

historians would hardly stop to notice facts which are not in the front rank of importance from their point of view. The facts which I shall lay before you to-day are gathered mainly from the Rev. Henry M. Baird's *History of the Rise of the Huguenots of France*, — a work in two octavo volumes, covering the history of only sixty-two years in all, and thus affording unusual room for minuteness of detail, although Mr. Baird is not a Churchman, and does not dream of making out the point of which he so unconsciously furnishes the evidence.

The two who are named first among the French Reformers, are the learned Lefèvre of Etaples and the ardent Farel. The third, he says, was Guillaume Briçonnet, Bishop of Meaux. His father had been a Cardinal, as well as Abbot of St. Germain-des-Prés and Archbishop of Rheims, and had anointed King Louis XII. at his coronation. As Cardinal, he had headed the French party in the Conclave, and in the service of his King had faced the dangers of an open quarrel with the Pope. The Cardinal was now dead, having left to Guillaume — born before his father had taken Holy Orders — a good measure of that royal favor which he had himself enjoyed. He was made Archdeacon of Rheims and of Avignon, Abbot of St. Germain-des-Prés, and lastly Bishop of Lodève and Meaux. He showed early his reforming tendencies by his efforts to make the luxurious inmates of St. Germain observe better discipline. Briçonnet was appointed Bishop of Meaux in March, 1516, and about the same time was sent by King Francis I. as special envoy to treat with the Pope. He had been at Rome on similar business in the time of King Louis XII. The knowledge thus gained of the way in which things were done at Rome, convinced him of the urgent need of reform; and he resolved to begin the work in his own Diocese.

He invited both Lefèvre and Farel to make their home at Meaux; and they came, followed soon by Michel d'Arande, Gérard Roussel, and others of the same sort. "A new era," says Baird, "now dawned upon the neglected Diocese of Meaux. Bishop Briçonnet was fully possessed by his newborn zeal. The King's mother and his only sister had honored him with a visit not long after Lefèvre's arrival, and had left him confident of their powerful support in his intended reforms. 'I assure you,' Margaret of Angoulême wrote him a month later, 'that the King and Madame are entirely decided to let it be understood that the truth of GOD is not heresy.' And a few weeks later the same princely correspondent declared that her mother and brother were 'more intent than ever upon the reformation of the Church.'" The effect of the new preaching at Meaux was great. The wool-carders, weavers, and fullers accepted it with delight; the day-laborers flocked from the neighborhood at harvest-time, and carried back the new enthusiasm to their secluded homes. Bishop Briçonnet himself was active in promoting the evangelical work, preaching against the most flagrant abuses, and commending the other preachers whom he had invited. He actually said to his flock: "Even if I, your Bishop, should change my speech and teaching, beware that you change not with me!"

Under Briçonnet's protection Lefèvre made and published (in 1523) a translation of the New Testament, and then of the whole Bible, into French, which was earlier than a similar work was done in England. The Bishop freely supplied copies to those who were too poor to buy. He introduced the French Scriptures into the Churches of Meaux, where the innovation of reading the lessons in a tongue that they could understand, astounded the common people. The delighted Lefèvre writes to a distant friend: "You can scarcely imagine with what ardor GOD is moving the minds of the simple in some places to embrace His Word, since the books of the New Testament have been published in French. . . . The attempt has been made to hinder the work, under cover of the authority of Parliament; but our most generous King has become in this matter the defender of CHRIST'S cause, declaring it to be his pleasure that his kingdom shall hear the Word of GOD freely, and without hindrance, in the language which it understands. At present, throughout our entire Diocese, on feast-days, and especially on Sundays, both the Epistle and Gospel are read to the people in the vernacular tongue, and the Parish Priest adds a word of exhortation to the Epistle or Gospel, or both, at his discretion."

All this was far stronger encouragement than the great Catholic Revival of our own day ever received from any Bishop in its earlier years. True, stern and formidable opposition soon arose. Briçonnet was cited by the Parliament of Paris to answer, in secret session, before a Commission. He was dealt with in such wise as to break his courage, and stop the public instruction of the people in the Holy Scriptures. He was acquitted of all charge of heresy, indeed, though they made him pay two hundred livres as the expense of bringing to trial the heretics whom he had helped to make. A man converted in that way is very likely to be " of the same opinion still."

But Briçonnet was not the only Bishop who sympathized with reform. He was a noble as well as a Bishop; but the same side was to be taken by one nobler than he, and higher both in Church and State. This was Odet de Coligny, the elder brother of the Admiral Coligny and of D'Andelot, of the blood royal, who was created Cardinal of Châtillon at the early age of *thirteen*, and afterward Archbishop of Toulouse, and Bishop and Count of Beauvais. He was at first a devout Romanist, but early showed sympathies with the Reformation, and ended by going over to it altogether. As early as 1551 he was pretty well known to be in sympathy with the " Lutherans." In Easter week, 1561, there were outbreaks of violence against the Protestants in many parts of France, one of the most noted of which was at Beauvais, Châtillon's own cathedral. He had openly fostered the preachers of reform in his Diocese. " But," says Baird, " even the personal popularity of the brother of Coligny and D'Andelot could not, in the present instance, secure immunity for the preachers who proclaimed the Gospel under his auspices. Incited by the Priesthood, the people overleaped all the bounds within which they had hitherto restrained themselves. The occasion was a rumor spread abroad, that the Cardinal, instead of attending the public celebration of the Mass in his Cathedral Church, had, with his domestics, participated in a private communion in his own palace, and that every communicant had, at the hands of the Abbé Boutillier, received *both* elements ' after the fashion of Geneva.' Hereupon the mob, gathering in great force, assailed a private house in which there lived a Priest accused of teaching the children the doctrines of religion from the reformed catechisms. The unhappy Adrien Fourré — such was the schoolmaster's name — was killed; and the rabble, rendered more savage through their first taste of blood, dragged his corpse to the public square, where it was burned by the hands of the city hangman. Châtillon himself incurred no little risk of meeting a similar fate. But the strength of the Episcopal palace, and the sight of their Bishop clothed in his Cardinal's costume, appeased the mob for the time; and before the morrow came, a goodly number of the neighboring nobles had rallied for his defence." Surely, one of the most striking incidents of those strange days was to see a Roman Cardinal receiving the Huguenot Communion, and afterward masquerading in his Cardinal's vestments to prevent his being torn in pieces by the rabble of his own people for the act!

Again, in the preparations for the famous Colloquy of Poissy, in the same year, 1561, when the assembled Bishops were about to join in the Holy Eucharist, we read that "Cardinal Châtillon and *two other Bishops* insisted upon communicating under both forms; and when their demand was refused, they went to another Church, and celebrated the Divine Ordinance with many of the nobility, all partaking both of the bread and of the wine, thus earning for themselves the nickname of Protestants."

Two years later, 1563, Pope Pius IV. issued a bull, calling for summary proceedings against sundry French Bishops, Cardinal Châtillon being at the head of the list, followed by seven others; but as he was rash enough to insert the Queen of Navarre also, the French Court made such a vigorous response that the bull was either recalled or dropped, and the proceedings against the Bishops were indefinitely suspended.

In the year 1565, the Pope's new Nuncio demanded that the red cap should be taken from the Cardinal of Châtillon. But the latter, who chanced to be at court, replied that "what he enjoyed, he enjoyed by gift of the crown of France, with which the Pope had nothing to do." And his uncle, the old Constable, was even more emphatic. "The Pope," said he, "has often troubled the quiet of this realm, but I trust he shall not be able to trouble it at this time. I am myself a Papist; but if the Pope and his ministers go about again to disturb the kingdom, *my sword shall be Huguenot*. My nephew shall give up neither cap nor dignity which he has, for the Pope, seeing the King's edict gives him liberty to keep them."

Three years later, 1568, it seems that Cardinal Châtillon had been excommunicated by the Pope, condemned of schism, and was dead in the eyes of the law,—as laid down by the Pope,— and Catherine de Medici had promised to surrender him into the Pope's hands. Châtillon had come to court, under the King's safe-conduct, to treat of peace after the second civil war. Cardinal Santa Croce, the Nuncio, entering the council-chamber, boldly demanded the performance of Catherine's promise then and there. Catherine did not deny the promise, but said that this was an unsuitable time for its fulfilment, owing to the King's safe-conduct. To this the Nuncio replied that no respect ought to be had toward Châtillon, for he was an "excommunicate person," condemned of schism, and dead in the eyes of the law. At this point the Duke de Montmorency broke out: "Madame," he said, "is it possible that the Cardinal Châtillon's delivery should come in question, being warranted by the King and your Majesty to the contrary, and I myself being made a mean therein? Wherefore this matter is odious to be talked of, and against the law of arms and all good civil policy; and I must needs repute them my enemies who go about to make me falsify my promise once made." After these plain words, Santa Croce departed, without attaining his most cruel and dishonorable request.

Later in the same year, 1568, it was in contemplation to seize Châtillon in his Episcopal palace at Beauvais. The third civil war was then raging. But he received timely warning, and escaped through Normandy to England, where Queen Elizabeth received him at court with marks of distinguished favor. She lodged him in Sion House, not far from Hampton Court, and never met him but she greeted him with a kiss; so that it was commonly said that the ambassador of Condé (then in rebellion against his King) was a much more important personage than the ambassador of the King of France. He succeeded in getting Elizabeth to send substantial help to his distressed friends in France.

In 1570, about two months after the declaration of peace, Cardinal Châtillon, who had been deprived by the Pope of his seat in the Roman Conclave, had also been declared, by the Parliament of Paris, on motion of the Cardinal of Bourbon, to have lost his Bishopric of Beauvais, on account of his rebellion and his adoption of Protestant sentiments. All such judicial proceedings had indeed been declared null and void by the terms of the royal pacification; but the Parliaments were very reluctant to yield obedience to the royal edict. The King sent orders to the first President of the Parliament to wait upon him with the records. And when, after a second summons, they were brought, the King, with his own hands, tore out and destroyed every page that contained any action against the Cardinal of Châtillon.

But we must be more brief in other cases; for these were not all. We find mention made of Michel d'Arande, who was Bishop of Saint Paul-Trois-Chateaux, in Dauphiny, and yet sympathized entirely with the Reformers, and was in confidential intercourse with them; also of Gérard Roussel, who was appointed by the Queen of Navarre to be her preacher and confessor, and rose to be Abbot of Clairac and Bishop of Oléron; yet he remained, to his death, a sincere friend of the Reformation. In his own Diocese he set the example of a faithful pastor. Even so bitter an enemy of Protestantism as Florimond de Raemond, contrasting Roussel's piety with the worldliness of the sporting French Bishops of the period, is forced to admit that " his pack of hounds was the crowd of poor men and women whom he daily fed; his horses and attendants a host of children whom he caused to be instructed in letters." Another prelate is mentioned, the Bishop of Senlis, as being so much in favor with the Queen of Navarre that he translated into French for her the book of " Hours," omitting all that most directly countenanced superstition. We read also of Cardinal Sadolet, Bishop of Carpentras, who readily certified to the falsity of the charges made against the Waldenses, exerted his influence with the Vice-legate to induce him to abandon an attack on one of their villages, and assured the inhabitants that he firmly intended, in a coming visit to Rome, to secure the reformation of some incontestable abuses.

Another prelate we read of, Châtellain, Bishop of Macon, who was at one time favorable to the Reformation, though his courage was not equal to his convictions.

Much better known, however, was Montluc, Bishop of Valence, who in 1560, when the Huguenots petitioned for liberty of worship, was their warmest and most uncompromising advocate. He " drew a startling contrast between the means that had been taken to propagate the new doctrines, and those by which the attempt had been made to eradicate them. For thirty years, three or four hundred ministers of irreproachable morals, indomitable courage, and notable diligence in the study of the Holy Scriptures, had been attracting disciples by the sweet name of JESUS continually upon their lips, and had easily gained over a people that were as sheep without a shepherd. Meanwhile, Popes had been engrossed in war, and in sowing discord between princes; the ministers of justice had made use of the severe enactments of the Kings against heresy, to enrich themselves and their friends; and Bishops, instead of showing solicitude for their flocks, had sought only to preserve their revenues. Forty Bishops might have been seen at one time congregated at Paris, and indulging in scandalous excesses, while the fire was kindling in their Dioceses. The inferior clergy, who bought their curacies at Rome, added ignorance to avarice. The ecclesiastical office became odious and contemptible, when prelates conferred benefices on their barbers, cooks, and footmen. What must be done to avert the just anger of GOD? Let the King, in the first place, see that GOD's name be no longer blasphemed as heretofore. Let GOD's Word be published and expounded. Let there be daily sermons in the palace, to stop the mouths of those who assert that, near the King, GOD is never spoken of. Let the singing of psalms take the place of the foolish songs sung by the maids of the queens; for to prohibit the singing of psalms, which the Fathers extol, would be to give the seditious a good pretext for saying that the war was waged, not against men, but against GOD, inasmuch as the publication and the hearing of His praises were not tolerated. . . . As to punishments, while the seditious, who took up arms under color of religion, ought to be repressed, experience had taught how unavailing was the persecution of those who embraced their views from conscientious motives, and history showed that three hundred and eighteen Bishops at the Council of Nice, one hundred and fifty at Constantinople, and six hundred and thirty at Chalcedon, refused to employ other weapons, against the worst of convicted heretics, than the Word of GOD."

This eloquent and bold harangue of the Bishop of Valence was followed, in the same discussion, by one still more cogent, from the aged and virtuous Marillac, Archbishop of Vienne. He urged " that it was in vain to expect a General Council, since, between the Pope, the Emperor, the Kings, and the Lutherans, the right time, place, and method of holding it could never be agreed upon by all; and France was like a man desperately ill, whose fever admitted of no such a delay as that a physician might be called in from a distance. Hence, the usual resort to a National Council, in spite of the Pope's discontent, was imperative. *France could not afford to die in order to please his Holiness.* Meanwhile, the prelates must be obliged to reside in their Dioceses, nor must the Italians — those leeches that absorbed one third of all the benefices and an infinite number of pensions — be exempted from the operation of the general rule. Would paid troops be permitted thus to absent themselves from their posts in the hour of danger? Simony must be abolished at once, as a token of sincerity in the desire to reform the Church. Otherwise CHRIST would come down and drive His unworthy servants from His Church, as He once drove the money-changers from the temple. Especially must Churchmen repent with fasting, and take up the Word of GOD, which is a *sword*, whereas at present," said the speaker, "*we have only the scabbard, — in mitres and crosiers, in rochets and tiaras.* . . . He warned the King's counsellors, lest the people, accustomed to have their complaints of grievances unattended to, should begin to lose the hope of relief; and lest the proverbial promptness and gentleness which the French nation had always shown in meeting the King's necessities, should be so badly met and so frequently offended as at last to turn into rage and despair."

Besides all these, we find Du Val, Bishop of Séez in Normandy, mentioned in the same group with Bishop Montluc of Valence, and that Abbé Boutillier who administered the Holy Communion in Genevan fashion to Cardinal Châtillon.

A very high authority gives us some other names. It is the bull of Pope Pius IV. already mentioned, in which, after Cardinal Châtillon, he adds S. Romain, the Archbishop of Aix, Montluc, Bishop of Valence, S. Gelais, Bishop of Uzès, Roussel, Bishop of Oléron, D'Albret, Bishop of Lescar, Guillart, Bishop of Chartres, and Caraccioli, Bishop of Troyes, who had resigned his Bishopric, and had been ordained a Protestant pastor, — *eight* prelates in all.

Besides all these, Jervis, in his History of the Gallican Church, gives us the names of Jacques Spifame, Bishop of Nevers, Pelissier, Bishop of Maguelonne, Etienne Poncher, Bishop of Paris and afterward Archbishop of Sens, as sympathizing with the Reform in the early period of the agitation; and Barbançon, Bishop of Pamiers, in the later.

We have now enumerated no less than *nineteen* prelates, among whom were *three* Archbishops and *two* Cardinals, who are shown to have sympathized with the Reformation; and of these, no less than *eight* are certified to us, by the Pope himself, as Protestant enough to be excommunicated. The Reformed party, therefore, had *Bishops enough* to have kept up the Apostolic succession, *had they chosen so to do*. The plea of necessity, because they *had* no Bishops, is utterly idle. They had them, but they *would not use them*. There is not recorded, so far as I have read, the slightest desire on the part of the sympathizing Bishops to retain the ancient rights of their Order in regard to government and ordination among the Reformed, nor the slightest desire on the part of the Reformed to have them do so. All consciousness of the importance of the question of Valid Orders seems to have been so utterly lost in the fiercer controversies of the times that it never once comes to the surface. Nay, so completely was it ignored that we find one of the above Bishops, and he an Italian too, Caraccioli, after resigning his See of Troyes, letting his own triple ordination go for nothing; and he (a Bishop) accepts a new ordination as a Protestant pastor!— about the most ridiculous ordination on record.

The books at my command do not enable me to go as minutely into the state of things in Germany, although the well-known position of Hermann, Archbishop of Cologne, is an indication that Reformation sympathies were not unknown among the prelates of Germany, any more than among those of France.

Why, then, if they had Bishops enough to continue the succession, did they not do it? Many reasons, doubtless, contributed, which we cannot consider here. One, doubtless, was that in *neither* country was any one of the great leaders of the Reformation movement a Bishop; and no one who was a true popular leader in so hot a popular movement was willing to defer to the authority of any Bishop less competent than himself to lead the people. Another was the prevailing impatience of the people under undeserved and cruel persecution.

II. And this leads me to the *Second* of the Three Points I am to touch upon, which is this: In England the Reforming party, as such, never drew the sword to defend themselves from persecution. They bore the persecution patiently, so long as it pleased GOD that it should last. All the rebellions that were made in England during the Reformation period proper — except the personal movement for Lady Jane Grey — were made by the opponents of Reform. As a reward for this patience and endurance, so it would seem, the good Providence of GOD accomplished the needed Reform, without disturbing a single foundation stone of the old Church. But in France and in Germany and in Scotland and elsewhere, impatience and persecution provoked civil war, and that of the most obstinate and hurtful kind. This caused *two* great evils. First, the religious question was tangled up and lost in the political question; and whenever they are thus tangled up, the politics of this world come out on top, and religion is sacrificed. The history of every civil war about religion will demonstrate the truth of this statement.

The other great evil is, that the going to war kills utterly all the *spiritual* fruit that otherwise would have been borne by persecution *patiently endured*. The early Church went through her ten persecutions — be they more or less — without once, even for a moment, resorting to armed defence against the most outrageous and cruel oppression. And this patient endurance — by the blessing of GOD — conquered the mighty Roman Empire. So in England, the burning of nearly two hundred of the Reformed party during the reign of Philip and Mary, *patiently endured*, turned the heart of the nation so strongly that after the accession of Elizabeth there was no serious obstacle to all the Reformation that was needed. In France, the glorious martyrdoms so bravely endured by Leclerc, Pauvan, De Berquin, Du Bourg, and innumerable others in the earlier part of the movement, produced a wonderful popular effect, which was spreading with astonishing rapidity. We read that "the curiosity to hear the preaching of the Word of GOD by men of piety and learning, the desire to hear those grand psalms of Marot solemnly chanted by the chorus of thousands of human voices, had infected every class of society. The records of the Chapters of Cathedrals, during this period of universal spiritual agitation, are little else, we are told, than a list of cases of ecclesiastical discipline instituted against chaplains, canons, and even higher dignitaries, for having attended the Huguenot services. At Rouen, the chief singer of Notre Dame acknowledged before the united Chapter that he had often been present at the 'assemblées,' — nay, more, 'that he had never heard anything there which was not good.'" Even Catherine de Medici herself, partaking of the general zeal, declared her intention to hear the Bishop of Valence preach before the young King and the Court, in the saloon of the Castle. In that same year, 1561, three weeks before the arrival of Beza to take part in the Colloquy of Poissy, this same Catherine de Medici wrote a remarkable letter to the Pope himself. "After acquainting him with the extraordinary increase in the number of those who had forsaken the Roman Church, and with the impossibility of restoring unity by means of coercion, she declared it a special mark of Divine favor that there were among the dissidents neither Anabaptists nor Libertines, for all held the Creed as explained by the early Councils of the Church. It was consequently the conviction of many pious persons that by the concession of some points of practice the present divisions might be healed. But more frequent and peaceful conferences must be held; the ministers of religion must preach concord and charity to their flocks; and the scruples of those who still remain in the pale of the Church must be removed by the abolition of all unnecessary and objectionable practices. Images, forbidden by GOD and disapproved of by the Fathers, ought at once to be banished from public worship, baptism to be stripped of its exorcisms, communion in both kinds to be restored, the vernacular tongue to be employed in the services of the Church, and private Masses to be discountenanced." Surely a wonderful letter to be written by such a person as Catherine de Medici, and to such a person as the Pope! From it we may easily estimate the force of the current by which she was surrounded. Again and again the Court seemed on the very point of taking sides with the Reformation; but every time, the mixing up of rebellion with Protestantism spoiled the prospect. A little more of patient endurance would have won the victory, and in such a way as to retain the ancient foundations of the national Church undisturbed. A few hundreds might have been added to the roll of martyrs in the mean time; but what was that compared to the tens of thousands that perished in the civil wars and massacres? Baird — as is to be expected — defends the Huguenots in their taking up arms. "Candidly viewing their circumstances at the distance of three centuries," he says, "we can scarcely see how they could have acted otherwise than as they did." Yet they had endured persecution for only about one generation, while the early Church endured it for nearly three hundred years. Even Baird, however, is compelled to admit that what he considers justifiable was actually destructive. And his language is so complete a demonstration of the truth, and so overwhelming a condemnation of those impatient Huguenots whom he defends, that we give it in full: —

War is a horrible remedy at any time. Civil war superadds a thousand horrors of its own. And a civil war waged in the name of religion is the most frightful of all. The holiest of causes is sure to be embraced from impure motives by a host of unprincipled men, determined in their choice of party only by the hope of personal gain, the lust of power, or the thirst for revenge, — a class of auxiliaries too powerful and important to be altogether rejected in an hour when the issues of life or death are pending, even if, by the closest and calmest scrutiny, they could be thoroughly weeded out, a process beyond the power of mortal man at any time, much more in the midst of the tumult and confusion of war. The Huguenots had made the attempt at Orleans, and had not shrunk from inflicting the severest punishments, even to death, for the commission of theft and other heinous crimes. They had endeavored in their camp to realize the model of an exemplary Christian community. But they had failed, because there were with them those who, neither in peace nor in war, could bring themselves to give to so strict a moral code any other obedience than that which fear exacts. Such was the misery of war; such the melancholy alternative to which, more than once, the Reformed saw themselves reduced, of perishing by persecution or of saving themselves by exposing their faith to reproach through alliance with men of as little religion or morality as any in the opposite camp.

And Baird goes on to state the full consequence of this terrible blunder of his friends, which, nevertheless, he attempts to justify. He says, —

The first Civil War prevented France from becoming a Huguenot country. [He forgets that he had just said that they were in danger of "perishing by persecution." They were in no danger of the sort. They were *growing* by persecution faster than they could ever grow by civil war. Nay, if persecution had not already made them so strong, they would not have thought it right to resort to civil war at all. But as to the fact that the outbreak of war destroyed the possibility of a reformation of the entire kingdom of France, he adds :] This was the deliberate conclusion of a Venetian ambassador, who enjoyed remarkable opportunities for observing the history of his times. The practice of the Christian virtue of patience and submission under suffering and insult, had made the Reformers an incredible number of friends. The waging of war, even in self-defence, and the reported acts of wanton destruction, of cruelty and sacrilege, — it mattered little whether they were true or false, they were equally credited, and produced the same results, — turned the indifference of the masses into positive aversion. It availed the Huguenots little, in the estimate of the people, that the crimes that were almost the rule with their opponents were the exception with them; that for a dozen such as Montluc, *they* were cursed with but *one* Baron des Adrets; that the barbarities of the former received the approbation of the Roman Catholic Priesthood, while those of the latter were censured with vehemence by the Protestant ministers. Partisan spirit refused to hold the scales of justice with equal hand, and could see no proofs of superior morality or devotion in the adherents of the Reformed faith.

The same evil consequences, only to a far greater extent, followed the terrible Thirty Years' War in Germany, — probably the most horrible civil war that has ever cursed any Christian country. And the same cause produced the same effects. It was not because the Reformed had no sympathizers among the Bishops, but because they were too impatient of persecution to be willing to wait until the LORD'S work should be done in the LORD'S way. And the same impatience — not *necessity*, by any means — led them to throw overboard the ancient authority of Bishops in the Church of GOD and originate a new ministry of their own.

Now we have seen, in our own day, though after a much milder fashion, the operation of the same general principles. The great Catholic Revival of the past half-century is one of the most wonderful that the Church has seen in any age or in any land. One great object of it was to revive the true doctrine that Bishops are in the Church by *Divine* right, and that the powers given to them by CHRIST and the HOLY GHOST cannot be taken away by any merely human authority. Yet at the beginning the entire Anglican Episcopate — with much fewer exceptions than we have found in France — was *opposed* to the Revival. Many were discouraged by this, lost heart, and left us. But a little reflection ought to have satisfied them. The primary instinct of the Episcopal Order is, and rightly, to hand things down to their successors exactly as they themselves received them. When, therefore, after the lapse of ages, the Church has gradually accumulated errors in certain directions, and the spirit of Reform is sent forth by the HOLY GHOST, that Reform must *always* expect to find the Episcopate, as a body, *opposed* to it. The Bishops, as a body, are rather more elderly men than the average of the rest of the clergy. They represent the age that is just ending, rather than that which is just beginning. And with their primary instinct of keeping things un-

changed, they oppose every improvement as an innovation.
This feeling of the Bishops was almost unbroken for a quarter
of a century after our Catholic Revival began; and even now,
when it is more than half a century old, a faithful and devoted
Priest in Liverpool, the Rev. J. Bell-Cox, has lately been sent to
prison by a Bishop — a Low Church Bishop, his *own* Bishop —
for his fidelity to that great Revival; he being the *fifth* Priest
who has cheerfully gone to jail in the same great cause. In all
these fifty years and more, all the persecution that could be
brought to bear on the Catholic Reformers has been cheerfully
borne, with *no* attempt to retaliate, or secede, or form a sect, or
usurp the canonical authority of the Bishops. Yet all the while,
preaching and teaching and writing and ritual and organizations for work among the poor, and the revival of the Religious
Orders, and much more, have gone on with unflinching energy
and courage, until at length we have fairly conquered the decided majority of the Anglican Episcopate itself. And that
Episcopate is now about as unanimous in commending the great
Catholic Revival as they were forty years ago in condemning it.
When one has mastered the *theory* that the Bishops will certainly, for at least a generation or two, oppose any and every
attempt at Reformation, from within and from below, he will be
less likely to lose heart and courage when he finds that the
theory is borne out by the *facts*. And it is well that it is so.
If changes could be brought about too easily, we should lose all
stability, — there would be nothing but change; whereas now,
when a change for the better has been slowly and painfully accomplished, it is a satisfaction to know that it will *last*. Moreover, when a movement is really begun by GOD the HOLY
GHOST, and is carried on with equal courage *and patience*, there
is no danger that any opposition by the Bishops of the day will
ever be able to put it down, no matter how hard they may try.
In a generation or two, the Reform will be represented and
maintained by the Bishops themselves. Let patience therefore
have her perfect work. With heavenly patience, the new life is
like leaven, that spreads its influence from soul to soul until the
whole Church is leavened. With *im*patience and Civil War,
that new life becomes rather like the destructive forces of
Nature, by which the solid mountain is rent into two opposing cliffs, which frown defiance on each other forever, and
unite no more.

III. I have left myself but little time for the *Third* Point, which is not so closely connected with the other two, but which, I hope, may be helpful to some minds.

When a metal bar freely suspended is rubbed so as to develop positive electricity at one end, it is always found that the same action has at the same time spontaneously developed an equal amount of negative electricity at the other end. The amount of electricity produced may thus be tested, with equal correctness, from the negative end as well as from the positive.

Now this third point is simply to compare the great Communions of Christendom *by their failures*. We are all familiar with the *positive* comparisons, — so familiar that sometimes the very familiarity makes us suspect that there must be some undiscovered fallacy about them. Let us, then, try the negative, for once.

But you may say, What do you mean by the negative? I will explain. Let us look at the three great Communions of Christendom, — the Roman, the Oriental, and the Anglican. So long as we are divided, no one of us has any authority from GOD to claim that we are *entirely* right in all points of difference, and that the others are *entirely* wrong. We *must* be, all of us, right in some things and wrong in other things. And in so far as we are wrong, we shall have our *failures*, as well as our successes. Now I propose to compare *our failures*. And — as we ought to do — let us begin with ourselves first.

Our failures, then, may briefly be described as the English-speaking Protestant denominations, so far as they have sprung out of the English Church. As for those which have sprung directly from the various Reformed bodies on the Continent of Europe, of course the Church of England is not responsible for *them*. All these denominations are without the Historic Episcopate; and this points to a great fault in the English Church, largely owing — as are most of her faults — to her union with the State. At the time of the Reformation, Cranmer earnestly desired to increase the number of Episcopal Sees in England from twenty-three to *forty ;* and King Henry VIII. gave him reason to hope that it should be done with endowments from the Church property taken by the Crown. But instead of that, only six new Sees were erected, — one of which soon ceased to exist; and there the increase stuck for three hundred years. If that proposed enlargement had then been made, it is highly probable that dissent from the Church of England would never have amounted to much. But when — with the steadily growing population — there was *no* growth in the Episcopate; when the time and attention of Bishops were absorbed to a large degree by their duties in Parliament; when their spiritual duties were more and more neglected, visitations being made only once in from three to seven years, and in some cases not at all; when the children from three, four, or five parishes were gotten together for Confirmation in one large Church, and the Bishop never visited the others at all, — what could be expected but that a type of earnest piety should largely prevail from which Bishops were entirely left out?

Then, again, in her Catechism, the Church of England has taught nothing about Confirmation or Holy Orders, or the organization of the Catholic Church, *not one word!* What wonder, then, that some of her people should easily come to think that Confirmation is of no great use, and that one kind of minister of the Gospel is just about as good as another, and that any and every sect is a Church? Other faults might be mentioned also, especially the suspension of the synodical action of the Church for nearly one hundred and fifty years. But no matter how great the evils of these divisions and losses, with all their controversies and jealousies, thus much must be allowed: On the whole, and with few exceptions, these denominations all accept the Bible, and use it in the version given them by the Church; they all profess to accept the Apostles' and Nicene Creeds; they all claim to keep up the ministration of the two great Sacraments; their Baptism is almost universally a valid Baptism; they are earnest and zealous in a great variety of good works, and not unfrequently, in liberality and zeal, they set *us* an example which we should do well to follow. They are, on the whole, a *very respectable set of failures.* And the separation from us is not so wide or so deep as in any of the other cases we shall mention; while the general confession of the evil of the disunion is more outspoken and sincere, and the prospect of final reunion far more promising, than we shall find anywhere else in Christendom.

Let us next look at the Oriental Church. Her great failure is Mohammedanism, — a far worse and more destructive failure than ours; for Mohammedanism is rather a heresy arising out of Christianity, than an original and separate religion. It includes a recognition of both the Old Testament and the New, — of Abraham and Moses and CHRIST. The faults that provoked this terrible reaction were rather the faults of the decaying and slavish absolutism of the old Pagan Roman Empire, which Christianity could not save; together with the picture-worship and saint-worship which grew naturally out of the other, aggravated by the irrepressible dialectics of the Greek mind in defining and over-defining the nature and relations of the Persons of the Blessed Trinity. Mohammed threw off Christian Baptism, and retained the old circumcision. He made one clean sweep of the Trinity and the Incarnation. He made GOD to be a simple unit, and himself to be GOD'S greatest and final Prophet, and the sword to be the chief propagator of his religion. The later organization of the Janissaries is a horrible travesty worthy of the Devil himself. The Turks levied a tribute on the Christians of *children*, — baptized Christian children, — who were violently taken from their parents before they were old enough to understand the truths of Christianity, and were then carefully trained up as Moslems, and were sworn to fight — as their life-work — that very religion into which they had been baptized in infancy. No wonder that such a weapon became ultimately intolerable even to the sultan who wielded it! There can be no question that Mohammedanism — the great failure of the Oriental Church — is incomparably worse than ours.

But the Church of Rome affords a failure far beyond either of us. As she has carried her practical corruptions, her additions to the Faith, and her passion for *absolutism* both in Church and State, to such tremendous lengths, so in the intensity of atheistic continental communism she has developed a failure incomparably worse than even Mohammedanism, and beside which our Evangelical Protestant denominations appear like positive blessings! The horrors of the first French Revolution were bad enough. The Commune of Paris has shown that it would improve on the old horrors, with greater ones of modern invention, the moment it should have a chance. The intense hatred of everything like Christianity, or even of a belief in a GOD, is startling. Only think what the condition of a man's mind must be who deliberately shoots dead a Priest who was standing at the altar and reciting the Apostles' Creed, — his only motive being *hatred* of the Creed which the Priest was reciting! Roman repression has been manufacturing the concentrated oil of vitriol, which threatens to destroy everything that it can get a chance to *touch*.

The comparison of our failures, then, while it ought to teach an Anglican modesty, and a deep sense of our own shortcomings, has in it also an element of comfort and encouragement. We have not been so long on the wrong course, and have not driven our errors so deep, and have not brought forth such desperate results as the others; and therefore as to what we still have to do, we may well " thank GOD, and take courage."

JOHN HENRY HOPKINS.

The Holy Eastern Church.

THE One Holy, Catholic, and Apostolic Church is composed, after all, of human particles; and it has always borne the marks of human weakness. It was never free from contentions. Even in our LORD'S time, and almost in His bodily presence, His disciples disputed as to which was the greatest; they undertook to forbid one to cast out devils in our LORD'S name, because he did not follow with them; and they were moved with indignation when the mother of James and John asked for her sons the highest rank in CHRIST'S kingdom. Paul contended against Peter and Barnabas because of their dissimulation; and while the Apostles yet lived there were divisions between Christians who claimed Paul, Peter, or Apollos as their leader. But the Church was not divided by any of these quarrels. For a thousand years, although contests abounded concerning certain refinements of doctrine, the relative rank of sees, and on other points, yet there existed a degree of unity to which in our day we can only aspire.

There never was a time known to the organized Christian Church when a difference in dignity was not conceded as between certain sees. In the earlier times, Rome being the political capital of the world, it was natural that all other bishops should yield a precedence of honor to the bishop of the world's metropolis; and when Constantinople, or New Rome, as it was called, became the metropolis of the world, it was natural that its bishop should expect the like pre-eminence; even as when it was the second capital, it had been granted the second ecclesiastical rank, superseding the See of Alexandria, which Saint Mark had founded. The Fourth Œcumenical Council did, in fact, declare Old Rome and New Rome to be equal. Canon XXVIII. of Chalcedon runs thus: " The Fathers fitly bestowed precedence upon the throne of Old Rome because it was the Imperial City; the one hundred and fifty bishops beloved of GOD [that is, the Fathers of the Second General Council of Constantinople], moved by the same consideration, rightly bestowed equal precedence upon the most holy throne of New Rome, wisely judging that the city honored by the seat of empire and by the Senate, and enjoying the same [secular] precedence as Old Imperial Rome, should be aggrandized like it in ecclesiastical matters also, ranking next after it." Precedence, it will be observed, was based solely on the political importance of the two sees, not on the supremacy of Saint Peter, for Constantinople claimed no Apostolic foundation.

So long as the civilized world was a unit politically, it was proper and natural that the hierarchy of the Church should also be an organized unit. When the Empire of the East became a State separate from that of the West, it was as proper and natural that the Church in each empire should have its own ecclesiastical head; and so, as nation after nation arose to independence carved out of the old empire, it would have been better and more consistent if the Church in each had also become self-ruled.

Happily, the world-wide empire and the world-wide Church existed together long enough to establish the fundamental doctrines of Christianity, to combat every form of heresy, and finally to embody in the Nicene Creed such points as were to be held as of Faith, and to agree that whoever added to or deducted from that creed should be *anathema*. The Pope and Church of Rome assented to that creed, and joined in the declaration of malediction; and if popes are really infallible, they are now excommunicate under this declaration.

So long as the true Nicene Creed was accepted as the universal symbol of the Christian faith, and so long as the canons of the Universal Church were acknowledged as the common law of all Christendom, the separation of the Church into eastern and western branches, with the like division of the Roman Empire, or its yet farther division into national churches, as nations arose from the ruins of both empires, could not have militated against the Divine unity of the Catholic Church. Neither political frontiers, nor distance, nor even war, could have destroyed the unity of one LORD, one Faith, one Baptism. Throughout Christendom a bishop, or a priest, or a deacon would have been acknowledged as such, and laymen everywhere would rightfully have claimed their Christian privileges, even among those whose tongue was strange, whose land was foreign, or whose political governors were at war.

If churches of different nations had sent missionaries to the same heathen land, there need not have been any mutual questioning of authority, or any demoralizing competition in the presence of converts; but whether Moscow planted or Rome watered, GOD would have given the increase to His One Holy Catholic Church, and we never should have seen the strange spectacle of holy treasure wasted in sending Christians to convert Christians.

This is the unity and the only unity which we of the American Church expect or desire. What shall be the ceremonial observances will be a matter of little consequence when such essentials as the Universal Church, in its unquestioned General Council, has decreed, are loyally accepted. Such unity existed in the Church throughout the first half of its history. It was not an ideal unity with absolute prevalence of harmony. Throughout Christendom there were many, some very bitter, contentions. Men are but fallible beings; and for some inscrutable reason controversies about religion, even among religious persons, seem to be attended with a degree of acrimony more intense than is common in merely secular discussions.

In the ninth century the words, "And the Son" (*filioque*), were in some countries inserted in the Nicene Creed where the Œcumenical Council had not inserted them; and this intrusion was finally authorized throughout the Patriarchate of Old Rome by Pope Nicholas I., although his predecessors, in spite of much importunity, had invariably refused to permit it, — one of them, the holy Leo III., having ordered the *filioque* to be omitted where the custom of using it had obtained, distinctly on the ground that no alteration could be made in the Church's creed by any less authority than that which had originally proclaimed the creed. To this violation of the common law of the Church we must attribute the final schism by which, in the year 1054, the Roman Church and its dependencies were cut off from the unity of the original Catholic Church.

After the separation, the Patriarch of Constantinople, who for more than six hundred years had been the declared equal of the Bishop of Rome, remained the chief dignitary of the Orthodox. Between the two patriarchates there have always existed these fundamental differences in character: (1) That whereas Rome has always striven to dominate the State, it has been usual in the East for the Church to defer to the State in matters not involving doctrine; (2) That while in the West Rome has always endeavored to centralize power in itself, breaking down all barriers to make the Church not national but Roman, the East has always recognized the right of a nation to hold within itself an autonomous Church, and the Patriarch of Constantinople has been content with his supremacy of honor merely.

In studying the history of the Patriarchate of Rome, we are for the greater part of the time among scenes which our education has made familiar, and we need only to acquire such languages as are taught in the seminaries about us. But the story of the Eastern Church leads us far afield to remote and unfamiliar, if not unknown, regions of the earth; and its literature is largely comprised in languages which are hardly spoken or taught in this hemisphere, — for of the one hundred millions of people who are comprised in the Eastern churches, eighty millions pray in the Sclavonic tongues, the greater part of them in tongues of that family now almost obsolete except for ecclesiastical purposes; and the number of American citizens who can read Hebrew far exceeds those by whom the Sclavonic types can be read and comprehended.

Again, it is comparatively easy to sketch the history of the Church of Rome by following down the list of popes and noting the prominent incidents of each reign; but in the East there is no such thread of connection, and it is necessary to tell, not one story, but many stories. It would occupy too much space, and perhaps outwear the patience of the reader, even to sketch in outline the annals of the Patriarchate of Constantinople, with what may be considered its dependencies of Alexandria, Antioch, and Jerusalem, of the Church in Russia and Greece and Cyprus and Montenegro, and of the Orthodox in Austro-Hungary; and even then there would remain undescribed the more or less unorthodox offshoots, — the Abyssinians, the Armenians, the Jacobites, and the Nestorians, as well as the curious forms of dissent in the Russian empire.

It would be an instructive but a sad narrative, touching upon the heresies and schisms which have warred within, and the fluctuating contests between the Crescent and the Cross; but nothing less than a volume would suffice to state even briefly the events which have marked the long centuries of the life of the various bodies which together compose the Holy Eastern Church.

The East is almost a different world from the West. Men's thoughts run in different channels; and whereas intense activity is characteristic of the West, passivity is the tendency in the East. The West delights in looking hopefully forward; the East revels in the past. From time to time Rome invents and imposes a new religious belief, claiming to have in itself the right to develop doctrine. The orthodox East abides by the ancient creed and reverences antiquity. Rome dates itself from S. Peter; but Constantinople regards the advent of CHRIST as occurring in the middle of Church history. Rome's saints are those only of the Christian dispensation, while the Byzantine calendar includes among the saints the prophets of the Old Testament, with Moses, Isaac, and Job the Just. Rome seeks always to acquire and extend power over secular rulers and affairs; but the patriarchs of the East claim no temporal power, and when they have mingled in secular politics have usually been stimulated by motives of patriotism, or have acted in defence of the Church.

But that is a very mistaken idea which counts the Eastern churches as having been indifferent to missionary duty and content to abide in their Dioceses. It is true that they never have pretended to own the earth and to parcel out heathen land among Christian princes; and it has not been their custom to compel submission to Christianity at the point of the sword, nor even to retaliate upon the Saracens such treatment as Christians had experienced at their hands. They have built on no man's foundation, nor have they attempted to lord it over GOD's heritage by sending missionaries to induce other Christians to submit to their rule, but have merely defended their own flocks against the intrusion of Papists and Protestants, whom they equally abhor.

And yet these Churches of the Eastern rite can give a good account of their stewardship. The habitable earth has been almost girdled by their missions. Passing westward into and through Germany and France, they seem to have been the first to establish the Episcopate in Germany, Gaul, and Britain, where traces still remain of the original Oriental influence. From Alexandria southward they carried the good news to Ethiopia, Abyssinia, and through regions even now unknown, south of the equator to the shores of the Indian Ocean. Eastward by sea along the coast they spread the Gospel as far as to Ceylon, and on the coast of Malabar the Christians of S. Thomas still celebrate their maimed rites in a Syrian tongue. Eastward by land through Persia and India they pressed on to a meeting with the sea-coast missions in Bengal ; and more yet to the north through Thibet and Mongolia, overcoming all obstacles, they penetrated into China, where the inscription of Sengan-fu attests their victorious presence and relates their annals for a century and a half, and where their churches are known to have existed for more than seven centuries. Northward the Orthodox Church moved to its greatest conquest; there it created the Empire of the Tsars, more extensive than that of ancient Rome, out of tribes known to old Romans only by half mythical stories; and by the waters of the Arctic Ocean they planted the monastery of Michael the Archangel. Skirting the frozen zone, they taught the Christian faith and established Apostolic vicars in the chief places; and their Bishop of Irkutsk in Siberia supplied priests to a Christian colony in Pekin whose descendants exist there to this day. Crossing the Behring Sea, they founded the bishopric of Sitka in Alaska, working wonders among the savage tribes and making converts even to within forty miles of the site of San Francisco, where the last Bishop of Sitka found his winter rest in the see city of our Bishop of California,—thus meeting on the coast of North America a successor of those bishops whom the same church had consecrated for Great Britain fifteen hundred years before. Even within the last twenty-five years the Orthodox have established a mission in Japan.

Much of this was accomplished by the Church while confronted and in places almost overwhelmed by the Moslem power. The origin of Mahometanism was in the tribes of Arabia in the centre of the Eastern churches. The forces of Islam at one time almost surrounded the waters of the Mediterranean. They reduced Spain to the condition of a Mahometan province, abiding within it for eight centuries, and they penetrated to the centre of France within two hundred miles of Paris. It was not until six centuries after their conquest of Spain that Constantinople fell into the hands of their generals; and the Turk will hardly have kept a footing in Turkey for one half the centuries that the Moor held Spain. But the struggle has been intense, and is not yet ended.

It was the policy of the Turks to kill or enslave all whom

they could not convert; and it is indeed a matter for wonder that under such tyranny the Eastern churches have been able to maintain even existence in their ancient territory. The Latin Church was practically exterminated in all that region on the southern border of the Mediterranean where once S. Augustine of Hippo and his contemporaries lived and ruled; and the names of ancient sees of the Roman Church in Africa survived merely as titles for ecclesiastics who never saw that continent; but the succession of patriarchs and metropolitans in Jerusalem, Antioch, Alexandria, Constantinople, at the foot of Ararat, and even in poor ignorant and isolated Abyssinia, has been maintained by bishops of whom many have been confessors and martyrs for the Faith.

It was in the centuries of her greatest troubles that the Orthodox Church effected the conquest of Muscovy. There too she was met by the followers of Mahomet; and as the tide ebbed and flowed, the Tartars would remove the Cross and place the Crescent above the captured churches. When these were recaptured, the Crescent was permitted to remain, but was surmounted by the Cross. Millions of Moslems, subjects of Russia, have been converted to Christianity; can Rome count its thousands? If the Turk yet keeps a foothold in Europe, it is only because the nations of Western Europe have tied the hands of the great Orthodox Empire whose people would willingly and long ago have driven him back to his native deserts, and relieved the provinces of the Levant from his obstructive reign. Within her own territory Russia has subdued the Turks; and beyond her borders of late, in Servia, Roumania, and Bulgaria, she has restored the Christian's rule.

The Holy Eastern Church has needed no unity of imperial autocracy to enable her children to preach the Gospel from the Arctic to the Indian Ocean, and from the waters of the Atlantic to the great Pacific Sea. By the tyranny of Moslem domination she has been fearfully disabled; and in many countries, for want of wealth and liberty, she has been unable to maintain seminaries of learning in theology, science, and the arts. Her people, oppressed, poor, ignorant, and consequently superstitious, have been troubled sometimes by heresies and always by Roman intrigues; but she never has been wanting in that seed of the Church, the blood of holy martyrs, by which perhaps her life has been maintained.

Within this nineteenth century an archbishop of Cyprus, his three suffragan bishops, and all the hegumens of the Cyprus monasteries were hung upon one tree; and so late as 1821, Gregory, Archbishop of Constantinople, was hung at the door of his cathedral.

In 1590 Poland was a State more powerful than Russia, and her people were divided in ecclesiastical allegiance between Rome and Constantinople. Roman intrigues and political influences led to the organization of the Uniat Church, which, consenting to acknowledge the supremacy of the Pope, was allowed to retain the rites, the customs, and the creed of the East. The concordat was basely violated, and the people shamefully abused, under the papal authority, so that at the first partition of Poland, of the Uniats who came under Russian protection, more than two millions in number voluntarily returned to their allegiance to the Eastern Church; and in 1839, the remainder of them, at least two millions more, on their own application, were received back with their bishops and clergy.

A List of all the Sees and Bishops of the Holy Orthodox Church of the East, compiled by the Rev. Charles R. Hale, S. T. D., and printed in 1872, names the various branches of the Church, and the titles of the head of each branch, as follows: —

1. The Most Entirely Holy Archbishop of CONSTANTINOPLE, New Rome, and Œcumenical Patriarch;

2. The Most Blessed and Holy Pope and Patriarch of the Great City ALEXANDRIA, Libya, Pentapolis, and Ethiopia, and of all the land of Egypt; Father of Fathers, Pastor of Pastors, Arch Priest of Arch Priests, Thirteenth Apostle, and Universal Judge;

3. The Most Blessed and Holy Patriarch of the Divine City ANTIOCH, Syria, Arabia, Cilicia, Iberia, Mesopotamia, and all the East; Father of Fathers, and Pastor of Pastors;

4. The Most Blessed and Holy Patriarch of the Holy City JERUSALEM, and all Palestine, Syria, Arabia, beyond Jordan, Cana of Galilee and Holy Sion;

5. The Most Holy Governing Synod of all the Russias;[1]

6. The Most Blessed and Holy Archbishop of NOVA JUSTINIANA and all Cyprus;

7. The Most Blessed and Holy Patriarch of SERVIA, Metropolitan of all the Servians residing in the AUSTRIAN EMPIRE, Archbishop of Carlovitz;

[1] This title is not from Dr. Hale's list.

8. The Most Reverend Archbishop of MOUNT SINAI;

9. The Metropolitan of Scanderia and the sea-coast, Archbishop of Tsettin, Exarch of the Holy Throne of Pek, Vladika of MONTENEGRO and Berda;

10. The Most Holy Governing Synod of the Kingdom of GREECE.[1]

Under these patriarchs and governing synods are more than three hundred and fifty metropolitans, archbishops, and bishops.

These, it should be remembered, are all undoubtedly Orthodox bishops. The Armenian Church is not recognized by the Orthodox as sound, yet there seems to be little doubt that its separation was the result of misapprehension and political disturbances; and as this body comprises a numerous people, — one perhaps the most active and intelligent of all Orientals, — it is greatly to be hoped that it may soon cease to be regarded as outside the true fold.

The chief ruler of the Armenians is " The Supreme Catholicos of all Armenians," and under him in 1874 were four patriarchs, forty-five archbishops and bishops, and some forty sees were in charge of vicars.

The number of people affiliated with these branches of the Church is somewhere between eighty and one hundred millions.

In ecclesiastical architecture the West far surpasses the East, but it was not always so. Those centuries which in the west of Europe were marked by the rise and development of Christian art and architecture, were those in which the whole mind of the Eastern Church was absorbed by the intensity of its contests with the power of Islam; and since then a large number of its Dioceses have existed within the Moslem dominions, where Christians who exhibited any evidence of wealth were sure to be the victims of tyrannic spoliation, and where to build a church of any peculiar attractiveness was simply to supply Mahometans with a mosque.

True, there has been a better state of affairs in the Russian Empire; but that sparsely settled country has only of late, if indeed it has even yet, extricated itself from a condition of crude civilization. Churches have been built there in almost incredible numbers, many of them at enormous cost, but architecture as an art has found in them no considerable development. We

---

[1] This title is not from Dr. Hale's list.

must bear it in mind that less than three hundred years intervened between the reign of Constantine and the opening wars with the Saracens, — that is to say, between pagan persecutions and the struggle with the infidels, — a short time for an Eastern people to create and establish a new architecture.

And yet the Church in the East has made its mark on the architecture of the world. The dome, — that feature without which neither S. Paul's, London, nor S. Peter's, Rome, would have great distinction, and which on our own Capitol at Washington crowns the noble edifice with glory, — the architectural dome is the outcome of the early artistic efforts of Eastern Christianity, although so many Oriental churches have been converted into mosques, and so many mosques have imitated this really Christian form, that people have come to regard the dome as a Moslem device.

Not many existing churches in Western Europe date back so far as to the sixth century of our era; but the middle of that century saw complete that marvel of costliness, the Church of the Eternal Wisdom, the patriarchal Cathedral of Constantinople.

The Temple at Jerusalem, built by Herod the Great, was forty and six years in building. S. Peter's at Rome occupied one hundred and seventy-five years, the reigns of twenty popes, and the service of twelve architects, in its construction; but in less than six years the Emperor Justinian began and completed a church which was for centuries the largest, and even now ranks among the most costly ecclesiastical structures that the world has ever seen. Its plan was the common one, — a Greek cross inscribed within a rectangle. Its measurement was two hundred and forty-three feet in width by three hundred and forty feet in length, and it covered nearly two acres of land. No timber was used for its construction, but the quarries of the world contributed sandstone, granite, porphyry, and marbles of every color, which were used in its walls, piers, and columns. Its aerial dome was of pumice-stone and light-weighing Rhodian bricks, and all was adorned with mother-of-pearl, jasper, alabaster, gold, silver, and precious stones. The altar was of solid gold and incrusted with jewels; the gates were of carved bronze; and the interior dome was decorated with mosaics of glass, crystal, amber, and precious stones.

Brilliant indeed must have been the appearance of what was then by far the largest and most costly cathedral of all Christendom, when it was presented for consecration by the zealous emperor, who in person had supervised the building; and one more than pardons his saying in the presence of the great congregation, " Glory be to GOD who hath accounted me worthy of such a work! I have beaten you, O Solomon!"

And this building yet stands, mutilated, desecrated, and degraded to be the mosque Aya Sofia, but still grand and beautiful, despite the passing of thirteen centuries and the neglect of Turkish rulers; and still the cherubim of the mosaics, peering through the covering which the Moslem attempted, wait for the day when the infidel shall be driven out of Europe, when CHRIST shall have His own again, and when His servant the Œcumenical Patriarch shall reconcile the Church and resume his throne after more than four centuries of exclusion.

The exterior of Eastern churches is not often satisfactory to eyes educated by the rich architecture of Western cathedrals. In Russia, where development has been greater than elsewhere, such a building as the Pokrovski Cathedral at Moscow, which is in fact a group of twenty-one small churches, presents a striking appearance as seen from without, — the multitude of domes and spires bright with color and gold and decorated with chains, globes, and crosses, all shining under the sunlight, — but there is wanting that stateliness, unity, and dignity which are characteristic of ecclesiastical edifices in the West. Churches of the Eastern rite are much smaller than those of Western Europe. There are cathedrals only sixty or seventy feet long, and many monastic and parish churches are of Liliputian dimensions; but the universal custom of standing during the service permits the compression of many people into a smaller space than would be possible if seats were provided.

The Cathedral of S. Mark, Venice, built in the tenth and eleventh centuries, was patterned after S. Sophia, and they who have seen it can imagine what Justinian's much larger church must have been. It speaks volumes for the Western estimate of Eastern architecture that an Italian church of such prominence should have been built five hundred years later than the Cathedral of Constantinople, and so closely after the same style.

The accompanying sketch of the ground-plan of one of the churches at Athens may be taken as typically representing the plan of most Eastern churches.

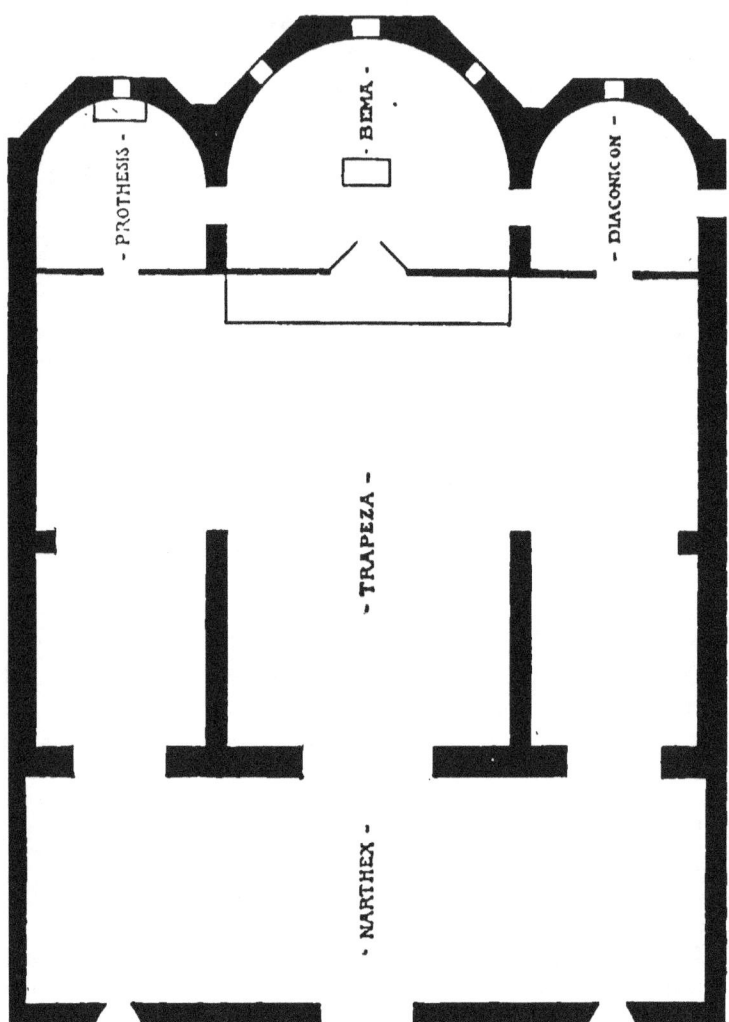

There is a Greek cross inscribed within a square, to which on the west (for Orientation is always observed) is added the narthex, which is a kind of vestibule, and which is often merely a lean-to in construction; the head of the cross is the bema or sacrarium; the intersection of the limbs of the cross is the choir, over which rises a dome; the bema and choir together may be considered as the chancel; the transepts and the trapeza, or nave, are about equal in length. The narthex, once the place for penitents and catechumens, is now often assigned to the women, who were formerly accommodated in galleries, the separation of the sexes being strictly observed.

Inscribing a cross within a square, there remain four exterior spaces. The two western spaces or corners are sometimes separate chapels; sometimes they open into the trapeza, or nave, as do our aisles, and are occupied by the congregation. The two rooms in the eastern corners have doors opening into the sacrarium and the transepts; often they are practically parts of the sacrarium. That in the southeast is the diaconicon, — that is, sacristy or vestry; that in the northeast is the prothesis, for which there is no equivalent name in our ecclesiastical vocabulary, for it is used for a purpose unknown to our rites, unless the table, which in it stands against the east wall, may be considered a credence.

The iconostasis separates the prothesis, the sacrarium, and the vestry from the rest of the interior. It is not a mere open-timbered screen, but is solid, high enough to prevent the officiating clergy being seen over it, but low enough to allow their voices to be heard across. It represents, not our chancel or rood screen, but rather our altar-rails, separating the sacrarium from the choir. The interior of the sacrarium is always apsidal at the east; and the altar stands on the chord of the apse and so detached that the deacon may, according to the ritual directions, at certain times cense it all around.

There is but one altar in one Church; over it is a canopy, and on it usually is the ark for the reserved sacrament, a cross, and a book of the Holy Gospels. Directly in front of the altar are the holy doors, opening into the choir; and on these and other parts of the iconostasis is lavished much decoration. Images are not allowed in the churches; but pictures, under limitations, are permitted. These are called icons; and on one side of the holy doors is the icon of our LORD; on the other, that of the Virgin Mary.

The floor of the bema is raised at least one step above the floor of the church; and this raised floor extends somewhat beyond, that is, west, of the screen, and is called the ambon. From it the Epistle and Gospel are read, and often there is no other place from which to preach; but sermons are not so common as to require any special provision for a preacher.

It is easy to discern in the plan of an Eastern church that of its model, the Temple at Jerusalem. The narthex represents the court of the Gentiles; the nave, the court of the Jews; the choir, the holy place; the screen, the veil of the temple; beyond which is the sanctuary, the Holy of Holies.

The priest's every-day dress is a cassock of any sober color he may prefer. The official vestments are often exceedingly rich, made of costly silks and velvets, and bright in color; some of those shown to travellers in Moscow are so incrusted with embroidery and jewels that they will stand upright alone. Except in Armenia, the mitre is never worn; but prelates wear a domed head-dress, — some of them a kind of crown. And these, as also the head-covering of the priests, — a brimless silk hat, — are very striking, and suit well with the long hair and flowing beards of the wearers.

Scarcely any rite is performed, whether by day or night, without lighted candles or lamps. A censer is in frequent use.

It is not the vernacular language that is used for the service in any Oriental church; but in the Orthodox communion it is the ancient, and in some cases the otherwise obsolete, language of the country, — that which was current when the Church was made known there, and one which the people can for the most part still understand. There is perhaps no exception to the statement that in every historical church the language used in worship is antiquated, if not archaic: what was once the vernacular has become an unused or altered tongue, and the formulas of the Church escape alteration. Our own Church shows this tendency, and even the extemporaneous prayers of denominational ministers are framed in language which is not used in common speech.

Latin, the ancient Italian vernacular, and the official language for centuries in all the west of Europe when the Church was planted there, is still the language of the Roman Church, and officially of the English Convocations. So in the East, the office-books of the Greek Church are in almost classical Greek. The Georgians use in the Church their old and statelier language, and the Russians the Sclavonic.

An attempt to reform the Russian books, although intended as a return to more ancient ways, was the cause of a great dissent in Russia; and our Church does not take to the Revised Version of the Bible, and has recently rejected a slightly modernized Prayer-Book.

The Oriental service-books are very numerous, — somewhere about twenty, — some very large; and although two of them are devoted to telling how the rest shall be used, a complete knowledge of that subject cannot be learned from books, but is acquired in part by oral tradition of unwritten rules. Among these books are lectionaries of the Old and New Testaments and the Psalms. The entire Bible is rarely seen in the churches. The most important book is that which contains the liturgies (that is, communion services) of S. Chrysostom, S. Basil, and the Pre-Sanctified. The two former are older than our Bible canon.

All the Eastern offices are very long, not to say tedious, representing rather the proper use in houses of the religious than a popular form. All of them are interspersed with interlocutions between the deacon and the priest, often as if the deacon were prompting the priest; and besides these troparia, short holy hymns not metrical are sung between the prayers. Prayer-Books are not used by the laity, most of whom cannot read; and the responses, except those by the choir, are limited to a few exclamations at well-known points in the service. The people stand, but are almost continually bowing and crossing themselves, *à la grecque*, and sometimes prostrate themselves.

The great length of the services, which were framed for use chiefly in monasteries, induces very rapid reading or singing, — so rapid that it is difficult, even for one who understands the language, to follow the meaning. No instrumental music is used. All singing is by men; and although it is peculiar, and at first not agreeable, it soon becomes acceptable and even attractive. The Constantinopolitan rites are those most widely used; but there are many, some very important, variations.

On the day of a child's birth, the priest goes to the house and says prayers for the recovery of the mother, for the child, for the mother, and for those who live in the house. On the eighth day the infant is taken to church, in the west end of which a short office is said, ending with "Hail, Mary!" On the fortieth day the child, its mother, and the sponsor or sponsors attend at the church. After the usual blessing follow prayers for the child and its mother. Then the priest, taking the child in his arms and standing in the west doorway of the nave, says, " N., the servant of GOD, is churched, in the name," etc. Taking the child into the church, he proceeds, " He shall come into Thine house, he shall worship before Thy holy temple." In the middle of the church he proclaims, " The servant of GOD is churched," adding, " In the midst of the church will I praise Thee." He then takes the child to the sanctuary, saying, *Nunc dimittis*, lays it down by the holy doors, whence a sponsor takes it up; and the priest giving the dismissal, all depart.

Very likely the child may have been previously baptized (in case of need any Orthodox person may baptize); but in such cases the child, if it lives, is afterward brought to church as with us, and the rest of the office is celebrated according to the ritual.

The sacrament of baptism is preceded by unction. After the oil has been blessed by the priest, the person about to be baptized is brought forward; and the priest takes of the oil and makes the sign of the cross upon his forehead and breast and between the shoulders, saying, " N., the servant of GOD, is anointed with the oil of gladness in the name of," etc.; and he signs the back and breast. When he touches the breast, he says, " For the healing of soul and body; " the ears, " For the hearing of faith; " the feet, " That thy steps may advance; " the hands, " Thy hands have made me and fashioned me."

The rule of the Eastern Church is that the person to be baptized should be immersed three times by a priest, who pronounces at the same time the formula, " N., the servant of GOD, is baptized in the name of the FATHER, and of the SON, and of the HOLY GHOST now and ever and ages to ages. Amen." While, however, trine immersion is the rule, it is not invariable; trine affusion is practised in Russia, Servia, and Montenegro, if not elsewhere. The leading features of the baptismal service resemble our own. The baptistery was once an entirely distinct building; later it was connected to the narthex by a passageway, and now is sometimes within the narthex. The font is usually a pool lined with wood or metal; in Russia it is sometimes movable.

Confirmation, called in the East the " Mystery of Chrism," immediately succeeds baptism, and is ordinarily performed by a priest. The Latin Church forbids priests to confirm, except under dispensation, and the Eastern Church makes the priest habitually the minister. But the episcopal authority is by no means absent, for the oil used is consecrated in both West and East by the bishop on Maundy Thursday; so that in both cases an episcopal act is required to make the rite valid. By the ritual of Constantinople the priest "anoints the baptized person with holy oil, making the sign of the cross on his forehead, eyes, nostrils, mouth, both ears, breast, hands, and feet, saying, 'The seal of the gift of the HOLY GHOST. Amen.'" After confirmation infants are immediately communicated, the priest dipping his finger in the chalice and touching the child's lips.

Auricular confession is theoretically the rule in all Eastern, as in all Western, churches. The Church expects it four times a year; but that at Easter is the only one really required. It is not a prerequisite for every communion. An office exists for the appointment of confessors by the bishop. Confession is not inquisitorial or suggestive as in the Roman Church. Unless mortal sin is confessed, no penance is imposed; nor does absolution necessarily follow. The Greek form of absolution is precatory, not positive, like that in the English Office for the Visitation of the Sick. In Russia an annual confession is required by law, — not rigidly enforced, however; and there absolution is authoritative. This annual confession is very perfunctory. During Lent the churches are crowded by the faithful, who, ranged in long *queues*, press one upon another with tapers in their hands, frequently bowing the head and making the sign of the cross. Each, advancing in turn, answers the priest's question with, "I am a sinner," receives absolution and a certificate, for which he pays, and passing on, lights his taper, reverently placing it before the holy pictures. A few days later he returns for the communion. There are no confessional-boxes; but usually, not always, a screen separates the priest and penitent from others. Real privacy is very uncommon. Confessions of well-to-do people are often received in their houses, the penitent sitting during confession, kneeling only to receive absolution.

Ordination is not necessarily for life; a priest may be relieved by dispensation. Parish priests must be married; bishops must be single; monks must be unmarried; and the bishops are selected from among the monks almost exclusively.

Marriage is indissoluble according to the Church; but the law in Russia permits divorce for certain reasons. The innocent party only is allowed to marry again. Third marriages are not considered respectable, and fourth marriages are forbidden. Marriages always take place in church, and none are solemnized in Lent.

Unction of the sick is practised everywhere in the East, — not extreme unction as in the Roman Church, but commonly in severe illness.

I have said that there is no name in our ecclesiastical language for the prothesis of the Eastern churches, because we have no rite like that for which that portion of their churches is used. The chief office of worship in the East is, as it should be everywhere, the office of the Holy Communion, — the Liturgy proper. In preparation for it five small loaves of leavened bread are provided. These are often made from selected grains of wheat, washed, ground, mixed, and sometimes even baked in the church. On each loaf is a stamp, — " JESUS CHRIST *conquers*," — commonly called the " Holy Lamb," or the " Holy Bread." These loaves and the wine are placed on a table which stands against the east wall of the prothesis. The priest and deacon, vesting in the diaconicon, pass through the sanctuary into the prothesis; and the office begins there with ablution of their hands, and proceeds with great formality and reverence.

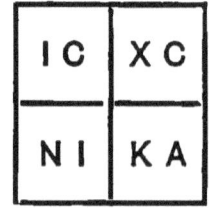

From one loaf the priest with a special spear-shaped instrument cuts out the Holy Lamb and places it in the centre of a disk. From a second loaf he cuts a portion and places it on the right side of the Holy Lamb, in honor of the Virgin Mary. From a third loaf he cuts nine portions, which are placed in three rows on the left of the Holy Lamb, in honor respectively of S. John Baptist, the prophets, apostles, fathers, martyrs, ascetics, saints, the parents of the Virgin, and for S. Chrysostom or S. Basil, according to the Liturgy to be used that day. From a fourth loaf the priest cuts portions, placing them in two rows below the Holy Lamb, — one row in memory of the dead, and the other in honor of the living. In these last two rows the deacon adds portions to commemorate such of the living and dead as he pleases. The whole is then reverently covered, and the clergymen return to the sanctuary, where this office ends, and the Liturgy of the Catechumens begins with a short litany, followed by an initial hymn.

Then occurs the "Little Entrance," which is the bringing in of the Gospel. The deacon takes the volume from the altar, and going before the priest, himself preceded by tapers, the little procession passes from the bema through the prothesis into the church, and so on to the holy doors, and through them back to the altar, where the Gospel is again deposited. Then the hymn of the trisagion is sung, — "Holy GOD, Holy and Mighty, Holy and Immortal, have mercy upon us!" After this come the lections.

The Apostle (Epistle) is read by one who stands at the holy doors. The Gospel is read from the ambon, — which may be a sort of pulpit, or only a part of the raised platform outside the screen. To this place the deacon goes, through the holy doors, bearing the volume, and preceded by tapers. As he passes out of the sanctuary, the priest, standing before the altar and facing the people, says, "Wisdom, stand up. Let us hear the Holy Gospel. Peace to all!" And after the reading, the Gospel is returned to the priest in the same order as was observed in passing out. After the reading of the Gospel there follows a prayer for the catechumens, who are about to leave, and thus ends what we might call the ante-communion, the deacon proclaiming, "Let all the catechumens depart. Catechumens, depart. Let all the catechumens depart. Let there be no catechumens. Let all the faithful."

After the departure of the non-communicants the service proceeds with prayers for the faithful, litanies, and hymns. After the Cherubic Hymn occurs the "Great Entrance." The priest and deacon pass from the sanctuary into the prothesis, where the priest, taking up the covered disk with the bread upon it, places it upon the head or shoulder of the deacon, who also bears a censer, and, himself taking the chalice, they pass from the prothesis into the church, and by the west end of the choir up to and through the holy doors, when the elements are placed upon the altar. In large churches and on high days this entrance is one of great pomp, the people bowing reverently as the procession passes by. In the sanctuary warm water is mixed with the wine in the chalice.

The principal characteristics of the communion service resemble those of our own, although they are interspersed with interlocutions between the priest and deacon in a way peculiar to the Eastern rite. There are the first prayer of oblation of the elements, the creed, the triumphal hymn, the commemoration of our LORD'S Passion and of the institution of the sacrament, the oblation of the body and blood, the invocation, the prayer for transmutation, the intercession for quick and dead, the LORD'S Prayer, the Sanctus, the breaking of the bread, the confession, the communion, and the thanksgiving.

The communion is administered to the people in both species, sometimes as it is in our churches, sometimes a sop of bread and wine from a spoon. The people receive from the priest standing, and the deacon, following, wipes each one's lips with a veil. The words of administration (Constantinopolitan rite) are: "N., the servant of GOD, is made partaker of the pure and holy Body and Blood of our LORD and GOD and SAVIOUR JESUS CHRIST, for the remission of sins and life everlasting."

Communion once a year is required of the laity, and is generally considered sufficient. Some very devout people receive every month; but even this is unusual. The priests communicate every day.

The burial offices are various, different services being used for the laity, monks, priests, and children. On the death of a lay person the priest goes to the house, and putting incense in his censer, gives the benediction. All present join in saying the trisagion, the LORD'S Prayer, and some collects. In the case of a person of rank relays of priests recite the office so long as the body remains in the house. When carried to the church, the corpse is placed in the narthex, and the service proceeds with prayers, hymns, versicles, and responses. The Epistle is 1 Tim. iv. 13 to the end; the Gospel is John v. 24 to 31. The kinsfolk, following the example of the priest, kiss the dead while a very solemn recitative is sung. The body is carried to the grave, the clergy singing, and when it is laid in the tomb, the priest casts upon it crosswise oil, earth, and the ashes from his censer. Among the troparia are these:—

"With just spirits made perfect give rest, O SAVIOUR, to the soul of Thy servant, guarding it to the blessed life that is from Thee!"

"In Thy repose, O LORD, where all Thy saints rest, give rest also to Thy servant, for Thou only art a lover of men!"

A common inscription on monuments is, "Good Christians are entreated to pray for the soul of N."

Absolution of the dead is clearly practised in Russia, and is suggested in the offices elsewhere; but the Roman doctrine of purgatory is not held, nor are purgatorial Masses used.

Among the minor offices are those for laying the foundation for a dwelling or a church; consecrating or reconciling a church; on washing the feet on Thursday in Holy Week; consecration of articles for use in a church; for a haunted house; planting; vintage; against blight; over a new vessel; in drought, plague, earthquake, and war; also one for children that have bad eyes.

The ecclesiastical year of the Eastern Church begins in January at what is called in our calendar the third Sunday after Epiphany, but which they name, as they do many others, for the Gospel of the day, the "Sunday of the Publican and Pharisee."

They have no Advent season; but there is a forty-day fast, from November 15 to Christmas Day, called the "Fast of the Nativity." There are two hundred and twenty-six days in the year scrupulously observed as days of abstinence. In Lent the use of meat, fish, cheese, eggs, butter, oil, and milk is forbidden; caviare and other preparations of fishes' eggs, shellfish, crabs, and lobsters, are allowed. On Saturdays and Sundays — the latter are fast-days in Lent — more than one meal and the use of oil is permitted. Wine may be used at all times.

Our first Sunday in Lent is called Orthodox Sunday; our Good Friday, the Holy Sufferings of our LORD; our Easter, Pascha, or Bright Sunday; our Whitsunday, Pentecost; our Trinity Sunday, All Saints' Sunday; our first after Trinity, second after Pentecost, and so forward. Between Easter and Pentecost kneeling is forbidden, and the usual posture at prayer is standing, which, no doubt, is primitive.

Monasteries and hermitages abound, and the ascetic or contemplative life is highly honored. There are no regular orders of monks as in the West, no rules like those of the Franciscans, Benedictines, etc.; but monks are governed by the canons of ancient councils, and by local tradition and custom.

Nunneries are much less common. In Russia women must

attain a certain age before being professed. Some monasteries are subject to an abbot, or archimandrite, and hold all things in common; in others, each monk lives as he pleases and can afford, the government being semi-republican, but in these the public opinion of the brotherhood prevents any departure from certain customs of the place.

Mount Athos, a peninsula on the coast of Roumelia, is entirely occupied by monks and always has been so since the time of Constantine; even the Turks have respected them. There are twenty monasteries on the Holy Mountain, as it is called,—some of them of very great size, including many chapels, and sheltering many hundreds of brothers; and some are very small. No female, human or animal, is allowed on the peninsula. The monks never cut hair or beard, and their life is for the most part one of simplicity and devotion, but there is now little learning or study. Here is preserved the custom of calling the people to service by striking a mallet on a board, the manner of sounding the call denoting the character of the approaching service.

Bishops usually are selected from among the dignitaries of the monasteries. In Russia, the Holy Synod nominates three persons to the Tsar, who chooses one of them to fill the vacant bishopric; and each bishop has a council, the members of which, nominated by him, must be approved by the synod. The selection of high ecclesiastics in Moslem countries is often the occasion of disreputable intrigues.

It is a rule of the Eastern Church that the parish priest — called pope in Russia — shall be married; and in order to be a parish priest, the man must first be married. So, too, if the wife dies, the priest often loses his parish and retires to a monastery; whence originates the Russian saying about being cared for as tenderly as a pope's wife. The priests' stipends are exceedingly small, and their living depends considerably upon fees, which are due to them at confession, baptism, unction, and burial, as well as at marriages; and in Russia, where these fees are not fixed, the people chaffer with their popes as to the amount to be paid on these occasions. As a rule, the popes have little education, and as a pope's children have the preference in the priestly schools, there is a tendency toward their becoming a separate class.

It is evident that in these Eastern churches the points of agreement with our own are many, and that fundamental differences are few. They acknowledge the propriety of the self-government of churches bounded by national lines; they own no single ruler whose commands are to be obeyed by all Christians, and whose decisions are infallible; they do not tie themselves to any one form of ritual, nor do they use the same language in their services, whatever may be the vernacular tongue, but, theoretically at least, recognize the propriety of their being understood by the people; they do not require celibacy of parish priests or deny the cup to the laity; to them the immaculate conception of the Virgin Mary is no article of faith, and by them the papal infallibility is held in derision. In such details as their belief differs from our own, the differences are matters, not of dogma, but of pious opinion, or else are merely the outgrowth of superstition resulting from imperfect education.

Why, then, should we and they be out of each other's communion? Why may we not make one great advance toward ecclesiastical unity, and break down one of those barriers which mar Christendom, by consolidating the holy Eastern churches with those of the Anglican rite?

In our yearning for Christian unity we are apt to limit our expectations to bringing back to our fold those who have strayed from our communion, and to centre our attention upon the sects which are scattered throughout America, or which use the English tongue. Now, in the East there is a communion whose antiquity, Apostolic succession, and ancient ritual no reasonable person questions. It occupies a large part of the habitable globe, one in which tradition is respected and where novelties are suspected; its people are Oriental in their adherence to what is old and their unwillingness to make changes. The oldest Christian sees are within its jurisdiction, and its bishops trace their descent in an unbroken line, — those of Jerusalem to James the brother of our LORD; those of Alexandria to S. Mark; those of Antioch to S. Peter, who undoubtedly ruled at Antioch before he possibly ruled at Rome; and they honor as their Œcumenical Patriarch the direct successor of the Bishop of Constantinople, the last capital of a world-wide empire. Their communion embraces one quarter of those who call themselves Christians; and if we could coalesce with this great church both of us would be strengthened for other fusions. In what, then, consist the obstacles?

There is no occasion to go back and study the controversies

of a thousand years ago; but we want to learn what are the present difficulties. As neither the Easterns nor the Anglicans have any unit of organization by which authoritative declarations can be made, it is necessary to gather the consensus of opinion in each, from acts in the recent past and from the declarations and other writings of learned men and high ecclesiastics of our own times.

Let us first understand that the spirit of the Eastern Orthodox churches is certainly not opposed to intercommunion; and they realize that it would strengthen them both in relation to the Latin and the Oriental schismatics.

In 1869 the Archbishop of Canterbury, at the request of the Southern Convocation of England, addressed to the Patriarch of Constantinople a letter asking, among other matters, in behalf of Anglican Churchmen dying within Eastern jurisdictions the kind offices of the Orthodox clergy in the absence of those of our own communion, and burial in consecrated ground, therein offering to reciprocate.

To this the patriarch replied by issuing an encyclical letter to his metropolitans, enjoining it upon them to assist at the burial of Anglican Churchmen in Orthodox countries where no Anglican priest or cemetery was at hand, and the Holy Synod of Athens also willingly granted the same privileges. When the Bishop of Gibraltar consecrated Christ Church in Constantinople, the patriarch sent the Bishop of Pera to represent him at the ceremony, and an archimandrite of Mount Athos attended in person. Soon after the Bishop of Gibraltar, by invitation of the Metropolitan of Athens, was present in his robes at a thanksgiving service in the Cathedral at Athens.

In 1870 the Archbishop of Syra and Tenos visited England for the purpose of consecrating a Greek church in Liverpool, and the archbishops of Canterbury and York were both represented there by clergymen; and while in England he of Syra was present in his robes at the consecration of two bishops of our communion.

This visit of the Orthodox archbishop to England, and the attentions bestowed upon him by the Church and the universities, excited great and grateful notice in the East. The Holy Synod of Greece, in acknowledging the hospitality and courtesies extended to one of their members, declared " that it smooths our way to mutual communion in CHRIST; and what we have long desired and now entreat of the Most High — to see divided members of CHRIST'S Church come together again — can appear to us no longer as a mere wish or a vain request, but as an aim which by GOD'S favor we may hope shall be realized."

Cyril, Patriarch of Jerusalem, said, "The most sweet auguries of a bright future have begun to dawn. May it be the pleasure of the Most High that it may be increased to a brilliant sun!" And Gregory, Patriarch of Constantinople, "These things straighten, smooth, and prepare beforehand the ways and the paths of the spiritual unity and fellowship of the faithful everywhere."

In 1871 Mr. S. G. Hatherly, an Englishman, was ordained to the priesthood at Constantinople, and started a congregation at Wolverhampton, in England, manifestly with a view to proselyting members of the Church. A remonstrance was made, and very promptly for Eastern ways the patriarch bade Mr. Hatherly to teach "duly the little Orthodox flock over whom you have been called and appointed by the Church to be priest, but never to think of assuming to proselytize a single member of the Anglican Church;" and he adds, "Our fervent desire is . . . that through sincere care, in the spirit of meekness, and by preparatory labor, all differences may be removed, and the unity of the churches may follow."

The differences to be removed as viewed from the Eastern standpoint are suggested from various sources.

The Patriarch of Constantinople, Gregory VI., having received from the primate of all England a Greek version of the English Prayer-Book, and having carefully perused the book, expressed it as his opinion that the statements in the Thirty-nine Articles concerning the eternal existence of the Holy Spirit, the Divine Eucharist, the number of the sacraments, the ecclesiastical tradition, the authority of the genuine Œcumenical Councils, the mutual relations of the Church on earth and that in heaven, and moreover, the honor and reverence due from us to those who are the contemplative and active heroes of the faith, the adamantine martyrs and ascetics, savored too much of novelty. And as to Article XIX., which says, "As the churches of Jerusalem, Alexandria, and Antioch have erred, so also the Church of Rome hath erred, not only in their living and manner of ceremonies, but also in matters of faith," the patriarch wisely comments, "Let us be permitted to say that depreciation of our neighbor is an intrusion in a distinguished confession of faith." "All these things," he says, "throw us into suspense. . . . So that we doubt what we are to judge of Anglican Orthodoxy."

It may be remarked here that inasmuch as the Thirty-nine Articles have been entirely ignored, first, by our own House of Bishops, and later by the all-Anglican Council in their declarations in behalf of unity, and as they have come to be universally regarded, not as a confession of faith, but rather as a monument of obsolete controversies in England, with Protestants on one side and Romanists on the other, the patriarch's objections to them are not to be considered as insurmountable obstacles.

Rome has been wise enough to see that the affiliation of the Eastern and Anglican churches would be a check to her claim to world-wide authority; and her emissaries always have been diligent to imbue the Eastern mind with doubts as to our orders. In this she has been so far successful that until within the last fifty years the Church of England was always classed by theologians of the East with the heretical Protestants; and one difficulty in reaching the mind of the Orthodox churches has been due to their isolation or separation by distance; but now, with more rapid general and frequent communication throughout the world, isolation does not exist, and as we come face to face with the East, difficulties grow less and a better understanding appears.

In 1874 a conference was held at Bonn under the presidency of the learned Dr. von Dollinger, the Old Catholic divine, at which attended several Old Catholics, three Russian, one Greek, and six English ecclesiastics, and "a brotherly concurrence more wide than had been expected was manifested as to several important doctrines." The validity of Anglican orders was one subject of discussion, Dr. von Dollinger declaring for himself and the Old Catholics as a body that they had no shadow of doubt as to their validity. A Russian present remarked that doubt had been expressed in the writings of Philaret; to which Canon Liddon replied that Philaret had told him that he had not examined the question for himself, but had accepted the testimony of Romish writers. The conference *unanimously* adopted this statement: "We agree that the way in which the *filioque* was inserted in the Nicene Creed was illegal; and that with a view to future peace and amity, it is much to be desired that the whole Church should set itself seriously to consider whether the creed could not be restored to its primitive form, without sacrifice of any true doctrine expressed in the Western form."

Perhaps the most interesting presentation of the points of difficulty is that to be found in the conference in England in 1870, between the Archbishop of Syra and the Bishop of Ely with other Anglicans.

The archbishop began by saying that in his opinion their churches were essentially agreed in basis; and he divided the points in which they differed under three heads: (*a*) Things to be corrected; (*b*) Things to be discussed; (*c*) Things to be tolerated. The things to be discussed it appeared were such as would easily result in things capable of toleration by one side or the other. These were, —

1. The number and form of the sacraments. This is merely a question of the definition of the word " sacraments." " Mysteries " is the name used by Easterns, and we should have no hesitation in allowing orders, penance, matrimony, confirmation, and unction to be classed as mysteries or as sacraments not generally necessary to salvation. Of course Syra stood for trine immersion; but inasmuch as affusion is the use in some parts of Eastern churches, and as Russians in our day do not rebaptize converts from Rome, immersion cannot be a *sine qua non;* and it should be remembered that immersion has the precedence in our rubric and is frequently practised in our Church. No other important difference was stated concerning the form of the sacraments.

2. The doctrine of the Holy Eucharist. Syra admitted that the idea of transubstantiation did not appear in Greek theology until the twelfth century; and his statement of his personal belief was not disputed by the English clergymen.

3. The priesthood and the marriage of the clergy. Syra remarked that priests ought to be spiritual enough to abstain from second marriages, and said that English orders had been questioned on account of the second marriages of bishops. He allowed that bishops were married down to the sixth century, and said that their marriage was forbidden partly as a check to nepotism, partly as a concession to Rome, which the Orthodox at that time wished to please. We may infer, then, that there is no reason why the Orthodox should not reverse the rule to please us. returning to the primitive custom, or at least tolerate it in us.

4. (*a*) Invocation of saints. Here, too, was a difference quite capable of toleration. Syra dated the introduction of such invocations from the fourth century. (*b*) Prayers for the dead. Here was no serious difference.

5. Icons and relics. The archbishop was clearly opposed to Eastern practices, but tried to maintain that the veneration of holy pictures might be useful in some regions.

The one only point which appeared definitely to be corrected on our part was the *filioque*. The archbishop owned that the English Church was sound in doctrine, but summed up the Eastern position by saying, "We cannot give up the original creed. . . . It contains the judgment of the Church in council from which the Orthodox cannot swerve."

On his return the Archbishop of Syra reported to the governing Synod of Greece that "in the Anglican Church there existed an ecclesiastical order totally different from other Protestants, and in conformity with the Primitive Church;" and as to the *filioque*, he said it "presents a serious and confessedly formidable difficulty. The English theologians, on the one hand, acknowledge that this addition is unfortunate, and that some unknown hand has put it in the creed; but still they very much hesitate to expunge it, fearing lest by so doing the consciences of men may be troubled, and may then begin to doubt respecting other dogmas of the Church," — and no doubt this statement by the archbishop as to the position of the English theologians is true, for they are a timid folk, and have other obstacles to surmount, growing out of the entangling alliance between Church and State in England.

All of the citations given above point to a gradually increasing amenity. It is evidently not the Eastern Church alone which will have occasion to tolerate. Perhaps the demand upon our charity may be even the greater; but much that we must object to in their practices will pass away with the progress of education in the East, as is evident from the experience of the last fifty years in the Church of Greece. History shows us that the Orthodox churches have often bent to outward influence or internal charity; and while individuals have expressed extreme views, — such as that of the Archbishop of Cavalla, that "according to our doctrine the Pope of Rome himself is neither more nor less than an unbaptized layman, and if he joined our communion would have to be baptized," — the Orthodox Church has been far from rigorous. In 1839 the Roman Church received the most severe check that it had experienced since the time of the Reformation, in the voluntary secession of the whole Uniat Church of Poland, numbering two and a half millions of people, with all their bishops and clergy, many of whom must have been baptized according to the Western custom; but the Orthodox Church imposed no terms of severity, exacted no rebaptism, no reordination, not even confession of error, but only the declaration that "Our LORD JESUS CHRIST is the one true Head of the one true Church." The Uniat Church had never received the *filioque*.

We are urging it upon both Protestants and Papists as a Christian duty to return to the old paths, to consult primitive custom, and to strive for Christian unity on the basis of ancient unity. No doubt there are motes in their eyes, but there is a beam in our own eye. The addition of the words "And the Son" to the creed of the Universal Church is utterly indefensible. It has been declared to be so by papal decision, and by judgment of doctors learned in theology; and it is a simple historical fact. That conservatism which characterizes minds ecclesiastically trained produces hesitation to make so marked a change, and inspires attempts to refine concerning the truth of the doctrine implied by the added words; but it is not a question of truth or untruth that is before us now. However correct may be the doctrine, the words have no business to be in that place in the creed. It was wrong to interpolate any words there; and if it was wrong, why should we not acknowledge the error and return to the original symbol?

We of the American Church are more favorably situated for considering and acting in such cases than is the Church of England. We are hampered by no State alliance, and have no need to obtain the consent of a secular parliament before correcting our formulas or negotiating with other churches; and the American mind, even when ecclesiastically trained, does not abhor change of itself.

Besides, we are not so committed to formulas which oppose Eastern prejudices as is the Church of England. Nobody, cleric or lay, is obliged by our canons to subscribe the Articles of Religion; but our Articles are less open to Eastern objections than those of the English Church, in that we have providentially omitted the Article XXI. of England, which by denying or limiting the authority of General Councils opposes the opinion of the Orthodox Church. Article VII. asserts that the Nicene Creed ought thoroughly to be received and believed; and it cannot be thoroughly received in an erroneous version. In the English Office of the Holy Communion the rubric reads, "And the Gospel ended shall be sung or said, the creed following;" and the creed following contains the *filioque*. In the same place in the American office the rubric reads, "Then shall be read the Apostles' or Nicene Creed;" and we are nowhere compelled to use the *filioque*.[1]

The Invocation which in the Orthodox churches is considered essential for the transmutation of the elements at the Eucharist, is not to be found, in a distinct form, in the offices of the Roman or English Church, and it is in the American Liturgy.

Again, the tendency to fraternization between the Eastern and the English churches, has no doubt been checked by the political antagonism existing between Russia and Great Britain, and their political rivalry in the East. Russia, comprising as it does more than two thirds of the Orthodox, has for a long time been the champion of the Eastern churches as against Mahometanism; while Great Britain is a Mahometan power in India, and has been the chief supporter of the Turks in Europe. This relation of the two powers to the Moslems has been an element of political strength in the East, which Russia is not anxious to lose, and which affiliation of the churches would weaken, if not destroy.

We in America not only have no such obstacle to overcome, but our relations with Russia are so friendly as to preclude prejudice; and our position in other Eastern countries is so negative as to forbid jealousies. May it not be, then, that the way for an alliance between the Anglican communion and the Holy Eastern Church will be opened by the precedence of the Church in America?

No doubt there will be obstacles to be surmounted. No doubt there will be occasion for toleration on both sides, perhaps on our part more than on the other; but there would be

---

[1] This was true when written, but since then the General Convention, notwithstanding its expressed desire for Christian Unity on the basis of the Nicene Creed, has for the first time ordered the insertion of the *filioque* in the Communion Office, thus adding a new obstacle to unity with what is by far the largest body of Christians outside of the Roman obedience.

no occasion for either church to change any of its ceremonies, either to discontinue any that it now uses or to adopt any from the other. The only serious change on our part, if indeed it would be a change, would be our adoption of the Nicene Creed in its true and original version. The space which separates us from the East is by no means so great as that which divides us from the Protestant denominations, and the basis of the recent declaration of our bishops would no doubt be accepted by the Orthodox churches.

What the desired unity would be was stated by Theophilus, Metropolitan of Athens in 1872, in these well-chosen words:

Unity, then, and union with the Orthodox Church, is not a fusion or a taking away of the national and ethical diversity inwrought by GOD ; it is not a slavish subjection of some to others; it is not a despotic raising up or a tyrannical levelling of national peculiarities and differences, but a certain brotherly harmonious binding together of spirit, manifested through a common creed, voluntarily accepted, of the fundamentals of the faith which the Divine Scriptures, the Apostolic Tradition, and the Œcumenical Councils of the undivided Church have defined for us. Those who in all places are thus bound one to another realize the ONE HOLY CATHOLIC AND APOSTOLIC CHURCH.

FRANCIS J. PARKER.

The Petrine Claims.

The Petrine Claims. A Critical Inquiry by RICHARD FREDERICK LITTLEDALE, LL.D., D.C.L. London: Society for Promoting Christian Knowledge. New York: E. & J. B. Young & Co. 1889.

THE REV. DR. LITTLEDALE is already the author of by far the best popular treatise to put into the hands of Church people who may find themselves befogged by any *ad captandum* arguments on the part of the Church of Rome. His *Plain Reasons Against Joining the Church of Rome*—the work to which we refer—is compendious in form, lively and interesting in style, very moderate in price, and unanswerable in its statement of facts. The attempt of Father Ryder, even with the subterranean assistance of Cardinal Newman himself, to answer this little book, was a total failure; though the attempt was a solid recognition of the importance of the work, which it thus did *not* dispose of. A few pages were all that Dr. Littledale needed in reply.

His present work, on *The Petrine Claims*, is of a very different scope. Instead of comparing the Anglican and Roman positions, he now does what our controversialists have seldom done. Instead of simply defending our own position, Dr. Littledale boldly carries the war into Africa, and shows that the Romanists themselves, on the requirements of their own Canon Law, have not a leg to stand on; that their whole succession came to an end four hundred years ago, and that there can be found no possible mode of starting it afresh! And he not only asserts this, but he *proves* it, by the Roman Canon Law itself, by Roman historians, and by the Bulls of Roman Popes.

But this, though the conclusion, is by no means all. He traces the question fully from the beginning, showing that the case is deficient in *every point* required for the establishment of a valid " privilege," according to the Roman Canon

Law itself: and that there have been quite a number of breaks—even if there had been anything to begin with—besides the last, and longest, and most complete of all.

This work has been so admirably and so thoroughly done, that we should be glad to give a condensed statement of the whole process: but our space will hardly permit of that.

In the "Preface," Dr. Littledale points out that this book "does not touch the theological side of the matters in debate, save incidentally and subordinately; and is *solely* occupied with the *legal* aspect of the claim laid by the Papacy to sovereign authority over the Church Universal." He goes on to say:

For this claim is much more than a mere speculative theory, or even than a dogmatic principle; it is a *legal maxim* of the widest range and the most detailed application, directly affecting every matter and every act within the spiritual domain, whether belonging to the sphere of faith or to that of discipline. The questions of the authority of Creeds and Councils, of the competence of all ecclesiastical officers, of the valid administration of Sacraments, of the legitimacy of forms of devotion, of the terms of Communion requisite to Church membership, and all cognate ones, are inextricably bound up with this single proposition, which is thus of *supreme legal importance*.

This being so, and the 'Privilege of Peter' being alleged as conveying no mere honorary Primacy, but as concentrating the whole government and jurisdiction over the Church Universal in the person of the Pope for the time being, it is removed from the sphere of dogma and from that of speculation into that of practical and legal action, and therefore must be examined and tested by legal methods, in order to ascertain its credentials.

The claim usually takes two forms : that it is based on and warranted by a Divine Charter, contained in Holy Scripture ; and that it has been in fact enjoyed and exercised, with the full recognition and approval of ancient Christendom, for a period so long and unbroken as to add a title by prescription to reinforce that conferred by the original charter.

The following pages are exclusively concerned with an investigation of these two theses, in their Scriptural, conciliar, and historical aspects; and the *principles* laid down by the *Roman Canon Law* have been *applied throughout* to guide the inquiry and determine the conclusions on *purely legal* grounds, as open to less dispute, and admitting of less evasion than the theological treatment of the controversy has usually proved.

We have here quoted the "Preface" *almost entire*, as giving, so clearly and succinctly, the leading difference between this work on *The Petrine Claims*, and our usual books of controversy against Rome. The issue is made more narrow, more definite, and more decisive than in any other we know of.

The first chapter is devoted to the Legal Evidence of Scripture, first setting down the teaching of the Council of Trent, and that of the Vatican, and the Creed of Pope Pius IV about Holy Scripture, the "unanimous consent of the Fathers," and the infallibility of the Pope. As to this last, the author says:

> As the entire claim of Papal Infallibility rests avowedly on asserted heirship to S. Peter, and right of succession to all his privileges, while no allegation is made that those privileges have been specifically re-granted to any Pope since his time, much less increased, developed, and amplified in any manner, it follows that the Pope can claim no more than is plainly discoverable as conferred upon and exercised by S. Peter himself. But the whole of the evidence now extant upon this head is confined to the books of the New Testament. The few meagre and uncertain notices of S. Peter's life which have come to us from uninspired writers, do not touch this question of his primacy, jurisdiction, and transmission of his powers at all. Consequently, the Gospel, Acts and Epistles contain not only his whole charter of privilege, but our whole means of ascertaining what he actually enjoyed and exercised in virtue of that charter.

It is indisputable, therefore, that the Roman claims—if they have any firm basis—must establish clearly and expressly, not by mere possible implication or inference, the following points:

> (1) That S. Peter was given, by CHRIST, a primacy, not of honor and rank alone, but of direct and sovereign jurisdiction over all the other Apostles.
>
> (2) That this primacy was not limited to S. Peter's person only for his lifetime, but was conferred on him with power to bequeath it to his successors.

And now we come to the bed-rock of the peculiarity of this entire book—the testing of the "Privilege of Peter." It is the phrase, not of *our* theologians, but of the Roman advocates themselves—their favorite phrase. Dr. Littledale contends that "an exclusively Roman claim" cannot reasonably or even plausibly refuse to be tested by *the Roman Canon Law itself*; as, for instance, by pleading that the Petrine Privilege, being older than the Canon Law, cannot be subject to its rules. for, as he says, the question is as to the devolution of this privilege *to the reigning Pope*, whose claim to it *must* be subject to the tests of contemporary

Canon Law; especially since the claim itself was not formulated definitely till the fifth century. He says also:

> The reason why the proof of it needs to be express and clear, is because *privilege*, being a private exception to the usual public course of law, either in the form of exemption from some burden generally imposed, or of enjoyment of some benefit generally withheld, is *essentially an invidious thing*, and requires *fuller proof than any other right* before it can be allowed as valid. Consequently, the Roman Canon Law has laid down the following broad rules (among others) to govern all cases of the sort :

Let the reader now mark well these *Seven Roman Rules*, which apply to all cases of *Privilege :*

(1) The authoritative document containing the privilege must be produced. [*Decret. Greg. IX.*]

(2) Its wording must be certain and manifest, not obscure or doubtful. [*Decret. Greg. IX.*]

(3) It must be construed in the most strict and literal sense. [*Reg. Juris.; Fagnan. de Past. et Prælat.; Zypæus de Privil. Consult.*]

(4) If personal, it follows the person [not the office]; and it dies with the person named in it. [*Boniface VIII.*]

(5) It may not be extended to any other person, because of identity or similarity of reason, unless such extension be expressly named in it. [*Decret. Greg. IX.*]

(6) It may not be so interpreted as to deny, interfere with, or encroach upon the rights and privileges of another. [*Decret. Greg. IX.*]

(7) It is forfeited by any excess or abuse in its exercise. [*Decret. ii, xi, 3, lx.*]

To one at all familiar with the Roman controversy, the tremendously destructive range of these Seven Rules, taken from the Roman Canon Law, is manifest at the first sight. They sweep the whole Roman fabric out of sight, like a house of cards. And this destructive sweeping is done with their own broom!

Dr. Littledale then quotes in full the three chief passages of Holy Scripture relied upon by Roman writers in proof of the Privilege of Peter: "Thou art Peter" etc., "When thou art converted, strengthen thy brethren," and "Feed my lambs, feed my sheep," showing how utterly they fail to comply with the Seven Rules, and giving further evidence besides of the impossibility of the Roman interpretation being the right one. In connection with the "Feed my sheep," Dr. Littledale alludes to S. Peter's question, almost immediately after, about S. John: "LORD, and what shall this man do?" with our LORD's reply, "What is that to thee?" and adds:

> It is obvious that if S. Peter had received jurisdiction over S. John only a few minutes before, his question was perfectly legitimate and reasonable, and merited a reply, as being his concern, because affecting one for whom he had just been made responsible. But the answer he actually receives can denote nothing short of S. John's entire independence, and the restriction of S. Peter's own commission to attending to his own specific and limited share of Apostolic work, with no right of control over S. John.

In commenting on the foundation on which the Church is built, it seems to us that Dr. Littledale might have made his position still stronger. He says, truly enough, that "even if we take S. Peter to be the rock, it appears that even this title does not stand alone in such sort as to constitute a gift of sovereign authority. For this same attribute of being foundations of the Church is in two other places ascribed to the Apostles generally, once by S. Paul: 'Now therefore ye are no more strangers and foreigners, but fellow-citizens with the saints, and of the household of GOD; and are built upon the foundation of the Apostles and Prophets, JESUS CHRIST himself being the chief cornerstone; in Whom all the building fitly framed together groweth unto an holy temple in the LORD " [*Eph.* ii, 19-21]; and again by S. John: 'And the wall of the city had twelve foundations, and in them the names of the twelve Apostles of the Lamb' [*Rev.* xxi, 14]; where, moreover," says Dr. Littledale, "it is not unworthy of notice, that the *first* stone, a jasper, is much inferior in beauty and value to some of the remainder, as the sapphire, emerald, and chrysolite which severally form the second, fourth, and seventh foundations." [*Rev.* xxi, 19-20.]

This word "foundation" is used in two very different senses, which must be carefully distinguished. One is, the great bed-rock, the Deity of the Son of GOD:—"Other foundation can no man lay than that is laid, which is JESUS CHRIST, the same yesterday, and to-day, and forever." The whole Church, the House of GOD, the living Temple, is built upon that Rock. The other sense is, not that Rock itself, but the first part of *the wall* that is *built* upon that Rock. It is in *this* sense that we read of the Church as being "built upon the foundation of the Apostles and Prophets," and, as above, of the "twelve foundations" in which are "the names of the twelve Apostles of the Lamb."

The former sense gives us the Deity of the Son of GOD, which S. Peter had just confessed: "Thou art the CHRIST, the *Son of the living* GOD." And *this* was the Rock of Deity on which the whole Church was to be builded. But where do we find the humanity of CHRIST in this great work? As *Man*, he is the corner-stone, the head-stone of the corner, the first stone laid in the foundation *wall*. This is in *exact* accordance with the language of S. Paul, who, after mentioning that we are "built upon the foundation of the Apostles and Prophets," immediately adds: "JESUS CHRIST *Himself* being the *chief corner-stone*," namely, of that same foundation wall. So that His Deity is the foundation of bed-rock on which the whole foundation rests: and His Humanity is the "chief corner-stone" of the wall built upon that Rock.

This then would make the *jasper*, which is the first stone of the twelve foundations, to signify, not S. Peter, but CHRIST Himself. It may not be so beautiful or so costly as some of the other stones mentioned. It was said of Him: "He hath no form nor comeliness; and when we shall see Him, there is no beauty that we should desire Him." But jasper is of the color of blood—the blood of His Atonement. And it is the jeweller's *touchstone*, by which the true quality of the precious metals is tested. Moreover, we find the statement, just *before* the enumeration of the twelve foundations, that the *entire wall*, resting upon the twelve foundations, was of this same "*jasper*:" "And he measured the wall thereof an hundred and forty and four cubits, according to the measure of a man, that is, of the angel. And the building of the wall of it was of *jasper*." Now we have heard of Romanists claiming from this that communion with the See of Peter was necessary; and it would look like it, if the "jasper" signifies S. Peter. But if the jasper is CHRIST, the understanding of the whole is much easier: for every baptised person is surely made thereby a "member of CHRIST," and therefore a part of the jasper wall.

But we never heard of anybody being made a "member of S. Peter."

One thing more. In the opening of the fourth chapter of the Revelation we read: "And immediately I was in the Spirit; and behold, a throne was set in Heaven, and One sat on the throne. And he that sat was to look upon *like a jasper* and a sardine stone. And round about the throne were the four and twenty elders sitting, clothed in white, and on their heads crowns of gold. And before the throne were the seven lamps of fire burning, which are the Seven Spirits of GOD. And before the throne was the sea of glass, like unto crystal. And the four living creatures, each of them with six wings, and full of eyes within, rest not day and night, saying: Holy, Holy, Holy, Lord GOD Almighty, which was, and is, and is to come!" Will any one dare to say that all this proves that *S. Peter* was upon that throne, because the *jasper* means S. Peter? Even papal blasphemy will hardly go as far as that, although Pius IX *did* assume to himself the words, "I am the Way, the Truth, and the Life."

To go back now to the beautiful words of S. Paul. He says that we are "built upon the *foundation* of the Apostles and Prophets, JESUS CHRIST Himself being the chief cornerstone:" and then he goes straight on: "In Whom"—that is, in JESUS CHRIST, not in S. Peter—in CHRIST, "*all the building*, fitly framed together, groweth unto an holy temple in the LORD." This covers the great bulk of the jasper wall. All the building is "fitly framed together" in CHRIST —not in S. Peter. It "groweth unto an holy temple *in the* LORD"—not in S. Peter. Holy Scripture is in perfect harmony with itself. But the Roman interpretation of these texts puts them in irreconcilable contradiction with similar expressions everywhere else in the Bible.

In the full discussion of the crucial text, "Thou art Peter, and upon this Rock I will build my Church," Dr. Littledale is peculiarly strong and clear. Cardinal Bellarmine was the author of an ingenious argument in favor of Rome. He *assumed* that our LORD was talking Syriac; and assured us that in Syriac there was only one word to represent the Greek *Petros* (Peter) and *Petra* (a rock). So that when our LORD said to Peter: "Thou art *Kipha*, and upon this *Kipha* I will build my Church," there could be no doubt that he meant what the Romanists would like to have him mean. This ingenious *guess* is unanswerably met by Dr. Littledale thus:

> The reply is direct and conclusive, that both the Hebrew *Cepha* and the Peshittâ Syriac Kiphâ, when they mean rock or stone, are of the feminine gender, which *Cephas* or *Peter*, as a masculine noun denoting a man's name, certainly is not, either in Syriac or Greek; and in the ancient Syriac version of this very passage, *S. Matt.* xvi, 18 (doubtless the most trustworthy gloss obtainable), the *feminine* pronoun is found united with the second *Cepha*.

Our Roman friends will therefore be compelled to abandon Cardinal Bellarmine's ingenious guess, unless they are prepared to assert that S. Peter was a *woman*, and that Pope Joan is the only *legitimate* successor of S. Peter on record! Yet Dr. Döllinger has proved that Pope Joan is a myth!

In considering [page 58] whether the "Babylon" mentioned at the close of S. Peter's first Epistle is the geographical Babylon on the Euphrates—a great stronghold of the Jews at that time—or is used mystically for "Rome," one consideration is omitted, which has always seemed to us conclusive against the Roman hypothesis. In Holy Scripture, whenever a number of different nations, countries or provinces is mentioned, the *order* is, to begin with that which is geographically nearest to the writer at his time of writing, and to end with the more remote. This order is the natural order, and it is *never* reversed. In S. Peter's Epistle, at the opening, he addresses it "to the strangers scattered throughout Pontus, Galatia, Cappadocia, Asia, and Bithynia," which is the *natural* order to one writing from Babylon on the Euphrates, for Pontus is the nearest to that Babylon; and Asia (the proconsular province of that name, which contained all the "Seven Churches of Asia" mentioned by S. John in the Apocalypse, and was at the western end of what we call *Asia Minor*) and Bithynia, were the most remote from Babylon, and therefore are mentioned *last*.

The chapter on the "Legal Evidence of Scripture" ends thus:

> So far, then, as the Papal claim is alleged to be of Divine Privilege, given by revelation, the Scriptures, treated as the chief document in evidence of claim, fail to satisfy the requirements of Roman Canon Law; for (1) they afford *no testimony whatever* as to the annexation of privilege to the Roman See, or its transmission from S. Peter to *any* of his successors; (2) the evidence as to his own primacy is obscurely and enigmatically worded; (3) so far as its wording does go, it is a personal, not an official, grant, and thus dies with the original grantee; (4) if continued in the Ultramontane sense, it encroaches on S. Paul's privileges, which are more clearly worded.
>
> Wherever the proof may be found, therefore, it is *certainly not* in the Scriptures.

The next point taken up is the "Legal Evidence of Liturgies and Fathers."

In the Liturgies, there is found much that, directly and indirectly, destroys the Roman claim. For instance:

In the Liturgy of S. James, or norm of Palestine, we find: "For the stablishing of Thy Holy Catholic Church, which *Thou hast founded on the rock of the faith*, that the gates of hell may not prevail against it:" which is not exactly the same as the Roman idea that the Church was founded on S. Peter. And we also find supplication made "Especially for the glorious Zion, *the Mother of all the Churches*," which is rather different from the idea that *Rome* is the Mother and Mistress of all the Churches.

In the Liturgy of S. Mark, the first place in the commemoration of ecclesiastical persons, is assigned to the Pope or Patriarch of *Alexandria* (not Rome) who is described in one passage as "pre-ordained to rule over Thy Holy, Catholic and Apostolic Church:" but not one word about the Pope of Rome!

But the strongest of all is the Roman Liturgy itself, which, in the Collect for the Vigils of SS. Peter and Paul runs thus:

> Grant, we beseech Thee, Almighty GOD, that thou wouldst not suffer us, whom Thou hast established *upon the rock of the Apostolic confession*, to be shaken by any disturbances," etc.

Even the Council of Trent itself, in its solemn decree upon the Symbol of Faith, speaks thus, after a long preamble:

Wherefore it (the Council) judged that the symbol of the Faith, which the Holy Roman Church uses, should be set forth in the full wording whereby it is read in all the Churches, as that principle in which all who confess the faith of CHRIST must needs agree, and as the *firm and only foundation, against which the gates of hell shall not prevail*, which is of this sort : " I believe in one GOD," etc.

Now, seeing that one clause of the Creed of Pope Pius IV binds all who accept it, to receive all the "apostolic and ecclesiastical traditions, and other observances and constitutions of the same (holy Roman) Church; and another binds him to the definitions of the Councils, and chiefly that of Trent: it follows that *no Romanist* is *free to hold that S. Peter* was "the *rock.*" He *must*—under pain of *anathema*—believe that the *faith*, or the *Creed*, is the "Rock" against which the gates of hell shall not prevail!

The summing up of the Liturgical Evidence is as follows:

The Liturgical Evidence is thus shown to be either positively against the Petrine Claims, or negatively incapable of being cited in their favor, although it is quite certain that, if any such view of S. Peter's peculiar rank as Head of the Church and Vicar of CHRIST had prevailed as unquestionably did prevail touching S. John Baptist's exceptional position as herald and forerunner of CHRIST, we should find abundant and conclusive proof of it in the Liturgies.

In passing from the Liturgies to the Fathers in general, Dr. Littledale confines himself mainly to citations from those who are recognized as " Doctors of the Church," whose authority is not open to criticism from Roman Catholics: and he reminds us—not for the first time—that "nothing short of the *unanimous consent* of the Fathers may lawfully be followed by any Roman Catholic in the interpretation of Scripture "—so says the Creed of Pope Pius IV. And in his summing up of this branch of the evidence, he shows that there is not merely no "unanimous consent" of the Fathers in favor of Peter being the Rock, but there is a powerful preponderance of adverse testimony. Only *seventeen* are for the Roman view, against *forty-four* who take the opposite, besides *eight* others who take *all* the Apostles to be the Rock: while there is *not one*, of the whole of them, who adds anything to connect the text with the Bishop of Rome as successor or heir of S. Peter!

As to another of the three chief Roman texts: "when thou art converted, strengthen thy brethren," Dr. Littledale tells us, that of *twenty* patristic citations made by Bellarmine in favor of his view, *all* are quoted *as from Popes*, and *eighteen* of the twenty are from the *False Decretals!*

We cannot resist the temptation to a long extract closing the Scriptural and patristic part of the examination. But then it is so clear and good, and the illustrations from modern usage are so apt!

> Thus an examination of the glosses of the Fathers on the three texts alleged for the Petrine Privilege results in one of two issues. Either *there was no such privilege*, as distinguished from the joint powers of the Apostolate, conferred upon S. Peter at all; or else—and this is the better way—his special privilege was limited to preaching the first Pentecostal sermon, and afterwards converting Cornelius—events which are absolutely incapable of repetition: even GOD HIMSELF (if it be lawful to say so) not being able to recall the past, so that no one else, after S. Peter had once done these two things, could be *the first* to teach Jews or Gentiles; just as no Pope can follow S. Peter in being *first* to confess Christ. No other distinction is named by the ancient Fathers, is claimed by S. Peter himself [*Acts* xv, 7], or is discoverable in Holy Writ. And, consequently, if this be the privilege of Peter, it did not merely die with him, but was possible for even himself to exercise not more than twice in his lifetime, so that is absolutely incommunicable and intransmissible, and incapable of serving as a precedent for any claim whatsoever based on alleged succession to his authority and primacy. If it could be strained to mean anything it would be that each Pope must needs start as a missionary pioneer to some country or nation which had not yet received the Gospel. But no Pope has ever done so. With this collapse of the alleged evidence, the *whole case* for the Divine character of the Roman privilege is *really gone*, and no mind trained in the investigation of testimony, and free from overpowering bias, can do other than dismiss it.

But what about the high-sounding, complimentary titles that are given to S. Peter in many ancient writings, which are *said* to imply some authority over the other Apostles? Is he not styled sometimes—especially from the fourth century, and by Eastern writers—"prince," "head," "president," "captain," and the like? Do these prove nothing? Hear the reply:

> Now what these epithets (none of which, by-the-bye, is found until the fourth century) *prove*, is the high estimation in which the ancient Church held S. Peter, and the fact that it believed him to enjoy some priority amongst the Apostles. They would be important evidence against any attempt to maintain that, owing to S. Peter's fall and denial, he had, in the belief of

early Christians, forfeited his office irreparably (as a strict Novatian might have taught), and had been looked on with a suspicion extending not merely to his rank, but to his teaching, such as we know to have existed against S. Paul.

What they do *not* prove, nor even seem to prove, is the Divine grant of *supreme jurisdiction*. For they are not authoritative titles, either found in Holy Scripture, or conferred by conciliar decree. The fact that nothing in the smallest degree resembling even the least exalted of them is discoverable in the New Testament deprives them of the mark of revelation; the fact that they are not common to the whole Church, leaves them without that of universal consent. They bestow nothing, and they define nothing. But what we are in search of is *an express bestowal of exceptional privilege*, as *divinely revealed* and *clearly defined*.

The matter may be illustrated thus: The title of Great *or* Grand Duke, in modern Europe, means one of two things, either sovereign authority, as in the case of the Grand Dukes of Baden, Saxe-Weimar, Oldenburg, Hesse, and the two Mecklenburgs, or else membership of the Russian Imperial family. But the celebrated Duke of Wellington was and is known as the Great Duke, and is frequently so described in English literature, notably in the Laureate's funeral ode. Let us suppose the case of a remote successor of his in the dukedom claiming this epithet as hereditary, and as conferring sovereign power, imperial rank, or even precedence, over all other English Dukes. How would it be treated? Not by a denial of the fact that the epithet was applied to the first Duke of Wellington, nor yet by an attempt to explain away the epithet itself as a mere piece of rhetoric—rather admitting its entire fitness—but by examining the original patent of the dukedom, in order to ascertain if a clause embodying this particular distinction were part of it. And, on its absence being certified, it would be at once ruled that, however deserved the epithet might be, it was not conferred by any authority capable of bestowing either civil power or social precedence, and must therefore be regarded as a mere personal token of popular admiration, conferring no rights whatever on its subject. Nor would the case for the claim to sovereign rank be mended by advancing proof that the first Duke of Wellington was Prime Minister of the Crown for part of his life, and Commander-in-Chief for a much longer period. For it would have to be shown, in the first place, that these posts connoted irresponsibility to any superior; and in the next, that the patents which bestowed them made them hereditary, and not merely personal. But in S. Peter's case, we have the original Divine patent, in which no clause of superiority or transmissibility occurs, and no expressions of individual human respect can read an additional title, article or section, into it.

In the second place, the great majority of these epithets occur in documents of the Eastern Church, which has never at any time admitted the Roman claims of supremacy, and which therefore obviously puts no such interpretation on its own language. The Western titles of S. Peter are fewer, and far less imposing.

And thirdly, not only are equally strong phrases used concerning S. John, and yet more forcible ones concerning S. James, but nearly every one of these special ones is applied to S. Paul as well as to S. Peter; so that even in the modern Roman Church they are grouped together as 'Princes of the Apostles.' So, too, when the full heraldic titles of an English Duke are set forth, he is described as the High, Puissant, and most Noble Prince—words which scarcely seem to allow of rivalry, but which are common to every Peer of the same grade; while all Dukes have to yield precedence to a mere Baron who happens to be Lord Chancellor, President of the Council, or Lord Privy Seal.

In a note, Dr. Littledale enumerates some of the sounding titles given by the Fathers to other Apostles than S. Peter—titles about which our Roman controversialists are singularly silent, while they pick out everything of the sort that they can find about S. Peter. For instance, S. Chrysostom speaks of the "pillar of *all the Churches throughout the world*, who hath the keys of the Kingdom of Heaven." If this had been said about S. Peter, we should never hear the last of it, as a proof of the universal sovereignty claimed for S. Peter. But as S. Chrysostom uses these words about *S. John*, the case is totally changed, and these strong words mean—*nothing at all*. So, again, the same eloquent Saint speaks of another Apostle as "the type of the world," "the light of the Churches," "the basis of the faith," "the pillar and ground of the truth;" which would mean full Ultramontanism *if* they were said of *S. Peter*; but as they are only said of S. Paul, they go for nothing. S. James, too, is called "bishop of bishops," in another place, "prince of bishops," in yet another, "bishop of the Apostles," and again, "chief captain of the New Jerusalem," "leader of the priests," "prince (exarch) of the Apostles," "summit of the heights," etc., all of which would be splendid jewels in the tiara of S. Peter; but, being only said of S. James, they all go for nothing.

The investigation of the three most ancient and important sources of testimony, Holy Scripture, early Liturgies, and the comments of the Fathers on the Petrine texts in the Gospels, having thus resulted in a clear failure to establish the "Petrine Claims," our author next turns to the "Legal Evidence of Conciliar Decrees." He begins by quoting the clause from the Creed of Pope Pius IV:

I likewise undoubtingly receive and profess all other things delivered, defined and declared by the Sacred Canons and General Councils, and especially by the Holy Council of Trent; and I condemn, reject and anathematize all things contrary thereto.

To this he adds the famous profession of S. Gregory the Great, embodied in the Canon Law, in which he receives the first four General Councils as he does the Four Gospels. And also, the solemn profession made by every Pope at his elevation, which is this:

> The eight Holy General Councils—that is, Nice first, Constantinople second, Ephesus third, Chalcedon fourth, Constantinople fifth and sixth, Nice seventh, and Constantinople eighth—I profess with mouth and heart to be kept unaltered in a single tittle [*usque ad unum apicem immutilata servari*], to account them worthy of equal honor and veneration, to follow, in every respect, whatsoever they promulgated or decreed, and to condemn whatsoever they condemned.

The Apostolic Canons, the most ancient of all, are of course silent about the Papacy. They say:

> It is fit that the Bishops of *each nation* should recognize their Primate, and treat him as Head, and do nothing of moment without his assent . . . . But neither let him [the Primate] do aught without the assent of all; for so shall there be concord, and GOD shall be glorified through the LORD in the Holy Spirit.

This is the rule throughout the entire Anglican Communion. We cannot allude here to all the Councils mentioned by Dr. Littledale: but there is a very important passage in regard to the famous third Canon of the Council of Sardica, which the Popes of Rome, on four different occasions, in four different places, and at four different times, tried to palm off as a Canon of the Great Council of Nice. Every time the fraud was exposed: yet with brazen front the attempt was renewed, whenever a difference of place or circumstance held out a fresh chance of success. That third Canon runs thus:

> If in any province a Bishop have a dispute with a brother Bishop, let neither of them call in a Bishop from another province as arbiter; but if any Bishop be cast in any suit, and think his case good, so that the judgment ought to be reviewed, if it please you, let us honor the memory of S. Peter the Apostle, and let those who have tried the cause write to Julius, Bishop of Rome, that if needful he may provide for a rehearing of the cause by the Bishops nearest to the province, and send arbiters; or if it cannot be established that the matter needs reversal, then what has been decided is not to be rescinded, but the existing state of things is to be confirmed.

Besides this Canon 3, their Canon 4 provides that a Bishop, deposed by a local Synod and appealing to Rome, shall not have his see filled up till the Pope has confirmed the sentence ; and their Canon 5 empowers the Pope either to commit the rehearing to the Bishops of the neighboring Province, or to send a legate of his own to rehear the cause. Now this Council of Sardica was held in the year 347, and yet these canons were never heard of until the year 419—*seventy-two years after*, and *then* the Pope tried to palm them off as *Nicene !* Even if genuine, they died with Pope Julius, according to the rules of the Roman Canon Law concerning privilege: "If personal, it follows the person (not the office); and it dies with the person named in it." *Julius* is the person *named*, and no one else. Also, "It may not be extended to any other person, because of identity or similarity of reason, unless such *extension* be *expressly named* in it." There is no extension expressly named in the Canon, nor even the least hint of such a thing. Therefore the Canon died with Pope Julius, more than 1,500 years ago. But Dr. Littledale has something yet more damaging to say about these famous Canons :

> No satisfactory evidence exists for the *authenticity* of these Canons, and there is much reason for suspecting them to be a sheer fabrication at Rome. For no hint of their existence occurs till they were falsely alleged in 419 as *Nicene* Canons by the Papal Legate at Carthage, while the African Bishops contented themselves with disproving that one fiction, but evidently knew nothing else whatever about them, not being able to assign them even to Sardica, obviously because they had never heard of them before ; whereas the invariable rule of the time was to send the Acts and Canons of Synods of more than provincial character round to all the great Churches for approval ; so that the Sardican Canons, if genuine at all, must have been known at Carthage, at any rate by 424, after attention there had been drawn to them five years previously, and a consequent search made, supposing no earlier information to have been accessible, as there *must have been*, since *Aratus of Carthage was at Sardica ;* and would have brought back any Canons.
>
> What is more, there is entire silence on this head in the Acts of Constantinople in 381, and of Chalcedon in 451, albeit both dealing with the question of appellate jurisdiction ; nor does S. Athanasius refer to these Canons. And though S. Augustine's silence may be explained away on the ground that he mixes up the Council of Sardica with the seceding Arian Synod of Philippopolis, no such excuse accounts for the equal silence of SS. Basil and Epiphanius, and of the three great ecclesiastical historians of the time, Socrates, Sozomen, and Theodoret, none of whom know of any Sardican document except the Synodical epistle. Seeing that the Canons, if genuine, altered for the West the system of appeals which had prevailed in the Church

up to that time, based as it was on the rule of the civil code that all cases should be ended where they originated, their legal and historical importance is such that this unbroken silence is nearly unaccountable. Nor is any example known of their having been avowedly acted on anywhere in the West—precisely where the canons of the Council must have been known and in many provincial archives, whereas they are *cited* only in *Papal* missives to Churches *whose Bishops were not at Sardica*. And as their Nicene character was alleged for the *fourth* time so late as 484 by Felix II, in his dispute with Acacius of Constantinople, it is obvious that this persistence in one falsehood makes the presence of another more likely. No one at Rome could have honestly believed them to be Nicene, because they expressly *name* Pope *Julius*, who did not begin to sit till 337, *twelve years after the Council of Nice* (a few Latin MSS. have *Silvester* here, an obviously fraudulent correction). The policy of urging them as Canons of a great Council like Sardica, when it proved impossible to gain credit for them as Nicene, is so evident that its not being adopted prompts a suspicion that they were well known at Rome not to be decrees of any Council whatever, so that any strict inquiry must tend to the same result, and that being so, it was more politic to keep up the Nicene claim. No Greek text is known earlier than the sixth century, and a very suspicious circumstance marks the three oldest Latin texts, the *Prisca*, that of Dionysius Exiguus, and the true Isidore. These, as a rule, give independent and various translations of all Greek Canons, but *they agree verbally for the so-called Sardican Canons*. The inference is, that there was never a Greek original at all, but only a Latin forgery. If so, *the whole fabric of Papal appeals falls*, for it has no other basis. Indeed, the non-Sardican origin of these Canons has been strongly asserted of late by a learned Italian theologian, Aloysius Vincenzi, in his treatise, *De Hebræorum et Christianorum Sacra Monarchia*, Vatican Press, 1875, who places them considerably later, and inclines to think them African.

The well-known case of Apiarius, an immoral African priest, who persuaded Pope Zosimus to back him up in an attempt to overrule the African decision against him, is thoroughly discussed by Dr. Littledale. It was in this contest that the Pope tried to pass off the so-called Sardican Canons as *Nicene*. The African Bishops at once challenged their authenticity, and sent special messengers all the way to Alexandria, Antioch, and Constantinople, and *all* the attested copies in these cities demonstrated the fraud of the Pope. They enacted a new Canon at once, forbidding all appeals beyond sea, or to any authority save African Councils and Primates, *under pain of excommunication throughout Africa*. And, finally,

> The Council sent a synodical letter to Pope Boniface by two legates, complaining of his conduct in reinstating Apiarius, disputing the genuineness of

the Canons alleged by Faustinus (the Bishop whom the Pope had sent on this business), and telling the Pope in the plainest language that nothing should make them tolerate his conduct, or suffer such insolence (*typhum superbiæ*) at the hand of his emissaries—a protest virtually aimed at himself, who had commissioned and despatched them. One of the signatories of this epistle was *S. Augustine*.

Just think of S. Augustine—that great saint—signing a letter like this addressed to the Pope of Rome of his day! And very probably he was the *writer* of it as well.

But the Pope stuck to his miserable Apiarius, who had been a *second* time deposed for immorality. It was Celestine I who undertook to rehabilitate him this time, and to send him back to Africa, with the same Bishop Faustinus, to obtain his reinstatement there. But his guilt was proved at the Council by his own confession, and his degradation confirmed:

> Hereupon the Fathers wrote to Pope Celestine, telling him that they had ascertained that the alleged Nicene Canons were not of that Council at all; that the Pope had transgressed the genuine Nicene Canons by interfering in another province; and that they could find no authority for his undertaking to send legates to them, or any other Churches, so that they begged him to refrain from doing so in future, for fear the Church should suffer through pride and ambition : and added that they were quite competent, with the aid of the Holy Spirit, to manage their own affairs on the spot, better than he, with less local knowledge, could do for them at Rome, ending by telling him that they had had quite enough of Faustinus, and wanted no more of him.

That was the outspoken and manly way in which the Church of North Africa resisted and repudiated the meddling of the Pope, when he first began to do business in that line. Would that *all* National Churches had had the courage to keep it up in the same strain!

The third General Council met at Ephesus only seven years later, in 431, and seems to give us a distinct echo of this African business in its Canon VIII, which enacts that no Bishop shall invade any province which was not from the beginning under his jurisdiction or that of his predecessors:

> And if any should so occupy one, or forcibly subject it to himself, let him make personal restitution, lest the statutes of the Fathers should be violated, *and lest the pride of power should creep in under the pretext of a sacred office*, and thus we might unknowingly and gradually *lose that freedom* which JESUS CHRIST our LORD and SAVIOUR of all men obtained for us with His precious blood, and bestowed upon us.

The next General Council, of Chalcedon, in 451—only twenty years later—gives further and unanswerable proof of the same great contest. The *Tome* of Leo—after full and close examination—was accepted as the correct statement of the doctrinal issue then pending. But as to disciplinary authority, the celebrated Canon XXVIII was the heaviest blow the rising Roman ambition had yet received:

> The Fathers with good reason bestowed precedency on the chair of Old Rome, *because it was the imperial city*, and the 150 God-beloved Bishops [the Council of Constantinople], moved by the same view, conferred *equal precedence* on the most holy throne of New Rome, rightly judging that the city honored with the Empire and the Senate should enjoy *the same precedence* as Rome, the old seat of Empire, and should be magnified as it was in ecclesiastical matters also, being second after it.

To make this still stronger, the Canon went on to confer upon the Patriarch of Constantinople the right of ordaining all the metropolitans of Asia, Pontus, Thrace, and the Bishops in barbarous regions—a larger domain of territory and population than then belonged to the Patriarchate of Rome. Now when this Canon was first read, the Roman legates—the only members present from the West—rose and left the assembly. The next day, when they returned and found that, without a word of objection from anybody, it had been *unanimously* adopted, they demanded another session for its abrogation, asserting that the Bishops had been forced by imperial pressure into that unanimity, and producing a forged version of the sixth Canon of Nicæa, in which the words "The Roman See hath always had the primacy" had been interpolated. But they failed utterly. Their forged interpolation was immediately exposed. Their charge of imperial pressure was scouted. The Canon stood, and has stood ever since. The then Pope, Leo the Great, resisted this Canon always, and pretended to nullify it, *not* on the ground that it contradicted the privilege of Peter— mark that!—but only because it conferred upon Constantinople the *second* place, till then given to Alexandria, and interfered besides with the rights of many metropolitans. But after long resistance, Rome herself has, in fact, swallowed her disappointment; and in the *three-fold* recognition

of the General Councils, makes no exception of the
XXVIII Canon of Chalcedon. Every Pope professes
that the acts of the General Councils are "with mouth and
heart to be kept *unaltered in a single tittle*," that he will
"account them worthy of equal honor and veneration,"
and will "follow, in every respect, whatsoever they promulgated or decreed, and condemn whatsoever they condemned." On this most important point, Dr Littledale
well says:

> Either the Council, in holding that the Roman primacy is a mere human
> and ecclesiastical dignity, conferred by the Church, and not a Divine and
> inalienable privilege, was *wrong* on the point of fact, or it was *right*. If
> it was *wrong* (apart from the objection that then the whole fabric of
> Conciliar authority falls, as no Council has ever been more authoritative
> than Chalcedon, or more definitely acknowledged by the Roman Church
> itself), then, since its *dogmatic* decrees are allowed to be the *standard of
> orthodoxy*, and yet as it must have *erred in dogma* if the Roman primacy
> be matter of *faith*, the conclusion is, that the said primacy is at best
> *not* matter of *dogmatic faith*, but only of *historical fact;* and so the Canon
> supplies proof that the Church of the fifth century did *not* hold the Papal
> claim to be of Divine origin or theological obligation. On the other hand,
> if the Council was right on the point of fact, there is nothing left to be said
> in favor of even the historical character of the alleged Petrine Privilege.

Dr. Littledale then tests the *principle* at issue, by looking at the position of the other great Sees. "If the allegation of the Council be true," he says, "that the civil
position of Rome was the sole cause of its ecclesiastical
primacy, then the same principle will be found to affect the
precedence of other great Sees. On the other hand, if the
Ultramontane contention be true, then the rival principle
will be seen at work, and the Sees will be found to rank
according to the dignity of their founders or the august
character of their traditions." He then shows that Jerusalem,
the Mother of all the Churches, when sunk into civil insig-
nificance, was only a suffragan See of Cæsarea, and when
afterwards elevated to a Patriarchate it was the last, and
not the first, in rank, though founded by CHRIST Himself
and the whole College of the Apostles. Then Alexandria
—which was the second city in the Empire for size and
importance—was not founded by any Apostle at all, but only
by S. Mark the Evangelist. Yet it always outranked

Antioch, the third largest city in the Empire, though S. Paul had labored there, and S. Peter was said to have been Bishop there for seven years before he translated his Episcopal chair to Rome. Ephesus, though Apostolic by at least two claims, through S. Paul and S. John, never rose to higher rank than that of exarchate or primacy. If, therefore, the greatness of the Bishop of Rome is to be traced to the greatness of the founder of the See, it is in *contradiction* to the principle which prevailed everywhere else throughout all Christendom: just as, if we are to interpret the "rock" to mean S. Peter, we must *contradict* the invariable use of that word in all the rest of the Bible, Old Testament as well as New. Dr. Littledale sums up the evidence:

> Thus the evidence of Church history amply justifies the Fathers of Chalcedon, and proves that they were right in alleging that the political supremacy of Rome as the capital of the Empire, making it the natural centre of all business affairs, and the chief resort of travellers from all quarters, made it also the most convenient centre for that great missionary organisation, whose battle was emphatically fought in the large towns, as the now significant word 'pagan,' once meaning 'rustic' or 'villager,' teaches us. And down to the middle of the third century all the extant evidence shows that the primacy was held to reside in the *Church* of Rome, not in its *Bishop*, who derived his importance from the See, not *vice-versa*. S. Clement, for instance, writes to the Corinthians in the name of the Roman Church, not in his own.

But we must shorten sail, or we shall never get through this masterly and most interesting work. We have thus far touched upon only 100 pages out of more than 350. And the further we go, the keener is the historical analysis, the more trenchant the criticism, the more unanswerable the refutation of Roman assumptions and deliberate frauds. The many doctrinal somersaults of Vigilius, and the palpable and notorious heresy of Honorius, are mercilessly shown up. Merely "local Italian Synods," not even professing to be œcumenical, are shown to have deposed Popes, and these depositions have always been counted valid. The acts of the Councils of Pisa, Constance, and Basle are carefully stated, and at the two former, the deposition of existing Popes and the election of Alexander V and Martin V are regarded as valid. Dr. Littledale keenly says:

It is obvious that if the 'privilege of Peter,' as affirmed in the Vatican Council, be a Divinely revealed verity, and the Pope be in truth the Head of the Church, his inferiors could not possibly sit in judgment upon him, nor could the body, without committing suicide, *cut off its own head.* Therefore, if the attitude taken up by the Councils were heterodox and unjustifiable, we should find their nominees to the Papacy rejected as pretenders, schismatics and heretics, and their acts disallowed as null and void.

Precisely so in English history, the whole Parliamentary annals of England under the Commonwealth are now a legal blank, ... and no Acts of Parliament nor decisions of the law-courts between 1641 and 1660 can be cited as of authority, or as having the smallest legal validity. But no such disavowal of Pisa and Constance exists in ecclesiastical history, and the claims of Alexander V and Martin V to be true Pontiffs and successors of S. Peter have never been disputed; albeit their title depends wholly on the validity of the deposition of their predecessors, which created the vacancies in their favor. Had there been any such collapse of the opposition at Pisa and Constance as that which left Eugenius IV ultimately victor over the Council of Basle, we should have merely proof that modern Ultramontanism was not then universally received, but none that it was not in the right, and entitled to be so received; but the triumph of Pisa and Constance over Papal resistance is *decisive of the controversy,* and refutes the Vatican decrees of 1870.

But, to our extreme regret, we must altogether omit from Chapter IV to Chapter VII, inclusive, though a most interesting and important article might be made from them alone. All the strong points are brought out so clearly and forcibly, and the underlying *principles* are set forth with such terseness and clearness. One such point we must quote, however, before we pass on. In quoting facts from history, as bearing upon Papal claims, Dr. Littledale most justly says:

It is to be distinctly remembered, that any *negative* examples are *very much more* to the point than *positive* ones can be. This proposition may strike persons unfamiliar with the rules of evidence as being unfair, for they may naturally suppose that at least equal weight should be given to the facts which make in favor of Papal supremacy, and to those which make against it. That would be perfectly true *if* the claim made for the Popes were simply that in virtue of their office they held the most prominent position in the early Church, and often exercised a preponderating influence in ecclesiastical affairs. Occasional proofs of their being unable to secure their ends, or enforce their authority, would establish no more against this view than the failure of many English Acts of Parliament to effect their object, or to obtain popular recognition and obedience, establishes against the general proposition that England is habitually governed by laws enacted in and by Parliament. Yet, in truth, no dispute exists so far, and, were nothing further demanded on behalf of the Popes, the controversy would die out for want of materials. But the claim is that of an *original and indefeasible Divine right* of *direct sovereignty and jurisdiction*, both in *matters of faith* and of *discipline*, exercised *from the first* by the Popes, and acknowledged by the whole Catholic Church. Every instance which makes against these pretensions is a flaw in the case, and is like a *gap in a pedigree* by which right of ownership to a title and estate is sought to be established. And if *several* such flaws and gaps be discoverable, they settle something further: for they not merely disprove the claim of special *privilege*, but make it impossible to sustain the Supremacy as a matter of *prescription*, and as having thus such ancient and universal consent on its side as to raise a strong presumption in favor of primitive Christendom having ranked it as a Church ordinance, equally with Infant Baptism and Sunday observance, for which no express Divine sanction is recorded. And any evidence which tends to show that the power of the Roman See did, in fact, become greater in the lapse of time, and gradually overpower resistance, at once helps to show its *purely human character*. For a *Divinely* bestowed authority is always strongest *at first*, growing weaker in popular regard as the memory of the original grant is weakened, which the instances of Moses and of the Apostles sufficiently prove; whereas a human authority, continually reinforced, often tends to grow, as the power of the French kings grew from Louis XI to Louis XIV, and as the power of the House of Commons has grown in England, from the Restoration to the present day.

Remembering this idea of *gaps* or *flaws* in a *pedigree*, which is exactly the one we have to deal with, let us turn to the chapter that closes this remarkable book.

In the idea of transmitted authority, all are familiar with the maxim that no one can convey to another a power which he does not himself possess. In consecrations to the Episcopate, *each* of the three or more Consecrators possesses that episcopate which, unitedly, they give to the one upon whom they lay hands. Any *one* of the three *could* do it: but for abundant security the Canons require *three at least*, so as to have a *three-fold* cord of *certainty*. There is, thus, the direct *touch of conveyance*, between those who have it, and him to whom, by that act, they give it. This is the Divine plan, followed in the Apostolic Church from the beginning, and kept up in all parts of the Catholic Church to this day.

To show how it operates, take, for instance, the case of any priest ordained by Bishop Doane of Albany. He himself was consecrated by *five* other Bishops. And following back the consecrations of these five, and so on, up to the reception of our Episcopate from England, eighty years before, it will be found that *every* priest ordained by Bishop Doane represents, in his own person, no less than *sixty-eight* Bishops of our American Succession, besides the original English prelates from whom we derived it, and several others who have taken part in subsequent American consecrations. The true idea of the Apostolic Succession is thus, not a simple chain of *single links*, where the breaking of a single link anywhere destroys the continuity of the chain: but it is a *complete network*, from which any one strand would never be missed. The destruction of the Apostolic Succession is simply a moral impossibility.

The idea of the Papal succession is the very reverse of all this, and is an absurdity in itself. As a channel for the perpetuation of *transmitted* authority, it is an impossibility, for no Pope *ever* gives it to his *successor*. No two successive links of the Papal chain *ever* interpenetrate. Sometimes weeks, or months, or even years have intervened between the death of one Pope and the election of his successor. And when the successor is chosen, from whence does he get his power as Pope? From his predecessor? No! His predecessor did not even *know* who should succeed him; never said a word to him about it; gave him no power, no symbol of investiture, no symptom even of *any*thing. Does the new Pope then get the power from the Cardinals who elected him? No! for *they never had it*. Only the previous Pope had it, and he died without giving it to anybody. *Where then does the new Pope get it?* The links of the Papal chain of transmission, it is thus seen, *never interpenetrate*. They can never even get close enough to one another to touch on the outside! There is a *total solution of continuity* on the death of *every* Pope, and there is no possible way to help it!

But this is not all. The Papal theory is beset by radical difficulties of its own, which would wreck it completely without any comparison with a better system. We all understand what is meant by the possession of power *de facto*, and consider that sufficient in temporal affairs, even if it be not at the same time *de jure*. But "it is an axiom of Latin Theology and Canon Law that *unlawful* possession of the Papacy confers *no rights whatever*, and that all acts done by one who is Pope *de facto* without being also Pope *de jure*, are *null and void.*" And "this nullity extends, of course, to the institution of all beneficiaries within the area of the quasi-Pope's domestic jurisdiction, and to the creations of Cardinals. That is to say, a false Pope may seriously affect the competency of the electoral body which will have to choose his successor." For Cardinals "are not specially ordained, as Bishops and Priests are." These latter may be possessed of perfectly valid orders, and yet have no legal right to a particular benefice or See. But no Cardinal has any shadow of claim to the red hat, or to be one of the electors of a Pope, unless the Pope who named *him* had *full powers.* And to make confusion worse confounded, "another maxim of Latin Theology is, that any *doubt* as to the rightful tenure of the Papal Chair by any claimant, is to be ruled *against* him, not for him, as is laid down expressly by Bellarmine, who says: 'A doubtful Pope is accounted *no* Pope.' This includes *all* cases of *disputed elections*, whenever there is not *full proof* of the valid election of the particular claimant who ultimately prevailed." And there were no less than *thirty-nine* anti-Popes before the Great Schism: a fact which proves, as Dr. Littledale well says, "that no Church is *so lacking* in the note of Unity as the local Roman Church. It has been the typical home of schism." And yet we are told that submission to the absolute despotism of Rome is the only thing that can preserve the unity of the Church!

But we have not yet reached the end. There are laid down for us, in the Roman Canon Law, *four* cases of *absolute nullity*, admitting of no dispute. They are these: (1) "Intrusion by some external influence, without any election by the constituency." (2) "Election by those only who are not qualified to elect." (3) "*Simony.*" (4) "Antecedent personal ineligibility of certain definite kinds, such as bastardy." And, as if all this were not enough, there are cases of "*highly probable nullity*," such as those of heresy, whether manifest *or secret*, and whether previous to, or after, election to the Papacy: and these are "highly probable only, and not absolute, because, while there is a *consensus* of theologians and canonists on the subject, there is no express decree of Canon Law to the same effect."

As we cannot give full attention to all these points, let us look for a moment to what is said of *Simony*.

Dr. Littledale gives a chain of authorities, from the Apostolic Canons down to Pope Julius II, including Canons of General Councils, *all agreeing* that simony is fatally destructive of Holy Orders. The Apostolic Canons declare that "if any Bishop, Priest, or Deacon obtain this rank by money, let him be deposed, and his ordainer also, and be altogether cut off from communion, as Simon Magus was by Peter." The General Council of Chalcedon ordains the same, and adds that "if any one act as go-between in such scandalous and illegal transactions, if he be a cleric, let him be degraded from his rank." A Roman Synod, under Gregory VII, declares that "All crimes are accounted as nothing in comparison with the simoniacal heresy. . . . Ordinations performed for money. . . . we decide to be null and void." Pope Leo IV will not admit that even penitence can avail, but that the deposition of simoniacs is "perpetual and irreparable." And, lastly, Pope Julius II, in the Bull *Cum tam divino*, " pronounces all simoniacal elections to the Papacy void, and incapable of being validated by any recognition accorded to the Pope as chosen. And Gammarus, Auditor of the Rota, in his commentary on this Bull, alleges it to be so worded as to be retrospective in effect, fully voiding all such former elections."

And now to the working of this principle. Omitting here all the numerous and more ancient cases, Dr. Littledale tells us that—

Innocent VIII was simoniacally elected in 1484, and his next successor, the infamous Cardinal Roderic de Borgia, was elected in the conclave of 1492 by a majority of twenty-two out of the then twenty-seven Cardinals, whose votes had been purchased by Cardinal Ascanio Sforza, as recorded by Von Eggs, the Roman Catholic historian of the Cardinals, in his *Pontificium Doctum* [p. 251] and *Purpura Docta*, in *Vita Card. Ascan. Sforzæ*, iii, 251. As Pope Alexander VI, Borgia *openly sold the Cardinalate* itself to the highest purchasers, so that both his own popedom and the membership of the Sacred College were *all void by reason of Simony*. But Julius II was elected in 1503 in a conclave of thirty-seven Cardinals, of whom twenty-six, or rather over the two-thirds necessary for a valid choice, were of Alexander VI's invalid creation, while the same Cardinal Sforza is known to have managed that conclave also, in the same simoniacal fashion as the previous one. And Leo X was elected in 1513, in a conclave consisting *entirely* of Cardinals created by either Alexander VI or Julius II, and *therefore incompetent to elect*. And Leo repeated the crime of Alexander VI in *selling the Cardinalate;* while, finally, Clement VII was simoniacally elected in 1523.

The electoral body was thus *utterly vitiated* and disqualified by Canon Law, at least so far back as 1513, and *no conceivably valid election of a Pope has taken place since that of Sixtus IV, in 1471*, even if every defect prior to that date be condoned, and it be conceded that the breaches in the tenth, eleventh and fifteenth centuries were made good *some*how.

Dr. Littledale pushes home, with the utmost boldness, the full conclusions from the facts which he has thus demonstrated:

> There has not been any retrospective action taken in regard to this final vitiation by Simony; and to Alexander VI belongs the responsibility of having made any assertion of unbroken and canonical devolution of a Petrine Privilege in the line of Roman Pontiffs *impossible for any honest canonist or historian* since his time. And, consequently, not only have the specific Divine privileges alleged to be attached to the person and office of the Roman Pontiff *all utterly failed*, but the whole ecclesiastical jurisdiction appertaining to, or derived from, the See of Rome, has *failed throughout the entire Latin obedience*. All acts done by the Popes themselves, or requiring Papal sanction for validity, since 1484 (just thirty-three years before the outbreak of the Lutheran revolt), have been *inherently null and void*, because emanating from *usurping and illicit Pontiffs*, every one of whom has been uncanonically intruded into the Papal chair by *simoniacal* or merely *titular* electors, having *no legal claim to vote at all*. Those orders and sacraments in the Latin Church which depend on the valid succession of the dispersive episcopate and priesthood may continue unimpaired, but all that is distinctively *Papal died out four centuries ago*, and continues now as a mere delusive phantom.

What can possibly be urged on the other side, is thus unanswerably dealt with by our Author:

> The defence set up on the Ultramontane side, against this proof that the Papacy has *ceased to exist* as a *de jure* institution is, that the mere fact of recognition and acceptance of an invalidly elected Pope by the Roman Church at large suffices to make good all defects, and to validate his position. But *this is in the teeth of all the legal facts*. For (1) there is no such provision to be found in the Canon Law, which could not omit so important a legal principle, did it exist; (2) no opportunity of expressing either assent or dissent is afforded to the dispersive Roman Church, seeing that the election in conclave is not conditional, but final, and the result is publicly signified at once, in words denoting that the new reign has begun; (3) the absence of

any schism, or any public challenge of the title of any one of the thirteen intruded Popes between 903 and 963 [the Pornocracy] is legally equivalent to acceptance of them all by the dispersive Roman Church, but Baronius is most precise in denying their status; and (4) there are Bulls of Julius II and Paul IV which *categorically contradict* this assertion, in that they enact that *no* recognition, homage, or obedience, shown to an invalidly elected Pope, shall avail to legitimate his status, when his disqualification has been either *simony* or heresy.

The transparent and impudent humbuggery of all this may be made plain by a suggestion which Dr. Littledale does not make. That same Julius II, who issued so tremendous a Bull against a simoniacal Pope, appears in the *table* of doubtful, intrusive, heretical and simoniacal Popes, as owing his own seat as Pope to that very *simony* which he so valiantly denounces! And what could be safer? He, of course, knew that he was *suspected* of it. And the Bull would—to the world at large—vindicate him. And what harm could it do? He, as Pope, had certainly no idea of unseating *himself*. And when the *briber* was so safe, there was little danger of the Cardinals, who were the *bribees*, making any real trouble about it. So that the Roman Cardinals, when that Bull was issued, must have found it as hard to keep their countenances sober, on meeting one another, as Cicero's heathen augurs.

Dr. Littledale says truly, that—

> The remarkable weakness of the line of Papal succession can be most clearly exhibited in a chronological table of the flaws in legitimate transmission of the Chair, which are precisely analogous to failures of proof of regular descent, or actual proofs of bastardy, in a family pedigree on which titles and estates depend. . . . . It is to be remembered that *intrusion* and *simony* are *absolute* disqualifications, heresy an almost equal one, and that all questions of doubt . . . . are ruled *against* the claimant by Bellarmine's maxim, 'A doubtful Pope is counted no Pope.' All persons reckoned, whether justly or unjustly, as anti-Popes, are excluded from the table; and merely legendary stories, such as that of Pope Marcellinus's apostasy, and rigidly technical objections, such as apply, for instance, to the orthodoxy of Nicolas I, and to the election of Gelasius II, are omitted also; so as to state the case for the prosecution as moderately as possible.

And with all this moderation, the entire list contains the names of *sixty-five* Popes, of whom no less than *thirty* were guilty of simony or intrusion such as, by Papal law, would render their claim to be *valid* Popes utterly *null and void*.

The *Table* ends with Clement VII, A.D. 1534, and only these words are added: "*No valid election has been possible since.*" The explanation of this is as follows:

> The Electoral College of Cardinals was completely vitiated by *simony* under Alexander VI; and thus, even if it could be conceded that the Papacy was saved somehow through former irregular transmissions, or was validly reconstituted by the Council of Constance, there has been, by *Roman Canon Law*, no *de jure* Pope since 1484 at latest, consequently no *de jure* Cardinal created, and thus *no means exist*, on *Ultramontane* principles, for *restoring the Petrine succession*.

We are sorely tempted to touch on other salient points. The question of Honorius is vigorously handled by Dr. Littledale, but is so familiar to all by this time, that there is less lost in passing it by once more. The horrible *Pornocracy* at Rome is another deadly blot on Roman history, far worse than can be found recorded of any other See in Christendom. Dr. Littledale thus outlines this dark and dismal period:

> In 903, Christopher, a priest of the Roman Church, rose against Pope Leo V, a few weeks after his enthronement, threw him into prison, and intruded himself into the Papacy. He was in his turn overthrown and imprisoned by Sergius III, who intruded himself similarly, and whose character is painted in the blackest colors by the chroniclers of the time. It is at least certain that it was under his auspices that the infamous triad of courtesans, the two Theodoras and Marozia, obtained the influence which enabled them to dispose several times of the Papal crown. They, or Alberic of Spoleto, son of Marozia, nominated to the Papacy Anastasius III, Lando, John X, Leo VI, Stephen VII, John XI, Leo VII, Stephen VIII, Martin III, Agapetus II, and John XII, the last of whom, a mere boy at the time of his intrusion, was deposed for various atrocious crimes by a Synod convened by the Emperor Otto I, in 963. This whole series, as Baronius declares, consisted of false Pontiffs, having no right to their office, either by election or by subsequent assent of the electors, each of them eager to undo the acts of his predecessors, and choosing persons of the same evil stamp as themselves for the Cardinalate and other dignities.

And the language of Baronius himself—the champion Ultramontane historian of the Church—is far more emphatic than that of Dr. Littledale:

> What was then the aspect of the Holy Roman Church? How utterly foul, when harlots, at once most powerful and most vile, bore rule at Rome; at whose will Sees were exchanged, Bishops appointed, and what is awful and horrible to hear, their paramours were intruded as pseudo-Popes into

the See of Peter, who are not set down in the catalogue of the Roman Pontiffs except for the purpose of fixing the dates. For who could assert that persons lawlessly intruded by such courtesans were legitimate Pontiffs? There is no mention anywhere of the clergy electing or subsequently assenting. All the canons were thrust down into silence, the decrees of Popes were strangled, the old traditions were banned, the ancient customs, the sacred rites, and the early usages in the election of the supreme Pontiff, were completely annulled. And what sort of cardinals, deacons, and priests do you suppose were chosen by these monsters?

Dr. Littledale, as a canonist, draws the following most serious conclusion from *the admitted* facts. It is, that—

> If any Petrine succession or privilege ever existed in the Roman Church, it was *extinguished irrecoverably* at the close of this period; for it extended over *sixty years*, during which *not one lawfully-elected* Pope ascended the Papal Chair. None of them could canonically appoint to any dignity or benefice in the Roman Church; many of them are known to have sold them. Consequently, it is certain that, at the close of the sixty years' anarchy, *not one single clerical elector in Rome was qualified to vote*, for *not one* could show a just title to his position; and the lay vote, even if it was given at all, was invalid by itself. The election of Leo VIII or of Benedict V (whichever be accounted the true Pope), in 963, was, therefore, void also; for even if conducted in due form, the clerical *voters* had *no status*. And as no act of indemnity was ever passed by any authority whatsoever—leaving out of account the very difficult problem of deciding what authority would have been competent for the purpose—the *defect* has been *incurable*. It is precisely analogous to a break of two generations of established bastardy in a pedigree by which it is sought to make good a claim to a peerage. Failing the production of some collateral heir (impossible in the case before us), there is no choice but to declare the family honors *extinct*. The Petrine line, *if* ever a reality, *ended in the tenth century*. The later Popes may just conceivably have been Bishops of Rome in some canonical sense for a few centuries longer, . . . but if so, they had no more connection with the older line than the Napoleonic dynasty has with the Carolingian emperors.

Another series of intruding Popes, who secured their places through simony, is found in the eleventh century, lasting *thirty-four* years—a very serious break. The "Babylonish captivity," at Avignon, is another very grave break:

> For the Roman contention is, that S. Peter, by his twenty-five years' *residence* and death in Rome, and by that alone—as no documentary proof exists—transferred his primacy from Antioch to Rome, his ultimate *residence* being the sole *nexus* between the Universal Primacy and the local bishopric. They admit that he might have fixed it in any other Church; but that by his final residence in Rome he established it forever there.

Accordingly, when the Popes went to Avignon, permanently resided there, and died and were buried there, they did in regard to Rome precisely what S. Peter is said to have done in regard to Antioch : they broke up the Roman succession, and created a new primacy at Avignon. For *residence* being an *essential condition* of the Episcopate, that condition failed utterly during the Avignon period, and its resumption could not rehabilitate the succession. The Popes living in Avignon could no more be considered Bishops of Rome, than S. Peter living in Rome could be considered as still Bishop of Antioch. And Pope Benedict XIV says : ' No one who is not Bishop of Rome can be styled successor of Peter, and for that reason the words of the Lord ' Feed my sheep,' can never be applied to him. . . . Furthermore, by the Canons of all the Councils, from Nice I to Trent, and from that to the Bull of Pius IV . . . . every Bishop, even of Patriarchal rank, is compelled to a *personal* residence, under pain of deprivation ; the Popes, therefore, as Bishops of Rome, and even as Patriarchs, fall under the universal law, and the See of Rome was *ipso facto* void during the Avignon Papacy.'

Besides all these gaps, there is the Great Schism, when there were two, and sometimes three Popes, each excommunicating all the rest, and all their adherents—a woful time, that paved the way for the Reformation, and did more to destroy the *prestige* of the Papacy than all other causes put together. But this, together with much else, we must pass over here, commending the reader to search it all out in Dr. Littledale's book. Notwithstanding the self-imposed narrowness of scope in that book, it contains the sum and substance of the whole controversy in a nutshell, with a masterly point and brevity and clearness, which are most refreshing. He appends a valuable "Note on the False Decretals "—forgeries of which we hear much said, but of which it is not easy to get a definite account such as is here given. This important *Note* thus closes:

So much will suffice to exhibit the general tone and object of the False Decretals, which revolutionized the polity of the Western Church, and which were formally embodied in the Canon Law (of which they had for centuries practically formed a large effective factor) in respect of all their legislative matter by Pope Gregory IX, under the editorship of S. Raymond de Pennaforte, in 1234. *They* are the *sole basis* and *justification* of those claims and exceptional powers asserted by the Roman Chair, which *culminated in the Vatican Decrees* of 1870.

We have dealt very largely in extracts from Dr. Littledale: and they are the best part of this article Our only object is to point out the solid merit, the singular strength, depth and brilliance of his work, so as to induce all to read it for themselves. And, as our last extract, we will give his own summing-up of the whole work done in this admirable little volume on the Petrine Claims:

The points successively raised, and (it is submitted) *proved*, in the foregoing inquiry, are as follows:

I. That the claim to teach and rule the Church Universal, as of privilege, in virtue of a special inheritance from S. Peter, made on behalf of the Popes of Rome, does not satisfy *any one* of the *seven* conditions required by Roman Canon Law in all cases of privilege. For,

(*a*) No document constituting them such heirs, and annexing the privilege to the inheritance, is producible, or so much as *thought* to have *ever existed*.

(*b*) The document alleged as conferring this privilege upon S. Peter himself is *not certain* and *manifest* in wording for this purpose, but obscure and enigmatic; so as to have been diversely interpreted from the earliest to the latest time since its promulgation.

(*c*) When strictly and literally construed, it contains *no express gift* of either teaching or ruling authority; which accordingly cannot be legally read into it.

(*d*) It is *exclusively personal* in wording, and is therefore *limited* to S. Peter singly.

(*e*) It contains *no* clause contemplating or empowering its extension to *any other person* than S. Peter.

(*f*) The interpretation actually put upon it by Ultramontanes *denies*, *interferes with*, and *encroaches upon*, the rights and privileges of all other Patriarchs, Metropolitans and Bishops of the Church Universal.

(*g*) It has been habitually exercised with *excess* and *abuse*, and has thus been *long since forfeited*, assuming that it ever existed.

II. Holy Scripture, construed as a legal document tendered in evidence of the Petrine Claims, not only fails to corroborate, but *directly contradicts*, them.

III. The Liturgies, as evidence of the mind of whole Churches, and remounting to remote antiquity, recognise no supreme authority as vesting in S. Peter himself, not to say any persons claiming to inherit from him.

IV. The great majority of the eminent Fathers of the Church interpret the three great Petrine texts, in S. Matthew xvi, S. Luke xxii, and S. John xxi, in a sense contrary to the Ultramontane gloss; and thus make that gloss untenable by Roman Catholics, who are bound to interpret Scripture *only* 'according to the *unanimous* consent of the Fathers.'

V. The Canons and Decrees of the undisputed General Councils of the Church, and those of a large number of provincial and other local councils, down to the middle of the fifteenth century, are wholly incompatible with any belief in the Petrine Claims having been currently received throughout the Church.

VI. The Acts (as distinguished from the formulated decrees) of the Councils, those of many Popes and of many eminent Fathers, are incapable of being reconciled with the Petrine Claims.

VII. No trustworthy or even probable evidence is adducible for the fact that S. Peter was ever Bishop of Rome.

VIII. Not only is the case for a Petrine Privilege destroyed, but the breaks in the chain of prescription are so numerous and serious as to make it impossible to establish the Petrine Claims on that basis.

IX. Even if there ever had been a Petrine succession, with devolution of the Petrine Privilege, in the See of Rome, it has been entirely annulled and voided by demonstrable and incurable flaws, so that *no valid Pope* has sat *for more than four centuries*, or *can* be *secured in the future* by *any* now existing machinery in the Church of Rome.

And now, what will our Roman friends do about this pungent book? It is simply unanswerable, and the wise among them know it. Hence the common saying among them, that to appeal to History is Heresy. With them, the "voice of the living Church"—that is to say, the latest novelty issued by the Pope of Rome—is the sole fountain of truth. If History does not agree with *that*, then so much the worse for *History!* If they would take our advice—which they are not likely to do—we should advise them to let it alone. It is the advice we should give to any dog who should meet a porcupine. The dog generally takes the other way. He barks furiously all around the porcupine—which does not hurt the porcupine in the slightest. But every attempt to *bite* the porcupine is sure to hurt the *dog!* We shall wait and see. Meanwhile, we rejoice that the great Society for Promoting Christian Knowledge has placed this admirable book upon its permanent list of standard publications, and long may it there remain!

J. H. HOPKINS.

What is

CASTORIA

Castoria is Dr. Samuel Pitcher's prescription for Infants and Children. It contains neither Opium, Morphine nor other Narcotic substance. It is a harmless substitute for Paregoric, Drops, Soothing Syrups, and Castor Oil. It is Pleasant. Its guarantee is thirty years' use by Millions of Mothers. Castoria destroys Worms and allays feverishness. Castoria prevents vomiting Sour Curd, cures Diarrhœa and Wind Colic. Castoria relieves teething troubles, cures constipation and flatulency. Castoria assimilates the food, regulates the stomach and bowels, giving healthy and natural sleep. Castoria is the Children's Panacea—the Mother's Friend.

Castoria.

"Castoria is an excellent medicine for children. Mothers have repeatedly told me of its good effect upon their children."

Dr. G. C. Osgood,
Lowell, Mass.

"Castoria is the best remedy for children of which I am acquainted. I hope the day is not far distant when mothers will consider the real interest of their children, and use Castoria instead of the various quack nostrums which are destroying their loved ones, by forcing opium, morphine, soothing syrup and other hurtful agents down their throats, thereby sending them to premature graves."

Dr. J. F. Kincheloe,
Conway, Ark.

Castoria.

"Castoria is so well adapted to children that I recommend it as superior to any prescription known to me."

H. A. Archer, M. D.,
111 So. Oxford St., Brooklyn, N. Y.

"Our physicians in the children's department have spoken highly of their experience in their outside practice with Castoria, and although we only have among our medical supplies what is known as regular products, yet we are free to confess that the merits of Castoria has won us to look with favor upon it."

United Hospital and Dispensary,
Boston, Mass.

Allen C. Smith, Pres.,

The Centaur Company, 77 Murray Street, New York City.

MISCELLANEOUS.

D. L. Dowd's Health Exerciser

For Brain-Workers and Sedentary People,

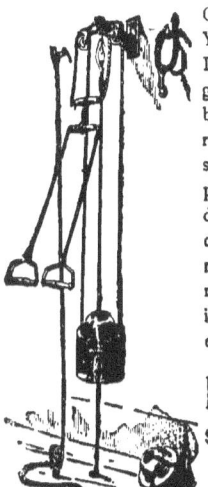

Gentlemen, Ladies and Youths, the Athlete or Invalid. A complete gymnasium. Takes up but 6 inches square floor room; something new, scientific, durable, comprehensive, cheap. Indorsed by 20,000 physicians, lawyers, clergymen, editors and others now using it. Send for illustrated circular, forty engravings; no charge.

Prof. D. L. DOWD

Scientific Physical and Vocal Culture,

9 East 14th St., New York.

"The Gladstone" LAMP

Is the finest lamp in the world. It gives a **pure, soft, brilliant white** light of **85 candle power.** Purer and brighter than gas light; softer than electric light—more cheerful than either. *A Marvelous light from ordinary kerosene oil!*

Seeing is Believing.
A "wonderful lamp" it is indeed. Never needs trimming, never smokes nor breaks chimneys, never "smells of the oil!" no sputtering, no climbing of the flame, no annoyance of any kind, and **cannot explode.** And besides all it gives a clear, **white** light, 10 to 20 times the size and brilliancy of any ordinary house lamp! Finished in either Brass, Nickel, Gold or Antique Bronze. Also

The Gladstone Extension Study Lamp,
for Clergymen, Editors, College Students, Teachers, Professors, Physicians and other professional men.
The Gladstone Banquet Lamps.
The Gladstone Piano Lamps.
Send for price list. Single lamps at *wholesale price*, boxed and sent by express. ☞ Get our prices. *"Seeing is believing."*
GLADSTONE LAMP CO.,
10 East 14th St., New York.

MARLIN REPEATING RIFLES

MODEL '81 REPEATERS.
MODEL '89 REPEATERS.

THE LATEST. MODEL 1889.

MARLIN SAFETY REPEATING RIFLE

using the 32, 38, and 44 Winchester cartridges, having a
SOLID TOP RECEIVER,
Excluding all dirt or moisture from the lock.
LOADING and EJECTING
from the side, away from the face of the shooter. Weighing but
6¾ POUNDS,
and a model of symmetry and beauty. Shoots with greater
ACCURACY
than any other. Don't buy until you see the
MARLIN SAFETY MODEL, 1889.

MODEL '81 REPEATERS
40-60 and 45-70 calibres.
LOW TRAJECTORY STRONG SHOOTING.

THE BALLARD
still remains the best shooting rifle in the world.

MARLIN'S DOUBLE ACTION AUTOMATIC EJECTING REVOLVER
in workmanship, finish and accuracy of shooting; second to none.

WRITE US
for information. All inquiries answered promptly.

ASK YOUR DEALER
to show you our rifles. For a complete description of the best Repeating Rifles in the world, write for Illustrated Catalogue D, to the

MARLIN FIRE ARMS CO.,
NEW HAVEN, CONN., U. S. A.

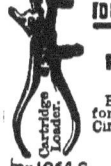

IDEAL RELOADING TOOLS
FOR ALL
RIFLES, Pistols
and **Shot Guns.**
BEST IN THE WORLD. Send for Illustrated Descriptive Circular.
IDEAL MF'G CO.,
box 1064 G   New Haven, Conn.

THE WINNER INVESTMENT CO.
◁ FULL PAID CAPITAL, $1,000,000. ▷

THIS Company does strictly an investment business and shares with investors the results of conservative and profitable investments. It offers a fixed income, large profits, and absolute security. Nearly $2,000,000 net profits paid to investors since 1883, from Kansas City (Mo.) real estate investments. At the present time opportunity is offered to invest in bonds, secured by first mortgage on one of the best office buildings in the West, yielding **6 per cent** guaranteed interest. A bonus of stock in the building company accompanies each bond. Also in bonds secured by first mortgage on residence property in and adjacent to Kansas City, in the line of immediate development, yielding **8 per cent** guaranteed interest. These bonds participate in one half the net profits and run five years. Send for pamphlet and monthly circulars.

KANSAS CITY BRIDGE AND TERMINAL RAILWAY

Six per cent Gold Bonds, due 1919, with bonus of stock in the Company that will yield an income in 1891. Central Trust Company of New York, Trustees.

☞ Other choice investments not obtainable elsewhere.

WILLIAM H. PARMENTER,
GENERAL AGENT,

Nos. 50 & 51 Times Building, New York City
No. 1 Custom House Street, Providence. R I

50 STATE STREET, BOSTON.

"Improvement the Order of the Age."

THE NEW SMITH PREMIER

TYPEWRITER.

Unequalled in all essentials of a perfect writing machine. Speed, ease of operation, permanent alignment and durability a specialty. *All type cleaned in ten seconds without soiling the hands.*

Illustrated Catalogue mailed free to readers of this Review.

The Smith Prem'er Typewriter Co.,
SYRACUSE, N. Y., U. S. A.

AGENCY OF THE CHEQUE BANK, LIMITED, OF LONDON,

ESTABLISHED 1873.

TRUSTEES: { The Right Honorable Earl Beauchamp.
John Edward Taylor, Esq., Proprietor *"Manchester Guardian."*

Head Office: 4 Waterloo Place, Pall Mall, London.

WINTER TRAVEL.

Travelers contemplating visiting the International Exhibition of Jamaica, in the West Indies, in January next, or any other part of the West Indies, Mexico, or Central America, will find the Cheque Bank Cheques available on board the Steamers that leave the port of New York for the West Indies, as well as at all the branches of the Colonial Bank, West Indies, and other places in Cuba, Mexico, etc.

Full information sent or given by

E. J. Mathews & Company, Agents,

No. 2 Wall St., New York.

The late Right Honorable John Bright was one of the original Shareholders and Trustees of this Bank, and remained such until the day of his decease.

 **RAILROADS.**

LEHIGH VALLEY
· RAILROAD ·
AND
AMERICA'S GRANDEST SCENERY.

| DOUBLE TRACK. | STEEL RAILS. |

THE POPULAR ROUTE
BETWEEN
NEW YORK, PHILADELPHIA,

EASTON,	WILKESBARRE,	GENEVA,	ROCHESTER,
BETHLEHEM,	PITTSTON,	WAVERLY,	BUFFALO,
ALLENTOWN,	SCRANTON,	WATKINS' GLEN,	NIAGARA FALLS,
MAUCH CHUNK,	ITHACA,	ELMIRA,	TORONTO,

DETROIT, CHICAGO, ST. LOUIS, AND ALL POINTS WEST.

PULLMAN PALACE CARS ON ALL THROUGH TRAINS.

ANTHRACITE COAL USED EXCLUSIVELY. NO DUST. NO SMOKE.

TICKET OFFICES.—NEW YORK: General Eastern Office, 235 Broadway; Depot, foot of Cortlandt Street; Depot, foot of Desbrosses Street. PHILADELPHIA: 836 Chestnut Street; P. & R. Depot, Ninth and Green Streets; P. & R. Depot, Third and Berks Streets.

The mountain and valley scenery traversed by this line is the most beautiful and picturesque in America, embracing the romantic valleys of the Susquehanna and Lehigh, and the historic Wyoming. Ask for Tickets via "Lehigh Valley Route."

E. B. BYINGTON,
Gen'l Pass. Agent, So. BETHLEHEM, PA.

JOHN WILSON.   CHARLES E. WENTWORTH.

University Press,

(ESTABLISHED 1639.)

JOHN WILSON AND SON,

Electrotypers and Printers,

CAMBRIDGE, MASS.

FOOD PRODUCTS.

Royal Baking Powder

The United States Official Investigation

Of Baking Powders, recently made, under authority of Congress, by the Department of Agriculture, Washington, D. C., furnishes the highest authoritative information as to which powder is the best. The Official Report

Shows the ROYAL to be a cream of tartar baking powder, superior to all others in strength and leavening power.

The Royal Baking Powder is absolutely pure, made from the most wholesome materials, and produces finer flavored, sweeter, lighter, more wholesome and delicious bread, biscuit, cake, pastry, etc., than any other baking powder or leavening agent.

Food raised by it will keep sweet, moist, fresh and palatable longer than when raised by yeast or other baking powders.

Being of greater strength than any other baking powder, it is also the most economical in use.

These great qualities warrant you, if you are not using the Royal Baking Powder, in making a trial of it.

FOOD PRODUCTS.

The Choicest Ever Imported.
Nothing like it ever known in
quality, prices, premiums, and
discounts.

BETTER NEWS TO LADIES AND ALL LOVERS OF FINE TEAS

A CHANCE OF A LIFE-TIME. GET PREMIUM NO. 27.

Latest and Best Inducements offered in Premiums and Discounts to introduce and get orders for our New Teas Just Received, which are *Picked* from the *Select Tea Gardens* of China and Japan, none but the Highest Grade Leaf being used. All guaranteed absolutely Pure. Handsome New Premiums of Imported China, Lamps, etc., given away with orders of $10.00 and upwards, or discounts made if preferred. Good Teas, 30, 35 & 40 cts. Excellent Family Teas, 50 & 60 cts. Very Best, 65 to 90 cts. per lb. Special—We will send by mail a *Trial Order* of 1½ lbs. of our very Fine Teas on receipt of $2.00. When ordering, be particular and state if you want Formosa or Amoy Oolong, Mixed, Young Hyson, Gunpowder, Imperial, Japan, English Breakfast, or Sun-Sun Chop. No Humbug. Remember we deal only in Pure Goods. Send at once for a *Trial Order* the *Old Reliable* and enjoy a cup of Good Tea. For particulars, address THE GREAT AMERICAN TEA CO., 31 & 33 Vesey St., New York, N. Y. P. O. Box 287.

The only **perfect substitute** for **Mother's Milk.** Invaluable in **Cholera Infantum** and **Teething.** A pre-digested food for **Dyspeptics, Consumptives, Convalescents.** Perfect nutrient in all **Wasting Diseases.** Requires no cooking. Our Book, **The Care and Feeding of Infants,** mailed free.

Doliber-Goodale Co., Boston, Mass.

Tomato, Mock Turtle, Terrapin,
Ox Tail, Okra or Gumbo, Macaroni,
Pea, Green Turtle, Consommé,
Beef, Julienne, Soup and Bouilli,
Vermicelli, Chicken, Mullagatawny.

RICH and PERFECTLY SEASONED.

Require only to be heated, and | Prepared with great care from | Have enjoyed the highest reputa-
are then ready to serve. | only the best materials. | tion for more than 32 years.

Send us 20 cents, to help pay express, and receive, prepaid, two sample cans of these Soups, your choice.

TEST FREE

SOLD BY ALL LEADING GROCERS.

J. H. W. HUCKINS & CO.,
Sole Manufacturers, Boston, Mass.

RICHARDSON & BOYNTON CO.'S
"PERFECT"
(Trade-Mark)

WARM-AIR
AND
HOT-WATER HEATERS

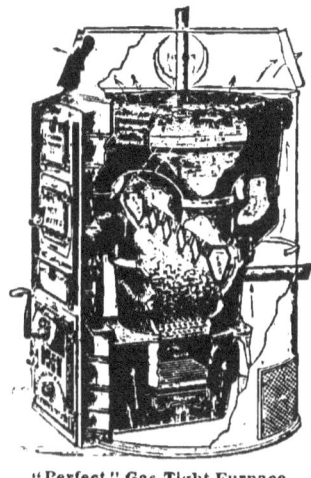

"Perfect" Gas-Tight Furnace.

are in construction and modern improvements greatly in advance of all others.

Correspondence solicited and Estimates furnished for heating

CHURCHES, SCHOOLS,

LECTURE-ROOMS,

HOSPITALS

or other buildings, PUBLIC or PRIVATE.

Send for Testimonials.

"Perfect" Hot-Water Heater.

RICHARDSON & BOYNTON CO.
Sole Manufacturers,
Nos. 232 & 234 WATER STREET,

Safe, | THE MOST AND BEST LIGHT FROM | Perfect,
Simple. | KEROSENE OIL. | Elegant.

THE "ROCHESTER" LAMP

HAVE YOUR FACTORY SAFE, YOUR STORE ATTRACTIVE, AND YOUR HOME CHEERFUL, WITH THE LIGHT OF THE "ROCHESTER."

No 148
ROCHESTER BRACKET LAMP.
An elegant Side Lamp for Residences, Churches, Halls, &c., &c. Projection, 14 inches. With Detachable Metal Fount. No. 2 Rochester Burner.

Antique Brass Finish.

We warrant every lamp. We have made more than ONE MILLION since 1835 (date of patent). We show over ONE THOUSAND varieties (our store is an art room) of Library, Hall, Piano, and Banquet Lamps, Chandeliers, Vase Lamps, etc., etc.

Every genuine lamp is plainly marked the "ROCHESTER." *Take no other from your dealer.*

MANUFACTURED BY

EDWARD MILLER & CO.

10 and 12 COLLEGE PLACE, ... NEW YORK.

THREE MINUTES' WALK FROM POST OFFICE. SEND FOR CIRCULAR.

STONE FILTERS.

NATURAL STONE WATER FILTERS

IN USE ALL OVER THE WORLD.

✻ ✻ ✻

FINE DECORATED CHINA

AND

GRAY STONEWARE JARS

TO

HOLD THE WATER.

———•———

A NATURAL STONE FOR A

FILTERING MEDIUM.

———•———

FITTED WITH SEPARATE PATENT

ICE CHAMBERS

TO COOL THE WATER.

———•———

As Easily Cleaned as a Water Pitcher.

Open cut shows filter disc used in our filters, and separate patent ice chambers.

✻ ✻ ✻

FOR USE IN OFFICES, HOMES, AND SCHOOLS.

For free descriptive price list, address,

GATE CITY STONE FILTER CO.,

J. A. DAVENPORT, Manager,

46 Murray Street, New York City.

 INSURANCE.

STABILITY, EXPERIENCE,

PROTECTION,

AND

PROVISION FOR THE FUTURE,

ALL COMBINED IN THE NEW POLICY OF THE

MANHATTAN LIFE

INSURANCE COMPANY,

OF NEW YORK.   ORGANIZED, 1850.

THIS OLD COMPANY

NOW OFFERS TO THE INSURING PUBLIC ITS NEW

SURVIVORSHIP DIVIDEND PLAN,

Which affords all the advantages of Life Insurance during the earlier years of life, and at the same time makes a provision for old age, as the Policy-holder can surrender his Policy at the end of the Survivorship Dividend Period and receive its Full Value in Cash — thus combining INVESTMENT *and* PROTECTION.

ANY INFORMATION CHEERFULLY FURNISHED.

HENRY B. STOKES, PRESIDENT.
JACOB L. HALSEY, VICE-PRESIDENT.

H. Y. WEMPLE, 2d VICE-PRES.   J. H. GRIFFIN, JR., ASST. SECY.
W. C. FRAZEE, SECRETARY.   E. L. STABLER, ACTUARY.

www.ingramcontent.com/pod-product-compliance
Lightning Source LLC
Chambersburg PA
CBHW022146300426
44115CB00006B/368